CRIMINAL BREACH OF TRUST

(A Comprative Socio-Legal Study of Indian and Islamic Criminal Laws)

CRIMINAL BREACH OF TRUST

التشريح الجنائى الخيانة بالا مانة

(*A Comprative Socio-Legal Study of Indian and Islamic Criminal Laws*)

By

DR. QAISAR HAYAT
Professor-in-Law,
Chairman and Dean, Faculty of Law,
Aligarh Muslim University, U.P.

KITAB BHAVAN
NEW DELHI-110002

Kitab Bhavan
Publishers, Distributors, Exporters & Importers
1784, Kalan Mahal, Darya Ganj
New Delhi-110002 (India)

Phone : (91-11) 3277392/93, 3274686
Web Site : www.kitabbhavan.com
E-mail : nasri@vsnl.com
Fax : (91-11) 3263383

First Edition : 2002

ISBN : 81-7151-329-8

Laser Typesetting at:
Laser Track
Darya Ganj, New Delhi-2

Published in India by:
Nusrat Ali Nasri for Kitab Bhavan
1784, Kalan Mahal, Darya Ganj
New Delhi-110002 [India]

Printed in India at:
Nice Printing Press
Khureji Khas, Delhi-110051

بِسْمِ اللّٰهِ الرَّحْمٰنِ الرَّحِيمِ

وَالَّذِينَ هُمْ لِأَمَٰنَٰتِهِمْ وَعَهْدِهِمْ رَاعُونَ.
وَالَّذِينَ هُمْ عَلَىٰ صَلَوٰتِهِمْ يُحَافِظُونَ.
أُولَٰٓئِكَ هُمُ الْوَٰرِثُونَ. الَّذِينَ
يَرِثُونَ الْفِرْدَوْسَ هُمْ فِيهَا خَٰلِدُونَ.

سورة المؤمنون (آيات ٨.٩.١٠.١١)

Those who faithfully observe
Their Trusts and their covenants,
and who (strictly) guard
Their prayers;—
These will be the heirs,
They will dwell therein for ever
(23:8,9,10,11)

ACKNOWLEDGMENT

Thanks Allah (SWT), with His blessings, mercy, benevolence and Hidaya, I have been able to complete the research work.

Prof. Mohd. Ishaque Qureshi's counselling proved very effective in taking a firm decision on the present topic. I am heartly thankful to him.

In fact, the source of inspiration to work on a comparative study are two learned and dynamic personalities.

Firstly the Honourable Rector, International Islamic Universities, Malaysia, for his scientific and systematic planned programmes for Islamisation of knowledge.

Secondly, the learned scholar Prof. Tan Sri Datuk Ahmad Ibrahim, Dean, Kulliyyah of Laws, International Islamic University, Malaysia for his untiring efforts to get elevated the position and dignity of Islamic Law, Shariah Courts and judges, and has the law its due recognition in the society which was relegated to the lower position during British rule.

Indeed, their devotion has attracted me to work on a comparative study so that I may be of some service to let the academics and jurists know the worth of Criminal Breach of Trust in Islamic Criminal Law as well as Indian Criminal Law. I am thankful to Allah (SWT) for giving me an opportunity to work under their able leaderships.

My thanks are also due to Prof. Rashiduz Zafer for the encouragement he gave to me from time to time in completing this work.

I will fail in my duty if I do not acknowledge my thanks due to Assoc. Prof. Dr. Mohd. Shokry A.G. El-Dakkak, from Egypt, Kulliyyah of Laws, IIU for his help in collecting the cases and relevant research literature in Arabic.

In the end I pray Allah (SWT) to forgive me for any error, if committed in explaining, interpreting, commenting and making observation on Islamic Law.

QAISAR HAYAT

CONTENTS

CHAPTER X

INTRODUCTION

قُلْ اِنَّ صَلَاتِی وَ نُسُکِی و مَحْیَایَ ومَمَاتِی لِلّٰهِ رَبِّ الْعٰلَمِیْنَ. لَا شَرِیْكَ لَهٗ وَ بِذٰلِكَ اُمِرْتُ وَاَنَا اَوَّلُ الْمُسْلِمِیْنَ.

(سورة الأ نعام، آیة : ١٢٦-١٦٣)

> Say: Truly, my prayer and my service of sacrifice, my life and my death, are (all) for Allah, the cherisher of the worlds: No partner has He: This I am commanded, and I am the first of those who submit to His Will." (6:162, 163).

This Totalitarian faith in God is the primary basis of Islamic Criminal Law. Allah asks His Prophet to say that his prayer, his sacrifices, his life and death are all for Allah-Subhanahu-wa ta'ala. He is the first to surrender, means supreme in submission and obedience to God in time and space. Everything of a believer is for God. This, infact, is the faith in God of all believers. Islamic Law is part of this integrated concept.

Islamic law is divine, the Will of God to be established on earth. Law is revealed by God, Who alone Knows what is absolutely good for mankind. The law is to be meticulously observed and interpreted in letter and spirit because Islamic law is what God in his wisdom has ordained for the well-being of all mankind. As God is the perfect being, so is His law, perfect and for all time. It is not a system of law to be judged and evaluated as good or bad in accordance with the changing views of the population or the policies of the State. Both the society and the State have ideally to conform to its dictates. Man sometimes, with his limited knowledge, maybe constrained to see the advantages of Islamic law, but, is a matter of faith that all advantages are there, may be hidden. It cannot be exposed to the vagaries in its ideal, that is, perfect form.

Allah says:

اِنَّـا اَنْزَلْنَا اِلَيْكَ الْكِتَابَ بِالْحَقِّ لِتَحْكُمَ بَيْنَ النَّاسِ بِمَا اَرٰكَ اللّٰه' ولا تكن للخائنين خصيما۔

(سورة النساء، آية : ١٠٥)

"We have sent down to thee the Book in Truth, that thou mightiest judge between people by that which Allah has shown thee: So be not an advocate for those, who betray their trust." (4:105)

Whatever guidance Allah has given to us, that is a trust, which we should not betray. Laws have to be obeyed as commanded by Allah.

Allah in Sura al-Maida commands:—

وَمَنْ لَمْ يَحْكُمْ بِمَا اَنْزَلَ اللّٰهُ فَاُولٰئِكَ هُمُ الْكٰفِرُوْنَ.

(سورة الما ئدة، آية : ٤٤)

"If any body fail to judge by what Allah hath revealed, they are unbelievers." (5:44)

This verse makes it clear that the believers have to obediently follow what Allah has commanded. Disobedience to Allah's revealed laws is a betrayal and those who act contrary to the command are unbelievers. These verses in definite and unequivocal terms, enjoin upon believer, a strict adherence to the law revealed by God to us. Thus believers, from cradle to grave, at every turn or movement in life are bound to follow what Allah has commanded. Law is inseparable from religion and faith. It is ideal.

وَمَا تَسْئَلُهُمْ عَلَيْهِ مِنْ اَجْرٍ اِنْ هُوَ اِلَّا ذِكْرٌ لِّلْعٰلَمِيْنَ.

(سورة يوسف، آية : ١٠٤)

"It is no less than a message for all creatures."
(12:104)

لَقَدْ كَانَ فِيْ قَصَصِهِمْ عِبْرَةٌ لِّاُولِي الْاَلْبَابِ، مَا كَانَ حَدِيْثاً يُفْتَرٰى وَلٰكِنْ تَصْدِيْقَ الَّذِى بَيْنَ يَدَيْهِ وَ تَفْصِيْلَ كُلِّ شَيْئٍ وَهُدًى وَ رَحْمَةً لِّقَوْمٍ يُؤْمِنُون. (سورة يو سف، آية ١١١)

"It is a detailed exposition of all things, and a guide and a mercy to any such as believe." (12:111)

Such a Divine ordained law has fascinated the author to compare with Indian Criminal law, a law made by man, based on man's intellectual reasoning, a secular law which does not recognize a system of natural and moral law ranking higher than State legislation. It is based on a firm belief that any competent legislative body can change all existing laws. Indian Law is based on the notion:

> "Crime is what society says is crime by establishing that an act is a violation of the criminal law. Without law there can be no crime at all, although there may be moral indignation which results in law being enacted."[1]

Infact, under Indian secular concept, it is said that law is a living creature that reflects the aims and needs of society it serves. An act is not a crime if it is not in violation of criminal law though it may be condemned as it is in disregard to moral and religious value. Thus morality, religion and law are separable.

---

1. Klare H.J., "Changing Concepts of Crime and its Treatment", p. 17.

As the study of Comparative Criminal Law as such would be very wide. It has, therefore, been narrowed down. The area of comparative investigation selected for present study is confined to "Criminal Breach of Trust under Islamic Criminal Law and Indian Criminal Law."

Breach of Trust is an area where development is rapid. Offences being committed are also of serious nature. Field is completely new. No work has been done, particularly in relation to Islamic criminal law.

About Islamic criminal law critics have gone to the extent of declaring as if there is no law. Under such circumstances comparative study explaining the similarities and dissimilarities is of much significance and importance. This fact has attracted the author to work on and let know the critics their worth.

A comparative study of Criminal Breach of Trust under Islamic criminal law with Indian Criminal Law is proposed because Indian law is supposed to be the modern comprehensive law. The text of Penal Code of India is not only applied in India but applied in different names in other countries as well, such as Sudan, Sri Lanka, Pakistan, Malaysia, Nigeria, Kenya, etc., the countries which were British colonies. Even after attaining Independence the same code is being applied in dealing with the crime problem. As it is supposed to be the most up-to-date and modern, it is selected for comparision with Islamic Criminal Law relating to criminal breach of trust so that the later's significance in modern context may also be tested and is made known.

Critics of Islamic criminal law are of the view:—

"That Criminal Law of Islam is not in tune with the fast developing scientific age. It does not suit to the modern advanced conditions, nor does it come up to the standard of modern laws."

The fact is that the Islamic Law which is part of modern syllabuses and curricular of colleges and universities is the one known as 'Personal Law'. This is the only part of Islamic Law which the modern scholars study.

Apart from this the Islamic Criminal Law has now become obsolescent and the modern scholars, are absolutely ignorant of the provisions of Islamic Criminal Law.

Western educated and brain washed secular scholars, generally attack Islamic traditions and its traditional values. To them western culture is the highest stage of men's spiritual and material development, and consider Islamic civilization and culture useless. They advocate the adoption of western civilization and culture without reservation as the only way leading to their advancement.

These westernized scholars not only attack Islamic culture and civilization but they make the Islamic Law also target of their criticism. They assert that law must be man-made if it is to fulfil the changing needs of the scientifically changing and developing society. They question the validity of Shariah for modern times.

However, the strict Muslims are of the opinion that westernisation of laws is serving no purpose. The introduction of western laws has corrupted society, bred immorality and destroyed the inherited and traditional values of Muslim society. Muslims realize that such modernization in the garb of western culture belongs to an alien ideal type. In all Muslim countries a new trend has emerged, especially manifested in religious movements aiming at mobilizing traditional Islamic Laws and values toward modernization, to give it sanction and strength. Conscious efforts are being made in the Muslim World now to eliminate all non-Islamic influences which have been introduced as part of western styled reform and modernisation and get rid of undesirable values of the west.

Muslim masses in all Islamic countries world over are demanding the introduction of complete Islamic code of criminal law replacing the existing British or European laws.

The contemporary Islamic world is full of crisis. History tells us that period of crisis often blossoms into periods of creative thinking. The role of Muslim scholars and Muslim intellectuals in this period is a crucial one. Their's is the onerous task studying, probing and discovering Islamic laws, particularly the Islamic criminal law in relation to the present day problem in the vastly complicated world of today.

Study of Islamic Criminal Law is also relevant in the present context because the western scholars consider Islamic criminal law harsh, barbaric and retributive, not-suiting to the modern civilised society.

Islamic jurists, on the other hand, consider Islamic Criminal Laws superior to other laws by virtue of its perfection. They are of the opinion that Islamic Criminal Law is modern in the sense that it contains all rules and relevant doctrines needed for law to be complete and comprehensive. It fulfils all the human requirements which a good law needs and is equally competent to meet new problems which may arise in future. The author will examine the above observation in relation to criminal breach of Trust comparing it with Indian law.

It is said that Islamic Criminal Law, breach of trust is a minor part of it, is permanent, stable, immutable and everlasting, eminated from Qur'ãnic revelation. Further they say that sublimity is another characteristic of Islamic Criminal Law which contains such principles and doctrines that will maintain superiority over other laws and its standard will always be loftier than human standards.

The specific offence of criminal breach of trust is selected with the aim to find out the truth and a solution to this debate currently undergoing between the traditionalists and western modern scholars.

In India before the advent of Britishes, during Muslim Rule, Islamic Criminal Law was the *Lex Loci*-the law of the land. Judiciary attained its highest honourable place during the Mughal period. The period is also known as golden period of the Indian History. Justice in criminal matters was being administered to all irrespective of caste, creed of religion.

Masses were satisfied with the standard of justice then being observed. However, the last period of Mughal Rule in India saw the downfall of the judicial system. The fact, the whole edifice of judicial structure was shattered. Some historians have criticised the criminal judicial system even of the golden period as a foreign system imposed upon Indian people.

In 1860s the present Indian Penal Code, prepared by Lord Macaulay was enacted and enforced in India completely replacing the Islamic criminal law. About this Penal code also it is said that it is a British Common Law alien to Indian conditions. However, even after 53 years since India achieved independence it is still in force and in practice.

With a view to have historical perspective the object of the present study is also to examine the efficacy of both the systems in relation to Criminal Breach of Trust in reference to the Indian conditions.

The entire study relating the Criminal Breach of Trust would have two dimensions:

First, theoretical, and

secondly, operational.

Under the first, efforts would be made to study nature and concept of criminal breach of trust in comparision to the Islamic criminal law and Indian criminal law. It would also examine liabilities of servants and hirelings, agents and partners. Under the operational part, procedure of the both the systems would be explored and examined. Arrests, bail, investigations, cognizance and institution of suits, court structure, judges, their appointments, qualifications and jurisdictions are to be studied and compared. Further such matter, as administration of oath, confession, and evidences are to be compared. Position of Muhtasib, position of non-Muslims under Islamic criminal, ijtihad and position of legal advisors are also to be studied. Lastly judgement and punishment, appeal, revision and reference are to be probed and compared. In brief, study would be comprehensive, examining both conceptual and operational dimensions of the subject.

The Book contains ten chapters. Some chapter are divided into Part A and B, and parts are further sub-divided.

Apart from there is a 'statement of the problem' in the beginnings, and recapitulation and projection at the end.

The scheme of the Book is so arranged that theoretical or conceptual and practical or operational aspects of the subject under study are given due representation, making the study to comprehend within it all answers to the questions agitating the minds of the scholars. It would be a novel-study and of great interest to scholars of a criminal law who are trying to analyze juristic problems intellectually and its translation into practical form in which they desire to shape the society. No doubt, study would be a good contribution to the academic world, particularly to India where heap of cases are pending in courts due to technicalities of laws. Justice is not being done because where justice is delayed justice denied. In fact, India needs its own indiginous judicial system.

CHAPTER I

"NATURE OF TRUST: INDIAN CRIMINAL LAW"

Word 'trust' has not been defined in the Indian Penal Code. In Under Hill's Law of Trust and Trustees,[1] the term 'trust' has been explained as:—

> "A trust is an equitable obligation, binding a person (who is called a trustee) to deal with property over which he has control (which is called the trust property), for the benefit of persons (who are called beneficiaries or cestuis que trust), of whom he may himself be one, and any one of whom may enforce the obligation."

Maitland explains trust as:—

> "When a person has rights which he is bound to exercise upon, on behalf of another or for the accomplishment of some particular purpose he is said to have those rights in trust for that other or for that purpose and he is called a trustee."[2]

Both the definitions are subjected to criticism. It is a fiduciary relationship with respect to property, subjecting the persons by whom the title to property is held to equitable duties to deal with the property is held to equitable duties to deal with the property for the benefit of another person, which arises as a result of manifestation of an intention to create it.'

---

1. 12th Edition, p. 3.
2. Maitland: Lectures on Equity (2nd Edition), p. 44.

Section 3, of Indian Trust Act,[3] defines the 'Trust' as:—

"Trust is an obligation annexed to the ownership of property, and arising out of a confidence reposed in and accepted by the owner, or declared and accepted by him, for the benefit of another, or of another and the owner."

A persual of the above definitions brings one to infer the following characteristics of the trust:—

1. A trust is a relationship;
2. It is a relationship of a fiduciary character;
3. It is a relationship with respect to property, not one involving merely personal obligations;
4. It involves the existence of equitable obligations imposed upon the holder of the title to the property to deal with it for benefit of another

   and
5. It arises out of a confidence reposed in and accepted by the owner, or declared and accepted by him, as a result of a manifestation of an intention to create the relationship.

   The combination of these things characterizes the notion of the trusts.

"Breach of Trust"

The next phrase which requires explanation is the concept of 'breach of trust'. It may be explained as 'any act or neglect on the part of a trustee which is not authorised or excused by the terms of the trust instrument, or by law, is called a breach of trust.

1.

Section 405 of the Indian Penal Code[4] explains 'breach of trust' as follows:—

---

1. Criminal breach of trust - Whoever, being in any manner entrusted with property, or with any dominion over property, dishonestly misappropriates or converts to his own use that property, or dishonestly uses or disposes of that property in violation of any direction of law prescribed the mode in which such trust is to be discharged, or of any legal contract, express or implied, which he has made touching the discharge of such trust, or wilfully suffers any other person so to do, commits "criminal breach of trust."

Explanation 1. A person being an employer, who deducts the employee's contribution from the wages payable to the employee for credit to a Provident Fund or Family Pension Fund established by law for the time being in force, shall be deemedd to have been entrusted with the amount of the contribution so deducted by him and if he makes default in the payment of such contribution to the said Fund in violation of the said law, shall be deemed to have dishonestly used the amount of the said contribution in violation of a direction of law as aforesaid.

Explanation 2. A person, being an employer, who deducts the employees' contribution from the wages payable to the employees for credit to the Employees' State Insurance Fund held and administered by the Employees' State Insurance Act, 1948, shall be deemed to have been entrusted with the amount of the contribution so deducted by him and if he makes default in the payment of such contribution to the said Fund in violation of the said conribution in violation of a direction of law as aforesaid.

ILLUSTRATIONS

(a) A, being executor to the will of a deceased person, dishonestly disobeys the law which directs him to divide the effects according to the will and appropriates them to his own use. A has committed criminal breach of trust.

(b) A is a warehouse-keeper, Z, going on a journey, entrusts his furniture to A, under a contract that it shall be returned on payment of a stipulated sum for warehouse-room. A dishonestly sells the goods. A has committed criminal breach of trust.

"Whoever, being in any manner entrusted......
criminal breach of trust."

In analysing the section in Isser Chander Ghoshe V. Peari Mohun Palit,[5] it was held that to constitute the offence of criminal breach of trust, there must be dishonest misappropriation by a person in whom confidence is placed as to the custody or management of the property in respect of which the breach of trust is charged.

(c) A, residing in Calcutta is an agent for Z, residing at Delhi. There is an express or implied contract between A and Z, that all sum remitted by Z to A shall be invested by A, according to Z's direction. Z remits a lakh of rupees to A with directions to invest the same in company's paper. A dishonestly disobeys the directions and employs the money in his own business. A has committed criminal breach of trust.

(d) But if A, in the last illustration, nor dishonestly but in good faith, believing that it will be more for Z's advantage to hold shares in the Bank of Bengal, disobeys Z's directions and buys shares in the Bank of Bengal for Z instead of buying Company's paper, here, though Z instead of buying Company's paper, here, though Z suffer loss and should be entitled to bring a civil action against A, on account of that loss, yet A, not having acted dishonestly, has not committed criminal breach of trust.

(e) A, a revenue officer, is entrusted with public money and is either directed by law, or bound by a contract, express or implied, with the Government, to pay into a certain treasury all the public money which he holds, A dishonestly appropriates the money. A has committed criminal breach of trust.

(f) A, a carrier, is entrusted by Z with property to be carried by land of by water, A dishonestly misappropriates the money. A has committed criminal breach of trust.

5. (1891) 16 W.R. (Cr.) 39.

There must be an entrustment of property or dominion over the property of another. In the absence of such a proof of entrustment or dominion over the property of another, this section will not apply. The entrustment may be in any manner.

Misappropriation or conversion must be to one's own use or use in violation of any legal direction or of any legal contract.

It must be proved that misappropriation or conversion was with dishonest intention. There is no criminal breach of trust if dishonest intention is not proved. Section 405 to 409 dealing with offence of criminal breach of trust are aimed to punish an offence of which dishonestly is the essence. Every breach of trust is not criminal. On the other hand every breach of trust gives rise to a suit for damages, however, it is only when there is a proof of a mental element of fraudulent misappropriation that the commission of misappropriation of any sum of money becomes a penal offence punishable as criminal breach of trust. It is in fact this element of mental condition of fraudulent misappropriation that distinguishes an act of embezzlement which is a civil wrong or tort, from the offence of criminal breach of trust.

While considering the cases of criminal breach of trust the distinction between civil and criminal wrong must be borne in mind. An act committed may be intentional without being dishonest, or it may apparently seem to be dishonest without really being so. Criminal breach of trust involves a civil wrong, the relief available to the complainant is that he may seek his redress for damages in the civil court, but every breach of trust in the absence of mens-rea cannot legally justify a criminal prosecution.[6] The determining factor in judging

6. Kanhaiya Lall (1937, 38 Cr. j) 491, Amritlal v. Bajrangdal, 1963, 11 Cr. Lj. 474.

whether a case is one of criminal breach of trust or of civil wrong or tort is whether the person proceeded against had acted dishonestly,[7] causing loss to the owner or possessor, or depositor. In every case of breach of trust, in the absence of requisite mens rea, is not criminal.[8]

Under English Law there is no exact equivalent to an offence of criminal breach of trust. Larceny by bailee and embezzlement in English law are the offences, which represent what, under the Indian Penal Code, is theft, criminal misappropriation or criminal breach of trust.[9]

As to scope the terms of the section are very wide. Section applies in cases where a person is in any manner entrusted with property or dominion over property. It is not required that the trust should be in furtherance of any lawful object. The only thing which the section, inter alia, provides that if a person dishonestly misappropriates or converts to his own use the property entrusted to him he commits criminal breach of trust. This part of explanation of trust is complete in itself. It does not refer to the provisions as to disposal in violation of any direction of law prescribing the mode in which such trust is to be discharged, or of any legal contract, express or implied, which he has made touching the discharge of such trust. Different modes are there in which criminal breach of trust may be committed.[10] In Kalaktar Singh,[11] case it was held that the entrustment may be in any manner, not necessarily what implies a trust to be in the sense of a law relating to trust. Further the accused

7. Halimuddin Ahmad v. Ashoka Cement Ltd., 1976, Cr Lj 449 Pat.

8. (1952) 52 Cr. Lj 1178 (1182) Lah.

9. (1957) Cr. LJ 575, Velagala Venkata Reddy v. Kovouri Chinna Ven Kata Reddy (1941) Ran. 547.

10. Nga Te (1904) 2 LBR 216: 1 Cr. LJ 760 (FB).

11. (1978) Cr LJ 663 Pat, Shob Nath, 1975, Cr. LJ 1122 (All).

may get dominion of the property in any manner. What is contemplated by the section is that the person charged for criminal breach of trust should receive the property.[12] All those offences not specifically provided for in sections 407, 408 and 409, as well as, offence committed by trustees with regard to entrusted property or dominion given over the property are covered within the scope of this section 405.

"Essential Ingredients"

The necessary ingredients of the section are:—

1. Entrustment of property or dominion over property to any person;
2. Such entrustment must be in trust;
3. Such a person misappropriates or converts to his own use such a property;
4. Using or disposing of that property, or wilfully offering any other person so to do in violation:—
   - (a) of any direction of law prescribing the mode in which such trust is to be discharged, or
   - (b) of any legal contract, express or implied, which he has made touching the discharge of such trust.
5. Such misappropriation or user or disposal must be dishonest.

"Analogous Law"

Before elaborating the ingredients, an attempt is made here to explain the controversy relating to some analogous

12. Surrender Pal Singh (1957) Cr. LJ 170.

laws. Section 5 (1) (c) of the Prevention of Corruption Act, 1947, is one such provision. It reads as follows:—

Section 5 (1) "A public servant is said to commit the offence of criminal misconduct in the discharge of his duty.

Section 5 (c) If he dishonestly or fraudulently misappropriates or otherwise converts for his own use any property entrusted to him.

or under his control as a public servant or allows any other person so to do."

A controversy was arisen in a Punjab case[13] as to the applicability of Section 405 in the presence of Section 5 (1), (c) which one is to prevail, whether the provision under the Prevention of Corruption Act repeals section Section 405. Does the provisions make the section 405 redundant? In Om Prakash's case, Supreme Court settled the issue overruling the Punjab High Court decision. Presence of Section 5 (1) (c) does not repeal Section 405 of the Penal Code. The offence in Section 5 (1) (c) referred above is a distinct and separate offence from the one committed under section 405 of the Penal Code.

Similarly Bombay High Court in a case[14] under Section 146 (o) of Maharashtra Cooperative Societies Act 1960 held that where an officer of the society wilfully sanctions or recommends for his persons use or benefit or for the use or benefit of a person in whom he is interested, a loan in the name of any other person, he will be guilty of an offence under the above clause. It is a different type of offence from criminal misappropriation.

13. A 1952 Punj. 89.

14. A 1968 Bom. 124 (125).

Distinction

A distinction between criminal misappropriation and criminal breach of trust would also help in making the concept of breach of trust more clear. Property under criminal misappropriation comes into the possession of the offender by some casualty or otherwise which he afterwards misappropriates it. Whereas the offender in the case of criminal breach of trust is lawfully entrusted with the property and he dishonestly or dishonestly uses or disposes of that property in utter disregard for the direction of law prescribing the mode in which such trust is to be discharged, or of any legal contract touching the discharge of such trust, or wilfully suffers any other person so to do.

Illustrations to Section 406 and 405 abundantly makes the difference quite clear.

"Entrustment of Property"

This is one of the most essential ingredient of the offence under this section. In the absence of evidence of entrustment of property or dominion over property, Section 405 has no application.[15] Implications of entrustment are: the person handing over the property or on whose behalf that property is handed over to another, continues to be its owner.

The person handing over the property must have confidence in the person taking the property so that fiduciary relationship is created between them.[16]

---

15. (1979), Chand LR (Cri, 43, 43, Punj; (1977) 1 Fac 236 (237) (Madh. Pra); (1977), Pun LJ (Cri) 208 (210); (1971) Cal 93 (99): (1971), Cr. LJ 361; 1955 Pat 338 (339): 1955 Cr. LJ 1096; (1952) Nag 255 (256).

16. Tata JRD v. Payal Kumar 1986 (2) Crimes 449.

The most significant implication is that the ownership or beneficial interest in the property against which breach of trust is alleged remains in some person other than the accused and he holds it on behalf of some person or for his benefit.[17] The law requires that the accused should receive the property, and hold it on account of another person, so that he should be trustee of the property.[18] A person cannot misappropriate his own property. Entrustment cannotes that property is handed over by one person to another in whom the first person reposes confidence in the later for a specific purpose.

Word trust used in the section is quite comprehensive, includes the relationship not only of trustee and beneficiary but also that of bailer and bailee, master and servant, pledgor and pledgee, guardian and ward, and all other relations which postulates the fiduciary relationship between the complainant and the accused and the word entrustment has a corresponding meaning and embraces all cases in which goods are entrusted for a specific purpose.[19]

In Somnath v. State of Rajasthan,[20] The Supreme Court observed:—

"The Expression 'entrusted' in Section 409 applies to cases of criminal breach of trust by Public Servant, or by Banker, merchant or agent, is used in a wide sense and includes all cases in which property is voluntarily handed over for a

---

17. Ibid, note II.

18. 1981 Cri. LJ 258 (259) Mad.

19. 1956 Raj. 20 (20, 21), 1956 Cr. LJ 107. 1934 Rang. 41 (42) (Waterproof coat supplied to Rly. Servant on condition that it should be returned on leavng service-pledge by servant). ILR (1952) Hdy. 753 (756, In Order to Constitute the offence to whom property is entrusted must act in a fiduciary capacity).

20. 1972, SC 1990 (1993): 1972 CR LJ. 897.

specific purpose and is dishonestly disposed of contrary to the terms on which possession has been handed over. It maybe that a person to whom the property is handed over may be an agent of the person to whom it is entrusted or to whom it may belong, in which case if the agent who comes into possession of it on behalf of his principle, fraudulently misappropriates the property, he is, nonetheless, guilty of criminal breach of trust because as an agent he is entrusted with it. A person authorised to collect money on behalf of another is entrusted with the money when the amounts are paid to him, and though the person paying may no longer have any proprietary interest nonetheless the person whose behalf it was collected becomes the owner as soon as the amount is handed over to the person so authorised to collect on his behalf."

It may be inferred from the above observation that a person entrusts property to another, continues to vest in the owner but the thing is in possession of the bailee to be restored to the bailor, or applied in accordance with his instructions.

The ownership or beneficial interest in the property must be in some person than the accused, and he must hold it on behalf of some person or in someway for his benefit.

Where jewellery is pledged in order to ensure the repayment of an overdraft there is an entrustment, it would amount to an entrustment."[21]

The accused falsely induced by making a representation to the complainant that they had sent some bonds for rectification to Bombay and as they had not arrived and the last day for completion of a contract with a Bank had arrived, entreated the complainant to give the complainant's bonds temporarily for a few days, assuming the complainant that

---

21. Supra N. P.

his bonds would be returned to him as soon as the rectified bonds returned from Bombay. On this assurance the complaint endorsed and delivered bonds to the accused. It was held that the bonds were not delivered to the accused absolutely but were entrusted to them. Though the accused when requested to the complainant to deliver certain properties had the intention of deceiving him, however, a subsequent misappropriation by them of the property to their own use would be considered a criminal breach of trust. "The fact that there was a complete offence of cheating when the property was received would not prevent the accused being guilty of the offence of criminal breach of trust."[22]

A mere transaction of sale cannot amount to an entrustment.[23] Similarly where goods are delivered to a person in pursuance of a contract for purchase, it would not amount to entrustment and the mere fact that the person denies receipt of goods delivered does not make him liable for criminal breach of trust.[24]

In Chanan Singh,[25] case, where a person was entrusted with property attached by an order of court, and he on demand refused to produce the property, it was held that his denial amounted to a breach of trust, hence held guilty.

A mere breach of contract or of the condition of a permit is not necessarily a criminal breach of trust.[26]

A secretary of a bank, authorised by the terms of a power of attorney to purchase government promissory notes for bank,

22. Melver, (1935) 49 MLJ 681.

23. Jaswantlal (1968) AIR SC 700.

24. Labhu (1930) 32 Cr. LJ 300.

25. (1934) 36 Cr. LJ 119.

26. 1970 Pat LJR 610.

obtains the notes, he is entrusted by the bank. He is under an obligation to pay them to the Bank and has no right to keep them with him even in satisfaction of any claim he may have against the bank. Such keeping of the Promissory Notes without authority amounts to misappropriation.[27]

The word entrusted has been used in a wide sense. Cases such as voluntarily handing over for a specific purpose and dishonestly disposing of in repudiation of any direction of law or in violation of the contract are all covered within the purview of entrustment. In Shob Nath,[28] money was deposited with the Post-Master for opening saving banks account was held entrustment. In Jage Ram,[29] a person borrowed a bicycle from the complainant with a promise to return within a period of two or three days. He failed to return the Bicycle as promised, disposed of the machine and converted the proceeds to his own use. It was held that the relationship between the accused and the complainant was of a bailor and bailee as the complainant had delivered his bicycle to the accused for a specific purpose and a specific period upon contract that after expiry of the said period the machine would be returned to him and is disposing of the machine dishonestly and appropriating money to his own the accused was guilty of an offence under this section.

In Jaswantlal Nathlal[30] their Lordships of the Supreme Court observed:—

> "The expression entrusted carries with it the implication that the person handing over any property

---

27. Ram Nath Dave 1932 OWN 485.
28. 1975 Cr LJ 1122 (All).
29. (1951) Punj. 286.
30. Jaswantlal (1968) Cr. LJ 803.

or on whose behalf that property is handed over the another continues to be its owner. Further, the person handing over the property must have confidence in the person taking the property so as to create a fiduciary relationship between them. A mere transaction of sale cannot amount to an entrustment."

According to this section property may be entrusted in any manner. It does not perceive the creation of trust with all its technical requisites. It simply conceive the creation of a relationship whereby the owner of the property hands over property to another person to be retained by him until the happening or not-happening of an event or to dispose of on such happening. However, ownership still remains with the transferer. The transferer has the custody of the property to retain or dispose of for the benefit of other party. The person so placed in possession has only a special interest by way of a claim for the same of the thing or such other accidental expenses as incurred by him.[31] There must be some entrustment. It matters little whether the complainant on whose behalf the property is entrusted is the owner thereof or not."[32] It is not requisite that the amount received should be the property of the person on whose behalf it is received. A person deems entrusted with the money and the amounts are paid to him. In Som Nath Puri,[33] it was held that though the person paying may no longer have any proprietary interest nonetheless the person on whose behalf it was collected becomes the owner as soon as the amount is handed over to the person so authorised to collect on his behalf. Mere use of legal terms are not sufficient to render a person liable for

---

31. Supra N. P.

32. Dahyalal Dalpartram (1959) 61 Bom LR 885: (1960) Cr LJ 217.

33. 1972 SCC (Cr) 897.

breach of trust. Merely the parties are calling a transaction a trust is not enough though it may be express and in writing. Actual entrustment of property should be there.

"Every payment of money by one person to another does not amount to entrustment unless there are circumstances attending it from which one can gather that it was an entrustment and not a mere payment.[34] In cases where a person gives gold to a goldsmith who has jewellery making business, for making some jewellery, or gives some money to the goldsmith to purchase gold and make jewellery, in both the cases there is an entrustment, if the goldsmith converts the gold or money into his own use, it would be a repudiation of implied contract between the parties, the goldsmith would be liable for breach of trust.[35] To Ratanlal Dhirajlal, a person cannot be said to be entrusted with property within the meaning of this section when he obtains possession of it by means of trick.[36] A trust implies confidence placed by one man in another. It implies necessarily that the confidence was freely given and that there is a true consent. There is no true consent if confidence is obtained as a result of a trick. If there was a trick or deceit, a true consent cannot arise; there can be no entrustment, and no offence under section 406,[37] because an essential element of that offence is an entrustment. The accused represented to the complainant that he was a tinner

---

34. Jairani Devi v. Khrisna Kumar Jauhari (1985) CRJ 64 (All).

35. Mithalal (1955) Raj 907.

36. Law of Crimes, Ratanlal & Dhirajlal, Vol. II, 23rd Edition P. 1529.

37. Punishment for criminal breach of trust. Whoever commits criminal breach of trust shall be punished with imprisonment of either description for a term which may extend to three years, or with- fine, or with both.

while he was in fact not a tinner. The complainant thereupon gave the accused certain utensils to be repaired which were neither repaired nor returned by the accused. It was held that it might be said, using the words of general import, that the complainant entrusted the accused with property, he was, in fact, tricked out of it. Therefore, the offence fell not under this section, but under section 420.[38]

When property is obtained by cheating there is no entrustment. Similarly under an agreement of sale where money is paid as part payment for the purchase of certain property, there is no entrustment and the person who receives the advance money may utilise that money in any manner he likes. Conversion of money to one's own use would not render him liable for breach of trust. But where the money is paid to him for a particular purpose and not as part payment of purchase money, the person who receives if converts into his own use, he would be liable for breach of trust, because there is a clear entrustment for a specific purpose.

In Sat Narain,[39] case, there was Chit Fund Scheme started by the accused company and the money collected from the depositors was to be utilised by the company as its own on condition that the members of the scheme would get the equivalent amount back after the completion of a particular specified period along with interest. It was held that there was no entrustment and if the company did not return the deposited amount to the member depositors. An action for breach of trust would not lie.

---

38. Arab Mihan (1942) Kar 284. Radhakanta (1954, Cr. LJ 429).

39. 1974 Cr. LJ 232 (P & H); Laxman Singh (1986) 1 Crimes 634.

The Sikkim Nationalised Transport[40] employed a person to act as bus conductor to collect fare from passengers. He collected a sum of Rs. 2,000/- as fare but failed to deposit the said amount inspite of repeated reminders, he was not held liable as there was no entrustment. The High Court held that one of the most important elements of entrustment is that the property in respect of which criminal breach of trust is alleged to have been committed must have been made over or transferred or handed over by the aggrieved person, who continues to be the owner thereof, to the accused. In this case there was no entrustment because the amount was not made over or transferred or handed over by any one on behalf of Sikkim Transport to the accused.

However, the above verdict of the High Court is not correct in view of the decision of the Supreme Court in Som Nath v. State of Rajasthan.[41] It was held in that case that a person authorised to collect money on behalf of another is entrusted with the money when the amounts are paid to him.

Where a superior officer delegates his authority to collect money to his subordinate staff, such a staff member gets a legal and during the exercise of such delegates power if he receives amount or paid to him would be considered entrustment as envisaged by Section 405.[42]

Where a Naib Tehsildar is authorised to collect rent and he lawfully authorises his Moharir to collect the same, the collection of rent by the Moharir is, under the

---

40. Puspa Kumar (1978) Cr. LJ 1379 (Sikkim)

41. Supra N.P.

42. Rajkishore (1969) Cr. LJ 995.

circumstances, under a delegated implied authority and the payment to the Moharir constitute entrustment.[43]

In Kesar Singh,[44] case a distinction was drawn between the person entrusted with property and one having control or general charge over the property. In the first case if the property found missing, with further proof, the person so entrusted would be held accountable, but in the second situation he would be liable only when either the misappropriation is shown or party to criminal breach of trust, committed in respect of the property by any other person. Illustrative cases may be referred where mere giving of keys of sub-treasury to the sonar on a holiday does not amount to giving charge,[45] and where the accused a cashier was in possession of the keys of the safe, the keys of the Inner Drawers were kept inside the safe and the cash disappeared from the safe, the inference was that the accused was party or privy to the extraction of the cash from the safe.[46]

The entrustment need not be for any lawful object.[47] Further it is immaterial and irrelevant that the accused could have been legally entrusted with the property.[48]

Justice Blair, in Queen Empress v. Gouri Shanker,[49] observed:—

43. (1969) Cr. LJ 1995.

44. 1969 Orissa 190.

45. Amreet Sakharam Sarup 1972 SCC (Cr.) 166.

46. Surrender Prasad Verma 1973 SCC (Cr.) 700.

47. 1958, Pat. 272 (275). It does not matter in the least whether the contract was legal or not so long as it was shown that, in some manner whatever there was an entrustment of the property in question (1927 Nag. 223).

48. 1958 All 698.

49. AIR 1968 SC 700.

"A person who accepts a trust cannot turn round and dispute the title of his trustee."

Sale of Cement by the government to the contractor solely for the purpose of its being issued for construction work is nothing other than sale and there is no entrustment which implies that the person handing over the property continues to be its owner.

The manner need not be proper or legal, it may be in any manner. Object should not necessarily be legal or trust created in execution of a lawful object. It shows that there may be liability for criminal breach of trust where the trust even is created in the course of illegal transaction. Ramappa's[50] case elaborates the point more clearly. In this case the accused, a servant of co., misappropriated a large sum of money made up of amounts which he received from the manager various times on the false pretence that they were required for paying coolies, it was held that he was guilty of criminal breach of trusts. When he receive the money, he did so as the servant of the company, for the express purpose of using it for his master's benefit in a particular way. He was, therefore, entrusted with the money and his misappropriation to himself amounted to criminal breach of trust.

The illustrations to the section 405 show clearly that property comes into the possession of accused either by an express entrustment or by some process placing the accused in a position of trust.[51]

"Such Entrustment must be in trust:—"

According to Ratanlal Dhirajlal, 'where there is no original confidence, there is no trust, and a misappropriation,

50. (1911) 22 MLJ 112.

51. AIR 1949 Cal. 207.

if punishable at all, will he under Section 403.[52] The illustrations to Section 405 clearly indicate that the property comes into the possession of the accused by some process placing the accused in a position of trust. The term trust under Section 405 had different implications in different circumstances. Expression of trust is comprehensive enough to include within its scope the relationship of trustee and beneficiary, bailor and bailee, master and servant, pledger and pledgee, banker and customer, graftsman and auctioner, director and company, spreader, guardian and ward, debtor and creditor and company, joint owner, pleader and ward, debtor and creditor, joint owner, pleader and client, husband and wife, partners, broker and customer, vendor and customer and all fiduciary relations between the complainant and the accused.[53]

In Shah Naim Ata,[54] it was explained that the terms of this section are wide enough to include trustees for every kind, that is, those who are such, not only by reason of some employment for which they receive remuneration, but by reason of some trust constituted by express deed, or even by mere implication of law, though the office may be gratuitious. However, if there is no trust, there will be no offence creating liability under Section 405 and Section 406.

Trust is a must. As explained earlier trust is an obligation annexed to the ownership of property, and arising out of a confidence reposed in and accepted by the owner, or declared or of another and the owner! These requirements

52. Supra N. P.

53. Supra N P.

54. (1930) 7 OWN 663: 3 Cr. LJ 1012.

should be satisfied first then violation or breach of trust would be taken into consideration.

"Breach of Trust and Breach of Contract":—

Mere breach of contract is not criminal breach of trust. Omission to return earnest money on failure to perform contract only creates a civil liability and does not amount to criminal breach of trust.[55]

Intention of the accused is to be seen at the time when an agreement or a promise is made and not afterwards. Accused who agreed to complete certain work within stipulated time and also took an advance and on failure to complete the work did not return the advance does not amount any offence under Section 406. It is a case of civil liability[56] and not of a breach of trust.

In the illustrations attached with section it has abundantly been made clear that where the person has committed the offence, the property in respect of which the offence has been committed must be the property of another person and not of the accused. He should also not be the beneficial owner, although in one case, that of executor, he had the legal title. In Ajoy V. Wadwani G.M.,[57] it was held that the property in respect of which criminal breach of trust can be committed must be either the property of person other than the person accused, or the beneficial interest in or ownership of it must be in some other person and the offender must hold such property on trust for such other person or in some way for his benefit.

---

55. 1977 Punj. LJ (Cri) 369 (373).

56. 1977 Punj. LJ 418.

57. 1965 II Cr. LJ 418. (See also AIR 1965 SC 1319 Mohd. Sulaiman v. Mohd. Ayub).

Example may be given where money advanced to a broker for the specified purpose of purchase and supply of paddy with an agreement that the broker is to suffer the loss or get the gains by the fluctuations in fall and rise of market price cannot be claimed as entrusted within the meaning of this section, though by the agreement the company bound itself to take delivery of the paddy purchased and an express trust was declared in regard to the amounts advanced.

Similarly, where a person instructed a jeweller to make a gold chain for him and paid Rs. 300/-, covering cost of gold and making charges, as advance, and the jeweller failed to prepare and deliver the chain on the stipulated date and did not return the money also. On prosecution it was held that 'though he was guilty of dishonest and dishonourable conduct in not making the chain, he could not be said to have misappropriated the money because when it was paid to him it became his. His obligation thereafter was to produce the gold chain. That he failed to do, and B could recover the money from A as money paid on a consideration which had wholly failed. That, however, would not make the act of A criminal, and as there was no entrustment there could be no question of an offence under this section.[58]

In Bhikari Charan,[59] a Sarpanch was supplied with seeds on credit, failure to pay amount within stipulated time did not amount to breach of trust but only a breach of contract.

On the other hand significant point under consideration is that mere breach of contract is not enough to make a person liable under the section, some sort of entrustment should be established to make a man guilty under this section. Therefore,

---

58. Kanailal Dutta (1951) 52 Cr. LJ 28.

59. 1982 Cr. LJ (Noc) 174 (Ori).

in case where a person took some gold jewels from the goldsmith for showing it to his wife for placing an order for similar jewel if approved by her, failed to give back to the goldsmith and retained the jewels with himself towards some debts due to him by the goldsmith, he was found guilty for criminal breach of trust.[60]

Again in another case where money was paid to a goldsmith with instruction that he should use it for purchasing gold from the market and preparing jewels as desired by the person making the payment, but the goldsmith dishonestly converted the money to his own use in violation of the implied contract, he was held guilty of criminal breach of trust.[61]

These later two cases referred above shows that there was some sort of entrustment, in both and the accused violated the condition for which he was given the money. However, in Mohinder Kumar,[62] case relating to transaction of 'trade sales', property in goods is delivered to the buyer without an element of entrustment. If the buyer fails to pay the price promised there is no breach of trust. We cannot impute any criminality in such cases.

The cases of craftsman and customer, important element is to establish entrustment and fiduciary relation between the two where a person hands over a gold to the goldsmith, transferring all his rights thereto on promise that goldsmith would give a certain amount of gold, the transaction is not an entrustment but a contract. On the other hand if he transfers the ornament for being melted and converted into gold and returned to him, in such a transaction there is entrustment, failure to give gold would amount to breach of trust.

Where property is entrusted for repair purposes and the repairer takes that in his own use instead of returning after the repair, is breach of trust. Allegations made in a complaint were that a truck was entrusted to the accused for the purpose of repairing it and he had agreed to return it in three days. The accused, however, instead of returning it started using the same. The allegations held constitute an offence under section 406.[63]

"Loan"

Whether a trust can be created in any transaction of loan depends upon the facts of each case. However, the relationship between a debtor and creditor is not a fiduciary one and the advance of a loan is not an entrustment of money.[64] Once the money advanced after the grant of loan, it becomes the property of the debtor. A failure to repay the loan is not a breach of trust much less, a criminal breach of trust. In Satyabrata Bhattacharya V. Jarnail Singh,[65] it was held that giving a loan to somebody for accommodating a person to have money for certain time is not entrustment of money with a direction that the money would be utilised in a particular manner. A payment by the debtor to the creditor in discharge of the debt is also not an entrustment. Further the failure by the creditor to give a receipt is not a breach of trust.

However, there may be transactions between debtor and creditor where there may be entrustment also, and breach of such entrustment either by one or the other party to such loan. For example the debtor pays an amount to the creditor with the intention to repose trust in him and expecting to dispose of the money in a particular manner, it would be considered entrustment of money. Where the accused borrowed jewels from the complainant for use in a marriage and pledged the

63. 1977 Punj-Lj 265 (267).

64. 1976 Cr. Lj. 446 (Ori).

65. Ibid N. 44.

same, raising a loan on it, it was held that he was guilty of criminal breach of trust."[66]

"**Pledge**": Pledge or pawn may be explained as a 'bailment of goods by a debtor with his creditor to be kept as security till the payment of the debt', and relationship thus resulted are fiduciary in character between the pledgor and the pledgee, a dishonest conversion or misappropriation of the property pledged, thus would amount to a criminal breach of trust. A dishonest use of pledged property by the pledgee in repudiation of any direction of law or of any legal contract related to the manner of use of the property would also amount breach of trust. Therefore like loan cases, there can be no general proposition of law that a pledgee cannot be guilty of criminal breach of trust where the contract between the complainant and the accused is that the pledged ornament would be returned to the complainant on payment of the entire dues and accused in spite of the payment retains it and uses and ornament as a pledge in respect of a completely independent transaction, he definitely uses the ornament in violation of the legal contract between the parties creating the trust.[67]

A sub-pledge by the pledge to the extent of his interest (in the absence of any condition to the contrary in the contract of pledge) would be fully within the rights of the pledgee and would not constitute a breach of trust. It may be otherwise if it is made in violation of a condition in the contract of pledge.[68]

In the absence of a condition attached to the contract of pledge, the pledgee has a legal right to deal with the pledged

66. (1905) 10 Mys. CCR. NO. 221, p. 913.

67. 1955 Cr. Lj. 1371 (DB).

68. 1942 Rang. 62.

property in any manner he likes in same way as can be exercised by a bailee under a bailment.

Under section 179 of the Indian Contract Act the pledgee has been given the right to sub-pledge of the goods pledged to him proportionate to his interest. Therefore, if the money lender during the regular course of his money-lending business, effects sub-pledges, with same amount, same date as the pledges made to him with a view to raise capital at a lower rate of interest, it would not amount to breach of trust. Provided there was no express contract prohibiting to make sub-pledges, secondly no proof to show that the sub-pledges were made with a dishonest intention. In a case where a person has been authorised to pledge some valuable belonging to another person for a specific amount, but pledges them for a larger sum and keep it secret from the owner, using the additional amount for his benefit, he would be liable for breach of trust. Here it is a clear case of entrustment.

In a case where the accused, who had pledged promisory notes with the complainant as security for a loan, dishonestly induced the letter to handover the same to him by pretending that he acquired the same to collect money from his debtors with the aid of which he would pay cash to the complainant and the accused disposed of the notes in violation of his contract with the complainant, it was held that there was both entrustment and dishonest misappropriation and the accused was guilty of criminal breach of trust.[69]

"**Hire Purchase Agreement**":- Under the hire-purchase agreement a person agrees to bind himself with the terms of agreement, that is, to pay the installments for the article purchased under the agreement, till the payment is made for

---

69. Vankatagurunatha Sastri v. 1923, 45 MLJ 133; 1923 AIR (M) 597.

the installments agreed, not to assign, underlet or part with the property during the period of hire, if he violates the terms, he would be guilty under section 406, because simply he is entrusted with the property, ownership still remains with whom he has entered the agreement for hire purchase. The title to the property si not transferred to the hirer during the period of hire. If the hirer during such period dishonestly disposes of the property contrary to the contract, he commits criminal breach of trust.[70] Where the hirer pledges or sells the hired property in violation of hire agreement, he is responsible for criminal breach of trust.[71]

Other illustrative cases may be, where a person hired a motor car under the hire purchase system, the terms of the agreement provided that until the installments were fully paid the car was to remain the absolute property of the company. Further the hirer agreed that during the period of hire he would not assign, underlet or part with the possession of the car in any way. While the agreement was still in force, the hirer pledged the car three to three different persons on three different occasions. It was held that the hirer is liable for criminal breach of trust.[72] This is a clear case of violation of the legal contract.

Assignments under the pledge to three different persons show that the hirer had a dishonest intention and absolute disregard, for the terms of hire-purchase agreement. In another case a person got a motor-lorry on hire purchase-agreement, stipulating conditions that so long as the amount of purchase price was not fully paid, the vehicle would remain the absolute

---

70. 1915 Bom. 206.

71. 1927 Bom. 38.

72. (1915) 17 Bom LR 670.

property of the transferor and the hirer would not dispose of it or deal with it. He also agreed that in case of default in the payment of instalment the owner could recover the possession of the car as well. The hirer, inspite of the agreement, sold the lorry before the installments were paid, it was held that the hirer is guilty of criminal breach of trust.[73]

However, in cases where there is a mere breach of condition of the hire-purchase agreement, such as, failure to pay an instalment of hire, without fault, would not amount to criminal breach of trust. For example where the complainant sold a gramaphone to the accused on instalment system but on his not paying installments the complainant asked for the machine and though it was not immediately produced, it had not been sold and was produced in court, it was held that the matter was of civil nature, and the mere-non-payment of the monthly installments could not be considered as a criminal offence.[74]

In Sunil Ranjan Ghosh Roy,[75] case the 'accused in violation of a hire purchase agreement removed certain parts from a truck, he would be guilty of breach of contract and cannot be proceeded under section 405. Similarly where the accused hired an electric motor which remained in his use for sometime and hire charges were paid for some months. Then he wrote a letter to the owner of the motor stating that he had purchased the motor on condition that it should be tried for three months and if it was found to be satisfactory the money would be paid and the purchase money and completed the purchase. It was held by the Supreme Court that the accused had not misappropriated or converted the property or used it

73. Cadd Cj. (1923) 45 All 588.

74 . Kalipade Mondal v. Kalikankar Chatterjee (1936) 38 Cr LJ. 113.

75. 1986 (2) Crimes 601.

or disposed of it in violation of the contract and that the letter merely raised a dispute of a civil nature between the parties and that there was no question of criminal breach of trust with respect to the motor.[76]

A hire purchase agreement is different from a contract of sale in which case the buyer promises to pay the price in installments. Distinction can be drawn on the leases that the hirer is entitled to terminate the agreement and return the property to the owner whereas the buyer under contract for sale cannot cancel the sale and return the article but is liable to the owner for payment of the installments. Further the buyer under the contract for sale will not be liable under section 406 even if he transfers it to another before the instalment are paid.[77]

Hiring is not entrustment and if a person fails to produce the article received on hire, will not be liable for breach of trust unless there is a proof that he acts dishonestly.[78]

"**Vender and Purchaser**":— To Supreme Court, a mere transaction of sale is not an entrustment. The fact that the purchaser subsequently denies receipt of the goods does not make him guilty of the offence of criminal breach of trust. The facts of the case are - that the government sold to the accused contractor, cement for the purpose of constructing a building, but the contractor used only a part of the centime for the building and disposed of the balance in other ways, it was held, 'that in the absence of evidence of any conditions or particulars of the agreement between the government and the accused, it could not be said that there was any fiduciary

---

76. Mohammed Sulaiman v. Mohd. Ayub (1965) II Cr. Lj. 421 Sc.
77. 1955 BLIR 144.
78. 1932 AIR (All) 324.

relation between the government and the accused or that the government had any proprietary rights over the cement after the sale, or that there was any entrustment of the property, so as to render the accused guilty under this section.[79]

In Dorabji F. Minwalla v. Sobraj Chellaram,[80] "A, a buyer, obtained from the seller certain documents of title under a "trust-receipt" whereby the buyer agreed to pay interest on the price of the goods purchased until payment was made, it was held that the seller did not intend to retain any ownership of the goods, that no entrustment was made and that A did not commit any breach of trust.

In criminal breach of trust cases the decisive test is: Firstly, there should be an entrustment, secondly presence of necessary dishonest intention, thirdly whether the property has passed or not passed to the buyer.

Where a person sells goods to another person with an understanding that property should pass to the buyer only on payment of price, and before such payment the buyer sells the property to a third person, it would amount to criminal breach of trust.[81]

Chitaley has referred other illustrative cases as follows:—[82]

1. A advances money to B to purchase and deliver to A grain within a certain time. B failed to perform the promise: Held that B was not guilty of an offence under this section as the transaction was in the nature of a debt.

---

79. 1969 SC 700 (702).

80. 1939 Sind. 27.

81. 1924 Cal. 816.

82. Indian Penal Code - Vol. 3, VR Mohar and WW Chitaley, P. 309.

2. A took ornaments from B on approval and promised to return the same in the evening of the same day but failed to do so: Held that A was not guilty of criminal breach of trust, but that the matter was a civil one governed by S. 24 of the sale of goods Act.[83]

3. A entrusts goods to B for sale and B sells them: a trust is created in respect of the sale proceeds also.[84]

"**Joint Owner**":— A co-owner of property cannot be considered to be entrusted with the joint property in the absence of an agreement of entrustment, hence cannot be liable for breach of trust. Muslim co-owners are not joint-owners of the property but own separate shares and thus the principle above noted that in the absence of an agreement of entrustment a co-owner cannot be guilty of breach of trust of the joint property cannot apply to them.[85]

"**Banker and Customer**":— In a current account deposited with bank, if a cheque is dishonoured it would not be considered a breach of trust but only a breach of contract,[86] because the money deposited with bank is not said to be entrusted. The relationship between the customer and banker is one of debtor and creditor as the money deposited is considered part of banks fund. But in cases of money dealing, between a bank and a customer sometime the transaction amounts to a bailement, not a deposit than violation would amount to breach of trust.

---

83. 1953 Nag. 301.

84. 1932 Sind. 169.

85. 1950 - Cal. 523.

86. 1991- Cal. 713.

"**Husband and Wife**":— A married woman may be convicted as a bailee, if she fraudulently converts to her own use or the use of any person other than the owner thereof.[87] Wife is in joint possession with her husband and cannot therefore be convicted of criminal breach of trust.[88] This decision is subjected to criticism. It is said that the decision is not sound. If the wife disposes of or deals with the separate property of her husband in any way prejudicial to his interest without of his consent is liable for theft, hence there is no reason why the wife should not be liable for criminal breach of trust in respect to such property.

In Anil Bhardway[89] it was held that where the exclusive property of one of the spouses is unwarrantedly taken away or misappropriated by the other and marriage breaks down, the offence of misappropriation can be made out.

It is wrong to say that a woman's stridha property becomes a joint property with her husband on entering into the matrimonial relations. Stridhan property of a woman may be placed in the custody of either of her husband or in-laws, but they are treated as trustees and are bound to return the same when demanded by her. If the stidhan is misappropriated or converted by the parent-in-laws, they would be deemed guilty for breach of trust.[90]

"**Sapurdar**":— When under the order of the court any property is attached and given in custody of any other person, such a person is known as sapurdar or custodian; he is in law

---

87. 31 LJMC 22 (Robson).

88. 1964 Weir 3rd Edd. 266.

89. 1985 Cr. Lj. 613 (Del).

90. Bhai Sher Jang Singh v. Virender Kaur, 1979, Cr. LJ. 493 (P & H).

bound to produce such property when called upon by the court. If he fails to produce when called upon by the court to do so, is guilty of offence under this section. In another case where there was no proof that the Sapundar misappropriated the entrusted property or converted in his own use and notice to account the property was given after the 6 years of entrustment, it was decided that accused was not guilty under this section.[91]

"**Auctioneer**":— In Baltharar[92] it was held that an auctioneer is not liable under this merely on grounds that he does not punctually carry out every condition of the agreement, that is the date of sale and the time of payment of the proceeds.

"**Disputed Claim**":— If the title of a property is in dispute, a criminal liability cannot be imputed. Right and title must be proved beyond doubt first, then there can be a liability.[93] In Raj Kishore Patter v. Joy Khrisna Sen[94] "The accuse was employed by the complainant and others to take their paddy for sale and he sold it to a Marwari. The complainant stated that the accused had withheld from him a portion of the money due from the sale of his paddy. There was a dispute between the parties as to the number of bags that were given to the complainant by the accused, and the defence was that some of the bags for which the price was claimed by the complainant, were bags given to the accused by another man who had filled a suit against him to recover their price. It was held that the accused could not be convicted of criminal breach of trust on refusing to give to the

---

91. 1960 All 380.

92. (1914) UI Cal. 844.

93. Superintendent v. Birendre Chandhe Chakravarty 1974 SCC (Cr) 191.

94. (1900) 28 Cal. 362.

complainant money, which claimed by another person as well as by the complainant.

"**Partner, Servant and Agents**":— As to the liability of Partners, servants and agents, we are having separate chapter, same thus would discuss the law in detail there.

"**Dominion over Property**":— Physical possession over the property of the accused is not necessary. All is required is:—

1. Accused should have dominion over the property.[95]
2. It could be disposed of under his direction.
3. Violation should be of any direction of law prescribing the terms of trusts.
4. The obligation to act in a certain manner in regard to the trust property having dominion over it may arise either expressly or impliedly.

Illustrative cases may where a municipal water works Inspector employed to control, supervise and check the distribution of water from the municipal supply pipes installed by municipal water works, it is considered that the Inspector has dominion over on behalf of the M. Water works. If there is a deliberate misappropriation or conversion of the water to his own use or for the use of his servant for which he does not pay any tax and also makes no information of such use of water to his employer, he is guilty of criminal breach of trust.

Supreme court in another case held that where a person has been given the power to deal with the funds in a bank, is

---

95. Bimala Charan Roy (1913) 35 All. 361.

considered to be entrusted with dominion over. The property any-Violation or misappropriation thereof would amount to criminal breach of trust.[96]

In an English Mortgage where the possession of Mortgaged Property continues with the Mortgagor, presumption is the mortgagor has dominion over the property belonging to the mortgagee and the mortgager if fraudulently allows the property be sold in execution for default of payment of revenue and purchased it benami in the name of another, he would be guilty for criminal breach of trust.[97]

Where a constable under reasonable suspicion seizes property to be stolen he is regarded as entrusted with dominion over it and misappropriation by him would make him liable under this section.[98]

If the municipal board employees customary sweepers for scavenging the rubbish and night soil from the house, and sanitary Inspector induces the sweepers to deposit the matter collected by them at a place not prescribed by the board and sells it for his own benefit, Inspector is liable for criminal breach of trust.[99]

---

96. A, 1962 SC. 1821 (1834): 1962, Cr. h. 805.

97. (1866) 5 Suthu WR 230 (DB). Property includes moable nad immovable property both. Supreme Court in Dalmia RK (1963) 1 SCR 253, over ruling Reg v. Gridhar Dharamdas 6 Bom. HCR Cr. 33, and Judgown Sinha (1895) 23 Cal 1372, and approving Bishan Prasad 37, All 128, Ramchandra Gurvala (1926) AIR Lah. 385, Manchester Ardeshir v. Ismail Ibrahim 60 Bom. 706 and Daud Khan 27. Cr. Lj. 17, observed "that the case law is more in favour of the wider meaning being given to the word "property" in sections where the word is not qualified by any expression like movable).

98. (1935) 36 Cr. Lj. 867.

Other illustrative case of 'dominion over property' may be where the employees of a society took delivery of levy sugar for the purpose of distributing to ration card holders, they committed criminal breach trust if they sold the sugar to persons other than ration card holders.[100]

In Vasant Moghe,[101] Tehsildar failed to deposit treasury amounts of land revenue, fines etc., under the circumstances he had dominion over the accounts and was entrusted with money. If he did not have any regard for the practice and procedure which was to be followed by him and the amounts were not entered in the account books, he was held guilty under this section.

In Journal Dass Aggarwal,[102] the Supreme Court questioned the order of conviction on grounds that the ingredients of criminal breach of trust were not proved. An over-seer was convicted by the lower courts for shortage of some articles from open godown which were in physical charge of chowkidars. It was not proved that the physical charge of go down was ever handed over to the overseer. Furthermore there was no evidence showing that the overseer misappropriated any article. It is a basic requirement that the prosecution must prove intrustment and misappropriation of the articles. Both the elements were absent in the present case, hence supreme court quashed the conviction order.

---

99. Horital, 45 All 381.

100. Ayyadurai devar, Inre (1981) Cr. LJ 258 (Mad).

101. 1979 SCC (Cri) 868.

102. 1981 SCC (Cri). 616.

"Dishonestly misappropriates or converts to his own use that property".

"**Dishonestly**":— Dishonest intention is the gist of the offence, both of criminal misappropriation as well as of criminal breach of trust.[103] This section is not applicable if the dishonest intention is absent.[104] The conduct which creates civil liability is distinguished from the criminal breach of trust on the basis of dishonest intention.[105] Breach of trust gives rise to a suit of damages, but it is only when there is a proof of a mental act of dishonest misappropriation that the commission of embazzlement of any sum of money becomes a penal offence punishable as criminal breach of trust.

The question is what constitutes dishonest intention. The term is not used in its popular significance, and need not always involve an element of fraud or deceit.[106] In order that the act has been done dishonestly, wrongful gain to one and wrongful loss to another is to be proved. These terms 'wrongful gain' and 'wrongful loss' have been defined in section 23 IPC, as gai by unlawful means of property to which the person gaining is not legally entitled, and the loss by unlawful means of property to which the person losing it is legally entitled. Hence section 405 is to be read in conjunction with section 23 of the Indian Penal Code. It is not necessary that to establish dishonest intention, both wrongful loss and wrongful gain by caused, intention to cause wrongful gain be caused, intention to cause wrongful loss would be sufficient.

---

103. 1959 Cr. Lj 1508.

104. 1965 (2) Cr. Lj 421.

105. 1976 Cr. Lj 449 (451) Pat.

106. Bodde Palli Laksh Minarayana v. Subbani Sanyasi Apparao, (1959) Cr. LJ 1141.

In Madhavan Pillai[107] (1966), it was observed that 'a person can be said to have dishonest intention if in taking the property it is his intention to cause gain by unlawful means of the property to which the person so gaining is not legally entitled or to cause loss by wrongful means of property which the person so losing is entitled. As observed by their lordships of the Supreme Court in Krishna Kumar v. Union of India,[108] "wrongful loss includes being kept out of the property. "It is not necessary or possible in every case of criminal breach of trust to prove in what precise manner the money was spent or appropriated by the accused because, under the law, even a temporary retention is an offence if it is dishonest."[109]

It is only the dishonest intention which is essential. Every breach of trust is not criminal. It may be international without being dishonest or it may appear to be dishonest without being really so. Actual results of wrongful gain or wrongful loss are immaterial.

"It is a consequence, but no essential part, of the offence, and a person is not accused of the offence by reason of it."[110]

Dishonest intention is proved when a postman, repays the amount of money order to the payee's mother subsequent to the filling of a complaint with the postal authorities.[111]

Accused giving a false statement of account of what he has done with the property received by him is a strong prove of his dishonest intention.[112]

---

107. (1966) Cr *Lj* 728 at 731).
108. 1959 Cr. *Lj*. 1508.
109. Ibid.
110. Mathura Prasad, (1946), PWN 192.
111. Salig Ram 1973 Cr. *Lj* 1030 (H.P.)
112. 1959, Cr. *Lj*. 1508.

Even in cases of retention an inference of dishonest intention may be drawn. However, mere retention of property without any misappropriation is not criminal breach of trust.

Where a person entrusts another person with some document for a specific purpose, and that another person hands over the document to a third person for a purpose prejudicial to the interest of the former, the second person would be guilty under this section.

The transfer of an account of another person to his own account is crime under this section.

Where a person takes from a goldsmith a gold jewel for showing it to his wife and placing an order for a similar jewel if she approved of it but fails to return it and retains it with himself towards some debts due to him by the goldsmith, he will be guilty of an offence under section 406 of the Indian Penal Code. He has utilized the jewel for a purpose not intended and against the express agreement. The mere fact that the jewel is intact is irrelevant.[113]

Even deprivation for a short period is covered by this section 406. A misappropriation is not a misappropriation merely because it is only for a short period.[114] However, it is not possible to lay down a hard and fast rule that retention would always and in all cases lead to an inference of misappropriation.

An intention to misappropriate in future is not within the scope of section 405.[115]

---

113. (1949) 2 MLJ 296 (K. Appanna).

114. (1907) 5 Cr. *Lj*. 5 (8) (DB) Bom.

115. (1934) 36 Cr. *Lj*. 165.

A mere delay or retention of money due to another cannot be a ground for inference of dishonest intention.[116] Although it is a circumstance against the accused.

In Jagroop Singh's case,[117] the accused was a graduate and a young man who was unanimously elected to the Panchayat of a village. He did much for the development of the village and also increased the income of the Panchayat. However, he was negligent in keeping proper accounts. The whole village was satisfied with his performance and honest functioning. But he was charged and prosecuted for keeping with him more than Rs. 21,000 cash contrary to Panchayat rule. It was observed that accused's criminal intention to misappropriate was not proved.

Wrongful remission of debt by company director, held no criminal breach of trust.[118] The gist is the dishonest misappropriation or the conversion by one to his own use of the property of another which has been entrusted to him.[119]

"**Misappropriates**":— To misappropriate means improperly setting apart for one's use to the exclusion of the owner. It also means 'wrongful setting apart or assigning of a sum of money to a purpose or use to which, it should not lawfully be assigned or set apart.[120]

For the offence under section 405, it is not necessary that to constitute misappropriation the money entrusted should have been applied or used in any particular manner: It is sufficient if the accused dishonestly intends to hold the

116. 1961 (1) Cr. Lj. 654.

117. 1936 Mad. WN. 825 (828).

118. 1980 Cr. Lj. 68 (P & H). 119 AIR 1963 Cal. 64.

120. Ram Khelawan (1919, 20 Cr. Lj. 654).

property as his own or to deprive another of his property and such intention is indicated by some overtact or conduct on the part of the accused.[121] Where any document has been entrusted to a person the document to third person to be used in a prejudicial way or harmful to the interest for which it was awarded, the person would be liable for misappropriation. It is not necessary to constitute misappropriation that the person should receive any money. It may be in any form but act done should be contrary to the interest to be achieved. To prove precise mode of conversion or misappropriation is also not necessary.

In misappropriation possession of the property comes innocently. If original taking is dishonest than it may be a case of theft rather than of criminal breach of trust.

For conviction it is not necessary that the accused should misappropriate the property to his own use. It may be misappropriated for the use of third person. If a person asserts that he is holding property for someone other than for whose benefit it was entrusted, his assertion amounts to dishonest misappropriation.

To constitute dishonest misappropriation actual loss is not necessary, mere intention to cause wrongful loss is sufficient. Misappropriation may be for a short period or long period, duration is not material.

Money may be misappropriated by a mental act without any actual expend of the money. However, some overtact and visible act must be established.

Where a secretary of co-operative society not depositing proceeds of sale of society property and spending some

---

121. 1941 Cr Lj. 824.

amount for his purpose commits misappropriation.[122] Delay in making payment of collection - is not misappropriation.[123] Withdrawal by an employee of the amount deposited by him as security during his appointment, without the permission of the employer and before adjustment of the accounts between them amounts to criminal misappropriation.[124]

Mere making of wrong entries in the receipt books by the licensee may not possible bring him within the purview of section 403 and 405 1 PC.[125] Similarly mere delay in making remittance of money collected on another's behalf is no evidence of misappropriation when there is no particular obligation to pay the same at a particular date.[126]

In Sardar Singh's case,[127] the accused a Patwari was entrusted with a receipt book. The accused failed to return this receipt book. It was held that mere omission or failure to return the entrusted property does not amount to breach of trust.

In Nirmalabai's[128] case it was held that mere retention of goods by a person without misappropriation does not constitute criminal breach of trust.

The most significant aspect of the offence of criminal misappropriation is that the property might have come to a person innocently but by subsequent change of intention or

---

122. (1974) 40 Cut. LT 873.

123. 1943, Cr. Lj. 445.

124. 1939, Cr. Lj. 961, (DB).

125. 1932, Cr. Lj. 300.

126. 1931, Cr. Lj. 1198.

127. 1977, Cr. Lj. 1158 (Sc).

128. 1953, Nag. 813.

knowledge with which the party was not previously acquainted, the retaining the same becomes wrongful.

"Dishonest Conversion":— To prove conversion it should be established that a man does an unauthorised act which deprives another of his property permanently or for an indefinite time. Mere preparation to convert is not an offence.[129]

In Durugappa's[130] case conversion has been defined as 'to appropriate and use another's property without right as if it is one's own'. The accused most not merely retain property to the physical exclusion of the real owner but also divert it to his own use.

In Gouri Shanker's case[131] a Magistrate handed over a pony to a person professing to be the secretary of a society for the maintenance of incurable animals. The pony belonged to Municipal Board which was declared by the authorities as unfit for work. Secretary agreed to take charge of the Pony, but afterwards he sold it to eka (one horse carriage) driver. It was held that the secretary was liable for conversion under this section.

Another illustrative case of conversion may be where a lady wishing to purchase a railway ticket, found a long queue before the ticket booking window and a person standing just near to the pay place. She asked him to get a ticket for her also and handed over some money to him for purchasing the ticket. He took the money and immediately after ran away with the money. Accused was held guilty under this section.[132]

---

129. 1950 Cr. Lj. 518 (DB).

130. 1956, Cr. Lj. 630.

131. (1894) 14 AWN 197.

132. Raghubir Kurmi, 1920 Cr. Lj. 413.

Misappropriation and conversion to one's use are not the same thing.

"In violation of any direction of law":— Liability under this section will be when there is a violation of legal direction prescribing the mode in which the person entrusted with the property is to excuse the trust or legal contract. In a case where the accused was entrusted with some silver for the purpose of making ornament and he mixed copper there in, it was held that the jeweller was guilty of criminal breach of trust.[133]

In Ganga Prasad's,[134] case A clerk who was incharge of government department Record Room, was having documents in his custody, handed over documents to a person who was entitled to the document in an illegal manner. It was held that the clerk was rightly convicted of the offence of criminal breach of trust by a public servant.

In another case where a secretary of society disbursed the money entrusted to him as such secretary in contravention of the bye-laws of the society was held liable for committing the offence of criminal breach of trust.[135]

A Managing Director of a Bank in contravention of Bank's Article of Association dishonestly disposed of bank money which was entrusted to him, was held liable under this section.[136]

A user of Property comes within the scope of section 405, IPC when such a user causes substanted loss to the owner

---

133. Babaji bin Bhau (1867) 4 BHC (Cr. C) 16.

134. 27 All 260.

135. (1970) 2 SCJ 461 (464).

136. 1958 Cr. LJ 518 (DB) (Conversion by Secretary of Cooperative Society).

of the property or gain to the accused. Illustration may be referred of the use by the printer of certain blocks entrusted to him to print the complainant's catalogue for the purpose of printing rival firm's catalogue, would be a breach of trust.[137]

In Kalaktar Singh's case a contractor under an agreement with the government was assigned to execute the construction work for which a particular quantity of cement bags were allotted to him. The agreement was that the government would supply all material to the contractor sold the unused bags outside and thus held liable under this section.[138]

It is sufficient for the prosecution to establish criminal breach of trust that the owner of the property has been deprived of its use and benefit for a time, and the accused has gained the benefit for a time. Permanent misappropriation is not to be established.

In the following cases there is no breach of trust:—

A court appointed a person as Receiver of a certain Mill and vested with process of management of its business in accordance with its Article of Association. He obtained illegal gratification for sale of articles belonging to the Mill. It was held that the illegal remuneration received by the accused was not entrusted to him on behalf of the complainant. Therefore, there was no breach of trust.[139]

Similarly a sum of money was given to a person in accordance with a lawful agreement, which later on became incapable of execution, the money was retained by him in

---

137. Keshab Chandra Boral v. Nityanund Biswas (1901) 6 CWN 203.

138. Kalaktar Singh 1978 Cr. LJ. 663 Pats.

139. A 1953 SC 478.

lieu of a debt due to him, he was not held guilty of criminal breach of trust.[140]

In another case a sum of money was given by the complainant to the accused as compensation for compromise of a criminal suit against the complainant, which could not be compromised due to the refusal by the court to grant permission. It was held that compensation was not entrusted and case did not fall within section 405.[141]

An employer who invests him employee's Provident Fund money in his own business transactions is not liable for breach of trust as there is no legal obligation to employ it in any particular manner.[142]

"**In violation of legal contract**":— The basic requirement is that the contract must be legal or valid, not for an illegal or criminal purpose. If the contract is for an illegal purpose such as for the purchase of stolen property violation thereof would not amount to criminal breach of trust. Further the contract must be in regard to the discharge of a trust. However, where there is no trust, merely money is advanced under a contract, a dispute arising out of violation of the terms of such a contract, will be of a civil nature. In such a case there is no breach of trust. A person must use or dispose of property in violation of any legal contract, express or implied, which he has made touching the discharge of such trust.

In Gurudas,[143] "the complainant deposited a municipal debenture with the accused on the occasion of his employment

---

140. Puran (1925) 27 Cr. LJ. 383.

141. Kamal Fakir (1949) 53 CWN (IDR) 79.

142. A 1956 Mad. 6 (61): 1956 Cr. LJ. 71.

143. 44 CWN 872.

as a security deposit. One of the terms of the deposit was that it would not be returnable before one year and thereafter only on fulfillment of certain conditions. The accused deposited the debenture with a bank as a security against a loan taken by him. There was not evidence to establish that the accused had no intention of redeeming it. It was held that the pledge of the security with the bank was not a breach of any legal contract, express or implied, and that therefore, the accused was not liable for breach of trust."

Illustrative cases may be where a jewel was taken from a "goldsmith for a particular purpose under a promise to return it, and the person, instead of returning it, claimed to retain it in live of a debt due to him and claimed the jewel as his own, he was held guilty under this section".[144]

"An officer who is engaged on contract for collecting land revenue on commission basis and converts the collections to his own use is guilty under this section".[145] Taking ornaments only for the purpose of approval but retaining the same dishonestly is an offence under this section.[146]

In Dani Sing's case, the wheat was supplied by the Government to a holder of Fair Price Shop with a condition to sell in a particular manner. The holder of Fair Price shop violated the condition. It was held that there was no breach of trust.[147]

"Post office employees are under an implied contract with the consigner to obey the V.P. rules and see that the

---

144. A 1950 Mad 49 (50).

145. 1937 ILR 1 Cal. 272 (DB).

146. 1964, (2) Cr. LJ. 117 (Raj).

147. 1963 AIR Pat. 52.

V.P. article is delivered in accordance therewith, Any delivery contrary to the rules is, therefore, a breach of this implied contract."[148]

In Khitish's case a person was held liable for criminal breach of trust when he took goods on approval under an agreement that property therein was to pass only if he exercised his option to take them and paid cash in full for certain articles and in part for others, the trust continued till the option was exercised and cash payments were made. He sold them without payment. Violation of the conditions made him liable.

"**False explanation or Accounting or Omission to account**"— "In criminal breach of trust failure to account for the money proved to have been received by the accused or giving a false account as to its use is generally considered to be a strong circumstance against the accused. But accused cannot be convicted on it alone. It is merely an inference as to dishonest intention, is to be taken into consideration along with other facts of the case.

It is servant's duty to account for and pay over the sum of money received by him at his stated times, his not doint so, intentionally, is considered misappropriation, a breach of trust.

If a person recovers the money which he is bound to account, his not doint so, would make him liable for this offence, although no precise time is stated within which he is to account for.

"The mental act or intent to deprive the master of his property is the gist of the offence of criminal breach of trust."[149]

148. 1927 AIR, Mad. 626.

149. Chaturbhuj Narain Chaudhury (1935) 15 Pat. 108.

In criminal breach of trust cases it is not possible to prove in every case the precise manner of misappropriation of money or how the money was spent, or retained for a temporary or permanent period. What is most important factor to be considered is dishonest intention.

In Som Nath Puri[150] the accused a traffic assistant in the office of Indian Airlines Corporation demanded on behalf of the corporation certain excess amounts for trunkcall charge from passengers for reservation of seats. After the amounts were received he passed receipts on behalf of the corporation. He, however, subsequently falsified the counterfol and fraudulently misappropriated the excess amounts. The accused was held guilty of breach of trust.

Mere retention is not conclusive proof, of criminal misappropriation or criminal breach of trust.[151] Appropriation if money assigned for one purpose but used for another purpose does not amount to misappropriation or criminal breach of trust. In cases where there is no dishonest use or disposal, a person would not be liable for breach of trust.

"**Wilfully suffers any other person so to do**":— "Willful" means deliberate or intentional and not accidential or in advertant.[152] Wilfully presupposes a conscious action. Where a person is incharge of a Record Room dishonestly gave the keys of the room to another person for giving access corruptly to the records, it was held that the person wilfully suffered the other person to dispose of property in violation of the direction of law touching the discharge of the trust and was guilty under this section.

---

150. 1972 Cr. LJ. 897 (SC).

151. Sardar Singh AIr 1977 Sc. 1766.

152. Kedar Neth (1865) Cr. LJ. 539.

"Attempt", "Abetment"

The offence of criminal breach of trust can be attempted.[153] A person who knowingly helps another to commit criminal breach of trust abets him.[154]

A negligence of rules by A which facilitates a criminal misappropriation by B, is not a wilful suffering B to commit criminal breach of trust.[155]

Section 406 provides for punishment. Any person who commits criminal breach of trust shall be punished with imprisonment which may extend to three years, or with fine, or with both. In Kaviraj's case a civil suit was filed and decreed. It was held that in such a situation criminal proceedings, and that after a long gap were not proper.[156]

Section 407 - deals with criminal breach of trust by carrier, wharfinger, warehouse-keeper. If the offence under this section is committed, the accused shall be punished with imprisonment of either description for a term which may extend to seven years, and shall also be liable to fine. The requirement of the section is that the property be entrusted to the carrier or whar-finger or house-keeper, and then they commit the offence of criminal breach of trust.

Section 408, criminal breach of trust by clerk or servant shall be the subject matter of discussion of the next chapter.

---

153. AIR 1934 Rang. 41.

154. 1913 Cr. *Lj*. 453.

155. 1958 Cr. *Lj*. 1071.

156. 1970 Cr. *Lj*. 632.

CHAPTER 2

"NATURE OF TRUST: ISLAMIC CRIMINAL LAW

The concept of trust under Islamic Criminal Law is very wide. It covers within its purview the violation of obligations in relation to covenant between God and His creature - human beings, or amongst human beings themselves, or treaties of war with enemies or relates to property, movable or immovable, goods or credits. It may also concern with plans, confidence, secretes, knowledge, talent, opportunities etc.

Its nature is spiritual, civil as well as penal and the redress available may be Divine chastisement, civil remedy or a criminal liability. According to Qur'ãnic Injunctions, it may be broadly divided into:-

1. Divine breach of trust;
2. Civil breach of trust; and
3. Criminal breach of trust.

Divine breach of trust can easily be distinguished from civil and criminal breach of trust but civil and criminal breach of trust are not distinguishable. Qur'ãnic Injunctions do not make any distinction between civil and criminal breach of trust. Some definitions may cover both aspects of breach of trust.

Islamic Law effects every aspects of life of mankind. It governs from cradle to the grave and its influence even extends from before the birth to after the death. Islamic Law thus governs spiritual and temporal aspects of life. It is Divinely Ordained System, the Will of God, revealed by God, Who alone Knows what is good and best for humanity. The Islamic Law is to be meticulously observed and interpreted in letter and spirit.

Unlike man-made laws, Islamic Law is static, not open to amendment, reform or repeal. As God is Omnipotent, the Perfect Being, so is His law, Perfect and Eternal, for all time to come. It cannot be exposed to the vagaries of human reasons and has to be observed in its ideal.

S.H. Amin rightly observes in his book,[1] "In Islamic Law there are set, fixed and ultimate values which are distinct and independent from the preferences and values of people. As such it is invariably the human being as the subject of law who has to adjust himself. It is the Islamic nation, the umma, which has to follow the rules of Islamic law as opposed to attempting to bring the law in line with people's attitude, or changing the law with a view to suit the desires and the wishes of the subjects of the law".

Allah Ta'ala in Holy Qur'ãn calls those who makes changes in His Revealed Laws as Unbelievrers, wrong-doers, rebellious and transgressors:-

وَلْيَحْكُمْ اَهْلَ الِانْجِيْلِ بِمَا اَنْزَلَ اللّٰهُ فِيْهِ وَمَنْ كَمْ يَحْكُمْ بِمَا اَنْزَلَ
اللّٰهُ فَاُوْلٰئِكَ هُمُ الفٰسِقُوْن.   (سورة املأ دة، آية : ٤٧)

> "Let the people of the gospel judge by what Allah hath revealed there in. If any do fail to judge by what Allah has revealed, they are those who rebel."[2]
>
> (5:47)

"If the Jews temper with their books they are unbelievers;

---

1. Islamic Law and Its Implications for Modern World, S.H. Amin, page 10.
2. The Holy Qur'ãn (English Translation of the meaning and commentary) printed at King Fahd Holy Qur'ãn Printin Complex. Al-Madinah al-Munawwarah under the auspices of the Ministry of Hajj and endowments, the Kingdom of Saudi Arabia.

if they give false judgement, they are wrong-doers. If the Christians follow not their light, they are rebellious." They cannot be called obedient servant of God. Same is with the Muslim Umma if they transgress, aimed, modify or change the Holy Qur'ãnic commandments, they would be considered as unbelievers, transgressors and rebellious. In the light of above Qur'ãnic verse, it is imperative on Muslims to strictly adhere to the revealed law in all affairs and at every turn or movement in life. Islamic umma has to follow the Islamic law as opposed to attempting to bring the law in line with peoples changing attitude, desires and wishes.

To understand the trust and breach thereof, an attempt to acquaint with the sources of Islamic Law is necessary. Generally the Islamic jurists are in the habit of classifying the sources of Islamic Law into the main classes:—

1. Chief sources, and
2. Supplementary or secondary sources.

Under the chief sources 'The Qur'ãn', the Holy Book of Islam, the 'Sunnah', the authentic Traditions of Prophet Muhammad (peace be upon him), the 'Ijma', the consensus of opinions of jurists of Islamic scholars, and the 'Qiyas', judgement upon juristic analogy are covered.

Supplementary or secondary sources includes, 'Al-Istihasan', deviation, one certain issue, from the rule of a precedent to another rule for a more relevant legal reason that requires such deviation, 'Al-Istislah', unprecedented judgement motivated by public interest to which neither the Qur'ãn nor, the Sunnah explicitly refer, and 'Al-Urf', or the custom and the usage of a particular society, both in speech and in action.

I. Qur'ãnic View (1st Chief Source)

Thus Islamic Law is derived from two main sources, the

Qur'ãn and the Sunna, supplemented by consensus of the orthodox Muslim Scholars, and reasoning by analogy. Companions of Prophet preferred analogical deduction to reason. They interpreted and applied the law by means of 'analogy' or 'Qias'. Analogy has been a source of law, but, in fact, it has a derivative value as 'declared by' Imm Shafi'i.

Holy Prophet (peace be upon him) says, "My community will not agree upon an error". From the above observation jurists consider Ijma, a source of law. However, it has to ensure the conformity with Holy Qur'ãn and the Sunna. It is also subordinate to original sources of Qur'ãnic and Sunna so that law may be protected against the encouragements of the fallible reason. Analogy is to discover the law and not to establish or enact it.

The analogical interpretation, and explanation of Holy Qur'ãn and Sunna has given birth to different schools of thought such as four Sunni Schools and a number of minority schools such as Ith'na-Ashari Shi't School, Zaidi Shi't School and Ibadi School. All agree that Ijma is to decide which of the views conforms to the text of Holy Qur'ãn, since the finality rests with the text alone.

Protection from facilely of the text of Holy Qur'ãn has been guaranteed by Allah Himself that

لَا يَاْتِيْهِ الْبَاطِلُ مِنْ بَيْنِ يَدَيْهِ وَلَا مِنْ خَلْفِهٖ، تَنْزِيْلٌ مِّنْ حَكِيْمٍ حَمِيْدٍ.
(سورة فصلت، آية : ٤٢)

"False hood-shall not approach this Book from what has passed or from lies ahead. It is a revelation from the wise, the praiseworthy." (41:42)

The passing away of Prophet Muhammad (peace be upon him) came after the declaration of the Qur'ãn:—

اَلْيَوْمَ اَكْمَلْتُ لَكُمْ دِيْنَكُمْ وَاَتْمَمْتُ عَلَيْكُمْ نِعْمَتِيْ و رَضِيْتُ لَكُمُ الاِسْلَامَ ديناً
(سورة الما ئدة، آية : ٣)

"This day have I perfected your religion (Islam)."
(5:3)

This verse was revealed chronologically, marking the approaching end of Prophet Muhammad's (peace be upon him) ministry in his earthly life which was emphasized by him in his last Sermon (Khutba):-

> "O people, bear in mind what I am saying, for I might not see you again. I have left two things, if you hold fast to them, never will you go astray after me. They are God's Book, and His Prophet's - Sunnah."

To understand the concept of Breach of Trust. It should be clear in the very beginning that law and religion are not separate under the Islamic Law as in the case of man - made law in India. Holy Qur'ãn contains number of injunctions explaining the concept of trust and breach thereof. These injunction are explained below:-

In al-Mu'minun trust has been explained as:-

وَالَّذِيْنَ هُمْ لِاَمٰنٰتِهِمْ وَعَهْدِهِمْ رَاعُوْنَ. والَّذِيْنَ هُمْ عَلٰى صَلٰوتِهِمْ يُحَافِظُون. أُولٰئِكَ هُمُ الْوٰرِثُوْنَ. الَّذِيْنَ يَرِثُوْنَ الْفِرْدَوْسِ، هُمْ فِيْهَا خٰلِدُونَ.
(سورة المؤمنون، آية : ٨-١١)

"Those who faithfully observe their trusts and their convenants and who (strictly) guard their prayers, these will be the heirs who will Inherit Paradise; they will dwell therein. (Forever)." (23:8-11)

This Ayat (آيت) shows that Allah promises heaven to those who preserve and observe their trusts and agreements, maintain the affairs with rectitude and fidelity.

Truth and fidelity are parts of religion in all relations of life. Every man of faith must discharge his obligations conscientiously. Trust is one such social obligation.

Trust may be express or implied. Express trusts are those where property is entrusted or duties are assigned by some one to some other when he trusts, to carry out either immediately or in specified contingencies, such as death. Implied trust arise out of power, or position, or opportunity, e.g., a king holds his kingdom on trust from Allah for his subjects. Covenants create obligations, and express and implied trust, and covenants taken together cover the whole field of obligations.

Almost similar view has been expressed about trust in Sura-al-Ma'arij) :- (70:29, 32, 33, 34, 35).

والَّذِيْنَ هُمْ لِفُرُوجِهِمْ حٰفِظُوْنَ، وَالَّذِيْنَ هُمْ لِاَمٰنٰتِهِمْ وَعَهْدِهِمْ
رٰعُوْنَ. والَّذِيْنَ هُمْ بِشَهٰدٰتِهِمْ قَآئِمُوْنَ، وَالَّذِيْنَ هُمْ عَلٰى صَلَاتِهِمْ
يُحَافِظُوْنَ، اُوْلٰئِكَ فِيْ جَنّٰتٍ مُّكْرَمُوْنَ.

(سورة المعارج، آية ٢٩،٣٢،٣٣،٣٤،٣٥،)

> "And those who respect their trusts and covenants and those stand firm in their testimonies and those who (strictly) guard their worship such will be the honoured ones in the gardens (of Bliss)."

In these ayat (the divine obligations as well as the human obligations, are referred. All the powers of man are the trust of God, and they should be utilized in those ways only that are told by the God, and man should not recede from the covenant he has made in eternity with God.

Obligation, created by trusts and covenants, express or implied are just as sacred in ordinary everyday life as they are in special spiritual relationships. In addition, our life itself, and such reason and talents as we possess, as well as our wealth and possessions are trusts, of which we must fulfil the duties functiliously.

"Sura-'al-Mu'minun' and Sura-al-Ma'airj', both explains the attributes and character of pious people who will be rewarded with paradise by Allah Ta'ala. One such attribute or characteristic is preserving and fulfilling the obligation of trust. This shows the significance attached to the term 'trust' under the Islamic Law.

Both social and spiritual aspects are covered in. Breach of trust would obviously deprive the believer all such benevolences promises by Allah Ta'ala.

Trust in Surah-al-Ahzab has been explained as follows:

(72)

إِنَّا عَرَضْنَا ٱلْأَمَانَةَ عَلَى السَّمٰوٰتِ وَٱلْأَرْضِ وَالْجِبَالِ فَأَبَيْنَ أَنْ
يَّحْمِلْنَهَا وَأَشْفَقْنَ مِنْهَا وَحَمَلَهَا ٱلْإِنْسَانَ، إِنَّهٗ كَانَ ظَلُوماً جَهُوْلاً.

سورة الأحزاب، آية :٧٢

(72) "We did indeed often the trust to the heavens and the earth and the mountains; but they refused to undertake it, being afraid thereof; but man undertook it. He was indeed unjust and foolish."
(33:72)

In this Ayat hypothetical sending down of the Qur'ãn to the ountains is mentioned, and it is mentioned that such parable are put forth in order to aid men to reflection.

The Heavens, the earth, and the mountains, other creatures of Allah, besides man, refused to undertake a trust or a responsibility, and may be imagined as happy without a choice of good or evil being given through their will. They preferred to submit their will entirely to Allah's Will, which is All-Wise and Perfect, and which would give them for more happiness than a faculty of choice, with their imperfect knowledge. Man was too audacious and ignorant to realise this, and the result has been that man as a race has been disrupted: the evil ones have betrayed the trust and brought punishment on themselves, though the good have been able to rise far above other creation, to be the 'Muqarrabin', the nearest ones to Allah.

Word 'Hamala', means to undertake, bear, carry (the trust or responsibility), to be equal to it. This is ordinary meaning, and the majority of commentators construe so. But some understand it to mean "to carry away, run away with, to embezzle (the thing entrusted); hence to be false to the trust, to betray the trust." In that case the sense of verses 72-73 would be: "Allah offered the trust to other creatures, but they refused, lest they should betray it, being afraid from that point of view, but man was less fait to himself: in his ignorance he accepted and betrayed the trust, with the result that some of his race became hypocrites and unbelievers and were punished, though others were faithful to the trust and received Allah's Mercy." The resulting conclusion is the same under both interpretations.

Word 'Zalum' used in the Ayat has been translated as 'unjust' and word 'jahul' as ignorant. Both the words in Arabic are in intensive form, as much as to say, 'man signally failed to measure his own powers or his own knowledge'. But Allah's Grace came to his assistance. Where men did his best, he won through by Allah's grace, even though man's best was but a poor good.

How did man generically undertake this great responsibility, which made him vicegerent on earth? Here came the doctrine of a covenant, express or implied, between Allah and humanity. A covenant (mithaq) necessary implies trust, and its breach necessarily implies punishment.

Duty of man is that he should not let this divine trust to be spoiled. He should carry this trust with full efforts, struggle, anxiety and care. Those individuals who fully keep that trust secure and develop it, may be rewarded and honoured, and those who commits the breach of trust out of heedlessness or mischief may be punished, and who somewhat commit fault in this connection may be pardoned and forgiven.

Allah-Ta'ala does not like those, who commit breach of trust. In 'Sura Anfal Khyanat', breach of trust has been explained as:-

وَإِنْ يُرِيدُوا خِيَانَتَكَ فَقَدْ خَانُوا اللّٰهَ مِنْ قَبْلُ فَأَمْكَنَ مِنْهُمْ، واللّٰهُ عَلِيمٌ حَكِيمٌ. سورة الأنفال، آية : ٧١

"But if they have treacherous design, against thee, (O Messenger!) they have already been in treason against Allah, and so hath He given (thee) power over them. And Allah is He who hath (full) knowledge and wisdom." (8:71)

In this ayat for word Khiyanat (breach of trust) has been translated as treachery or treason. Breach of trust has been equalled here as treacherous designs and treason against Allah.

Some prisioners of war were trusted by Holy Prophet when they declared to have had adopted Islam. Kindness were shown to them but they committed breach of that trust when abused the kindness shown to them and their declaration of Islam was merely by way of treachery and hypocracy. Allah says that it is not a matter for discouragement to those who showed the kindness. Such persons have already committed breach of the First Covenant which they had made in the spiritual world before coming into this world of matter. Second, some Bani Hashim had promised to support the Prophet in the life of Abu Talib but they committed breach of trust when they joined with the opponents of the Holy Prophet (peace be upon him) and came down in Badr to fight. This was another Khinayah (breach of trust) against God. The result was that they suffered defeat and disgrace, and were now in the hands of Muslim who had full power over them. Thus they have seen by their own eyes the result of khiyanat (breach of trust) against God. Allah knows all, and in His Wisdom will order all things for the best. Allah is all powerful punish them for any such Khiyanat against Him and His Prophet. They cannot hide their hidden intentions from God because God knows the heart of every soul in the world.

The believers have done their duty in showing clemency as they could in the circumstances of war. For them "Allah sufficceth" (viii.62).

In Sura-Yusuf, it is made clear the Allah never guide the snare of the false one. Khiyanat has been prohibited and Khai-neen (those who commit breach of trust) are disliked by Allah. Ayat 52 from Sura Yusuf is quoted below which deal with Khai-neen:-

ذٰلِكَ اَنِّى لَمْ اَخُنْهُ بِالْغَيْبِ وَاَنَّ اللّٰه لَايَهْدِى كَيْدَ الْخَائِنِينَ.

(سورة يوسف، آية : ٥٢

(52) "This (says), in order that He may know that I have never been false to him in his absence, and that Allah will never guide the snare of the false ones."

In this Ayat Hazrat Yusuf was referring to his fidelity to the Aziz, that he had never taken advantage of his absence to play false with his wife, although he was human being and liable to err. The confidence which Aziz reposed in Hazrat Yusuf by keeping him in his house was preserved. Even in Aziz's absence no breach of trust committed because Hazrat Yusuf knew that Allah did not like the Khaineen.

As to the characteristics of a good servant, trust is one such attribute. Servant employed should be trustworthy. Sura-Qasas explains servants trustiness as follows:—

"Said one of the (damsels): O my (dear) father! Engage Him on wages: truly the best of men for thee to employ is the (man) who is strong and trusty."

(28:26)

One of the daughters said to the father, keep Hazrat Moose as servant, indeed the best servant whom than desireth to keep is the one who is strong and trusty. The inference is that Allah likes those servants who are strong and trusty. Hazrat Moose had both things - he was strong as well as trusty. From Hazrat Moose's purity and selflessness she understood his trustiness.

Ayat 283, Sura al-Baqara, is another injunction on breach of trust. It reads as:-

وَاِنْ كُنتُمْ عَلٰى سَفَرٍ وَّلَمْ تجدُوا كَاتِباً فَرِهٰنٌ مَقبُوضَةٌ فَاِنْ اَمِنَ
بَعْضُكُمْ بَعْضاً فَلْيُودّ الّذِى اُوْتُمِنَ اَمَانَتهٗ وَلْيَتقِ اللّٰهَ رَبَّهٗ وَلَا تَكْتُمُوا
اللشَّهَادَةَ وَمَنْ يَّكْتُمْهَا فَاِنَّهٗ اٰثِمٌ قَلْبُهٗ وَاللّٰهُ بِمَا تَعْمَلُوْنَ عَلِيْمٌ.

(سورة البقرة، آية : ٢٨٣

"If ye are on a journey, and cannot find a scribe, a pledge with possession (may serve the purpose). And if one of you deposits a thing on trust with another, let the trustee (faithfully) discharge His trust, and let him fear Allah his Lord. Conceal not evidence; for whatever concels it, his heart is tainted with sin. And Allah knoweth all that ye do." (2:283)

Another translation: "And if you are upon a journey and you do not find a writer then pledge in hand. Then if there is a mutual confidence the trusted one should deliver the trust in full and fear God his Lord. And do not conceal the evidence and who so conceals it then no doubt his heart is sinful. And God well your action."

According to this Ayat, pledges and securities are also covered under trust. Violation of such securities and pledges would amount to breach of trust.

The law of deposit implies great trust in the depository on the part of the depositor. The depository becomes a trustee, and the doctrine of trust can be further developed on that basis. The trustee's Wduty is to guard the interests of the person on whose behalf he holds the trust and to render back the property and accounts when required according to the terms of the trust. This duty is again linked to the sanction of religion, which requires a higher standard than law.

This Ayat explains that if you make a contract of debt while in journey and you do not find a writer to write the document, then the debtor should put some thing as pledge with the creditor. In journey the necessity of pledge in hand would be more than in stay, hence the order of pledge is given in journey, otherwise in stay and in the presence of writer pledge is lawful according to tradition. And if the creditor relies on the debtor and as such does not demand the pledge in hand, it is incumbent on the debtor to repay the demand in full and fear God and should not commit breach of trust.

Ayat 58, Sura al-Nisan is another injunction on trust. It reads as:—

إِنَّ اللّٰهَ يَأْمُرُكُمْ أَنْ تُؤَدُّوا الْاَمٰنٰتِ إِلٰى أَهْلِهَا وَإِذَا حَكَمْتُمْ بَيْنَ النَّاسِ
أَنْ تَحْكُمُوا بِالْعَدْلِ إِنَّ اللّٰهَ نِعِمَّا يَعِظُكُمْ بِهِ إِنَّ اللّٰهَ كَانَ سَمِيْعًا
بَصِيْرًا.

(سورة النساء، آية :٥٨)

(58) "Allah doth command you to render back your trusts to those to whom they are due, and when ye judge between people that ye judge with justice: verily how excellent is the teaching which He giveth you! For Allah is He Who heareth and seeth all things."

Another translation of the above quoted verse:—

> "No doubt, God bids you to deliver the trusts to their owners and when judge between the people, that you judge with justice. God gives you a good admonition. No doubt, God is All hearing, All seeing."

It means the admonition which God has given you - the delivery of trust to their owners and the doing of justice in all matters is much beneficial. God knows all the hidden and public affairs, and the present and future circumstances, so if you fail on some occasion when you consider that justice and integrity shall not be conclusive to your tagible expediency, then you consideration shall not be reliable and commendable in the presence of this Divine Admonition. Expediency shall be subservient to the Divine Commandment and not the divine Commandment shall be subordinated to expediency.

Under the same Sura, that is Sura-e-Nisa there is another commandment of Allah Ta'ala:—

اِنَّآ اَنْزَلْنَآ اِلَيْكَ الْكِتٰبَ بِالْحَقِّ لِتَحْكُمَ بَيْنَ النَّاسِ بِمَآ اَرٰكَ اللّٰهُ
وَلَاتَكُنْ لِّلْخَاۤئِنِيْنَ خَصِيْمًا (سورة النساء، آية : ١٠٥)

(105) "We have sent down to the Book in truth, that thou mightest judge between people by that which Allah has shown thee: so be not an advocate for those who betray their trust."

The general lesson is that the righteous man is faced with all sorts of subtle viles, the wicked will try to appeal to his highest sympathies and most honourable motives to deceive him and use him as an instrument for defeating justice. He should be careful and cautious, and seek the help of Allah for protection against deception and for firmness in dealing the strictest justice without fear of favour. To do otherwise is to betray a sacred trust; the trustee must defeat all attempts made to mislead him. Then the non-administration of justice is a breach of trust for which a man would be liable for punishment. Khaineen are disliked by Allah, they are those who betray the trust-reposed in them.

In Sura Anfal, Ayat 27 Allah Ta'ala commands:—

يٰٓاَيُّهَا الَّذِيْنَ اٰمَنُوْا لَا تَخُوْنُوااللّٰهَ وَالرَّسُوْلَ تَخُوْنُوا اَمٰنٰتِكُم وَ اَنْتُمْ تَعْلَمُوْنَ۔ (سوره الانفال، آية : ٢٧)

(27) "O ye that believe! Betray not the trust of Allah and the Messenger, nor misappropriate knowingly things entrusted to you."

Another translation:—

"O believers! Betray not God and the Messenger and misappropriate not your trusts knowingly."

Men may betray the trust of Allah and His Prophet by misusing property, or abusing the confidence reposed in them, or the knowledge or talents given to them. On that special occasion, when the plans for the protection of Allah's worshippers against annihilation were of special importance, the Prophet's trust and confidence had to be guarded with special case. Occasions for scrupulously respecting the trust and confidence of our fellow-men occur every day in our life, and few of us can claim perfection in this respect. Hence the special distinction of the Prophet of Allah, who earned the title of 'Al-Amien', the one who true to every trust reposed in him.

Prophet Muhammad (peace be upon him) has said that "when a covenant is made with a certain people no knot should be untied and no knot should be tied till the term of the covenant is completed, or the other party should be informed that the covenant is returned and they are no longer bound by the contract.[3] No doubt, God is not pleased with the Khaineen, those who commit the breach of trust.

Khiyanat has been explained in Surah Maedah also. Ayat 13 reads as:—

In Sura al-Mumin, breach of trust has been explained as:—

يَعْلَمُ خَائِنَةَ الْاَعْيُنِ وَمَا تُخْفِي الصُّدُوْرُ

(سوره المؤمن، آية: ١٩)

(19) "(Allah) knows the treachery of the eyes, and all that the hearts (of men) conceal."

Sura An-Nisa explains trust in relation to orphan's property as:—

وَاٰتُوا الْيَتٰمٰى اَمْوَالَهُمْ وَلَا تَتَبَدَّلُوا الْخَبِيْثَ بِالطَّيِّبِ وَلَا تَاْكُلُوْا اَمْوَالَهُمْ
اِلٰى اَمْوَالِكُمْ اِنَّهٗ كَانَ حُوْبًا كَبِيْرًا۔ (سورة النساء، آية: ٢)

(2) "To orphans restore their property (when they reach their age) nor substitute (your) worthless things for (their) good ones and devour not their substance (by mixing it up) with your own. For this is indeed a great sin."

The guardian of the orphans, whose father has died, is ordered to restore them their property when they become mature. The guardian of the orphans is prohibited to take any good thing from his wealth and put a bad thing in place of the good thing. The

3. Hazrat Umar bin Anbara (God is pleased with him) a follower (Sahabi) of the Prophet (peace be upon him).

guardian is also forbidden to devour the wealth of the orphans by mixing the things of the orphans with his own things, e.g., the guardian is allowed to manage the meals of the orphan with his own meals in common, but in this management the orphan should not be given any loss. Under this pretence the wealth of the orphan should not be devoured, because devouring the wealth of an orphan is a great curse whose effects are very destructive in both the worlds. Such a breach of trust is a very great crime and a great sin.

The commandments dealing the orphans have great significance because orphans deserves more care and kindness owing to his helplessness, feebility and meekness. A careful management of the property of an orphan is enjoined so that the orphan may not suffer any loss, whatsoever. Islam does not allow breach of trust in such cases with a view to oppress or deprive the weak and meek of their rights. In the days of Prophet (peace be upon him) orphans were deprived of their property and were left in destitution. The Holy Qur'ãn came and gave a strong below to such evil practices.

Ayat 6, of Sura An-Nisa, is another injunction-prohibiting misappropriative of orphan's property. Injunction reads as:—

وَابْتَلُوا الْيَتٰمٰى حَتّٰى اِذَا بَلَغُوا النِكَاحَ فَاِنْ اٰنَسْتُمْ مِنْهُمْ رُشْدًا فَادْفَعُوا
اِلَيْهِمْ اَمْوَالَهُمْ وَلَا تَأْكُلُوهَا اِسْرَافًا وَّ بِدَارًا اَنْ يَّكْبَرُوْا وَمَنْ كَانَ غَنِيًا
فَلْيَسْتَعْفِفْ وَمَنْ كَانَ فَقِيْرًا فَلْيَأْكُلْ بِالْمَعْرُوْفِ فَاِذَا دَفَعْتُمْ اِلَيْهِمْ
اَمْوَالَهُمْ فَاَشْهِدُوا عَلَيْهِمْ وَ كَفٰى بِاللّٰهِ حَسِيبًا۔ (سورة النساء، آية:٦)

(6) "Make trial of orphans until they reach the age of marriage; if then ye find some judgement in them, release their property to them; but consume it not wastefully, nor in haste against their growing up, if the guardian is well-off, let him claim no remuneration, but if he is poor, let him have for himself what

is just and reasonable. When ye release their property to them, take witnesses in their presence; but all-sufficient."

Another translation:—

"And train the orphan well till they reach the age of marriage. Then if you perceive in them right judgement deliver unto them their property, and devour not the wealth of the orphans more than necessary and before need are they are grown.

And who has no need he should abstain from the wealth of the orphan and he who is poor may consume according to custom. And when you deliver to them their property take witness over them and god is sufficient for reckoning."

The orphans should be trained and educated and tested till the age of adolescence. If you find after adolescence that they are able to understand fairly well, deliver their property unto them. If the orphan does not show right judgement or wisdom of management even after adolescence, he will be waited till the age of twenty five years. If he attains right judgement and wisdom of management before the age of twenty five years, the property shall be delivered to him forthwith, whether he attains to wisdom or not. This is the religion of Imam Abu Hanifa (Be mercy on him).

The wealth of the orphan should be managed properly and must be spent when necessary. The unnecessary or more than necessary expenditure is prohibited. For example, where one dollar can do, two dollars should not be spent. It would amount to breach of trust.

Moreover, the wealth of the orphan should not spent hastily their thinking that this wealth will be returned when he is grown up. This would also be considered misappropriation and breach of trust.

As to rich and poor guardian there is a difference of approach. If the guardian is a rich man he should not consume the wealth of the orphan for his own personal benefit or for the benefit of his dependants. If the guardian, is poor he may take as remuneration of his service from the wealth of the orphan, but the wealth of the orphan should not be used by the wealthy man in any case.

When the father of child has died a list of his property should be prepared before some Muslims and handed over to the trustee. When the orphan is adolescent the property should be returned to him according to the list, and the expenditure adjusted. And what is being returned to the orphan should be given before the witnesses to remove possible future disputes. And God knows well the accounts of every individual. He does not require the accounts of the human beings. All these instructions are to avoid litigation, relating to misappropriation or breach of trust.

In Ayat 10, Sura an-Nisa, warning for punishment in case of misappropriation of breach of trust is given. It reads:—

اَنَّ الَّذِيْنَ يَاْكُلُوْنَ اَمْوَالَ الْيَتٰمٰى ظُلْمًا اِنَّمَا يَاْكُلُوْنَ فِى بُطُوْنِهِمْ نَارًا وَ

سَيَصْلَوْنَ سَعِيْرًا۔

(سورة النساء، آية: ١٠)

"Those who unjustly eat up the property of orphans, eat up a fire into their own bodies, they will soon be enduring a blazing fire!" (Sura an-Nisa : 10)

It means those who misappropriate the property of the orphan without right, they devour but fire in their bellies, and shall roast in a blaze in near future.

In Ayat 29, Sura an-Nisa, there is a general commandment to human being, prohibiting misappropriation and breach of trust of property entrusted. It says:—

يٰاَيُّهَا الَّذِيْنَ اٰمَنُوْا لَا تَاْكُلُوْا اَمْوَالَكُمْ بَيْنَكُمْ بِالْبَاطِلِ اِلَّا اَنْ تَكُوْنَ

تِجَارَةً عَنْ تَرَاضٍ مِّنْكُمْ وَ لَا تَقْتُلُوْا اَنْفُسَكُمْ اِنَّ اللّٰهَ كَانَ بِكُمْ

رَحِيْمًا۔

(سورة النساء،آية: ٢٩)

"O ye who believe! Eat not up your property among yourselves in varieties but let there be amongst you traffic and trade by mutual good-will. Nor kill (or destroy) yourselves: for verily allah hath been to you most merciful! (Sura an-Nisa : 29)

Misappropriation of someone's wealth wrongly by means of breach of trust, falsehood and theft is prohibited. But if there is trading or business by mutual consent - buying and selling by agreeing together - then there is no harm in consuming the wealth or good, of one another. Further prohibition is that you should not kill each other. God is very kind to you that he sent such orders which protect your life and wealth from the oppressors, exploiters, violators of trust and tyrants.

There are three verses from Sura Al-Imran which are also related to breech of trust. Ayat 75 says:—

وَمِنْ اَهْلِ الْكِتٰبِ مَنْ اِنْ تَاْمَنْهُ بِقِنْطَارٍ يُّوَدِّهٖ اِلَيْكَ وَ مِنْهُمْ مَنْ اَنْ تَاْمَنْهُ بِدِيْنَارٍ لَّا يُؤَدِّهٖ اِلَيْكَ اِلَّا مَادُمْتَ عَلَيْهِ قَائِماً ذٰلِكَ بِاَنَّهُمْ قَالُوا لَيْسَ عَلَيْنَا فِى الْاُمِّيّنَ سَبِيْلٌ وَ يَقُوْلُوْنَ عَلَى اللّٰهِ الْكَذِبَ وَهُمْ يَعْلَمُوْنَ۔ (سورة آل عمران، آية: ٧٠)

"Among people of the book are some who, if entrusted with a hoard of gold, will (readily) pay it back; others, who, if entrusted with a single silver coin, will not repay it unless thou constantly stoodest demanding, because they say: "There is no way over us to the unletteted people, but they tell a lie against Allah, and (well) they know it."

(Sura Al-Imran : 75)

Every race imbued with race agrrogance resorts to this kind of moral or religious subturfage. Even if its members are usually honest or just among themselves, they are contemptuous of those outside their circle, and cheat and deceive them without any quelms of conscience.

The people of the book were so much avaricious of worldly wealth that they had change the laws and injunctions of the Heavenly Books e.g., they had forged this law that thee was no sin in misappropriating the wealth of the Pagau Avabs because they were ignorant people and did not possess heavenly knowledge, so heavenly law did not apply in their case, as if heavenly law was their special concern. They are knowlingly forging against God a false thing. God has never allowed the breach of trust. Even today this is the law of Islamic Fiqh that misappropriation of a trust is not lawful whether the trust is of a Muslim or unbeliever.

In the second Ayat 76, commandment is:—

بَلٰى مَنْ اَوفٰى بِعَهْدِهٖ وَاتَّقٰى فَاِنَّ اللّٰهَ يُحِبُّ الْمُتَّقِيْنَ۔

(سورة آل عمران، آية:٧٦)

"Nay, those that keep their plighted faith and act aright, verily Allah those who act aright."

(Surah Al-Imran : 76)

Ayat 161, is and the commandment on breach of trust. It relates to the person of Holy Prophet. It reads:—

وَمَا كَانَ لِنَبِيٍّ اَنْ يَّغُلَّ وَمَنْ يَغْلُلْ يَاتِ بِمَا غَلَّ يَوْمَ الْقِيٰمَةِ ثُمَّ تُوَفّٰى كُلُّ نَفْسٍ مَّا كَسَبَتْ وَهُمْ لَا يُظْلَمُوْنَ۔ (سورة آل عمران : ١٦١)

"No Prophet could (eer act dishonestly if any person acts dishonestly he shall, on the day of judgment, restore what he misappropriated; then shall every soul receive its due whatever is earned, and none shall be death with unjustly."

(Sura Al-Imran : 161)

Besides the gentleness of nature of Prophet Muhammad (peace be upon), he was known from his earliest life for his trust worthiness. Hence his title of Al-Amin. Unsempulos people often read their own low motives into other men, and their accusation, which is meant to injure, fastens on the various virtues for which the man they attack is well-known. Some of the hypocrates after 'Uhud' raised some doubts about the division of the spoils, thinking to sow the seeds of poison in the hearts of the men who had deserted their post in their craving for booty. Those low suspicions were never believed in by any sensible people, and they have no interest for us now. But the general principles here declared are of eternal value.

1. Prophets of Allah do not act from unworthy motives.

2. Those who act from such motives are the lowest of creatures, and they will make no profit.

3. A Prophet of Allah is not to be judged by the same standard as a greedy creature.

4. In Allah's eyes there are various grades of men, and we must try to understand and appreciate such grades. If we trust our leader, we shall not question his honesty without cause. If he is dishonest, he is not fit to be a leader.

Holy Prophet is an epitome of all moral virtues and an embodiment of all human perfections; any misunderstanding about his character is a great, sin which is tantamount to Kufr (كفر). To quote an Ayat from Holy Qur'ãn:—

مَاضَلَّ صَاحِبُكُمْ وَمَاغَوٰى وَمَا يَنْطِقُ عَنِ الْهَوٰى اِنْ هُوَ اِلَّا وَحْىٌ يُّوحٰى۔ (سورة النجم، آية : ٤-٣)

"Yours companion Muhammad (peace be upon him) errs not, nor is he deceived. Whatever he utters, it is not his own whim and fancy. It is naught else but a divine revelation revealed unto him." (53:2-4)

In Sura Bani Israil, it is said:—

وَقُرْاٰنًا فَرَقْنٰهُ لِتَقْرَاَهٗ عَلَى النَّاسِ عَلٰى مُكْثٍ وَّ نَزَّلْنٰهُ تَنْزِيْلًا۔

(سورة الا سراء، آية : ١٠٦)

(106) "(It is) Qur'ãn which we have divided (into parts from time to time), in order that thou mightest recite it to men at intervals: we have revealed it by stages."

Allah-Ta'ala trusted Prophet (peace be upon him). Prophet in turn presented to mankind whatever revealed to him. He never committed any breach of trust or betrayal with Allah. Islamic law is revealed law, which was revealed upon Prophet in stages so that he could explain the revelations to the mankind. Allah's revelation comes as a light to illuminate out difficulties and show us the way in actual situations that arise. Prophet never committed any mistake.

Some people alleged that Qur'ãn was composed by Prophet himself, it is not God's revelation. It is false allegation Prophet never deviated or mixed any thing from his side. Whatever Allah revealed that is as presented before mankind. Trust of God in His Prophet was never shaken. The above allegation has been challenged by God in the Qur'ãn itself. If it is composed by man, the people may rival it. Qur'ãn says:—

اَمْ يَقُوْلُوْنَ افْتَرٰىهُ قُلْ فَاْتُوا بِعَشْرِ سُوَرٍ مِّثْلِهٖ مُفْتَرَيٰتٍ وَّادْعُوْا مَنِ
اسْتَطَعْتُمْ مِنْ دُوْنِ اللّٰهِ اِنْ كُنْتُمْ صٰدِقِيْنَ۔ (سورة هود، آية : ١٣)

(13) "Or they may say, "He forged it". Say, "Bring ye then ten suras forged, like unto it, and call (to your aid) whomsoever ye can, other than Allah! If ye speak the truth!" (11:13)

Those who doubt they are challenged to produce ten verses like Holy Qur'ãn. If they could not then they should accept it as an outstanding Revelations of Allah.

Some view has been expressed in Surah al-Baqarah:—

وَاِنْ كُنْتُمْ فِى رَيْبٍ مِّمَّا نَزَّلْنَا عَلٰى عَبْدِنَا فَاْتُوا بِسُوْرَةٍ مِّنْ مِّثْلِه
وَادْعُوا شُهَدَاءَ كُمْ مِّنْ دُوْنِ اللّٰهِ اِنْ كُنْتُمْ صٰدِقِيْنَ۔
(سورة البقرة، آية : ٢٣)

(23) "And if ye are in doubt as to what we have revealed from time to time to our servant then produce a sura like thereunto; and call your witnesses or helpers (if there are any) besides Allah, if ye are truthful." (2:23)

In fact all true revelation is itself a miracle, and stands on its own merit. No one can produce any parallel to the revealed verses of Holy Qur'ãn. This challenged was never met by those who exhausted all their means to crush Muhammad (peace be upon him) and his religion.

From the above study of Qur'ãnic injunctions it may be, inferred that 'trust's range is varied and wide. It includes within it's scope spiritual as well as social obligations, dealings and affairs of mankind.

It should be admitted that Qur'ãn being basically a book of religious guidance, is not an easy reference to legal studies. However, whatever revelations are there the Islamic law whether penal or civil is to be interpreted in accordance to that revealed text.

Sura-al-Baqarah, Ayat 27, and Sura-al-Rad, ayat 25, are also relevant here. In these verses Allah has cursed those who commit the breach of Trust. They do nothing but cause loss to themselves, and warns that there is a terrible home for them. Terrible home is the opposite of the state of blessed, and eternal home, the gardens of perpetual bliss.

II. Ahadith (2nd Chief Source)

Sunnah is an Arabic word meaning by 'method', applied by the Prophet (peace be upon him), as legal term comprising what he said, did and agreed to.

Sunnah is the human, though prophetic, clarification of the Qur'ãn by Prophet Muhammad (peace be upon him). Its authority is derived from the prophethood of Muhammad, as expressed in Holy Qur'ãn. Qur'ãn says:—

بِالْبَيِّنٰتِ وَالزُّبُرِ وَاَنْزَلْنَا اِلَيْكَ الذِّكْرَ لِتُبَيِّنَ لِلنَّاسِ مَانُزِّلَ اِلَيْهِمْ وَلَعَلَّهُمْ
يَتَفَكَّرُوْنَ۔ (سورة النحل، آية : ٤٤)

(44) "(We sent them) with clear sings and scriptures and we have sent down unto thee (also) the message; that thou mayest explain clearly to men what is sent for them, and that they may give thought." (16:44)

This verse shows the supreme authority of Prophet Muhammad (peace be upon him) in the interpretation of the Holy Qur'ãn. Interpretation may have been by his words or by his actions all are included within the preview of 'Sunnah'. This authority is binding on all Prophet Muhammad (peace be upon him) is called.

Authority of sunnah or Ahadis as main second source of Islamic law i.e., shariah is proved by different Ayats from Holy Qur'ãn.

Surah al-Hashar, Ayat 7, is an example approving the authority of Sunnah that is the sayings and doings of Prophet Muhammad (peace be upon him) are to be strictly followed. It says:—

مَآاَفَآءَ اللّٰهُ عَلٰى رَسُوْلِهٖ مِنْ اَهْلِ الْقُرٰى فَلِلّٰهِ وَلِلرَّسُوْلِ وَلِذِى الْقُرْبٰى وَالْيَتٰمٰى وَالْمَسٰكِيْنَ
وَابْنِ السَّبِيْلِ كَىْ لَا يَكُوْنَ دُوْلَةًۢ بَيْنَ الْاَغْنِيَآءِ مِنْكُمْ وَمَآ اٰتٰكُمُ الرَّسُوْلُ فَخُذُوْهُ وَمَا نَهٰكُمْ
عَنْهُ فَانْتَهُوْا وَاتَّقُوا اللّٰهَ اِنَّ اللّٰهَ شَدِيْدُ الْعِقَابِ۔(سورة الحشر، آية : ۷)

(1) "So take what messenger gives you, and refrain from what he prohibits you and fear Allah, for Allah is strict in punishment." (59:7)

Surah al-Ahzab, Ayat 21, is another example of authority of Sunnah proved from the verse of Holy Qur'ãn. It reads as:—

لَقَدْ كَانَ لَكُمْ فِىْ رَسُوْلِ اللّٰهِ اُسْوَةٌ حَسَنَةٌ لِّمَنْ كَانَ يَرْجُوا اللّٰهَ
وَالْيَوْمَ الْاٰخِرَ وَذَكَرَ اللّٰهَ كَثِيْرًا۔ (سورة الا حزاب، آية : ۳۱)

(2) "Ye have indeed in the Messenger of Allah an excellent exampler for him who hopes in Allah and the final day, and who remember Allah much."
(33:21)

Surah al-Imran, Ayat 31, also proves the authority of sunnah:—

قُلْ اِنْ كُنْتُمْ تُحِبُّوْنَ اللّٰهَ فَاتَّبِعُوْنِىْ يُحْبِبْكُمُ اللّٰهُ وَيَغْفِرْ لَكُمْ ذُنُوْبَكُمْ
وَاللّٰهُ غَفُوْرٌ رَّحِيْمٌ۔ (سورة آل عمران، آية : ۳۱)

(31) Say: "If ye do love Allah, follow me: Allah will love you and forgive you your sins; for Allah is oft forgiving, most merciful." (3:31)

Ayat 32, Surah al-Imran says:—

قُلْ اَطِيْعُوا اللّٰهَ وَالرَّسُوْلَ فَاِنْ تَوَلَّوْا فَاِنَّ اللّٰهَ لَا يُحِبُّ الْكٰفِرِيْنَ۔
(سورة آل عمران، آية : ۳۲)

Say: "Obey Allah and His Messenger", but if thy turn back, Allah loveth not those who reject faith." (3:32)

Other Verses, on authority of Sunnah are:—

اِنَّماَ كَانَ قَوْلَ الْمُئو مِنِينَ اِذَا دُعُوا اِلَى اللّٰهِ وَرَسُولِهِ لِيَحْكُمَ بَيْنَهُمْ اَنْ
يَقُولُوا سَمِعْنَا وَاَطَعْنَا وَاُولٰئِكَ هُمُ الْمُفْلِحُوْنَ۔ (سورة النور، آية : ٥١)

(5) "The answer of the believes, when summoned to Allah, and His Messenger, in order that he may judge between them, is no other than this: they say, "We hear and we obey". It is such as these that will prosper." (24:51)

Similarly Ayat 63, says:—

لَا تَجْعَلُوا دُعَاءَ الرَّسُوْلِ بَيْنَكُمْ كَدُعَاءِ بَعْضِكُمْ بَعْضاً قَدْ يَعْلَمُ اللّٰهُ
الَّذِيْنَ يَتَسَلَّلُونَ مِنْكُمْ لِوَاذاً فَلْيَحْذَرِ الَّذِيْنَ يُخَالِفُوْنَ عَنْ اَمْرِهِ اَنْ
تُصِيْبَهُمْ فِتْنَةٌ اَوْ يُصِيْبَهُمْ عَذَابٌ اَلِيْمٌ۔ (سورة النور، آية : ٦٣)

(63) "Deem not the summons of the Messenger among yourselves like the summons of one of you to another: Allah doth know those of you who slip away under shelter of some excuse: then let those beware who withstand the Messenger's order lest some trial befall them, or a gravious chastisement be inflicted on them." (25"63)

Approving the authority Surah al-Nisaa, Ayat 59, says:—

يٰاَيُّهَا الَّذِيْنَ اٰمَنُوا اَطِيْعُوا اللّٰهَ وَاَطِيْعُوا الرَّسُوْلَ وَ اُولِى الْاَ مْرِ مِنْكُمْ
فَاِنْ تَنَازَعْتُمْ فِى شَىءٍ فَرُدُّوهُ اِلَى اللّٰهِ وَالرَّسُوْلِ اِنْ كُنْتُمْ تُوْمِنُوْنَ بِاللّٰهِ
وَالْيَوْمِ الْاٰ خِرِ ذٰلِكَ خَيْرٌ وَاَحْسَنُ تَاْوِيْلاً۔ (سورة النساء، آية : ٥٩)

(59) "O ye who believe! Obey Allah, and obey the Messenger, and those charged with authority among you, if he differ in anything among yourself, refer it to Allah and His Messenger, if ye do believe in Allah.

And the last day: That is best, and most suitable for final determination." (4:59)

Ayat 65, Surah al-Nisaa says:—

فَلَا وَرَبِّكَ لَا يُؤْمِنُونَ حَتّٰى يُحَكِّمُوْكَ فِيْمَا شَجَرَ بَيْنَهُمْ ثُمَّ لَا يَجِدُوافِي اَنْفُسِهِمْ حَرَجاً مِمَّا قَضَيْتَ وَ يُسَلِّمُوْا تَسْلِيْماً۔

(سورۃ النساء، آیۃ : ٦٠)

(65) "But no by thy Lord, they can have no (real) faith. Until they makes thee judge in all dispute between them and find in their souls no resistance against. Thy decisions, but accept them with the fullest conviction." (4:65)

The test of true faith is not mere lip profession, but bring all over doubts and disputes to the one in whom we profess faith. Further when a decision is given we are not only to accept it, but find in our in most souls no difficulty and no resistance, but on the contrary a joyful acceptance springing from the conviction of our own faith.

These are some of the authentic proves approving the authority of Sunnah as second main source of Islamic Law or Shariah.

Believers are bound to follow the Sunnah is made clear by the Holy Qur'ãn:—

يٰاَيُّهَا الَّذِيْنَ اٰمَنُوْا اَطِيْعُوا اللّٰهَ وَرَسُوْلَهٗ وَلَا تَوَلَّوا عَنْهُ وَاَنْتُمْ تَسْمَعُوْنَ۔

(سورۃ الا نفال، آیۃ : ٢٠)

(20) "O ye who believe! Obey Allah and His Messenger, and turn not away from him when ye hear (him speak)." The binding of the authority of interpretation by prophet upon all Muslims is also expressed by another Ayat:— (4:80)

مَنْ يُطِعِ الرَّسُوْلَ فَقَدْ اَطَاعَ اللهَ وَمَنْ تَوَلّٰى فَمَا اَرْسَلْنٰكَ عَلَيْهِم حَفِيظًا۔ (سورة النساء، آية : ٨٠)

(80) "He who obeys the Messenger, obey Allah."

It means that obedience to Prophet is the obedience to Allah. Prophet's duty is to convey the message of Allah. If men perversely disobey that message, they are not disobeying him but they are disobeying Allah. This recognition of Sunnah by Holy Qur'ãn makes the saying and actions of the Holy Prophet authority text of Islamic law.

Practice has been that whenever there is a problem, it is to be solved in the light what the Holy Qur'ãn says. If Qur'ãn is silent then to seek the help from Sunnah. Hazrat Abu Baker, the first Caliph whenever he had to pass a judgement, looked into the Qur'ãn, if he found an applicable text therein, he would apply it. If not, he would ask the people whether any of them knew of a judgement passed by the Prophet on the particular issue. It sometimes happened that some people would come forward and state that the Prophet had passed a judgement on it. If nothing found then he used to consult the chief representatives of the people. Umar, the second caliph did the same.

With this brief background let us turn how the Prophet looks at the trust and violation thereof. Prophet Muhammad (peace be upon him) explains trust in relation to divine and religious obligations, and moral and social obligations. We may note down some of the Sunnas or Ahadis as followers:—

Hazrat Abu Huraira narrated that Prophet (peace be upon him) said:—

"The signs of a hypocrite are three:

1. Whenever he speaks, he tells a lie.

2. Whenever he promises, he always breaks it (his promise).

3. If you trust him, he proves to be dishonest. (If you entrust something as trust with him, he will not return it)." (Bukhari, Ref. 1.032).

The above hadith shows that entrustment is the requirement and whatever is entrusted must be returned honestly. Breach of trust places a person in the category of a hypocrite.

In the following Hadis or Sunnah entrustment to administer the property is again a basic requirement.

Concerning the wakf of 'Umar', Hazrat Amr Ibn Dinar al-Makki narrated that prophet (peace be upon him) said:—

> "If was not sinful of the trustee (of the wakf) to eat or provide his friend, from it, provided the trustee had no intention of collecting fortune (for himself)."
>
> (Bukhari, ref. 3.507).

Ibn 'Umar was the manager of the trust of "Umar and he used to give presents from it to those with whom he used to stay at Makkah". Here again under this hadis misappropriation of entrusted property is prohibited. No one appointed as trustee of wakf property should administer or manage the affairs in such a way by which he commits the breach of trust and thus makes his own fortune.

Entrustment creates an obligation which has to be fulfilled. Hazrat Az-Zubair, a Sahabi (follower of Prophet) whenever entrusted with property by someone, he used to refuse the acceptance. Instead of taking the responsibility of trust he preferred debt because he was afraid of managing the entrusted property.

To quote Abdullah bin Az-Zubair, he said that his father Hazrat Az-Zubair preferred debt than the trust. He says:—

> "If somebody brought some money to deposit with him (Hazrat Az-Zubair), he would say, "No, (I shall not keep it as a trust), but I shall take it as a debt, for I am afraid it might be lost." (Bukhari, ref. 4.358).

This shows the significance attached to the trust property and fear of breach of trust. He used to prefer debt rather than take the responsibility as a trustee.

Abu Dharr has reported that when he asked Prophet (peace be upon him) would he not appoint him to public office, Prophet stroked his shoulder and said:—

> "Abu Dharr, thou art weak and authority is a trust, and on the day of judgement it is a cause of humiliation and repentance except for one who fulfils its obligations and (properly) discharges the duties attendant thereto."
> (Sahih Muslim - ref. 4491)

According to the above hadis, entrustment of public office is also a trust. Those who are assigned to execute the duties attached thereto if fails in due performance they commit the breach of trust.

Assingment of duty to teach Sunnah and al-Islam is also kind of trust. Non-performance of such a duty properly would also amount to breach of trust.

The people of Yemen came to Allah's Messenger (may peace be upon him) and said:—

> "Send with us a person who should teach us Sunnah and al-Islam, where upon he (the Prophet) (peace be upon him) caught hold of the hand of 'Ubaida and said: he is a man of trust of this ummah."
>
> (Anas Ibn Malik, Sahih Muslim, ref. 5948).

Who is a Muslim and a believer? According to Prophet (may peace be upon him) the person who respect his trust, does not misappropriate things entrusted. In other words a person who does commit breach of trust.

Allah's Messenger (peace be upon him) said:—

> "A Muslim is one from whose tongue and hand the Muslims are safe and a believer is one in whom people trust in regard to their lives and wealth."
>
> (Hazrat Abu Huraira, Mishkat al-Masabih, ref. 0033 - Transmitted by Tirmidhi and Nasa'i).

Again relating to believer there is another Hadis Abu Sa'id al-Khudri narrated that Allah's Messenger (may Allah bless him and grand the peace) said:—

> The believer in the world are in three classes: those who believe in Allah and His Messenger and do not doubt, but strive with their property and their person in Allah's cause; the man whom people entrust their properties and their persons; and the man who, when he is about to display greed, abandons it for the sake of Allah, who is great and glorious."
>
> (Mishkat al-Masabih, ref. 3854, Ahmad, transmitted it).

Allah's Messenger (peace be upon him) in another Hadis emphasised that the things entrusted must be returned to the claimant of the things honestly. To quote Hazrat Aisha, Prophet (may Allah bless him and grant him peace) wore two coarse stripped garments, and when he sat and sweated he found them heavy. A certain jew received a consignment of cloth from Syria, so, I suggested he should send for him and buy two garments from him and to be paid when circumstances were easier.

He did so, and when the man replied, "I know what you what is to go off with my property", Allah's Messenger (peace be upon him) said:—

> "He has lied, he knows I am one of the most pious of them and most accustoned to pay what is given on trust."
>
> (Mishkat al-Masabih, ref. 4361, Tirmidhi and Nasa'i, transmitted it).

Prophet guaranteed a believer to achieve paradise if he fulfils certain virtues, one of them is to fulfil the trust. According to Ubada Ibn as-Samit, Prophet (peace be upon him) said:—

> "If you guarantee me six things on your part I shall guarantee you paradise. Speak the truth when you talk, keep a promise when you make it, when you are entrusted with something fulfil your trust, avoid sexual immorality, lower your eyes, and restrain your hands from injustice."
>
> (Mishkat al-Masabih, ref. 4870, Ahmad and Baihaqi, in Shu'ab al-Iman transmitted it).

Again Prophet (peace be upon him) mentioned, certain virtues a pious man who loves and be loved by Allah and His Messenger should fulfil includes fulfilment of trust also.

Hazrat Abd ar-Rahman Ibn Abu Qurad narrated that Prophet (peace be upon him) performed ablution one day and his companion begins to wipe themselves with the water he had used.

The Prophet (peace be upon him) asked them what induced to do that, and when they replied that it was love for Allah and His Messenger (peace be upon him) he said:—

> "If any one is pleased to love Allah and His Messenger (peace be upon him) or rather to have Allah and His

Messenger (peace be upon him) love him, he should speak the truth when he tells anything, fulfil his trust when he is put in a position of trust, and be a good neighbour." (Mishkat al-Masabih, Ref. 4990. Baihaqi transmitted it in Shu'ab al-Iman).

Condemning the breach of trust, according to Abu Said al-Khudri, Prophet (peace be upon him) while addressing after the afternoon prayer about the happening on the day of resurrection without mentioning it warned:—

"The world is sweet and verdant and Allah is putting you as successors in it, so consider how you act. Be on guard against the world, and be on you guard against women. He warned that everyone who committed breach of trust would have a banner on the day of resurrection to the extent of his commission of breach in the world."

(Mishkat al-masabih, Ref. 5154, Transmitted by Tirmidhi).

Houring the trust is one of the virtues of a good and piousman. Mentioning the virtuous of a good man Prophet (peace be upon him) said:—

"If you have four characteristics, whatever worldly advantages passes you by does not matter to you: keeping a trust, speaking the truth, a good character, and abstemiousness in food."

(Abdullah, Ibn Amar, Mishkat al-Masabih, transmitted it by Ahmad and Baihaqi, in Shuab al-Iman).

In the following hadis, just see how Allah Ta'ala curses and punishes those who commit their breach of trust. According to Hazrat Abu Huraira, Allah's Messenger (peace be upon him). said:—

> "When the booty is taken in turn, property given in trust is treated as spoil, zakat is looked upon as a fine.... look at that time for a violent wind, and earthquake, being swallowed up by the earth, metamorphosis, pelting rain, and signs following one another like bite of a necklace falling one after the other when its string is cut."
>
> (Mishkat al-Masabih, Ref. 5450, Tirmidhi transmitted it).

As to breach of trust relating to moral obligations, Hazrat Abu Huraira narrated that Prophet (peace be upon him) asked Abdul Haitham Ibn al-Tayyihan if he had a servant, and when he replied that he had none, he told him to come to him when captives arrived. Two captives were brought to the Prophet, and when Abdul Haitham came to him he told him to choose one of them.

He asked Allah's Prophet (peace be upon him) to choose himself for him, the Prophet said:—

> "The one who is consulted is in a position of a trustee. Take this one, for I have seen him praying, and treat him kindly."
>
> (Mishkat al-Masabih, Ref. 5062, Tirmidhi transmitted it).

Again on violation of moral obligation, Hazrat Jabir Ibn Abdullah narrated that Prophet (peace be upon him) said:—

> "When a man tells something and then departs, it is a trust." (Abu Dawud, Ref. 4850).

On Violation of moral obligation Prophet (peace be upon him) said:—

> "The sanctity of the wives of Mujahids is like the sanctity of their mothers for those who sit at home (i.e., do not go out for jihad). Anyone who stays behind looking after the family of a Mujahid and commits breach of trust will be made to stand on the day of judgement before the Mujahid who will take away from his meritorious deeds whatever he likes. So what do you think (will he leaves anything)?"
>
> (Buraida Ibn al-Hasib, Sahih Muslim Ref. 4673).

One cannot imagine how dreadful a punishment would be for a believer who commits breach of trust under situation referred in the above quoted Hadis. His life long worldly meritorious deeds would be taken away in one stroke.

Treatise entered with enemies and resulted obligations therefrom are also covered under the head of trust. If the enemies commit breach of trust by violating the terms then there is no obligation on believers to observe them. Whatever harm is caused by enemies, reciprocity is the principle. The following Hadis may be referred as an example of trust created by a treaty.

Salma Ibn al-Akwa narrated that we arrived at Hudaibiya with the Messenger of Allah (may peace be upon him) and we were fourteen hundred in number.....when all companions had sworn allegiance to the Holy Prophet (peace be upon him), the polytheists sent messages of peace, until people could move from our camp to that of the Makkans and vice-versa. Finally, the peace treaty was concluded. I (Salma Ibn al-Akwa) was a dependant of Talha bin Ubaidullah, I watered his horse and rubbed its back. I served Talha (doing odd jobs for him) and partook from his food. I had left my family and my property as an emigrant in the cause of Allah and His Messenger (peace be upon him). When we and the people of Makkah had concluded a peace treaty and the people of one side began to mix with those of the other, I came to a tree, swept away its thorns and lay down (for rest) at its base.

While I lay there, four of the polytheists from the Makkans came to me and began to talk ill of the Messenger of Allah (may peace be upon him). I got enraged with them and moved to another tree. They hung their weapons (to the branches of the trees) and laid down (for rest). (While they laid there), somebody from the lower part of the valley cried out: run up, O Muhajirs! Ibn Zunaim had been murdered. I drew my sword and attacked these four while they were asleep. I seized their arms and collected them up in my hand, and said: "By the Being Who has conferred honour upon Muhammad, none of you shall his head, else I will smite his face."

(Then) I came driving them along to the Holy Prophet (may peace be upon him). At the same time, my uncle Amir came (to him) with a man from Abalat called Mikraz. Amir was dragging him on a horse with a thick covering on its back along with seventy polytheists. The Messenger of Allah (may peace be upon him) casted a glance at them and said:—

> "Let them go (so that) they may prove guilty of breach of trust more than once (before we take action against them)." (Sahih Muslim, Ref. 4450).

Messenger of Allah (may peace be upon him) forgave them.

Where a person is entrusted with property or dominion over property, discharges his obligations, honestly, his social status is exalted. Hazrat Malik Ibn Anas narrated that someone said to Luqman, "What has brought you to what we see? (Meaning his high rank). Luqman said:—

> "Truthful speech, fulfilling the trust, and leaving what does not concern me." (Al-Muwatta, Ref. 56, 7.17).

To sum up, the jurists in the light of above noted Ahadith and Qur'ãnic injunctions and commandments developed the whole edifice of the nature of trust and breach thereof. The whole discussion may be summed under the three heads:—

1. Trust (ودیعت) results from divinine and spiritual covenant between Allah Ta'ala and his servants (human beings);

2. Trust results from covenants or without covenants between human beings.

3. Trust results from covenants or without covenants between human beings.

The present study is confined to the last category noted above.

III. Ijma and Qayas (3rd Chief Source)

Under this source of Islamic criminal law we refer here consensus approaches of Islamic jurists and scholars and judgements based upon juristic analogy.

Muslim scholars or jurists (Faqih) have explained criminal matters in the light of Qur'ãnic verses, injunctions and commandments of Allah-Ta'ala, and Sunnah or Ahadith of Prophet Muhammad (peace be upon him). They attempted to interprete the Qur'ãnic ayat and Sunnah, and thus made analogical deductions in the form of fatwas and judgements and also propounded definitions of specific crimes and laid down general principles governing them in conformity with Qur'ãn and Sunnah. Thus explaining any matter they strictly adhere to the injunction, and commandments of Allah and Sunnah of Prophet Muhammad.

The nature of trust, and breach of trust have also been defined and explained by the jurists. Here we will refer some authentic fatwas, judgements and definitions of trust for our comparative study purposes. Muslim jurists have used word 'Emanat (امانت) or vadiat (ودیعت) for the word 'Trust'. For 'Breach of Trust' they use the word Khyanat (خیانت).

"Fatawa-e-Maulana Hazrat Ashraf Ali Thanwi"

Maulana Hazrat Ashraf Ali Thanwi, an eminent Islamic Faqih (jurists) has explained 'Emanat' and Khyanat as follows:—[4]

Mas-ala 1. (مسئلہ) keeping of Emanat is a great responsibility according to religious code. If anyone deposits something with someone and he accepts it, then it becomes essential for him to keep it safe and protected. If it is lost due to negligence or was stolen the trustee is liable to the depositor's claim. But without negligence where the entrusted property is burnt due to the house being set on fire, then the depositor cannot claim its compensation. Even if the keeper had promised it in case of loss also, the depositor is not entitle to any compensation."

"Mas-ala 2. "if anyone while going away asked someone else to keep his articles with in and he agreed to it or did not say anything and the man left leaving the article with him, then it has become a deposit (Emanat). But if the man clearly refused to accept it and even then the man left the article with him then it is not a deposit. But if the person took up the article after the other person has left and kept it, then it became a deposit."

"Mas-ala 3, the condition - that is - one who keeps the deposit with him - may keep the deposit in his own custody or

4. 'Bahishti Zewar', Maulana Ashraf Ali Thanwi, page 362, English translation by Mohammed Mansoor Khan Sarohe, M.A., L.L.B. Aligarh.

with some of his relatives who live in the same house and with whom he can keep his own deposits and is trustworthy. But it should not be kept with an unreliable person because in case of its being lost he will have to give its compensation. It is not proper to keep it with any other person without the permission of the owner."

"Mas-ala 4"; if the custodian forgot the deposit and it was lost, ;then he is responsible to compensation the article."

"Mas-ala 5", if fire break out in the home of custodian, then the deposit may be kept with someone else. But it should be immediately taken back when the cause is removed. It is also permissible to entrust the deposits to someone else at the time of dying if no relation or member of the family is present."

"Mas-ala 6", if anyone has deposited some cash with someone, then it is essential to keep the same cash, coins or notes etc., in safe custody. It is not permissible even to mix this amount with one's own money or to spend it. It is wrong to presume that all money is the same and spend it thinking that the amount will be paid when demanded. The deposit may be used if permitted by the owner. But in such a case it would become a debt. If the same money is kept and somehow it is lost, then the custodian will not be liable to pay the compensation. But if the money was spent with the permission of the depositor, then it shall have to be paid in every case."

"Mas-ala 7", if any one deposited Rs. 100/- with someone and the custodian with the permission of the depositor mixed Rs. 100/- with his own hundred rupees, then this amount of Rs. 200/ - became a joint property. If these are stolen then both will suffer and the custodian shall have to pay nothing to the depositor."

"Mas-ala 8", if anyone deposited milk animal with someone, then it is not permissible to use its milk without the permission of the owner. If it is used without his permission, then its price shall have to be given to the owner."

"Mas-ala 9", the same is true about ornaments, clothes and other domestic goods. These should also not be used".

"Mas-ala 10", if some gave some money as deposit to a person and while keeping the money in his pocket, or purse it fell down and the custodian believed that he had kept it in his pocket or purse, then no compensation will be due on him due on him.

"Mas-ala 11" - whenever the depositor demands back, it is essential to be returned immediately. It should not be delayed without any legitimate cause as it is justified and improper. If the depositor agree, to take it after sometime, then it is permissible.

"Articles Taken on Loan" - Articles taken on loan for temporary use also amount to deposit and are covered by the same injunctions. These should also be kept safely. It is a common practice that clothes, ornaments or utensils etc., are taken for temporary use on the understanding that the same will be returned when not needed. These are also deposits. If inspite of all precautions, any such article is lost, then the owner is not entitled to any compensation even if the debtor had promised to compensate in case of loss. But if it was lost due to carelessness, there compensation is essential. Such article should also be returned when demanded."

A persual of the above referred mas-a-el shows that these are answer to given situations. They determine whether in a given situation there is a trust or not, and when does it amount to breach of trust and the liability arising therefrom. Generally the liability is civil where compensation is awarded. But such cases are covered by penal liability also. The aggrieved party may apply to criminal course for the prosecution of the wrongdoer also.

From these fatwa, we infer the following essentials of trust and of breach of trust:—

1. Two parties, the depositor, the person who entrusts the goods or property, and secondly, the trustee, to whom the goods or property is entrusted.
2. Entrustment of property or giving dominion over the property by the depositor to the trustee, and acceptance by the trustee for the property entrusted.
3. Emanat (Trust), is a great responsibility. Once accepted it is the responsibility of the trustee to keep it safe and protected.
4. If the trustee is negligence, property is burnt due to the house set on fire, trustee not liable to the depositor. Depositor under such a situation is not entitle to claim any compensation or seek any redress in Shariah criminal courts.

6. In a case where someone is going away asks another person to keep his property with him and the second person does not say anything and the man left having his property with the second person, then the property so left becomes trust (Emanat) with him. However, where the person refused to accept the entrustment, it would not amount to trust (Emanat). But inspite of refusal he leaves behind his property and goes away and the second persons keeps it with him it becomes a trust.

7. Entrusted property may be kept in the trustee's custody or trustee may keep with some of his relative who live in the same house and with whom he also keeps his own deposits and the custodian is a trustworthy person. The trustee should not keep the trust property with an unreliable person. In the later situation if the property is lost, the trustee would be liable. Further, it is not proper to keep the trust property with any other person without the permission of the owner.

8. In case where due to the forgetfulness of the trustee, property is lost, he would be liable for.

9. In case where fire breaks out in the house, property entrusted may be kept with someone else ealso. But immediately after the fire is extinguished it must be taken back by the trustee.

10. It is also permissible to entrust the property to some third person at the time when the trustee is dying and neither his relative nor a family member is present near him.

11. It is also obligatorty on the trustee to keep the property as it is. In other words if the deposit is in cash, the same coins or notes should be preserved. He should not mix the trusted property with his own unless so permitted by the depositor. It is wrong to presume that all money is the same and spend it thinking that the amount would be returned when demanded.

12. The trusted property may be used by the trustee if so permitted by the owner. But in such situation it would become a debt. Further if the entrusted property is mixed with his own property then it becomes a joint property. If the joint property is stolen the trustee has to pay nothing to the depositor because in such a case both of them suffer.

13. If the entrusted property is such which has daily returns and profits then it is not permissible to utilize such usufructs without the permission of the owner. If the usufructs are used without the permission of the owner, the trustee, has to pay the price thereof to the owner.

14. Where the entrusted property is in the nature of oranaments, clothes and other domestic goods, they are also not to be used by the trustee.

15. In a case where the property entrusted is kept in the pocket or purse falls down and the impression of the trustee is that he has kept it properly, in consequence lost, then trustee is not answerable as there is no fault of him.

16. Where the entrusted property is demanded back by the depositor, it must be returned immediately. There should not be any delay unless there is a legitimate cause to the contrary. But if the depositor agrees to take the property after sometime, then it justified.

17. Property taken on loan for temporary use also amount to trust and is subject in it's governance to the same principles above noted.

These are possible inferences which governs trust. Misappropriation results in breach of trust and in consequence makes a person liable for the such violations of the general principles laid down in fatwa.

"Fatwa-e-Kazee Khan"

For elaborating further we may refer some fatawa from Fatawa-i-Kazee Khan also.[5]

These fatwas relate to breach of trust.

- "Amount of deposits should be faithfully restored". (Page 126).

- "There should be no Khyanat or misappropriation of Emanat or trust property" (Page 219).

- "Bizaut, or entrusting another to sell a thing is jaiz." (Page 266).

5. Tagore-Law-Lectures-Translated by Honourable Moulvi Mohammed Yusuf Khan Bahadur, and Moulvi Williyat Hussain.

- "It is Haram to misappropriate property."

- "It is unlawful to eat, if edible, misappropriated thing." (Page 27).

These fatwas from Fatwa-e-Kazee Khan show that there is an absolute prohibition for misappropriation of trust property. It has been declared Haram. If a thing is edible its use is prohibited.

Trust Explained: Fatawa-e-Hindia-'Fatawa-e-Alam-Giri

Where an owner assigns another person to look after for the safe keeping of his property, in shariah, it is known as 'Eida' (ایدا). Whereas the property is left with trustee (متولی), in shariah, it is called a "Trust" (ودیعت). Kanz (کنز)

Trust (ودیعت) requires proposal and acceptance (تجویزوقبولیت), that is 'depositor' (موو‌جیع) should say to the 'Trustee' (متولی) that he has entrusted him with the property or use such words or does such deeds which may represent his intention, and the 'Trustee' (متولی) should accept the 'Trust' (ودیعت) either by his words or by his action, or by deeds only. 'Tabe-yeen'. Further 'trust (ودیعت) is created sometime by proposal and acceptance (تجویز وقبولیت) and sometime inferred by implication (امانت بذریه کنایت).

When the depositor (موو‌جیع) says, "I entrust this thing as trust to you", and the trustee (متولی) in response says, "I accept it", trust is created. In cases, however, where property has been transferred for safe-keeping, without proposal and acceptance (تجویزوقبولیت). 'Eida' (ایدا) would not be complete. Whereas in 'Trust' (ودیعت) mere proposal is enough. Exception to this rule is 'usurpation'. Where the owner of the property says to the 'usurpur', "I entrust the thing usurped he is responsible for safe-keeping and his acceptance in such a case is necessary".

"Trust by implication (امانت بذریہ کنایت) has been explained as: "Where a person entrusted the property to another, and said nothing, or said that property had been made 'Trust' (ودیعت) to him, and that person remained silent, did not say any word in response thereto, he becomes a 'Trustee' (متولی) because his keeping silent amounted to acceptance (قبولیت), though, thereafter, that person absconded and property was lost. For any loss he would be responsible. (Khazanat-Ul-Mufteen).

According to this explanation there should be depositor (مووجیع) and trustee (متولی). For trust (ودیعت). For entrustment proposal and acceptance (تجویز وقبولیت) are required. Proposal and acceptance by depositor (مووجیع) are required. Proposal and acceptance by depositor (مووجیع) and trustee (متولی) may be express or implied by implication (کنایہ). Sometime for trust (ودیعت) mere proposal (تجویز) is enough but to this there are exceptions.

Apart from the above requisites. The things entrusted or made should be capable of possession. Thing, like absconded slave, a bird flying in the air, and a thing fallen into the dept. of sea cannot be the subject matter of trust (ودیعت). (Behrul-Ra-Eq).

In Hedaya[6] the term trust (ودیعت) has been explained as:—

"Widda, in the language of the law, signifies a person empowering another to keep his property, the proprietor of thing is styled modee (مودحیح), or the depositor;

- the person so empowered, the mode (مود) or trustee: and the property so left with another, for the purpose of keeping it, is styled widdeeyat (دویعت) because Widda (ودہ)

---

6. (Hedaya-Commentary on Islamic Law, Translated by Charles Hamilton. Page 471 (Shorter Edition).

( ) literally means to leave, and thing in question is left with the mode or trustee."

"Abdul Qadir Oudah Shaheed's views on trust":-

Abdul Qadri Oudah Shaheed has explained 'breach of trust' in his book - "Criminal Law of Islam,"[7] by referring the Qur'ãnic verses and Sunnah of Prophet Muhammad (peace be upon him). He has referred the following Aayat explaining the trust and breach of trust:-[8]

1. Surah al-Ahzab (33-72)
2. Surah al-Nisan (4-58)
3. Surah al-Anfal (8-27)
4. Surah al-Nisan (4-2)
5. Surah al-Nisan (4-6)
6. Surah al-Nisan (4-10)
7. Surah al-Nisan (4-29)

Besides Qur'ãnic Ayat, above noted, Qadir Oudah Shaheed in explaining "Breach of Trust" takes the help from, Ahadith also. He quotes 'Holy Prophet where he mentions the distinguishing characteristics of a hypocrite" as:—

A man having four qualities is a hypocrite to his finger tips. If he possesses one of the four qualities, he has then one quality of inpostor unless he shakes it off. The qualities are: he commits breach of trust whenever something is kept in his custody; whenever he tells something it is a lie; whenever he enters into a transaction, he is dishonest, and whenever he picks up a quarrel, he abuses."

---

7. Criminla Law of Islam, Vol. I, Abdul Qadir Oudah Shaheed.
8. These Aayat have a already been discussed in details under the head First main Source of Shariah or Islamic Law.

Abdul Qadir's approach is to explain the breach of trust in the light of Qur'ãnic injunctions and Sunnah. If the case is covered under the above sources then it may be trust. Whoever breaks, the law would be liable.

The governing principle under Shariah is that both crime and punishment pre-suppose the existence of provision (injunctions and sunnah)

"Trust explained in The Mejelles:"-[9]

Apart from the criminal law of Islam by Abdul Qadir Oudah Shaheed, we have the Majelle also wherein an attempt has been made to define and explain the nature of trust in accordance to Qur'ãnic injunctions and Sunnah. Articles 762[10] defines Emanat (trust) as follows:-

"Emanat is a thing found with someone, who is considered to be in charge of it. Whether it is made an emanet by a court requiring the safe keeping of property, like property entrusted to another for safe keeping (Vedie, Article 763), and whether it be an emanat in a contract requiring compensation for loss, like a thing taken on hire, are thing received as a loan for use, and whether it passes as an emanat into the hands of someone without contract existing or a design formed. As, if the property of a neighbour falls into the house of someone on account of the wind, by reason there being no contract, that property is not property deposited

---

9. Majelle Ahkame Adliye, represents an attempt to codify part of hanafi fiqh which treats of muamalat (transactions between people). The codification was the work of a commission of jurists, headed by ahmed Djevdet Pasha, the Minister of Justice in Turkey approved by Sheikh al-Islamic and other. This compilation is used as a guide and useful book of reference both in civil as well as criminal matters. (Page ii).

10. Book VI, Article 762, The Mejelle, translated in English by C.R. Tyser B.A.L. President, District Court of Kyrenia.

with another for safe keeping (Vedie, Article 763), but it is an emanat (plural emanat)."

For entrusting the property either by way of contract or without contract, different specific terms have been used with the intention to show the variety of processes of entrustment of emanet (trust), such as:-[11]

Vedia, Ida, Ariyyet, Mu'ar, Musta'ar, L'are, Mu'ar, Isti'ire, and Musta'ir.

This definition has been propounded in inconfirmity with the Qur'ãnic verses as well as the Ahadith or Sunnah. According to this definition the following requisites should be there for creating a trust or calling a thing to be emanat:—

Broadly speaking emanat or trust may be created either by contract or without contract.

1. The first requisite is that there must be a thing or property.
2. Thing or property should be found in possession of someone.
3. The person having custody over or dominion over is considered to be the incharge of it.
4. Emanat or trust may be the creation of a contract.
5. A contract may be for safe keeping the property or thing.

---

11. Article 763 - 'Vedi'a is property deposited with someone for safe-keep.
Article 764 - 'Ida' is to deliver to another the safe keeping of own property. To the person who deliver it, the name Mudi is given to the person who accepts it, the name 'Vedi' and 'Mustevde.
Article 765 - Ariyyet is property the use of which is granted, gratuitously, that is to say, without a price. It is called 'Muar and Musta'ar.
Article 766 - 'h' are is to give an Ariyyet. To the person who gives it, the name Muir' is given.
Article 767 - Ishti' are is to take an Ariyyet. To the person taking it, the name Musta'ir is given.

6. Property may be made widdeeyat or entrusted to another person for safe keeping.
7. The person whop creates the trust or transfer the emanats for safe keeping is known as 'mude', and the person who accepts the trust or emanat is known as 'vedi' or 'mustevda'.
8. A thing may be emanat in a contract requiring compensation for loss. Under this requisite cases of taking thing on hire or received on loan for use are covered.
9. Ariyyet case where the use of property is permitted gratiutiously and without price one also covered under the scope of the term emanat; the person who gives the property on Ariyyet is known as Mu'ir and the taking the property is known as Musta'ir.
10. Property is emanat or trust into the hands of someone even without contract or entrustment for example when the property of neighbour falls into the house of someone on account of the wind, by reason of there being no contract. Property in such a case is not entrusted vediat (ودیعت) with another for safe keeping but it is an emanat (trust). In other words there can be a trust (emanat) even without entrusting the property to the trustee or delivery of possession thereof or giving dominion over it for safe-keeping.

Inference from the above analysis is that the scope of trust (emanat) under shariah or Islamic law is very wide. Obligations resulted either by contract or without contract are convered within it's purview.

IV. "Rules Governing Breach of Trust"

The rules governing emanat (trust) are enumerated in mejelle Ahkeame Adilya in Book VI, under three chapters, from Articles 768 to 832 which are quite exhaustive. Significance of these Articles lies, in fact, that they are all inconsonance with the spirit of Qur'ãnic injunctions and Sunnah. Violation of these rules would amount to Khiyyanat (breach of trust). Articles are considered below.[1]

No Compensation Without Fault "Article 786"

An emanet is not a thing for which compensation has to be made.

That is to say, in case of the destruction or damage of an emanet without any fault being committed by the person entrusted (Emin), it is not necessary to make compensation. It means that a person (emin) would be liable for breach of trust when he is at fault. For making Emin liable, his negligence or carelessness which is responsible for the destruction of property, is to be proved. If it is proved he would be liable for breach of trust.

"Finder's Liability:" "Article 769"

If someone finds a thing on the road, or in any other place, and takes it for the purpose of making it his own property, he becomes like a wrongful appropriator (ghasib).

Therefore, in case that property has been destroyed or damaged, although there may not be any fault of his own, he is responsible.

But in case he has taken it for the purpose of giving it to its owner, if its owner is known, in his hands, it is a pure emanet (trust). It is necessary that he should deliver it to its owner.

And if it owner is not known, it is a thing picked up by a chance, and it is an emanet (trust) in the hands of the person who picks it up, that is to say, who finds and takes it.

---

1. Rules Governing Trust: Hedaya Commentary on islamci Law, Charles Hamilton, Like Majelle 'Rule Governing Trust' have also been explained in Hedaya. The details are as follows:-

---

Of Widda, Or Deposits

A trustee is not responsible a deposit unless he transgresses with respect to it. A DEPOSIT remain in the hands of the person who receive charge of it, as a trust, that is to say, he is not answerable for it. If, therefore, a deposit be lost or destroyed in the trustee's hands, without any transgression on his part, he is not in that case responsible for it, because the prophet has said, "an honest trustee is not responsible", and also because there is a necessity, amongst mankind, for deposits; and this necessity could not be answered in case of making trustees responsible, as no one would then accept the trust.

He may keep it himself, or commit the care of it to and of his family. A TRUSTEE may either keep the deposit himself, or commit for that purpose to some one of his family such as his wife, his son, his mother, or his father; because it is evident that a trustee does not engage to keep the property of another with more care than he does his own; and he sometimes keeps his own himself; and sometimes commits it to one of his family. besides, there exists an absolute necessity for committing the trust to his family, since it is neither possible for him to remain always in the house, or, when he goes out, to carry the deposit with him - for all those reason,s therefore, the consent of the proprietor is understood to extend to the trustee's commiting the deposit to the care of his family.

But if he give charge of it to a stranger he becomes responsible. BUT if the trustee should commit the deposit to the charge of any other than a member of his family (as if he were either to hire some person out of his family, for the purpose of keeping it, or to give it in deposit to some one out of his family), he is then responsible, in as much as there is a difference between the care of different people, and it was his own care, and not that of another, to which the proprietor assented. Besides, a thing does not involved its similar; and hence a trustee is not empowered to constitute another the trustee of the same thing; in the same manner as an agent is not permitted to constitute another agent. (By the term family, in this place, is to be understood all such as live with the trustee, or whose maintenance is incumbent upon him, or his upon them, as a wife or adult son).

And so also, if he lodge it in a place of custody belonging to another. If a trustee lodge the deposit in a place of custody belonging to another, he becomes responsible for it; b ecause the lodging it in another's place of custody is, in effect, depositing it with that other, it is otherwise, however, if he hire the said place; for in that instance his lodging it there is considered in the same light with his keeping it himself and therefore does nt induce responsibility.

He is not made responsibile by putting it out of his own possession with a view to the immediate preservation of it. If the house of a trustee take fire, and he deliver the deposit to his neighbour or if, being in a boat on the point of sinking, he throw the deposit into another boat, and it in either case be lost he is not responsible, since he acted only for the preservation of it, and consequently according to the consent of the proprietor. But the assertion of the trustee, in such cases, is not to be credited unless supported by witnesses since, upon the establishment of a cause of responsibility, be pleads the existence of a necessity, which invalidates the responsibility, and the case therefore the same as if he were to plead that the proprietor had empowered him to consign the deposit to another.

He becomes responsible on neglecting to deliver it on demand. If the proprietor of the deposit demand it from the trustee, and he neglect delivering it to him, being at the same time caable of such delivery, he becomes in the case responsible for it, since his neglecting or refusing to deliver, under a capacity to do so, is a transgression. The ground of this is, that the demand of the proprietor clearly indicates his dissent from the trustee's retaining possession any longer, and is therefore a dismission of him from the trust. Hence the trustee is responsible, because of his retaining possession after such dissent.

If he mixes it insperably with his own property, he must make the proprietor a compensation - If the trustee mix the deposit with his own property, in such a manner that a separation becomes difficult, he must in that case make an adequate compensation, and the proprietor (according to Haneefa) has not the option of sharing the mixed property, whether the mixture be of a homogeneous nature (such as milk with milk, wheat with wheat, or white dirms with white dirms), or of a heterogeneous nature (such as oil of sesame with oil of olives, or wheat with barley). The two disciples allege that where the mixture is of homogenous articles not of a liquid nature (such as white dirms with white dirms, or wheat with wheat), the proprietor of the deposit has the option either of becoming a sharer with the trustee, or of taking a compensation for the value; because although it be impossible in such a case, for the proprietor to receive his right with respect to apperance, still it is possible for him to receive it with respect to reality (that is in effect), by making a division, since, in all articles of weight, or measurement of capacity, a delivery of the actual article, according to all authorities. Such, therefore, being the case, it appears that mixtgure, in the instance in question, is a destruction in another respect; and consequently, that the proprietor of the articles placed in deposit has the option either of taking a compensation on the principle of the mixture being a destruction, or of becoming a sharer (if he please) on the principle of its not bein a destruction. The argument of Haneefa is that mixtgure is in every respect a destruction, because of its being an action which occasions an impossibility of returning the thing to the proprietor in its original substance, - In regard to what the two disciples advance, that "it is possible for the proprietor to receive his right with respect to reality, be means of a division", it is answered that the proprietor cannot attain his actual right by means of division. Besides division has been instituted from necessity, merely as a mode of advantage in cases of partnership. Division, therefore, is merely an effect of partnership, and is incapable of being a cause of it, for otherwise the principal would become secondary, and the secondary principal. The result of this disagreement is that if the proprietor should exempt the trustee, where he according to Haneefa, his right becomes entirely cancelled, since (agreeably to his tenets) the proprietor's right is limited to the compensation, which he expressly forgog; where as, according to the two disciples, the proprietor's right of option to a compensation ceases in consequence of such exemption, and resolves itself into a share in the mixed property; because observed that the mixtgure of one liquid with a different liquid (such as of oil of Sesame with oil of lives) it to a compensation, according to allow destroys the right of the proprietor to a participation in the mixed property, and fixed and determines it is a compensation, according to all our doctors, as such a mixture is a destruction with respect both the same class, according to the Rawayet Saheeh, are all cases of an admisxture of different articles, not liquids, where the separation is difficult, as in the mixture of wheat with barley. In cases where the separation requires a process, or is attended with some difficulty (such as if dirms should be melted and incorporated with others), the depositor's right to the substance ceases, and he is entitled to a compensation, according to Haneefa, as before stated. Aboo Yoosa holds that in this case the smaller is subordinate to the greater (for, according to his tenets, superiority must be regarded), and that therefore, the person who possessed the largest share of the property becomes proprietor of the whole, and liable to compensate to the other for the value of his quantum. Mohammed, on the other hand, maintains that the proprietor of the deposit becomes a participator with the other in either case, because according to his tenets, species cannot acquire a superiority over the same species, as has been already explained in treating of fosterage.

If the mixture be occasioned by accident, the properitor becomes a proportionate sharer in the whole. If a deposit be mixed with the property of the trustee, not be any act of the latter, but by accident (as if a bag containing the deposit, and another containing property of the trustee, should both be torn, and the contents mingled together), in that case the trustee becomes a sharer in the property with the depositor, and is not responsible for a compensation, since he did not commit any act inducing responsibility. They therefore become partners in the whole according to all our doctors.

If the trustee expend a part, and supply the eficiency, by mixture, from his own property, he is responsible for the whole. If a trustee expend part of the deposit, and then produce a similar to what he had expended, and mix it with the remaining part, in such a manner that a separation is difficult, he is, in that case, responsible for, the whole of the deposit; because the part expended is a debt due by him, which he cannot otherwise discharge than in the presence of the owner. When, therefore, he mixes his own property with the remainder of the deposit, he in fact destroys that remainder; as was before explained.

In case of transgression report to the deposit, the trustee is responsible so long as the transgression continues. If a trustee transgress with repsect to the deposit, by converting it to his own use (as if, being a quardruped, he should ride upon it, or, being a gown, he should weat it, or being a slace, he should use his services), or by committing it to the case of a stranger, and he afterwards refrain from the use of it, or receive it back from the stranger, his responsibility thereupon ceases. Shafei maintains that he does nt become exempted from responsibility; because the contract of deposit ceases and determines immediately on the extence of responsibility, since responsibility and deposit are irreconcileable: the trustee, therefore, in such case, cannot be exempted until he made actual restitution to the proprietor. The argument of our doctors is, that the order of the depositor to preserve the property restitution to the as it was absolute, and not restricted to any particular time; it being understood, in this case, that the proprietor had generally desired him to preserve the property, without restricting such desire to any particular time. As, therefore, the order is still in force, it follows that the trustee, after abstaining from the transgression, becomes again trustee, because the object of the contract was preserrvation. The contract, moreover, was suspended in its effect merely from the necessity of establishing a branch of it: when, therefore, the branch is removed, the contract becomes revived in its effect; in the same manner as where a person hires another to guard his property for a month, and the person so hired remits his guard for part of the month, in which case he is entitled to wages in proportion to the number of days he did watch. In answer to Shafeis assertion, that "the trustee cannot be exempted from responsibility until he make actual restitution his transgression, a recovery of the deposit is obtained into the possession of the trustee, who is the substitute or confident of the proprietor; and as this recovery is equivalent to a restitution of it to the proprietor himself, he [the trustee] is consequently not responsible for it on the ground of destruction.

If the trustee deny the deposit, upon demand, he is responsible in case of the loss of it. If the proprietor of the deposit demand it of the trustee, and the trustee deny the deposit, and it be afterwards lost, the trustee is in that case responsible: because, as the depositor, in making the demand, dismisses the trustee from his charge, if follows that the trustee, in retaining the deposit after such demand, is an usurper, and is cnsequently responsible. If also, after the denial, the trustee should acknowledge the deposit, still he does not thereby become exempted from responsibility, because the contract had been previously done away, inasmuch as the demand of restitution by the depositor was a dissolution on his part, and the denial of the deposit was a dissolution on the part of the trustee; in the same or of sale either by the buyer or seller, is a dissolution on their part - Now when a dissolution takes place on both sides, the contract to which it relates is done away; and cannot afterwards be revived, unless by a new formation, which does not appear in the case in question. In this case, therefore, a recovery into the possession of the proprietor's substitute cannot be understood. It is otherwise where the trustee deviates from his instructions by transgressing upon the property, and afterwards ceases from such deviation and conforms to his orders, for in this case a recovery appears into the possession of the proprietor's substitute, as was before explained.

But not if the denial be made to a stranger.

If the trustee deny the deposit to some other than the proprietor, he is not responsible, according to Aboo Yousaf (contrary to the opinion of Ziffer), because denial to any other than the proprietor may be for the sake of preservation. The trustee, moreover is not competent to his own dismission, unless in the presence of the depositor, or unless the depositor claim his property from him. The order for keeping the property, therefore, still continues in force - contrary to where the denial is made to the depositor.

A trustee is at liberty to carry the deposit with him upon a journey. A trustee is at liberty, according to Haneefa, to carry the deposit with him when he travels, although carriage and other expenses be thereby incurred. The two disciples maintain that is not permitted to him where carriage or other expense is incurred. Shafei, on the other hand, maintains that it is not allowable in either case, because he considers an order to keep the article in the common acceptation of keeping, namely keeping in cities, in the same manner as where a person hires another for the preservation of his goods for a stated time, in which case the person hired is not at liberty to travel with the goods, or, if he should do so, becomes responsible for them. The argument of Hanafeea is, that the proprietor's commission for preservation is absolute and unconfined; and that a plain is a place of preservation, provided the road be secured; on which principle it is permitted to a father or guardian to travel with the property of their ward. The reasoning of the two disciples is that, in case of travelling, where carriage for the deposit is necessary, the expense of it must fall on the depositor; and as it is probable he may not assent to this, his commission for keeping the article must, in such a case, be considered as limited to a city. The answer to this is taht the cricumstance of the expense of remoment, as it may be a consequence of an attention to the preservation of his property, and the fulfilment of his commission - the answer to Shafei is that although are articles cheifly abound in cities, still the keeping or preserving of them is not particularly confined to cities, but extends alike to cities and to plains; since the inhabitants of plains must necessarily keep their property in plains - Besides, a removal of the deposit may sometimes be a desirable object to the proprietor: as where it is made from a city in danger to one in security; or to the particular city in which the proprietor dwells, now as the keeping of an article is not, in its common acceptation limited to cities, it follows that a commission for keeping is not limited to any particular city, it is otherwise in a case of hire for keeping, as hire is a contract of exchange, which requires a delivery of the subject of the contract (namely, keeping or guarding) in the place where the contract is executed.

Provided the contract be absolute, the road safe, and the journey necessary, It is to be observed that this case proceeds on a supposition of the contract being absolute, the road which the trustee travels safe, and the journey necessary: for, if the road be dangerous, or the journey not necessary, the trustee travel with all his family, he is not responsible: but if, the journey not being necessary, he should leave his family behind, he becomes responsible, as in that case it was his duty to have left the deposit with his family.

Unless this be expressly prohibited. If the proprietor expressly prohibit the turstee from carrying the deposit out of the city, and he nevertheless carry it out, he becomes in that case responsible for it, as the restriction so imposed is a valid one since keeping the article in a city is most eligible.

In case of a deposit by tow persons, the trustee cannot deliver to either his share, but in presence of the other. If two men deposit something jointly with another, and one of them afterwards appear, and demand his share of the deposit, the trustee must not gie it, unless in the presence of the other depositor, according to Haneefa. The two disciples maintain that the trustee must deliver the claimant his share; and the same is also said in Kadooree's compendium. In the Jama Sagheer is said that if three men deposit one thousand dirms with a particular person, and two of them afterwards disappear, the third is not entitled to take his share, according to Haneefa; but according to the two disciples he is entitled to take it. (It is to be observed taht this difference of opinion relate solely to articles of weight, or measurement of capacity). The argument of the two disciples is that the depositor claims his own share only, and is therefore entitled to receive it, where it is attainable in the same manner as a copartner in a debt. The argument of Haneefa is that the person present, in claiming his absentee's since he claim a separate and deteerminate portion, whereas his right is indefinite. Now where a right is mixed indefinitely with another, it is to be rendered separate and determinate only by means of divission; but the trustee has no power to make a division; and accordingly, if he were to give the present claimant his share, it is not account a division by any of our doctors - it is otherwise in a case of a participated debt, because in that instance, the present creditor claims from the debtor a delivery of his right, which may be made without a division, since debt is discharged by means of similars. With respect to what is advance by the two disciples that "the depositor is entitled to receive his share where it is attainable" it may be answered, that it does not from hence follow that the trustee is liable to any compulsion on that head: in the same manner as where for instance, a person deposits one thousand dirams with another, who is indebted in one thousand dirms to a third person; in which case although it be lawful for the creditor to take his due wherever it be attainable, still it is not lawful for the trustee to pay him with the said deposit.

Two person receiving a divisible article in trust, must each keep on half. If a peson deposit. with two men, an article capable of division, it is not lawful for either of these trustee to commit such article entirely to the other, but they must divide it, and retain each and half; whereas, if the article were incapable of division, either might lawfully keep it entirely with the consent of the other. This is the doctrine of Haneefa; and such also is the law, according to him, in a case of two pawnees, to whom a thing incapable or a division is jointly pledged; for in that case either of them, with the consent of the other, may retain sole possession of it, and so likewise, in the case of two agent empowered to buy anything, and entrusted jointly with the purchase money, for in that case, also one of the parties may retain the whole of the money with the consent of the other. The two disciple allege that it is lawful for one of the parties to the take entire charge, with the consent of the other, in either case; for as the proprietor has manifested his confidence in the integrity of both, it, is therefore lawful for either, to deliver the deposit to the other without being responsible, in the same manner as where the deposit is incapable of division. The argument of Haneefa is, that the proprietor has vien his approbation to the charge being united in two, but not to its being vested entirely in one; because the act of keeping, where it relates to a divisible article applies only to a part of the article, not to the whole. The delivery therefore, of the whole by either party to the other is without the proprietor's consent; and the party who makes such delivery is accordingly responsible. But the receiver is not responsible, since (according to his tenets) the trustee of a trustee is not subject to responsibility. It is otherwise where the deposit is incapable of division; for where an article of that nature is deposited with two persons, it is impossible for them jointly to be concerned in the case of it every hour of the day and night, unless by turns; and the approbation of the proprietor, with respect to the whole, is therefore of necessity construed to extend to either of them in particular.

Restrictions are not regarded where they are repugnatn to custom or convenience. If the proprietor of a deposit say to the trustee "deliver not the deposit to your wife" and he nevertheless deliver it to his wife, he becomes in that case responsible, it is recorded, in the Jama Sagheer, that if the proprietor prohibit the trustee from delivering the deposit to any one of his family and he nevertheless

> deliver it to one of his family from any unavoidable necessity, he is not made responsible by having so delivered it; as if, for instance, the deposit be an animal, and the proprietor prohibit the trustee from giving charge of it to his slave, or as if, being of the description of things usually committed to the care of women, he should prohibited him from delivering it to quoted from the Jama Sagheer restricted, the first ought also to be understood as restricted; for this reason, that it is impossible to manage to conservation with an observance of the condition, which is therefore nugatory. But if the trustee should not act from necessity, as if, having two wives, or two slaves, the proprietor should prohibit the delivery to one particular wife, or to one particular slave, and the trustee nevertheless commit the deposit to the particular wife or slave so prohibited, he becomes responsible, since the condition in this case is usuful, as same of the family may not be trustworthy; and, as the conservation of the deposit is not incompatible with the observance of the condition, it is therefore valid.

Or where they relate to the particular apartment in a house. If the proprietor say to the trustee. "Keep the deposit in this apartment of theSarai", and he keep it in another apartment of the same Sarai, in that case he is not responsible for it; because the condition was useless, inasmuch as there is no difference with respect to keeping in different apartments of the same Sarai. (If, on the contrry, he were to keep it in a different Sarai, he is responsible; because as a difference of Sarai's occasion a difference in the keeping, the condition is therefore of use, and the restriction is consequently valid). If, however, there be an evident different between two different apartments of the same Sarai (as if, the Sarai being extensive, the apartment prohibited should be full of holes and crevices), the condition so made is valid, and the trustee becomes responsible in case of preserving it in that apartment.

> evidence, no superiority would have been given to either evidence on the gound or priority, to also in the present instance - The defendant must also give a compensation of another thousand dirms to the claimants, since in paying them the one thousand which was present hje only pays each half his due-supposing that the Kazee, in consequence of a refusal to take the first oath, should immediately pass a decree in favour of the first claimant, without waiting to tender an oath with respect to the claim of the other, in

---

this case Imam Alee Yezadee, in this commentar upon the Jama Sagheer, says that an oath must be tendered with regard to the second: and if the difendant refuse to take it, a decres must then be passed jointly, in favour of both claimants, in an equal degree; because the decree in favour of the first claimant ws not destructive of the right of the second, since the procedence, in the administration of the oath, was determined either by the will of the Kazee, or the chance of the die; and neither of these have power to destroy the second's right - Khasaf has substituted a slave in this case; that is, instead of one thousand dirms, he has supposed the dispute to related to a slave, and he maintains that the sentence ought to be executed in favour of the first claimant, since the matter is uncertain, in as much as several of the learned have given it as their opinion, that a decree should be passed in favour of the first without waiting for the second, as a denial to take on oath is equivalent, by implication, to an acknowledgment. He, moreover, remarks, that the oath with respect to the oath with respect to the second claimant must not be administered to this effect, "this slave is not the slave of such as one", because a refusal on the part of the defendant to take such an oath is of no consequence, after the slave in question had been proved to be the property of another. The tenor of the oath, therefore, must be "there is nothing due from me to to this man, not this slave, nor less than the said value". He also observes, tht it is requisite this oath be administered, according to Mohammed; but not according to Aboo Yoosaf; because if a tustee should make an acknowledgement of the deposit in favour of a certain person, and the thing acknowledged should by a decree of the kazee be given to another, then, according to Mohammed, the acknowledger is responsible but not according to Aboo Yoosaf. Now the case in question is a bracnh of this case relative to the acknowledger here alluded to, is where a person first acknowledges a particular person, and afterwards denies it, averring that another person had deposited the slave with him, and a decree is passed in favour of the first acknowledge, because of the second acknowledgment being a retraction of the first; in which case, if he should have given the slave to the first without a decree of the Kazee he is responsible, in the opinion of all our doctors; or if he should have given the slave by the decree of the Kazee, in that case

---

also, according to Mohammed, he is responsible, because he acknowledges his obligation to keep the slave on account of the second and yet he destroys the said slave (that is, so far as relates to the claim of the second), by means of his acknowledgment, and is consequently responsible. According to Aboo Yoosaf he is not responsible in this instance, because he as holds, it is not the immediate act of acknowledgment that destroys the slave, so far as relates to the right of the other hand, maintains that it was he who urged the Kazee to pass that decree; whence he is reponsible. Now the reason for assimilating the case in question with this one is, that the acknowledgement in favour of the second claimant, after the first had acquired a right to the thing, is useful to the second claimant in as much as (the opinion of Mohammed, it induces a responsibility in his favour. Hence in this case, it is requisite, according to Mohammed.. to administer an oath to the second claimant, notwithstanding the slave have been proved to be the right of the first, because the object from it is to obtain a refusal to take the oath, which is equivalent to an acknowledgment; and an acknowledgment, even in that case, is useful, as it induce responsibility. According to Aboo Yoosaf, on the contrary, on oath is not to be administered; because, in this same manner as the defendant is not made responsible by an acknowledgement, so neither is he by a refusal to swear, and hence that tnedering of an oath is useless.

Where the deposit is transferred to a second trustee, and lsot, the proprietor receives is composition from the original trustee. If a person deposit something with another, and that other again deposit it with a third person, and it be lost in this person's hands, in that case the proprietor of the deposit, according to Haneefa, must take a compensation from the first trustee, not from the second. The two disciples allege that the proprietor is at liberty to take the compensation either from the first or second trustee; and that, in case he should take it from the first, be [the first] is not empowered to take an indemnification from the second; but that, in case of his taking it from the second, then is second then entitled to take an indemnification from the first. The reasoning of the two disciples is that the second trustee has received the deposit from the hands of a person who has himself become responsible (in consequence of

---

the deviation from is trust) and is therefore responsible; in the same manner as the trustee of an usurper; that is to say, if an usurper deposit with any person the goods he has usurped, and they be lost in the trustee's hands, the properietor is, at liberty to take a compensation either from the urusper or the trustee; and so also in the case in question. The ground of this is, that the proprietor of the deposit not having given his approbation to the second deposit; the first trustee was guilty of a transgression; and the second trustee was also guilty of a transgression in having received it without the consent of the proprietor. The proprietor, therefore, has to option of taking a compensation from either. If, however, he take the compensation from the first trustee, he [the first trustee] is not in that case entitled to indemnify himself from the second trustee is not responsible for the deposit. If, on the contrary, the proprietor take the compensation from the second trustee, he [the second] is in that case entitled to an indemnification from the first; because, as not being a legal trustee; he must be considered merely as an agent fro conservation on behalf of the original trustee; and as such he is entitled to an indemnification for whatever losses he may sustain, connected with the agency. The reasoning of Haneefa is, that the second trustee received the article from the hands of a trustee, and not of a responsible person; because the first trustee be separated from the second trustee; since so long as it is in existence with him, the wisdom and judgement of the first trustee are considered to be, as it were, extent and at hand with regard to it. The proprietor, moreover, is supposed assenting to any mode of keeping his property which may be agreeable to the trustee's judgment; and as that still continues to be exerted, it follows that no transgression whatever has as yet taken place. But, upon the article being lost by the second trustee, on the othr hand, continues in his original predicament; that is, his seisin is a seisin of trust in the end, in the same manner as it was at the beginning; and as he is not found in any transgression, he therefore is not responsible for the deposit; in the same manner as where the wind blows a gown near to any person, and it is after wards destroyed - in which case that person is not responsible.

Case of claim advanced by two persons to a sum of money in the possession of a third. If two persons should separately claim a

---

thousand dirms in the possession of a third; each asserting that he had deposited them with him; and the possessor deny their claims, but refuse to take an oath to that effect, the thousand firms must, in that case, be divided between the two claimants, and the defendant remains answerable to them for one thousand more. The reason of this is, that the claim of each several claimant is valid, as the claim of each has the probability of truth - Hence each is entitled to exact an oath from the defendantl, who, on his apart, is required to make a separate deposition with respect to each, as the right of each is distinct. The kazee, in administering the oaths, may lawfully being with either, since it is impossible to administer both at the same time, and neither has ground of preference over the other. If however, a contention should take place between the claimants on this point, the die must be thrown in order to satisfy them, and to remove any suspicion of partiality on the part of the Kazee. If he then take an oath in denial of the claim of one, let another oath be administered to him in denial of the second's claim; and if he thus made oath, denying the claims of both, nothing is due from him, for want of proof. If he should refuse to take the second oath, a decree must be passed in favour of the second claimant, since the proof is established. If, on the contrary, he refuse to take the first oath, a decree must not be passed in favour of the first claimant, but an oath must be tendered to him with regarded to the claim of the second it were otherwise if, at the time of refusing, he were be make make an acknowledgement in favour of the first; for in that case a decree would immediately pass; since acknowledgment is proof and a cause of property in itself; whereas a refusal to takean oath is neither proof: nor a caused of property, unless in conjunction with the decree of the Kazee. It is therefore lawful for the Kazee, in such a case, to suspend his decree until he shall have tendered the second oath, that he may apprised of the full extent to which his decree is to go: and if the defendant refuse to take the second oath, that he may be apprised of the full extent to which his decree is to go: and if the defendant refuse to take the second oath also, the Kazee must then pass a decree equally in favour of both; becase neither party has a superiority over the other in point of proof; and no regard whatever is paid to priority of refusal [to swear], since the two refusals do not constitute proof separately, but together and at one period, namely, at the period of the decree of the Kazee, and as, if both had adduced

In Hedaya[2] same vies has been taken as in Article 769 noted above about a thing found on the road or in any other place. It has been termed as "LOOKTA". If the finder takes away for the purpose of preserving it would be considered as "Trust" (وديعت). It has been explained as:—

> "Lookta signifies property which a person finds lying upon the ground, and takes away for the purpose of preserving it, in the manner of a "Trust". It is proper, to observe that the terms "LAKEET" and "LOOKTA" have an affinity with respect to their sense, the difference between them being merely this, that Lakeet is used with regard to the human species, and Lookta with regard to any thing else.

A LOOKTA, or TROVE property, is considered as a "TRUST" in the hands of the "MOOLTAKIT" or finder, where he has called persons to witness that "he takes such property in order to preserve it, and that he will restore it to the proprietor", because this mode of taking it is authorised by the law, and is even the most eligible conduct - (That is to say, the taking up of the proper is permitted by the law, and is even more eligible than suffering it to remain where it is found) according to many of our doctors. This is where there is no apprehension of the property being damaged or destroyed - but where is to be apprehended, "the taking of it up is incumbent, according to what the learned in the law have remarked upon this point. Now such being the case, the property is not a subject of responsibility; that is indemnification for the trove property is not incumbent upon the finder, where it happens to perish in his hands: and in the same manner, the finder is not responsible in acase where himself and the proprietor both agree that he had taken the property avowedly "for the owner"; because their agreement in this point is a proof with respect to poth; and hence the declaration of

---

2. Hedaya, Book XI, page 264, Vol. II.

the proprietor that "he (the finder) had taken them for the owner" - amounts to the same as if the finder were to produced evidence that he had them for myself", responsibility is incumbent upon him according property of another without that other's consent, and without the permission of the law". Rest of the rules governing finder's liability for breach of trust are same as referred below from Majelle.

Liabilities relating to above situation are enumerated in Article 770 noted below:—

"<u>Article 770</u>"

A person, who finds a thing picked up by chance, causes advertisement to be made, and until the owner appears, he keeps it with himself as an emanet (trust). If someone appears and proves that it is his own property, it becomes necessary to give it up to him.

The two articles enunciate the principle that where a thing is found on the road or any other place and picked by the finder such a thing is emanet (trust) in his possession. These articles deal with three different situations:—

Firstly, someone finds the thing and converts it in his own use. He commits criminal breach of trust and is considered as misappropriator of property. In case after the misappropriation of the picked up thing property is destroyed or damaged though without his fault he would be liable.

Secondly, the finder has taken the property for handing over it to the true claimaint whom he knows. It is an emanet (trust). He must find out the claimant or the owner of property. Property on efforts to inform the owner. If he falls to take necessary measures for ascertaining and informing the claimant, he commits breach of trust and is liable.

Thirdly, if the claimant or owner of the property is not known of the thing picked up by chance. It is still an emanet. Converting to his own use would be misappropriation. For ascertaining the claimant of the lost article he should make advertisement. It may be pronouncements of the picked up thing in public or private gathering or any other possible way by which the true claimant may announcement someone comes and identifies the lost article or thing, it must be handed over to him. Under such situation advertisements, he may claim them from the claimant. Making no efforts to know who is the claimant or no proper steps taken to amount to breach of trust for which the finder would be liable. According to Article 770, it is the duty of the finder to ascertain the whereabouts of the owner of the lost property by making due advertisement, failures subject him to liability as it amounts to breach of trust.

"Liability for damage to things in one's possession"

"<u>Article 771</u>"

Article is self-explanatory. It deals with different situations where a person deems to have committed Khiyyanet (breach of trust) and is liable. It also lays conditions where inspite of the fact that harm is caused to the emanet (trust property) but a person is not liable. Article is quoted below:—

> "In case the property of another destroyed, by accident, while in someone's possession, if he has taken without the leaves of the owner, in every case he is responsible."

And if he has taken it with the leave of the owner, by reason of its being an emanet in his hands, there is no responsibility.

But in case it was on approval for sale at a fixed price, and the price was named, compensation becomes necessary.

For example - if someone takes a bastin from a china shop, of his own accord, and it falls from his hand and is broken, he is responsible. And, if he takes it by the permission of the owner, and while is he looking on it, it by chance falls to the ground and is broken, compensation does not become necessary. And if that bastin falls on a quantity of others basins, and is broken and also breaks them, compensation must be made for those basins, but no compensation is necessary for that basin, by reason of its being an emanet.

But if he says "how many piastres is this basin? And after the shop-keeper has said, "take it. It is so many hiastries", he takes it in his hand and it falls and is broken. He is responsible.

Likewise, when one is drinking sharbat, and the cup of the sharbat seller falls from his hand and is broken, by reason of its being an emanet of the class "Ariyyet (Art 765), no compensation is necessary. But if it has fallen in consequence of the bad manner in which he himself used it, he is responsible."

"Express and Implied Permission"

"Article 772"

This article deals with permission which may be either express or implied. But in cases where there is an express prohibition for doing a thing implied consent cannot be a defence. A person would be liable if he has committed breach of express prohibition. Article lays down the rule as follows:—

"Permission by indication is the same as permission explicitly given. But, if there is an explicit prohibition, permission by indication cannot be considered."

For example - when a person has entered the house of another with his leave, he has by indication leave to drink water from a tumbler standing openly. And while the person is drinking, if the glass in his hand falls by accident, and is broken, compensation does not become necessary.

But when the owner of the house says "do not touch that tumbler" and makes a prohibition, if the person takes it in his hand, and it falls, and is broken, he is responsible."

In this article words indication leave used for implied or constructive consent, and explicit leave are used for express consent.

"Contract How Made"

This chapter dealing with contract how made is divided into two parts. Part I sets out precepts relating to the contract and condition for making a delivery for safe keeping (Ida).

"Article 773" - lays down the principle as follows:—

"A delivery for safe keeping becomes a concluded contract, by a proposal and acceptance, expressly made or indicated. For example, if the owner of the thing delivered say, "I have delivered this thing to you for safe-keeping" or "I have made it an emanate", and the person who accepts it says, "I have accepted" there is a concluded contract of delivery for safe-keeping expressly made.

A person is having a cloth in his hand. Another person asks the holder of cloth to give it to him. The holder of cloth gives the cloth to him. It is a trust. If any loss caused to the cloth. It would amount to breach of trust. (ZAHEERIA).

Also, if someone enters an inn and says to the inn keeper "Where can I tie up my animal?" And the Inn keeper shows a place, and the person ties it there, a contract of delivery for safe-keeping is concluded by implication.

Same illustration has been reported in 'FATAWA-E-AHLE-SUMERQAND (فتعائے اہلِ سمر قند) that a person with horse came to an inn and asked the Inn Keeper where should he tie his horse. The Inn Keeper pointed out a place to tie the horse there. The Inn Keeper himself tied the horse. Thereafter that person went away. On return back that person found that his horse was not there. On inquiry the Inn Keeper replied that his companion had carried the horse for providing it the drinking water. That person had no companion.

It is a breach of trust. The Inn Keeper is liable for the loss of horse. (MUHEET).

Likewise, if someone leaves his property with a shopkeeper, and goes away, and the shopkeeper sees it and is silent, that property becomes a thing delivered for safe-keeping (vedia') with the owner of that shop.

But if the owner of the shop says "I do not accept" and returns it, there is no contract of delivery for safe-keeping.

Similarly, a thing is kept with another person and asked him to take care of it. He refuses to look after. Property is lost. That person is not liable. Because of his refusal there is no trust created. (MUHEET).

And, likewise, someone leaves his property with a number of persons, intending to deliver it for safe keeping, and goes away, and they also see it and keep silence, that property becomes a thing delivered for safe-keeping with all of them.

But if one by one they get up and leave that place, by reason of its being clear that the person remaining after the others is the guardian, it becomes a thing delivered for sake keeping (Vedica), with him."

If a person sitting in a gathering gets up and goes away leaving behind his books, then all those persons remained there they would be considered as trustee (متولى). If all of them left behind those book and thus lost, all of them would be liable. But one by one left the place, then the last person who remained there would be responsible for any loss ensued to the books. He would be considered as trustee. (MUHEET SERKH-ASI).

Some persons were sitting on a shop. The shop-owner in their presence went away leaving behind the doors of his shop open. They also left the shop one by one. Thereafter, some articles were lifted from the shop. The last person who left the shop would be responsible. (MULTAQIT).

Analysing this article it can be inferred that there must be entrustment (Vadiat, by delivering the thing. It must be effected by contract which requires proposal and acceptance by the parties concerned. Proposal and acceptance may be express of implied.

"Either Party Can Annual The Contract"

The next article authorises the 'mudi', the person who delivers the thing, and the 'vedi', the person who accepts the thing as emanat to revoke the contract at any time at will. Once revoked there is no liability on the vedi for any loss caused to the property. Article is referred below:—

"Article 774": "Both, the person who delivers his property for safe keeping, and the person, who accepts it to keep safely, have the rights to annual the contract for save keeping at any time they like."

The word right shows the significance that either party may revoke or annual the contract at anytime. It is all discretionary with the parties to continue the contract or to resind it any time they like.

"Article 775": This article deals with the nature of these which can be made subject matter of emanat (Trust). Article reads as;—

"It is a condition that the thing delivered to kept, be suitable for receipt and capable of being taken.

"Therefore, the delivery for safe keeping of a bird, which is in the air, is not good."

"Who can deliver and accept a thing for keeping":-

Article 776": This article deals with the competency of persons, one who delivers the thing and another who accepts the thing. When are they competent to contract? Article 776 explains:—

"It is a condition that the person, who delivers the thing to be kept, and, the person, who accepts it, be of sound mind and capable of contracting (Mumeyyiz, Article 943). It is not a condition that they should be of full age.

Therefore, it is not lawful for a madman or on infant who is not capable of contracting (Article 943),[3] to deliver a thing for safe keeping, or, to accept a thing delivered for safe keeping. But a delivery for safe keeping, and the acceptance of a thing delivered for safe keeping by one infant, who is capable of contracting and freed from control (Me'zun), is good".

Thus according to this article to be competent to contract the requirements are:—

1. Firstly, that a person be "Sagir Mumeyyiz", capable of knowing the nature of transaction. It is not necessary that

---

3. Art. 943. "Sagir Ghayr Mumayyiz" is a young person not understanding selling and buying, that is to say, not knowing that by sale rights of ownership are lost, and that by purchase they are acquired, and not being able to distinguish from a small deceit, a deceit which it is clear has been an excessive deceit. Like being deceived five in ten." A young person who can distinghish these, is called "Sagir Mumayyiz".

the parties should be major. Even the person who is accepting may be minor but should be capable of knowing the effects of the contract. If he is incapable than he would be deemed to be an infant, a person not competent to contract.

2. Secondly, parties should be of sound mind. If a person is made, is not competent either to deliver the thing or accept the thing as emanat (trust).

3. Thirdly, the person who delivers and the person who accepts should be free from control. (Me'zun).

If the above three requirements are satisfied any contract entered into would be binding and effective on the parties.

In Fatawa-e-Alam-Giri, the competency to deliver and accept the trust has been explained as:—

1. Trustee (متولی) should of sound mind.

2. Madman or infant, incapable of understanding thing should not accept trust.

3. If infant is capable to understand thing, he is competent. It is not necessary that he should of age of majority.

4. A boy who has the permission to consume thing, he can accept the trust. It is not necessary that he should be independent. Thus a thing can be entrusted to a slave.

5. A boy who is prohibited to consume things on his own acceptance of trust is not proper.

6. For contract of trust it is not necessary that the trustee (ودیعت) should be independent.

7. A slave (غلام) can make a thing "Tust" (ودیعت) and acceptance of such from him is proper. Rules governing

trust would be applied in such a case. But acceptance of trust from slave (غلام) is not proper. (BADAI-). بدائی

If these elements are satisfied then the parties are competent to deliver and accept the trust.

Part II is about the rights and liabilities in respect of property delivered for safe keeping as emanet (Trust).

"Liability for loss or destruction": "Article 777- "The thing delivered for safe-keeping is like an emanet (Art. 762), in the hands of the person who accepts it.

Therefore, if it be destroyed or wasted without any default of the person who accepts it, and without any fault in the keeping of it, it does not become necessary to make compensation.

"Where trustee is paid":- "But if the contract for delivery has been made for payment to be made for the safe-keeping, in case it is destroyed or wastered by a cause which it is possible to guard against, it becomes a cause of compensation.

For example - if a watch, which is delivered for safe keeping, is destroyed by falling accidentally from the hands of someone, compensation does not become necessary.

But if he tramples the watch under foor, or if something falls from his hands and the watch is destroyed, compensation becomes necessary.

Likewise, if, after someone has delivered his property to another, and paid him a wage for its safe keeping, it suffers damage arising from a cause which it is possible to provide against, like theft, it becomes necessary for the person, who accepts the property to keep, to make compensation.

"Liability of Several of Trustee"

"Article 778" - If something falling from the hands of the servant of the person, who accepts the property, destroys the property delivered for safe-keeping, the servant is responsible.

"Treatment of Property"

"Article 779" - It is a fault to do things in respect of the property delivered to be kept, if there is no permission from the owner.

"Keeping of the Property by Whom"

"Article 780" - "The person who accepts the property to keep, takes care of it himself as if it were his own property, or causes it to be kept by someone, who is trustworthy.

And if without fault or neglect on the part of the person entrusted by him, it is destroyed or wasted, neither the person who accepted the property to keep, nor the person entrusted by him, is liable to make compensation."

"Article 781" - "The person, who undertakes to keep the property, can kept it were he keeps his own property." Trustee" (متولی) can entrust the trust property to his family members. To whom the trustee gives the property whether wife, son, daughter or parents, it is subject to the condition that the person must be trustworthy. Thee should not be any doubt about her or his safe-keeping. (Fatawe-Qazi-Khan).

If the trustee has two wives. Both the wives have one son each from their former husbands. They also live with them. They would also be included in the family of the trustee. If the trustee entrusts the "Trust" (ودیعت) to them and is lost. The trustee would not be liable. (ZAHEERIA - ظہیریہ).

The trustee hands over the trust property to his wife and thereafter he divorces her. Iddat period is passed but he does not take back the rust property. If the property is lost, some Islamic jurists are of the opinion that he would be liable because it was his responsibility to take back the trust property from her. (FATAWA-E-ALAM-GIRI - Page 84).

"Manner of care to be taken"

"Article 782" - "The thing delivered to be kept must be taken care of in the same way which things like it, are taken case of.

Therefore, to place things like money and jewellery in places like a stable, or strawshed, by reason of its being a neglect in keeping them, if, in this case, they are wasted or destroyed, compensation becomes necessary."

"When Two Persons Entrusted"

"Article 783" - "When there are different persons who undertake to keep the thing, if the thing is not capable of division, by the leave of one the other keep it, or they keep it in turns, and in that case, if the thing, delivered to be kept, is destroyed without fault or neglect, neither is compelled to make compensation.

And, if the thing is capable of division, the persons, who accept the charge of it, divide it equally in their possession, and each one takes care of his share.

And one cannot give his share to another while the permission of the person, who delivered the thing to them, is not given. If he does give it, and it is destroyed or wasted, without fault or neglect, while in the hands of the other, the person, who takes it, is not liable to make compensation, but the person who gave it, is liable to make compensation for his own share."

If the trustees are two persons and the trust is divisible, both of them have right to divide between them the trust half and half with a view to keep the trust (ودیعت) safe. If one of the trustees entrusts the whole trust to the other trustee and trust is lost. The trust and the other one would not be liable. (IMAM AZAM [Rahmatullah Aleh]).

If thing entrusted is not divisible. Both of the trustees would be responsible for its safe keeping. Any one of the trustees of entrusts the property to the other trustee, the other trustee would not be responsible for the whole trust. (Shareh-TANAWI).

"Article 784" - "A condition in a contract of safe keeping is observed, if the restriction is possible to be observed, if not, it is void.

For example - when an agreement for the safe-keeping of a property has been made, with a condition that it must be kept in the house of the person entrusted, if a necessity has arisen for removing it to another place in consequence of a fire having occurred, no attention is paid to the condition. And in this case when the thing entrusted is removed to another place, if it is destroyed or wasted without fault or neglect, compensation is not necessary.

Likewise, if the person, who delivers the property to keep, gives an order to the person, who accepts it, to keep the property, and forbids him to give it to his wife, or his child, or his servant, or the persons who keeps his own property, if necessities, compelling him to give it to that person, arise, the prohibition is not considered.

In this case if the person entrusted gives the thing, entrusting to his keeping, to that person, and it is destroyed or wasted without fault or neglect, compensation is not necessary. And if he gives it while there is no necessity he is responsible.

Likewise, when a condition has been made for keeping in a creation room of a house, in case the person entrusted has kept it in another room of that house, if those rooms are equal for the purpose of safe keeping, the condition is not regarded.

And in this case, "if the thing entrusted is destroyed, again, compensation does not become necessary.

But if there is an unequality between the rooms, like one being constructed of masonary and the other of wood, the condition is no observed. The person entrusted is compelled to kept the thing in the room agreed upon. And if it is destroyed when put in a room inferior to that room as regards safe keeping, compensation is made.

The significant point under consideration is that the condition imposed by the Depositor (جمع کرنے والا) should be practicable. It should be implemented. But if the condition is such implementation is neither possible nor beneficial than it would not be valid. Under the circumstances of the condition imposed not followed, the trustee (متولی) for breach of it would not be liable. (BADA-E- بدائع).

If the conditions imposed by the depositor (جمع کرنے والا) are:—

1. That the trustee should keep the trust (ودیعت) in his pocket and not put it at any place, or

2. That he should keep safe the trust by his right hand and not use his left hand, or

3. That the trustee should see the trust (ودیعت) by his right eye and not by his left eye, or

4. That he should not carry the trust (ودیعت) out of Koofa (name of the city) and not transfer from Koofa, or

5. That he should keep safe the trust (ودیعت) in a box in a specific house.

Such condition would not be valid. Breach of such conditions by the trustee would not made him liable for. (TAMER-TASHI).

"Duty of Trustee when Death of Depositor Doubtful"

"Article 785" - "When the owner of the thing delivered for safe custody is absent it is not known whether he is dead or alive, the person entrusted keeps it, until the death of its owner is certain.

But, in case the thing being taken care of is one of those things, which will spoil by keeping, he may sell with the leave of the judge, and can keep the price of the thing as an emanet with him. But if he does not sell and it perishes by keeping, compensation does not become necessary."

"Feeding of Thing Being Kept"

"Article 786" - The feeding of the thing delivered to be kept, when it has need for food, like a horse or a cow, falls on the the owner when the oner cannot be found, the person who has accepted the thing to keep may make no application to the judge, and the judge of orders the carrying out of arrangements which are safer and most beneficial for the owner of the thing, then the letting of the thing is possible. The person, who has charge of it, lets it with the approval of the judge, and from what is received he may provides the food. And if the letting is not possible, likewise with the approval of the judge, immediately, or after he has provided food from his own property for three days, he sells for the equivalent value. And he can demand from the owner what he has expend for thrce days at the outside.

But if he has incurred expense without the leave of the judge, he cannot recover it from the person who delivered the thing to keep.

"Fault or Neglect"

"Article 787" - "If there is any fault or negligent on the part of the person entrusted, and destruction or loss of value comes on the thing in his charge, compensation becomes necessary.

Therefore, if the custodian destroys money, delivered for safe keeping with himself, by diverting it into his business, he becomes responsible.

In this case, when he has in his way divered a sum of money which was an emanet (Art. 762), with him, and afterwards, after he has put in its place some of his own property, if it is lost without fault or neglect, he cannot escape liability.

And also, if, while the person entrusted goes riding an animal, delivered into his hands for safe-keeping, without leave, whether by extra-ordinary riding, or other cause it is destroyed, or of during the journey it is stolen, the person who undertook to keep the animal becomes responsible.

Likewise, when the person who accepts the care of the thing, is bound to remove it to another place in case of fire, he does not remove it and it is burnt by a fire, compensation is necessary.

Imam Muhammad (Rahmatullah Aleh) says that if the house of trustee catches fire and under necessity if the trustee hands over the trust property to a stranger, in case of loss he would not be responsible. But after extinguishing the fire if he does not take keep the trust property and is lost, he would be liable.

Same views have been expressed by Sahabe Muheet (صحابه مهيت) and Imam Qazi Khan (FASUL-Amadia).

The trustee would not the responsible for any loss caused to the trust if he handed over the trust to someone else for safe-keeping under urgent necessity. For example, the trustee's house catches fire and fear is that the trust would be burnt, or the trust property is in the boat and the fear is that boat would be sunk, or thieves or dacoits come and fear is that trust property would he taken away by them. Under these condition of necessity if the trustee hands over the trust to another person and is lost, the trustee would not be liable. (Fatawa-e-Kazi Khan).

Article 788 - It is a wrongful act to mix the property delivered for safe-custody with other property, without the leave of the owner, in case their separation from one another cannot be made.

For example - when the person who has taken charge of them has mixed a quantity of gold Yuz Likes (T.L.) delivered to him to keep, with gold Yuzlik, of his own, or with gold Yuzliks which have delivered by someone else to be kept, without leave, if they are destroyed or stolen, he becomes responsbile:

And again if someone, other than the person who has taken charge of them, mixes the said gold coins in that way, that person is liable."

"Mixing by Leave or Accident"

"Article 789" - "If the person who has undertaken the safe keeping of the thing, with the leave of the owner, mixes it with other property as mentioned in the last article, or without any act of his, two properties become mixed, in a way that they cannot be separated from one another (like a purse of gold, which has been put for safe-custody in a chest, being torn, and the gold inside it being mixed with other gold), as regards the whole, the shares of the owner of that delivered for safe custody and of the custodian are up to the amounts belonging to each.

In this case, if it is lost, or destroyed without fault or neglects no compensation is payable.

"Trustee cannot Delegate His Charge"

"Article 790" - "The custodian cannot give the thing, which is in his charge into the custody of another, without leave. If he does, and afterwards it is destroyed, he is responsible.

And if it is destroyed by the fault or neglect of the second custodian, the owner, if he wishes, he can make the first custodian compensate him, and the first custodian recovers it back from the second custodian.

Delegation of Charge by Leave"

"Article 791" - If the custodian has delivered the thing in his custody to the safe-keeping of another, if the owner permits it, the first custodian drops out, and that person becomes custodian.

"Letting, Lending, or Pledging by Trustee"

"Article 792" - The custodian can let for hire, or lend for use, or pledge the property delivered to him to keep, just as he can use it, with the leave of the person who delivered it with him.

But if he lets, lends or pledges it, without the leave of the owner, if the thing is destroyed or perished in the hands of the hirer, borrower or pledgee, or if there is a diminution in its value, the custodian must make compensation.

The trust (ودیعت) cannot be made to another person. It cannot be given as Arriyat (عاریته) nor can be let out on hire or be pledged. If the trustee (متولی) does any of the above referred acts he would be responsible of breach of trust. (BEHRUL - RAIQ).

"Lending or Paying Money by Trustee"

"Article 793" - If the custodian lends and pays money, which is an emanet (Art. 762) to another, without leave, if the owner does not permit it, the custodian is responsible for that money.

Likewise, if the has paid the debts of the owner, owed to another, with money delivered to him to keep safe personally, he is responsible.

"Return of thing to owner, Expense of Return"

"Article 794" - When the owner of thing, entrusted to be kept, demands it, it must be returned and delivered to himself, and the provision for the return and delivery, that is, the care and expense falls on the owner.

And if the custodian does not give up the thing entrusted to him, when the owner demands, if it is destroyed, or perished, he is responsible.

But if he does not give it up in consequence of some valid excuse, like the thing being at a distant place at the time of the demand, in that case, if it is destroyed or perished, it is not necessary for him to make compensation.

"Return How Made"

"Article 795" - The custodian returns and delivers the thing given into his charge, either personally or by some trustworthy person.

And in case he has returned and despatched it by a trustworthy person, if, before arrival, it is destroyed or perished, without fault or neglect, compensation does not become necessary.

If the trustee (متولی) brings the trust (ودیعت) to the house of the depositor (جمع کرنے والا) and is lost there, then trustee (متولی) would be liable. Similarly if the trustee hands over the trust (ودیعت) t3. Art. 943. "Sagir Ghayr Mumayyiz" is a young person not understanding selling and buying, that is to say, not knowing that by sale rights of ownership are lost, and that by purchase they are acquired, and not being able to distinguish from a small deceit, a deceit which it is clear has been an excessive deceit. Like being deceived five in ten." A young person who can distinghish these, is called "Sagir Mumayyiz".o the son or slave of the depositor (جمع کرنے والا) or to someone who is a family member (فیملی ممبر) of the depositor, and is lost or destroyed, even then the trustee (متولی) is liable. Fatawa Qazi Imam Abu Hashim Aamir-Rahmat-Allah - JAWAHAR AFLATI).

However, other jurists differ from the above fatawa. To some jurists (faqih) if the trustee gives the property to someone who is a member of his family (فیملی), the trustee (متولی) would not be liable. (TATAR KHANIA).

If the trustee sends back the trust (ودیعت) to the depositor through his son who is not a part of his family (فیملی) but the boy is major, then any loss caused to the trust (ودیعت) during transit, the trustee (متولی) is liable otherwise not. If trust (ودیعت) is sent back through a minor, the trustee would not be liable under conditions when the minor knows how to keep things safe or keep things. Safe but if he does not keep things safe, the trustee (متولی) would be liable. (MUHEET)

"Return to one of two Depositors"

"Article 796" - When two persons have delivered to someone their common property to be kept, and one of those part owners, in the absence of the other, demands his share from the custodian, of the thing in his charge is of the sort

Misly (Art. 145),[1] the custodian gives him his share of the thing. If it is of the sort Qiyami (Art. 146),[2] he does not give it.

"Place of Return"

"Article of Return" - In the giving back of the thing entrusted, the place, where the delivery to keep was made, is regarded.

For example - Merchandise, which must be returned at Istamboul, the custodian cannot be compelled to return it at Andrianpole.

"Usurfructs Belongs to Owner"

"Article 798" - The benefits derived from a thing entrusted for safe keeping belong to the owner.

For example, when an animal is an emanet, its young, milk and wool are for the account of the owner.

"Payment to Person Dependent on Owner In Owner's Absence"

"Article 799" - When the owner of the thing delivered to be kept cannot be found, and the judge, on the application of a person, who has a right to support from him, has directed that provision be made for that person from the money being kept for the person who cannot be found, if the custodian diverts it to the maintenance of that person, part of the money delivered to him to keep, which is in his hands, he is not liable.

---

1. Article 195 - "Kisly" is a thing found in the Bazars and weekly markets, that is to say, a thing to be matched without any difference causing an increase of price."
2. Artical 146 - "Qiyami" is a thing which cannot be matched in the markets or Bazars, or if it is found, there is a difference in the price."

But if he diverts the money to this purpose, without the order of the judge, he is liable.

"Madness of Trustee"

"Article 800" - If madness seizes the custodian, and there is fear that he will not recover and get rid of it, and if there does not exist the property itself, which has been delivered to him to keep before his madness, the owner, on producing a satisfactory surety has a right to claim compensation from the property of the madman.

But after he has god well, if he declares, that the thing delivered to be kept was returned to his owner, or that it was destroyed, or perished without fault or neglect, he proves it by oath, and takes back the money has been received.

"Death of Trustee"

"Article 801" - When the custodian dies, in case there is clearly found to be property, delivered to him to keep, in his estate (tereke), it is returned to its owner, but reason of its being an emanet (Art. 762), also in the hands of the heirs.

But if it is not found itself in his estate (tereke), if the heirs prove that the custodian made a statement and declaration in his lifetime of the condition of the thing entrusted, as by saying "I returned that thing delivered to me to its owner" or that it was destroyed without any fault, it does not become necessary to make compensation.

Likewise, if the heirs say "We know the thing which was delivered to be taken care of. It was like this. It was like that, describing and explaining it, and if they assert that it perished, without fault or neglect after the death of the custodian, and affirm it on oath, compensation does not become necessary.

And if the custodian has not declared the condition of the thing delivered to him, by reason of its being considered that he died in ignorance, like other debts, it is paid from his estate (tereke).

Again of their heris say only "We know the thing which was delivered to be kept" and do not describe it, and say that it has perished, what they say has no weight. In case they have not proved the way in which it perished, compensation becomes necessary from the estate (tereke).

If the trustee (متولی) dies and the trust (ودیعت) thereafter subjected to identification or gets identified, the trust (ودیعت) would become debt. It would be adjusted the 'trustee's estate (ریاست). Trust debt would be treated at par with other debts of the period when the trustee was healthy. Whatever will be the position of deceased's life time debts. Same will be of trust debt.

(KAZA-FIL-TEHZEEB-)

This fatawa is applicable in a situation when the trustee (متولی) dies and trust is not known to anyone.

If the trustee (متولی) entrusted the trust (ودیعت) to his wife and thereafter died, then trustee's wife would be responsible. If the wife said that the trust (ودیعت) was lost or stolen, then, she had to give statement on oath. Her swearing would be acceptable and nobody would be responsible for.

However, if the wife said that she returned the trust to the trustee before his death, she is to swear for. Her statement on oath in this connection would be acceptable but the trust would be a debt on the estate whatever she had inherited from her husband (trustee). Thus the extent of the value of trust debt would be taken out from the property succeeded from her deceased husband. (MUHEET SARKHAST).

"Death of the Owner"

"Article 802" - If the person, who delivered the thing to be kept, dies, the thing is given to his heirs, but if the estate (tereke) is submerged with debt, application is made to the judge.

And if, without making an application to the judge, the custodian gives it to the heirs and if it is destroyed, the custodian is responsible.

In case when the Depositor's (جمع کرنے والا) where about are not known whether he is alive or dead, the trustee should continue the safe-keeping of the trust (ودیعت) until he gets the information either of his death or comes to know the whereabouts of deceased's heirs. (KAZAFIL-WAJEEZ-IL-KARDARI).

If the owner of the trust is deed, and has not left behind any debt due against him, the trust (ودیعت) should be returned to the deceased's heirs.

However, if he left behind debt (قرض) due against him, then the trust (ودیعت) be given to executor (ودیحیع) and not to his heirs. (WAJEEZ KARDARI).

If the trustee (متولی) gives the trust to the deceased's (متولی) heirs and the estate (ریاست) is subject to the payment of debts, then the trustee would be liable to the creditors to compensate them. The trustee (متولی) would not be immuned from liability because of the fact that he returned the trust to the deceased's heirs. (KHAZANATUL-MUFEEN).

These are the detailed conditions under which the trustee is liable for breach of trust if he violates them in the manner above enumerated.

V. "Arriyyat"

Chapter III or Mejelle Ahkamae-Adliya, is devoted to the discussion on Ariyyat, the property which is lent gratuitously to be used.

Arriyyet is an emanet (trust). Article 813, explains it as:—

"The thing lent for use is an emanet (Art. 762), in the hands of the borrower."

The nature of Arriyet (عاریت) has been explains as:—

"Arriyyet (عاریته) according to our doctors, signifies an investiture with the use of a thing without a return - the person who so grants the use is termed as "Moyeer' (معیر) or the lender, the person receiving it, 'Moostayar' (مستعار), or the borrower, and the article of which the use is granted, 'Arriyyat' (عاریت), or the loan - Koorokhee".

Imam Shafei (Rahmat-ulla Aleh) defines "Arriyyet to signify simply, a licence to use the property of another because it is settled by the world IBAHIT, signifying licence or permission". (Hedaya).

To quote Hazrat, Abu Baker Razi "To make a person owner" of usufructs (یوزوفرکٹ) without consideration (کنسیڈریشن), in Shariah is known as "Arriyyat" (عاریت). (SIRAJ-UL-WAHAJ).

Arriyyat is an investiture where the borrower is made entitle to use and utilise the usufructs arising from the property borrowed without return. There is no consideration. A loan gratuitously given by the (مستعیر), the person who grants it and received by the (بوروواز), the borrowers.

By proposal and acceptance, and by delivery a lending for use becomes a concluded contract. If someone says to another, "I have given this property to you as a loan for use" or "I have given a loan for use" and the other says "I have accepted", or, if he takes it without saying anything, or, if one says to another "give me this property as a loan for use "(Arriyyet)", and he gives it, the giving of the property as a loan for use is a completed contract and thus loan given is Arriyyet.

The silence of the person who gives the loan is not regarded as an acceptance.

Therefore, if a person asks from another for a thing as a loan for use, if the owner keeps silence, and the person takes it, he is a wrongful appropriator. (Art. 805).

The receipt of the property lent for use is necessary. Without receipt there is no right over it. It must be a definite and defined thing. There should not be an ambiguity. However, if the lender gives a choice to the borrower to take whichever he likes, the loan for use is good. The same rule is to be applied in cases of period for which the thing has been given in loan for use must be definite and defined. Without specification either of the thing or the period the full extent of the use cannot be ascertained, and an investiture with anything uncertain is invalid.

The use of a thing without return is lawful as being a species of kindness because God has said, "Do kindness to each other" and also the Prophet (peace be upon him) borrowed a suit of armour from Sifwan.

The loan (Arriyyet) as said earlier is a trust. Both in Hedaya and Fatawa-e-Alamgiri, it has been recognized as trust (emanat). Now let us discuss conditions governing Arriyyet and violation thereof amounting to breach of trust.

"Liability of the Borrower"

The borrower is not responsible for the loss of value, or the thing perishes or destroys, without fault or neglect or the borrower does not make any transgression in respect of it. Under such conditions there is no necessity to make compensation. If, therefore, it be lost in the hands of the borrower, without any transgression on his part, he is not answerable for it, whether the loss happen, at the period of his using it, or otherwise.

For example - if a mirror lent for use, by falling, accidentally, from the hand of the borrower, or by his knocking it himself in consequence of his foot slipping, is broken, borrower is not responsible.

Similarly, in another situation where a carpet has been lent and the value of the carpet is diminished by its being spotted by something split on it accidentally, compensation is not necessary. (Art. 813).

Hazrat Imam Shafei (Rahmatullah Aleh) maintains that he is responsible for it in case the loss should take place at a time when he is not using it; because he has taken possession of property of the another without a right in it; and also, because as the borrower is liable to the charges of removal, in case of the substance, as also he is answerable for the value, in case of its destruction, in the same manner as an usurpur the article standing, in the same predicament with merchandise detained with a view to purchase - with respect to the permission of seisin, established on the borrower's behalf that was granted merely with a view to enable him to enjoy the use; and hence, where the use ceases it no longer operates; in other words, where the loan is destroyed during his enjoyment of the use; he is not responsible, because of the existence of the necessity; where-as it be lost at a time when he is not using it, he is responsible, because of the non-existence of the necessity; where-as it be lost at a time when he is not using it, he is responsible, because of the non-existence of the necessity at the time. The argument of our doctors is, that the term Arriyyat does not indicate responsibility, for (according to their exposition) it is an investiture with the use without return or (according to Hazrat Imam Shafie (Rahmatullah Aleh) and Koorokee), a permission of the use; and the seisin of it is not a transgression on the part of the borrower, since it was made with the consent of the lender; and although that consent was merely with a view to enable the lender to use the article, still to borrower did not make the seisin with any other intention, he therefore, is not guilty of any transgression, and consequently is not responsible. (Hedaya).

There are observations against Hazrat Imam Shafie (Rahmatullah Aleh) also. The expense attending a removal of the article is incumbent on the borrower, merely on account of the advantage he derives from it, in the same manner as the maintenance of a loan is incumbent upon the borrower, on account of the advantage he derives from it, and not on account of any defect in his tenure. It is otherwise in the case of usurpur, where the charges of removal are due merely because of the defect in his tenure - with respect to seisin with a view to purchase, the responsibility in that instance does not arise from the seisin, but from the design with which it was made; for as seisin in virtue of a contract of sale induces responsibility, as also seisin with an intention of purchase induces responsibility, since seisin with a view to contract is subject to the same laws with that contract. (Hedaya).

In Article 814, it has been explained that in case of fault or neglect on the part of the borrower, then, from whatever cause it maybe, whether the thing lent by destroyed, or its value diminished, borrower is responsible.

Example may be referred that where the borrowe goes for one day, with an animal lent for use, to a place of two days journey distance and the animal is destroyed or becomes weak and its value is diminished, the borrower is responsible for breach of trust.

Likewise, where an animal is borrowed to go to a certain place, he has arrived at that place with it, and after he has gone beyond that place, the animal dies a natural death, the borrowe is responsible for breach of trust.

Again, if a necklace has been borrowed for use, put it in the neck of an infant and leaves the infant without anyone to look after him and the necklace is stolen, the borrower is responsible for the loss.

In case where the thing borrowed is an animal than responsibility to feed - the borrowed animal lies upon the borrower. Therefore, where the animal dies because no fodder was given to it, the borrower is responsible.

When a loan for use has been made without any restriction that is to say, in case the lender has not made any condition as to time, and place, or any way of user, the borrower can use it at any time, or place, he wishes, and in anyway, he wishes. But he is bound by use and custom. (Art. 816).

However, where there is a restriction as to time and place, the borrower cannot use the thing contrary to the restriction. The violation would amount to breach of trust.

In case where loan for use is restricted to one particular type of use, the borrower cannot use against - the restriction. For example, iron or stone cannot be loaded on an animal lent to be loaded with corn. But he can put on it a load equal to corn or lighten than it.

"Unrestricted User Power to Lend"

Article 819, explain that if a loan for use is made, which is unconditional, without fixing the person who is to use it, the borrower has right to use of the thing in an unrestricted manner, that is to say, if he wishes, he uses himself, and, if he wishes, he causes, another to use it by lending it to him. Whether the thing lent for use, be one which is not changed by a change of persons who use it, like a room, or whether it be one that is changed, like a riding horse.

For example - "when someone has said, "I have lent you my room to use", the borrower, if he wishes, stays in it himself, and, if he wishes, he causes another person to inhabit it.

In another illustration jurists has taken a same view. For example, when a person has said, "I have lent you this horse" the borrower, if he wishes, rides the horse himself, and, if he wishes, he makes someone else ride it.

However, if the lender has prohibited its being given to another, the borrower, while the prohibition lasts, cannot cause the Arriyyet to be used by another.

"Loan By Wife"

Article 822 lays down that come one asks from a lady a thing, which is the property of her husband, as a loan for use, and she, without leave, gives it, in case that thing perishes, "if it is one of those thing which in the house by custom in the hands of the wife, then neither wife nor borrower would be responsible. If the thing is not found in the hands of the wife, like a horse, the husband can make them - wife and the borrower, liable for breach of trust.

"Letting or Pledging thing Lent"

The borrower cannot let or pledge a thing lent to him for use, without the leave of the lender.

A property which lent to be pledge for a debt in one town, the borrower cannot pledge for debt in another town. If the borrower does and the thing lent is destroyed or perished, he become liable because it is a breach of trust.

Same view has been taken in Hedaya. It is not lawful for a borrower to let out a loan. If, therefore, he should let it out, and it be afterwards lost, he is in that case responsible for it. As the act of lending does not comprehend hire, it follows that such delivery is an usurpation (misappropriation) lending to breach of trust.

"Borrower can deliver thing to another to keep"

Borrower can deliver thing for use to another for safe keeping and if any harm caused of the property without fault or neglect, there is no responsibility. When a thing is lent for use as conveyance for going and returning to a place and the thing has been handed over to another to keep that, the property so delivered if it is damaged without fault, then the borrower would not be liable. For example a horse is given for riding, the horse being tired stops and given by the borrower to another person for safe-keeping, dies a natural death. The Borrower is not responsible because there is no negligence or fault.

"Return of thing Borrowed"

Article 827 lays the law for the return of a thing lent for a particular purpose. When the purpose of lending is accomplished it must be returned to the (لينڈر) lender. Because thing in hand is an 'emanat' (tust). Therefore "When a thing has been borrowed for use in a business, on the completion of that business, the thing lent becomes like a property deposited for safe keeping (vedic) in the hands of the borrower. He must no longer use it. And he cannot keep it longer than it is usual to keep it. And, if he does and it is destroyed, he is responsible." Keeping longer would amount to breach of trust, for which the borrower would be liable.

"Manner of Return"

The borrower may return the thing lent for us to the lender either personally, or by someone he trusts that is hireling or his servant. Person through whom the borrower is returning must be a trustworthy person. If he sends through a person in whom he has no trust, any loss caused to the vedie (وديع) before it is delivered to the lender, he is responsible. In cases where the thing lent for use are ornaments with precious stones, these must be returned to the lender personally. (Art. 829). "But other thing lent for use, sending them to a place considered delivery by use and custom, and giving them to the servants of the lender, is a return and delivery."

If a person has borrowed an animal from another, he should restore it to the stable of the lender, and if it is afterwards lost, in that case the borrower is not responsible. There is no breach of trust in such cases making persons liable. The animal may also be delivered to his groom as well. However, analogy would suggest that he is responsible, since he has neither restored it to the proprietor nor his agent, but merely to is ground. The reason in favour to put an animal on the proprietor's stable is that a restitution has been made according to general custom, since it is customary to restore loans to the house of the proprietor as where, for instance, vessels or utensils belonging to a house borrowed, in which case it is ususal to return them, not into the proprietor's hands, but merely to his house. Besides, if the borrower had returned the animal to the proprietor, he (proprietor) would have sent it to the stable and therefore his doing so at once is considered as a valid return. (Hedaya).

If the borrower sends the animal borrowed for use through his servant getting yearly wages and is lost during transit in the way, he is not responsible. The reason is that a loan is in the nature of trust and the borrower may commit it, for the sale of preservation, into the hands, of any of his family, in which relation an yearly wage earner servant stands. It is otherwise with respect to a daily servant, as he is not held to be one of the family.

If the borrower sends back the Arriyyat (عاريت) which is in the nature of Vedia (ويديه) trust to the proprietor through his (proprietor's) servant and it be lost or destroyed on the way, the borrower is not responsible. It is subject to the condition that the thing so consigned should be one to whom the care and management of it is always given. Other jurists are of the opinion that it matters not whether it be consigned to such a servant or to any other servant or slave of the proprietor. This later rule is the most approved doctrine.

However, in cases where the borrower returns the vedio to the proprietor by the hands of the stranger, he becomes in that case responsible for it, and must make good the value in the event of its lost, otherwise would be liable for breach of trust.

"Expense of Return"

The charges or expense and care of returning a thing lent for use must be defrayed by the borrower. As he took the thing for his own benefit, therefore, the restitution is incumbent on him and whatever expenses maybe incurred, in such restitution, he is responsible for them. (Art. 830).

"Revocation of Loans or Arriyat[3] in the Nature of Trust for Building and Planting"

It is lawful to borrow land as loans for building or for plantation purposes. However, it is permitted to the lender to resume the land and receive it back in the state in which he lent it,

---

3. Note: Arriyyat and Qarz are, in common conversation, used indiscriminately to denote a loan, but there is a distinction in law with regard to them. Arriyyet is used with respect to such things as, after being lent to another, are indentically, but equal point of number, weight,or measurement of capacity. Thus where a person, having borrowed a book, and read it, afterwards return it, it is considered Arriyyet. But if a person should borrow one hundrd dirms, from another, and after using them should return another hundred dirms, it is considered a Qarz (قرض).

English Language makes no distinction between the term Qarz (قرض) and Arriyyet (عاریت) although both are essentially different on their effect.

he is therefore, empowered to compel the borrower to remove his houses or tree1s. If there has been a fixed time for the loan, and the buildings and trees have been pulled down, whatever difference there may be between their value if they had stood to the end of the time, and their price, as pulled up, at the time when they were pulled up, the lender is responsible for it. Jurists have observed that if the removal of the trees and buildings be detrimental to the ground, the choice of the alternative rests with the proprietor of the ground, as he is the principal, and the borrower the secondary, and a preference is always given to the principal.

In case where the land has been borrowed for the purpose of tillage, it cannot be taken back by the lender until the crop be reaped from it.

VI. (i) "Pledge - Rehn"

We referred Ayat 283 Surah al-Baqarah No. 3, earlier explaining the pledge deposited for safe-keeping is a trust. Law relating to pledge entrusted is elaborated below.

Pledge is to make property a security for the return of debt borrowed. It is a security in respect of a right of claim. In case of default in repayment of the debt, it can be claimed or realised from property so pledged.

The pledge becomes a concluded contract by the offer and acceptance of the pledger and the pledgee. But, until the pledged property is received by the pledgee, it is not complete and irrevocable.

(ii) "Pledge Deposited with Trustee":- Pledge, like deposit, loans, or Mozaribat, or partnership stocks, cannot be taken as trust. However, it is lawful, that both pledger and pledgee may agree to deposit the pledge with an honest, upright person. Such a person known as 'Adil' would act as trustee for both. But Imam Malik (Rahmatullah Aleh) is of the opinion that it is not lawful.

Imam Malik (Rahmatullah Aleh) explains his view that taking possession by the trustee over the pledge is the same as that of the pledger. He argues that the trustee has recourse to the pledger for indemnification where the pledge is lost in his possession, and another, having proved a right to it, takes a compensation from him for it's loss. He further says that such being the case, no account is made of taking of possession by the pledge.

Contrary view of the jurists is that they argue that the possession of the trustee is apparently the same as that of the pledger, with respect to preservation (substance of the pledge being a trust), and with respect to worth it is the same as that of the pledgee. The reason given in support of the later argument is that the trustee is subject to responsibility in case of its loss, a pledge being insured with regard to its worth. Therefore, the trustee stands in the place of two parties, the pledger and the pledgee. He strengthens the object of both, that is, the agreement of pledge.

In short, the trustee acts as a deputy of the pledger for the conservation of the substance of the pledge, and as to the worth of the pledge he acts in the same may as pledgee.

Once pledge is entrusted to the trustee, neither of them is at liberty to take it out of the trustee's hand. The pledgee is not at liberty to take the pledgee from the trustee, in as much as the right of the pledger is still connected with it, in this way, that the pledge is a deposit (جمع) in the trustee's hands.

Similarly, the pledger is not at liberty take it, because of pledgee's right being connected with it for the purpose of obtaining repayment of his debt. Non of the parties can violate the rights of the other attached with the pledge property so deposited or entrusted.

"Responsibility of the Trustee (for Breach of Trusts)"

In case the pledge is destroyed while in the possession of the trustee, the pledgee is responsible for such destruction because the possession of the trustee is the same as that of the pledgee in regard to the worth of the pledge. The responsibility is attached with only on account of its' worth. However, if the trustee has transgressed and violated the trust himself, then in that case he is responsible.

Again, in case the trustee delivers the pledge either to the pledge or to the pledgee, he is responsible if any destruction is caused. The reason is that he cannot transfer the pledge to either of them. Trustee is the pledger's trustee with respect to the substance of the pledge, and the pledgee's trustee with respect to its worth. Both the parties, that is, pledger and pledgee stand as stranger to each other. Thus delivering the pledge to either of them, is a transfer to a stranger.

It is further argued by the jurists that the trustee, therefore, being in such a situation responsible, cannot retain the value by way of pledge in his own possession; because he becomes indebted for the value if he retains by way of the pledge, he becomes at once the claimant and claimee, and the payer and receiver, in which is implied an obvious inconsistency.

Rules to be observed in this instance has been elaborated as follows:-[4]

> "The pawner and pawnee must therefore, in this case, concern to take the value from the trustee, and deliver again to him, or to any other person, in place of the original pawn. If however, they should not concern in so doing, either of them may in that case refer the matter to

4. Hedaya, p. 644.

the Qazi, who may take the value from the trustee, and again deliver it to him, or to any other, in the place of the original pawn. If the Qazi does so, and the pawner afterwards discharge his debt, then, supposing that the responsibility for the value had attached to the trustee in consequence of his having restored the pledge to the pawner, the value in question remains secure to the trustee, as the pawner here appears to have recovered his pledge, and the pawnee his debt. If, on the contrary, the responsibility had attached to the trustee in consequence of his having surrendered the pledge to the pawnee, the pawner, upon discharging the debt, is entitled to take from him the value in question; for as, in case of the existence of the pawn, he would immediately on payment of the debt resume it, he is by consequence at liberty to take the substitute. It is to be observed, in this case, that if the trustee given the pledge to the pawnee in loan or trust, and it has been destroyed without any transgression on his part, he (the trustee) is not entitled to take the value from him (the pawnee), whereas, if the pawnee has occasioned the loss, he is so entitled; for as the property of the thing has before vested in him in virtue of his having compensated for its loss, it was of course his own property that he lent; and the borrower is therefore liable for its when occasioned by himself, but not otherwise. If also, the trustee gives the pledge to the pawnee, "in order that he may preserve it himself as a security for, his debt", and it be afterwards destroyed, he is entitled to take the value from the pawnee, whether he (the pawnee), were the occasion of its loss or not, for it was not given to him in the nature of trust or loan, but on terms which implied a liability to make compensation."

Further the trustee cannot sell the pledge without such an authority given by the parties concerned. If he sells without such an authority, it would be a breach of trust. He would be held liable for the pledge so entrusted to him for safe-keeping.

CHAPTER 3

PART A

SERVANT'S LIABILITY : INDIAN CRIMINAL LAW

In the earlier chapters the offence of breach of trust generally was discussed under sections 405 and 406, I.P. Code. The Remaining Section 407, 408, and 409 dealing with Criminal Breach of Trust are confined to the commission of crime by particular classes of persons, such as, carrier, wharfinger, warehouse-keeper, clerk or servant, public servant, or banker, merchant or agent. The scope of our study confines to assess the provisions relating to servant, public servant, agent and partners.

Servant is to be studied under two heads: servant under section 408, IPC, and public servant under section 409 IPC.

"Who is a Servant"

Servant is a person bound by an express or implied contract of service to execute the orders and submit to the control of his master in the course of business. It is his duty as a servant to transact the business as directed. The generally accepted test of the relationship of master and servant is that of a control,[I] and contract of service is thought to be one by virtue of which the employer "cannot order or require what is to be done, but how it shall be done"[II] The control test probably

---

I. Yewens V. Noakes (1880) 6 Q.B.D. 530.

II. Collins V. Hertfordshire Country Counsil (1947, K.B. 598).

retains a good deal of importance in case to which it applied,[I] but in modern conditions the notion that a master has the right to control the manner of work of all his servants, save perhaps in the most attenuated from,[II] contains more of a fiction than of fact. It is clearly the law that such professionally trained persons as the master of a ship, the captain of an aircraft and the house surgeon at a hospital are all servant for whose torts their masters are responsible, and it is unrealistic to suppose that a theoretical right in a master, who is as likely as not to be a corporate and not a natural person, to control how any skilled worker does his job, can have such substance.[III] It has therefore, not been conclusive proof against the existence of a contract service.[IV]

Various attempts have been made to lay down a more suitable test. Often quoted statement is that of Lord Thankerton. According to him, there are four indicia of a contract of service:

(a) The master' power of selection of his servants.

(b) The payment of wages or other remuneration.

(c) The master's right to control the method of doing the work, and

(d) The master's right of suspension or dismissal.[V]

I. Argent V. Minister of Social Security (1968, IWLR 1749).

II. Whittaker V. Minister of Pensions and National Insurance (1967, 1 Q.B. 156).

III. Kahn-Freund, "Servant and Independent Contractors" (1951) 14 MLR 504.

IV. Market INvestigations Ltd. V. Minister of Social Security (1946, 62 TLR 427).

V. Short V. J & W Henderson Ltd. (1946, 62 T.L.R. 427).

However, the above statement is subjected to criticism in Ready Mixed Concreate (South East) Ltd. V. Minister of pension, and National Insurane,[I] on grounds that the statement does not carry the matter much further; the first and the last, and perhaps also the second, are indicia rather than of the existence of a contact than of the particular kind of contract which is a contract of service'.

Denning L.J's statement is more helpful in this connection. To quote:

> "It is often easy to recognise a contract of service when you see it, but difficult to say wherein the distinction lies. A ship's master, a chauffeur and a reporter on the staff of a newspaper are all employed under a contract of service; but a ship's pilot, a taximan, and a newspaper contributor are employed under a contract for services. One feature which seems to run through the instances is that, under a contract of service, a man is employed as part of a business, and his work is done as an integral part of the business; whereas under a contract for services, his work, although done for the business, is not integrated into it but is only accessory to it."

Another important judgement which elaborated the test was delivered by MacKennaj, where the learned judge held that for the existence of a contract of service three conditions must be fulfilled:

(1) the servant agrees that, in consideration of a wage or other remuneration, he will provide his own work and skill in the perfection of some service for his master;

I. (1968, 2 Q.B. 497).

(2) he agrees expressly or impliedly, that in the performance of that service he will be subject to the other's control in a sufficient degree to make that other master;

(3) the other provision of the contract are consistence with its being a contract of service.

This statement is also subjected to criticism. It is said that it is probable that no more complete general test exists. It is not possible even to compile an exhaustive list of all the relevant consideration.[I]

However, the control will no doubt always have to be considered, although it can not be said as only determining factor. One has not to minimize the significance of others factors such as:

(1) the man performing the services provides his own equipment;

(2) he hires his own helpers;

(3) degree of financial risk he takes;

(4) degree of responsibility for investment and management he has, and

(5) the opportunity of profiting from sound management in the performance of his task.

Another important factor to be taken into consideration is that the criminal misappropriation or criminal breach of trust by the servant must be within the course of servant's employment. A wrongful act falls within the scope of employment if it is expressly or impliedly authorised by the

---

I. Market Investigations Ltd. Minister of Social Security (1969, 2 Q.B. 173).

servant, or doing something in an unauthorised manner or necessarily incidental thereto. It is difficult to decide whether an act is or is not within the curse of employment. No single test can be claimed as appropriate to cover all cases. Question is ultimately one of fact differing from case to case.

After considering who is servant and course of employment let us examine the liability as enshrined in section 408 IPC. The requisites for the application of section are:

(i) Being a servant or accused employed as servant;

(ii) A servant in any manner entrusted with property in such capacity; or

(iii) Servant commits criminal breach of trust in respect of that property.

The basic requirement is that the accused must be servant, if he is not a servant of the complainant, the section will not be applicatble.[I]

The offence is committed where the act of the servant is to cause wrongful loss to his master for a temporary period even.[II]

Word 'whoever' used in the section includes a minor over 12 years of age, so long as his case is not covered under section 82 and 83 IPC. He can be guilty under this section. If the person is above 12 years of age, the question of sufficient maturity of understanding to judge the nature and consequences of their acts does not arise. The significant consideration for the application of this section is the actual entrustment of property. It is not material whether the property

---

I. 1919 Gi zj. 967.

II. Tulsides Chhagaulal (1906, 8 Bom. L.R. 95) : 5)

could have been legally entrusted or not, or dominium over the property could be given or not, a person is liable when he dishonestly misappropriates it.[I]

A servant is bound to carry out all orders of his master subject that the orders must be reasonable, and in the course of the business. In fact a servant acts under the direct control and supervision of his master. 'A person hired by a market gardener to do a day's work, and sent by him to sell vegetables at market and who brings back proceeds is a servant' to his employer in respect of such employment'.[II]

In Pyo Gyi,[III] a Trading Firm employed a person on commission for making purchases for the firm as directed is a servant of the firm.

A person is not a servant whose duty is to receive orders when and where he likes and forward them to the principal for execution. However, a person is a servant of the contract of employment is for a specified period but continue, even after the expiry of such a period because the presumption in such a situation would be that employment after the expiry is on the same terms as of the previous contract.

Similarly a person is not less a servant because he is working under others also[IV] or the servant gets the commission share of profits of a business, or works only on certain occasions. In all such situation a person so acts is a servant of his master. If he is dishonesty misappropriates whatever assigned to him would be liable under section 408 IPC. 'A commercial traveller was engaged by a shirt making

I. Kalka Prasad (1959, Cr. L.J. 1264).

II. 1920 Cr. L.J. 513.

III. 1919, 10 L.B.R. 31.

IV. (1861, 30 Ljmc 142 - Queen V. Tite).

firm on commission basis. The person received samples and during his journey received the sums which he misappropriated. He never returned the samples'. He is liable under this section as servant.

'A Director of company may be a servant of the company if he is employed by the company as such.[I] But, where a Director is not so employed, he cannot be charged under this section for criminal breach of trust with regard to the company's money, aggleged to have been entrusted to him.[II]

'A, Court Inspector, improperly delegated to a constable the custody of government money and the latter dishonestly converted the money to his own use. It was held that the constable was employed as a servant of the Inspector and was guilty under this section'.[III]

Where a person serves as servant, though there is no contract binding him to work, so long as he performs the duties his acts would be covered by this section.[IV]

Even is cases where an employer has no right to receive money or he is wrong-doer in receiving but if the servant on behalf of his master receives such a money and dishonestly misappropriates, servant would be liable under this section.[V]

Section 408 is general in its connotation and applies to servants whether 'public servant' or not. Section 409 deals with criminal breach of trust by public servant only. In

---

I. Rr. Stuart, (1894, 1Q.B. 310).

II. 1980 Chand L.R. (Gr) 18 (23) Delhi.

III. (1867) 8 Suth WR, Gr, 1 (2) (DB).

IV. Karimuddin (1918, 40 All 563).

V. Beacall (1824, lc IP 454).

considering the guilt of a person accused under section 408, it is irrelevant to consider whether the accused is a public servant within the definition of section 21. In this view, the case[I] in which it was held that the secretary of a co-operative society was not a public servant within section 21 and hence was not governed by this section does not seem to be correct.

Servant entrusted with property

For the application of section 408, it is necessary that property must be entrusted to a person in his capacity as servant otherwise a person would be liable under section 406. Entrustment may be either express or implied. If implied entrustment is there then it is to be inferred from the circumstances of a case.

Entrustment can be distinguished from control or charge over the property. In Kesar Singh's case,[II] it was held that of the property is found missing, the person entrusted with the property is liable without any further proof, but in the case of control or charge over the property he will be liable only when it is shown that he misappropriated it or was a party to criminal breach of trust committed by any other person.

A servant under a legal contract made by him with his master to realise money on his behalf and render account to him, fails to give account inspite of such a repeated demand from his master and also uses the money in violation of service contract, would be guilty under this section.[III]

In an English case,[IV] 'if servant secrets money, which

I. 1974 BBcj (227) (Pat), 1975 Cr. Lj. 326 (Him. Pra).

II. State V. Kesar Singh, 1969 Cr. Lj. 1595.

III. Brj. Kishore V. Pandit Chandrika Presad (1936) 12 Luck. 77.

IV. Headge's case (1809) 2 Leach 1033.

his maser has marked and sent by a friend to make a purchase at his shop, with a view to try the honesty of the servant, it is a felonious breach of trust'.

A secretary of a co-operative society entrusted with society fund is a servant and any dishonest misappropriation would render him liable for criminal breach of trust.

In Dina's case a person was employed as Tonga Driver on a fixed monthly salary. Further it was agreed between the employer and employee that the later would be driving the Tonga on hire basis within the Municipal locality of a particular city and was to bring back the tonga every evening and pay over his earnings to the complainant. He did not comply with the conditions, failed to return one evening. The next following day he was pursued and arrested at a place several miles away from that specified city driving tonga with fast speed. The accused was convicted under this section by the magistrate. However, acquitted by the session judge on ground that driver did not commit any criminal breach of trust as the accused had not disposed of the tonga. In appeal before the High Court, the leaned judge held 'that there was no doubt that the accused intended to deprive his master of the tonga and that this intent or mental act of his was the gist of the offence of criminal breach of trust and he was therefore guilty of an offence under this section'.[1]

Where the money is given to a person as loan there is no entrustment. Similarly money deposited with Bank cannot be considered as entrustment.

In a case where accused had general supervision over the goods, and another person who was having a charge over

---

1. Dina (1925) 6 Lah. 257.

those goods made false report which was later endorsed by the accused, it was held that the accused was not liable under this section.[I]

A mere entry in the account book showing payment to the accused, without any other proof, would not amount to entrustment.[II]

A person employed in a firm not authorished to receive or encase cheques of the firm induced another employee to identify him as a partner before the Treasury officer so that he might deliver him money on certain cheques, held that his act amounted cheating rather than the criminal breach of trust.[III]

When a person was charged for committing a criminal breach of trust on grounds that a mistake was made by entering a false figure in the account book, defence pleaded for oversight and prosecution failed to prove guilt beyond reasonable doubt, it was held that the person was not liable under this section.[IV]

A servant who was instructed by his master to burn. Waste papers but he sold them, was held not guilty under this section.

'The entrustment to the servant must be in his capacity as such servant. A charge which omits to state thesis imperfect.[VI]

I. 1969 Cr. Lj. (1595) (Raj).

II. A 1974 Sec. 388; 1974 Cr. Lj. 447.

III. A 1955 NUC (Pat, 4900).

IV. 1979 Gri. L.R. (Guj) 42.

V. A 1930 All 449: 1931 Cr. Lj. 865.

VI. (1865) 3 Suth WR (Cr. Letters) 12.

With Dominion over property

A servant having dominion over the property of his maser in any manner misappropriates or converts to his own use such property is guilty of criminal breach of trust. In such cases physical possession of the accused is not necessary. Al that is required is that he should have dominion over it and can be disposed of by him in violation of law laying the mode of discharge of such trust. Where a person has been empowered to operate on the funds in a Bank, it is said that he is entrusted with dominion over it.[I] Here a case of Municipal Wahter Works Inspector authorised to supervise and check the water distribution may be referred where he has dominion over water on behalf of his master. If he diverts water for his own use or his tenants without paying the tax and gives no information to the employer of such use, he is guilty of criminal breach of trust.[II]

'Dominion over property must be as a result of entrustment, whereas dominion of a partner over partnership property is to an entrustment even when working as an employee of the partnership and he cannot be held guilty under this section.'[III]

In mortage cases where possession even after mortgage executed continues with the mortgagor, he has dominion over the property on behalf of the mortgagee and he allows the property to be fraudulently sold in default of payment of revenue and purchases benami in the name of another, the morgagor is liable under this section.

I. 1962 SC (1821).

II. Birmala Charan Roy (1913) 35 All 361.

III. Abhai Singh 1980 Cr. Lj. (NOC) 98 (All).

Where a police constable under lawful justification seizes property suspected to be stolen and later misappropriates to his own use, is said to have dominion over the property and for such misappropriation is liable for criminal breach of trust.

Entrustment or dominion over the property must be in any manner either by operation of law or by act of parties. Mere dominion over property is not enough. President of co-operative society along with other office-bearers was charged for misappropriation of society-store on the ground that the Key of store at night used to remain with the President. In this case it was held that the circumstances of the face were not sufficient to convict for the charge.[I]

"Property"

Word property under this section includes movable as well as immoval property. The view that the property under this section includes, only movable property is incorrect. Controversy whether this section covers movable only and not immovable property was set al rest after the decision of Supreme Court in R.K Dalmia V. Delhi Administration. Their lordships have held that the word property is used in the code in much wider sense than the expression movable property. There is no good reason to restrict the meaning of the word property to movable property only when it is used without any qualification in section 405 and other section of the Indian Penal Code'.

'Where a person receives a letter by post, and after reading the letter, throws away the envelop, the envelop cannot be considered property.[II] Another illustration may be given

I. Jagan Nath 01976 Cr. L.j. 847 (SC).

II. 1919 Cr. L.j. 174.

of rice which had become rotten and which had been ordered. To be destroyed is not a property.[I] Where a Municipal Inspector was ordered to destroy certain begs of condemned rotten rice but he sold it and used the proceeds for himself, it was held that no property was entrusted to the Inspector and that he could not be convicted for criminal breach of trust.[II]

However, in Moti's case,[III] a different view was taken A currency note was cancelled by tearing off certain parts, but the further process of cutting it into pieces and then destroying to by burning remained, it was held that such a note though cancelled, was not resnullius (not property) and could be the subject matter of theft. The court observed; "A very clear distinction must be drawn between to destroy and to abandon and an actual destruction and abandonment. The very fact that the owner of the property intends to destroy or abandon that property and hands it over to some person to effect those purposes is in our opinion a clear indication that he still maintains his rights as the owner of that property and those rights subsist until the abandonment or destruction is completed......as long as the destruction or abandonment is not fulfilled and as long as it is still in the hands of the owner to counter and such destruction or abandonment the property is still the property of the owner and the taking it out of his possession is theft, and improper use of it is breach of trust."

Earlier case was criticised and it was not based on sound reasons. But in the present case his lordship has given thought where there is in property, there is no loss and gain, no dishonest intention, hence no liability.

I. (1898) 2 Cal WN 216.

II. Ibdi.

III. Moti (1923) 17 SLR 260, 262: (1925), AIR (s) 21.

In determining whether a thing is 'property' the value of it is immaterial.[I]

Conversion by servant under special trust

When a servant deputed to receive money for a particular object and spent on did not utilize it for that object inspite of the fact that he was called to account for, but gave a false statement that he used the received money for that particular object was held to have committed criminal breach of trust.[II]

A salesman employed by a co-operative society was charged for shortage of clothes entrusted to him. He admitted the shortage of clothes as also his liability to pay the value of clothes. Further admitted that he alone was responsible for the shortage. He was convicted under this section.[III]

In a case where a servant employed by a firm to purchase paddy of a specific quality on a specified price for which he was to receive commission for work and also was given the necessary money for such purchase and all expenses to be incurred in purchasing the paddy and bringing up to the mill, diverted the greater part of such money to his own use, was held guilty under this section.[IV]

A munsiff in a village authorised to collect the repayment of loan due to the government, failed to remit the money to the treasury for a few months. Government issued notice to him to collect and remit the same to the treasury. He denied any collection of repayment loans, and also demanded

I. (1904) 1 Cr. LJ. 603 (605) All.

II. Wallson & Co. V. Golab Khan (1868) 10 WR (Gr.) 28:

III. Ramchandaran A.K. 1972 Cr. L.J - 698 (Mad).

IV. Pyo Gyi (1919) 1LBR 31 : 20 cr. L.J. 513.

a second payment from the depositors. Munsiff under the circumstances was held liable for misappropriation and breach of trust.[I]

In Sapneshwar Thappa's case, a certain sum of money was with drawn from the Depositor's Account. The accused in this case admitted that he passed the necessary pay order. Entries in the register, and cash book also indicated the withdrawal. However, it was clear that the application for withdrawal was not moved by the depositor, instead by the accused himself. Accused failed to give any explanation about such entries and withdrawal application, it was held that the accused himself withdrew the amount and misappropriated.[II]

'Where a railway servant was supplied with a water-proof coat on condition that if it was damaged or lost it would be renewed at the cost of the railway servant. Delivery of water proof coat was an entrustment, and when he attempted to pawn the garment, he was liable to conviction under this section read with section 511.[III]

An accused a paid servant, supervisor of a society, connected with the co-operative movement, debited Rs. 2/- as the pay of a sweeper woman, took the thumb impression of his nephew against the debit entry, certified the thumb impression to be that of the sweeper woman, and appropriated the amount to himself, it was held that he committed the offence of criminal breach of trust.[IV]

I. Vijayaraghava Reddiar (1956) mwn 79.

II. State V. Sapneshwar Tappa (1987), G. Lj 612 (Ori).

III. Nga Aung Thein (1933, 35 Cr. L.j. 788).

IV. Keshaoarao (1934), 36. Bom. LR. 1120.

Public Servant

Section 409 deals with criminal breach of trust cases committed by public servant in the capacity of a public servant. A property entrusted to a person happens to be a public servant is not sufficient. For the application of section 409, it is necessary that the property must have been entrusted to a public servant and he has authority to receive the property in his capacity as public servant.

Separate section has been devoted because the responsibilities of public servant are of highly significant character. It involves greater control and care because of secrecy and confidentiality. If there is breach of trust, it may lead to serious public and private calamities.

"Who is Public Servant?"

Section 21[1] Indian Penal Code enumerates the various functionaries who are designated as public servant. In fact

---

1. Sectin 21 - Indian Penal Code:

"Public Servant" - the words "public servant" denote a person falling under any of the descriptions hereinafter following namely:

First - Rep.

Second - Every Commissioned Officer in the Military, Naval or Air Force of India;

Third - Every Judge including any person, empowered by law to discharge' whether by himself or as a member of any body of person's any adjudicatory functions;

Fourth - Every officer of Court of Justiece (including liquidator, receiver or commissioner) whose duty it is, as such officer, to investigate or report, on any matter of law or fact, or to make, authenticate, or keep any document, or to take charge or dispose of any property, or to execute any judicial process, or to administer any oath, or to interpret, or to preserve order in the Court, and every person specially authorised by a Court of Justice to perform any of such duties;

Fifth - Every juryman, or member of a panchayat assisting a Court of Justice or public servant;

Sixth - Every arbitrator or other person to whom any cause or matter has been referred for decision or report by any Court of Justice, or by any other competent public authority;

Seventh - Every person who holds any office by virtue of which he is empowered to place or keep any person in confinement;

Eight - Every officer of the Government whose duty it is, as such officer, to prevent offences, to give information of offences, to bring offenders to justice, or to protect the public health, safety or convenience;

Ninth - Every officer, whose duty is, as such officer, to take, receive, keep or expend any property on behalf of the Government, or to make any survey, assessment or contract on behalf of the government or to execute any revenue process, or to investigate, or to report, on any matter affecting the pecuniary interest of the Government or to make, authenticate or keep any document relating to the pecuniary interest of the Government, or to prevent the infraction of any law for the protection of the pecuniary interest of the Government.

Tenth - Every officer whose duty it is as such officer, to take, receive, keep or expend any property, to make any survey or assessment or to levy any rate or tax for any secular common purpose of any village, town or district, or to make, authenticate or keep any document for the ascertaining of the rights of the people of any village, town or district;

Eleventh - Every person who holds any office by virtue of which he is empowered to prepare, publish, maintain or revise an electoral roll or to conduct an election;

Twelfth - Every person.

(a) in the service or pay of the Government or remunerated by fess or commission for the performance of any public duty by the Government.

the section does not define the term 'public servant'. It may be said that the general characteristic of a public servant is that he performs certain public functions. The Supreme Court in G.A. Montario's[1] case laid down the test whether a person is a public servant as follows:

(1) Whether he is in the service or payoff the government, and

(2) Where is entrusted with the performance of any public duty.

Essential to be proved in a charge against a public servant under this section are:

(1) Being entrusted with property, or dominion over property.

(2) In his capacity of public servant.

(b) in the service or pay of the local authority, or corporation established by or under a Central, Provincial or State Act or a Government Company as defined in Section 617 of the Companies Act, 1956.

Illustration

A municipal Commissioner is a public servant.

Explanation 1 - Person falling under any of the above descriptions are public servants whether appointed by the Government or not.

Explanation 2 - Wherever the words 'public servants' occur they shall be understood of every person who is in actual possession of the situation of a public servant, whatever legal defect there may be in his right to hold that situation.

Explanation 3 - The word 'election' denotes an election for the purpose of electing members of any legislative, municipal or other public authority, of whatever character the method of selection to which is by, or under, any law prescribed as by lection.

1. 1957 A.I.R. SC. 13

(3) Commits criminal breach of trust.

Criminal breach of trust under this section is to be construed in the light of the provisions of section 405. Dishonest intention, disposing of the property in violation of law prescribing the mode of discharge of such trust or violation of terms of contract for the execution of such trust or conversion to one's own use of such property are all part of study under this section as well.

Criminal liability under this section must be strictly proved. Initial entrustment of property and subsequent dishonest conversion by a public servant must be proved. The mistaken belief of the person delivering the property, or of the person accepting it, or of both, that the letter was authorized to receive it in his public capacity cannot alter the facts and supply the deficient and requisite authority so as to convert simple breach of trust into breach of trust by a public servant.[I]

A public servant is not ip-so-facto guilty of the offence of criminal breach of trust if he is negligent in seeing that the rules about remitting money to treasury are not observed, but something more, that is, dishonest intention is required. If a person opens a current account in the bank it would not amount to entrustment because the relationship between the bank and the customer is one of creditor and debtor. Bank may invest the money so deposited in any project it likes. There will be no violation of any provision dealing with criminal breach of trust.[II]

Misappropriation of property at a future date is not covered by this section.[III]

I. Bhag Singh (1876) PR No. 24 of 1876, at p. 46.

II. Gopesh Chandra V. Nirmal Kumar (1950, 1 Cr. L.J. 388).

III. Ahmed Din (1934) 36 Cr. L.J. 165.

It is not necessary that misappropriation should take place after the creation of a legally current entrustment of dominion over the property. 'Official capacity' of the public servant should also not be strictly constructed. 'A legal defect in the scope of ostensible authority of an public servant does not stand as a bar if the facts of the case establish a nexux between his acts and capacity.[I]

"Section 409 and related provisions"

"Section 409 and Section 34 IPC"

For an offence under section 409, physical presence for participation in the commission of crime is not an essential ingredient.[II] Where criminal breach of trust under section 407 has been committed involving participation of number of persons, all such persons, shall be charged under section 409 read with section 34, penal code. Essential requisite to be established by the prosecution is the entrustment of the property to all jointly.[III] Where two persons participating in diverse acts that led to criminal misappropriation both accused held would be liable under section 409/34 I.P.C. even though the other accused was not present when final act was committed.[IV]

"Section 409 and Section 5(1) (c) Prevention of Corruption Act 1947"

Both section are limited to the offence committed by the public officers. Question is whether section 5(1)(c) of

---

I. 1974 SCC. (Cr.) 359 (Som Nath), 1975 Cr. L.j. 1122.

II. A 1960 Sc., 889.

III. 1967 Cr. L.j. 1429.

IV. ILR (1976) 1 Bom. 203 (244).

Prevention of Corruption Act, 1947 repeal or abrogate Section 409 I.P.C.? Supreme Court has clearly laid down that section 5(1)(c) neither repeals nor abrogates section 409 I.P.C.[I] The offence under section 5(1)(c) is distinct from the offence committed under Section 409 I.P.C. There can be a trial and conviction under section 409 of the code even though the accused may have been acquitted in a trial for on offence under section 5(2) of the Prevention of Corruption Act.[II]

In another case the Lordships of Supreme Court observed, "The preamble of Prevention of Corruption Act makes it clear that the intention was to make effective provision for the prevention of bribery and corruption. From this itself, it is clear that the legislature was alive to the ;fact that something more stringent and drastic than section 409, Penal Code was necessary in the case of bribery and corruption by public servants and it was to effectuate that intention that the Act was put the statute book".[III]

"Conviction under section 409, I.P.C. and also under section 5(2) read with section 5(1)(c) of the Prevention of Corruption Act is not illegal".[IV]

Under section 5(1)(c) of prevention of Corruption Act, 1947, a person is liable for misconduct if he dishonestly or fraudulently misappropriates or otherwise converts for his own use any property entrusted to him or under his control as a public servant, or allows any other person so to do."

Punishment for violation of above provision is provided in section 5(2) of Prevention of Corruption Act. Further sub-

I. A 1960 SC. 889.

II. A 1957 SC 593.

III. A 1957 SC. 458 (461).

IV. 1978 Cr. L.j. (NOC) 175 (Goa).

section 4 of that section clearly lays down that the provisions of section 5 shall be in addition to and not in derogation of any other law for the time being in force and that nothing contained therein shall exempt any public servant from any proceeding which might, apart from that section be instituted against him'. 'It is open to the prosecution to proceed against the accused under either provision'.[I]

Under both the sections, that is, for prosecution of a public servant under section 5(2) of the Prevention of Corruption Act, and section 409 IPC it is necessary that the 'sanction to prosecute' must be obtained from the government. Section 409 I.P.C. is governed by section 197, Cr. P.C. which lays down that a public servant not removable from his office save by or with the sanction of the government is accused of any offence alleged to have been committed by him while acting or purporting to act in the discharge of his official duty, no court shall take cognizance of such offence except with the previous sanction of either central or state government.

A case under section 161 and 5(1)(c) was lodged. Police reported that no offence under section 161 I.P.C. and section 5(1)(c) had been made out against the accused. The special judge accepted the report but observed that an offence under section 409 was made out. It was held by the High Court that the special judge had no jurisdiction take cognizance of the offence under section 409.[II]

"Section 409 and 477 A"

Section 477 A deals with falsification of books and accounts even though there is no proof of misappropriation.

I. A 1955 Bom. 451 (454) (FB).

II. 19785 Cr. L.j. 978 (Raj.)

Such falsification of accounts or books must be by a clerk, officer or servant and is distinct from misappropriation and criminal breach of trust. However, an accused may be guilty under both the sections 409 and 477 A I.P.C. but a single charge is illegal, unless the offences form the part of same transaction under section 235 of Criminal Procedure Code.[I] 'The acquittal of a person of an offence under section 477 A is no bar to a trial under this section'.[II] Falsification of accounts may be an evidence of misappropriation or breach of trust'.[III]

When a clerk or servant is being prosecuted under section 409, no sanction for prosecution is required. But a case falling under section 477A, sanction for prosecution is required.[IV]

"Section 104 and 105 Insurance Act and 409"

Section 104 and 105 of Insurance Act are not identical in content and scope with section 409 I.P.C. Offence under section 409 is not the same offence as under section 105 Insurance Act and hence Article 202, of the constitution or section 26 of the general clauses (X of 1897 cannot be applied.[V] For the prosecution under section 409 I.P.C. cannot be said to be instituted in order by pass the requirement of sanction under the Insurance Act.[VI]

Section 242 of the Companies Act, is another which is distinct from section 409 I.P.C. 'If it appears to the central

---

I. A 1956 SC. 149 (153).

II. A 1956 Mad 130.

III. 1955 Cr. L.j. 1520.

IV. 2940 Cr. L.j. 468.

V. 1961 Cr. L.j. 725 (SC).

VI. A 1969, Delhi 330 (349) (DB).

government that any person referred to three-in under section 242 of the Companies Act has been guilty of any offence for which he is criminally liable, the central government may prosecute the person for the offence. However, this section 242 is an enabling section and does not deprive a Police Officer of his jurisdiction to investigate into a complaint of an offence under sections 406 and 409 I.P.C. and initiate proceedings in the court, even if the acts in respect of which the offences arise were committed in relation to the affairs of a company.[I]

"Section 409 I.P.C. and Section 52, Post Office Act, 1898"

Both the sections above referred are different in nature and scope. A magistrate is not competent to try an offence under section 52 Post Officer Act. While under section 409 I.P.C. magistrate has jurisdiction to try the case. If a case under section 52 tried by magistrate, trial would be void as being without jurisdiction. Offence under the section falls within the juridiction of a Session Court. A trial for the offence under section 52 Post Office Act would not be barred by virtue of section 461 of the Criminal Procedure Code.[II]

Section 409 and Section 14 of the Employee's Provident Fund Act

Offence under section 409 I.P.C. and section 14 of Employee's Provident Funds Act may not be considered as same offence so as to bar fresh trial.[III]

I. 1957 Cr. L.j. 205.

II. A 1970 Goa 7 (12).

III. 1976 Cr. L.j. 868 (Pr. 5).

Section 409 I.P.C. and Section 420 I.P.C.

To constitute an offence of breach of trust property must come into the hands of the accused in a lawful manner of with the consent of the owner. Entrustment implies handing over in a lawful manner. It also implies that the person entrusting the property has confidence in the person taking the property. Thus it creates a fiduciary relationship between them. This confidence would be lacking if the property has been acquired by a deceit. If there is false representation or deceit applied for obtaining the property from the owner, it would not amount entrustment which is essential igredient for the offence of cheating. Instead the act would fall under section 420 I.P.C. Deception is the basic requirement for the application of section 420 I.P.C. If the property is obtained for one purpose lawfully and later used for another, the offence is one under section 406 and not under section 420 I.P.C.[I]

Being Entrusted with Property

As studied earlier under section 405 and 406 I.P.C., property must have been entrusted to the accused. Without entrustment section 409 would not be applied. Whether the property is entrusted or not depends upon the facts and circumstances of a case. If nature of the transaction is loan, even the parties to the transaction in writing call it a trust, it would not be covered by section 409. It is not a trust. For example A financed the accused B at his business of purchase and sale of gunny bags. As security the bags were stored in the godown of A for which B had to pay rent and the sale proceeds had to be paid to A. B had to pay interest to A on the loan advanced. It was held that neither the money advanced nor the goods purchased were entrusted to B'.[I]

I. 1974 Cr. L.j. 207 (Ker.)

In another case the accused was working as a post-delivery agent. "A postal insured cover allegedly containing Rs.1000/- currency notes was handed over to the accused for delivery to the addresses. After delivery the cover was open in the presence of the addresses by the accused but instead of the notes some pieces of paper were found therein. It was held that the conviction of the accused could not be sustained as the essential ingredient of entrustment was not proved by the prosecution by clear or cogent evidence that at the time the cover was handed over to the accused it contained the notes".[II]

Similarly, in Tapan Kumar Mitra case, where a partner of firm was charged for criminal breach of trust,. held not liable. Facts of the case were that the accused partner opened a bank account in the name of partnership firm in another bank showing himself as its sole proprietor and uncashed the cheques payable to the partnership firm and got the amount deposited in his account he cannot be charged under this section because in the absence of an agreement between him and the other partners specifically authorised the accused to collect the money in question, there was no entrustment of property within section 409 I.P.C.[III]

Illustrative cases of breach of trust by public servant may be cited below:

Money handed over to the money-order issue clerk in a post office is money entrusted to him.[IV]

I. 1938 Suid 57 (58); 39 Cr. L.j. 399.

II. Fakria Nayak 1987 Cr. L.j. 1479 (Ori.).

III. 1987 Cr. L.j. 483 (Cal.)

IV. A 1957 Orissa 268.

Money given to the post-master for opening a new saving bank account is money entrusted to him.[I]

Where under an agreement between the accused and the government, the accused is under a duty to sell to persons grain stored in government building and pay the sale proceeds to the government, the accused is entrusted with the property.[II]

An employee of the government bound to keep custody of, and to account for, the receipts and disbursement pertaining to government funds without and power of disposition over them is entrusted with the property.[III]

Where the accused, a petty officer with salt department was empowered to sell salt at reduced prices only to ticket holders, but he really bought the salt himself at the reduced rates and entered the sales in the government books as if sold to ticket-holders, it was held that the accused was entrusted with salt and that what he did was a breach of trust.[IV]

V.P.P. article handed over to a postman for delivery to the addresses, are property entrusted to him.[V]

A constable who was given the pay of his Thana Police is entrusted with the amount.[VI]

Where the President and sales clerk of co-operative society were entrusted with levy sugar for distributing it to ration-card holders, however, they sold it to persons other

---

I. (1957) 1 All L.R. 166.

II. A 1956 Hyderabad 180.

III. (1908) 8 Cr. L.j. 492.

IV. I. Weir 467 (468) (DB).

V. A 1959 Mys. 185.

VI. (1863) 3 Suth WR Cr. (44) (DB).

than the ration-card holders; they would be guilty of offence under this section.[I]

Where a sub-post-master had forged the thumb impression of a party and misappropriated the money order amount he would be guilty under this section.[II]

Entrustment implies:

(1) handing over the property to another person.

(2) placing confidence.

(3) Creating fiduciary relationship between them.

Above noted requirements must be proved for a valid entrustment. If entrustment with above requisites not proved, there would be no criminal breach of trust. Where the ownership has passed with the transfer of goods, a person cannot be said entrusted with the property.[III]

A purchaser of property is not a trustee.[IV] A booking clerk recovering in excess of legal charge and not crediting excess to railway-excess amount not held entrusted to him.[V] Where money or other property is obtained by practising deception there can be no question of entrustment because where the custody is made over, the property or right there in pass to the recipient.[VI]

I. 1981 Cr. *Lj*. 258 (Mad.)

II. Naujappa DC 1971 Scc (Cr.) II.

III. A 1967 Cal. 568.

IV. A 1968 SC 700.

V. A 1923 Lah. 295 (1).

VI. (1970) 36 Cut. L.T. 39 (52).

(All illustrative cases are noted from Indian Penal Code, Vol. 3, by V.R. Mohar and W.W. Chitaley page 349).

For entrustment it is not necessary that the property given possession should be the property of on whose behalf it is received. Where the possession of the property given for a specific purpose or to deal with in a particular manner, the ownership of property being vested in some person other than the accused, he can be said to be entrusted with the property.

'Where goods are entrusted to A for sale and A sells them, the sale proceeds also must be regarded as property entrusted to him'.[I] Similarly where money is given to a person to purchase paddy, the paddy purchased with the money can be said to be entrusted to A.[II]

'The property must have been entrusted to the accused personally. A person who is the manager of a firm cannot be said to be entrusted with property which was entrusted to the firm'.[III]

As to property, concept should be clear. It must be a definite property or sum of money than only the elements of criminal property or sum of money than only the elements of criminal breach of trust, this is, entrustment of property, or dominion over property and dishonest misappropriation or conversion etc., can be the basis for conviction. 'Property under this section does not include immovable property.'[IV] Further property must belong to some one, not necessarily the entrusting person should be the owner of it. It is also not the aim of the section that the entrustment should fulfil all the legal formalities needed for the creation of a tust. It may be entrusted in any manner. Direct entrustment to the accused is also not necessary. It will be sufficient if a person received

---

I. A 1932 Sind 169; 34 Cr. L.j. 51 (DB).

II. A 1955 Trav. Co. 271 : 1955 Cr. L.j. 1539 (DB).

III. A 1930 Rang 332 : 32 Cr. L.j. 149, (1975) 1 Andh. Pra. L.j. 119.

IV (1954) 56 Punj. L.R. 521.

the control over the property under circumstances whereby he becomes entrusted. Therefore, where a parcel registered and delivered at the post office for transmission each of the postal employed authorised to receive and handle it for the purpose of its transmission becomes entrusted with it.[1]

Dominion over Property

The phrase dominion over property has earlier been discussed in detail. Here some cases selected to public servant would be discussed. A public servant is liable in case either he has been entrusted the property or has dominion over it and violates the conditions of his duties assigned to him in regard to such property. A public servant responsible for spending a certain sum of money for specific purpose but has no dominion over the money other then passing the orders for payment thereof. The person under whose the certain sum of money is, dies, and the public servant cannot produce voucher for the actual expensed incurred by him due to his death and owner of money himself is also satisfied with the payment made, there is no case of criminal breach of trust.

Capacity of a Public Servant

Entrustment of property must be to a public servant in his capacity as a public servant. If the entrustment is made in a private capacity of public servant section 409 I.P.C. will not apply. Receipt of the property may be fraudulent or improper or innocently made. The mode is not material what is significant is the entrustment to public servant than only the provision of section 409 I.P.C. are attracted.

"Although in order to bring a public servant within this section, the entustment should have been made a him in his

---

I. 1973 Kash L.j. 79 (81) DB.

capacity of public servant, it is not necessary that the misappropriation should have been made in not necessary that the misappropriation should have been made in his capacity of public servant.[1] Even if a public servant in his private capacity misappropriates but entrusted property in his capacity of public servant, he would be liable under section 409 I.P.C. A patwari in his capacity as public servant collecting various sums of money on behalf of state paid lesser amount in the treasury, would be liable under this section.

Property entrusted to a public servant need not be a government property. In a case where a public servant is under a duty to receive money and enter the cash balance in the register day today but fails to do so and misappropriates the money, and also does not hand over the money to his successor, he will be convicted for criminal breach of trust under this section.

Where a public servant relinguishes his office and hands over the charge to his nominee who has not been appointed to the post, would not be considered a public servant, and any misappropriation made by such nominee would not under him liable for criminal breach of servant under this section because he is not a public servant. But if a person is appointed by the government for a temporary period, entrusted with property dishonestly misappropriates, he would be punished under this section.

"A Lambardar came to deposit amount collected by him as land revenue in the treasury and treasury officer was on leave. To avoid coming over again he paid the amount to the accused, a Jamadar, for depositing in the treasury. The accused did not deposit the amount. It was argued that since it was no part of the official duties of the accused to accept this type of

1. (1962).

money, hence the Lambardar wrongly paid this amount to the accused no criminal offence much less on offence under section 409 was made out".

It was held that the requirement of the law is that a person should be a public servant and in that capacity he should receive property or dominion over property in the form of entrustment and in that situation it becomes his bounden duty to discharge that trust in the manner undertaken by him or at least to deal with that property in an honest manner and, if he acts in violation of those directions or dishonestly misappropriates the same, he is guilty of the offence even of that entrustment was made to him under an erroneous assumption. The accused was thus convicted under section 409 I.P.C."[I]

For the application of section 409[II] I.P.C. following persons, under different decided cases by different High Courts, have been held to be public servants.

(1) A Naib Nazir.

(2) an extra department branch post-master.

(3) a person temporarily carrying on duties but under a letter of appointment from the government.

(4) the officiating Kukarni of a village.

(5) an employee of Shipping Corporation of India.

(6) Railway material clerk in charge of stores.

(7) a Mouzadar in Assam.

(8) a Quirq Amin.

I. State V. Wazira Ram (1986) Cr. L.j. 995 (HP).

II. Law of Crimes by Ratanlal & Dhirajlal, Vol. II, 23rd Edition, p. 1564.

(9) a Sanitary Inspector of Municipality.

(10) Person appointed by government and his salary paid through the collector.

(11) a patwari collecting various sums on behalf of state, etc. etc.

The listing all by designation will become quite exhaustive. The test is that a person should have a letter of appointment. He should be under the control of government receives the salary from the government. Further he is entrusted with the property as a public servant, and dishonestly misappropriates or converts the same to his own use.

Controversy as to the applicability of Section 409 I.P.C. to Public Servants

As discussed earlier controversy was arisen with Gurucharan Singh's[I] case, in which the Punjab High Court took a view that after the enforcement of section 5 of the Prevention of Corruption Act 1947, this section 409 I.P.C. concerning offences by public servants was "pro-tanto repealed". This view has been dissented by Madras High Court,[II] Rajasthan High Court,[III] Hydrabad High Court,[IV] Bombay High Court,[V] Calcutta High Court,[VI] Lucknow Bench of Allahabad High Court,[VII] Pepsu High Court,[VIII] and Madhya

I. Gurcharan Singh (1954), Punj. 35.

II. Satyanarayane Murthy 1952 MWN 957.

III. Gulab Singh (1954) U. Raj. 910.

IV. Jayarama Iyer 1954 Cr. *L.j.* 464.

V. Pandurang Baburao (1955) 57 Bom. L.R. 784.

VI. Amarendra nath Rao (1955) Cr. L.j. 784.

VII. Om Prakash 1955 Cr. *L.j.* 754 (FB).

VIII. Raj Kumar 1956 Cr. *L.j.* 100.

Bharat High Court.[I] The gist of different dissenting decision is: section 5 (1) (c) of the Prevention of Corruption Act, after its enforcement does not repeal section 409 I.P.C. Pro-tonto. After the amendment of section 5 inserting sub-clause (4) it has been made abundantly clear that section 409 has not been repealed. Even before amendment section 5 (1) (c) cannot be held to have impliedly repealed section 409, as a special law does not repeal the general law unless the intention is made clear in that law. A public servant can be prosecuted under section 409, notwithstanding section 5(2) of the Prevention of Corruption Act. In case of criminal breach of trust by a public servant, it was open to the prosecution to launch prosecution either under section 409 or under section 5(2) of the Prevention of Corruption Act.

The controversy ultimately rested with the decision of Supreme Court in Veereshwar Rao.[II] It held "that the offence of criminal misconduct punishable under section 5(2) of the Prevention of Corruption Act, is not identical in essence, important and content with an offence under section 409 of the Penal Code. The offence of criminal misconduct is a new offence created by that enactment and does not repeal by implication or abrogate section 409 of the Penal Code". Supreme Court further held, "that the view taken by the Punjab High Court in Gurcharan Singh's case is not sound and it has approved of the view taken by the Bombay High Court in Pandurang Baburao, by the Madras High Court in Satyanarayana Murthy, and by the Calcutta High Court in Amarendra Nath Rao". With this decision the controversy has now been finally set at rest.

I. Madhoprasad 1953 MLR Cr. 38.

decision is: Section 5(1) (c) of the Prevention of Corruption .

II. 1957 SCJ. 519 : (1957) Cr. *L.j.* 892.

PART B

"LIABILITY OF SERVANTS UNDER ISLAMIC LAW"

Qur'ãnic View

Employing servant to work in according to the directions of the master is justified and legal under the Islamic law. Justification can be inferred from Allah's commandments in Qur'ãne-Pak and Prophet's (peace be upon him), Sunnah. Allah-Ta'ala in Ayah 26 and Surah 28 says:

قَالَتْ اِحْدٰهُمَا يٰٓاَبَتِ اسْتَاْجِرْهُ اِنَّ خَيْرَ مَنِ اسْتَاْجَرْتَ الْقَوِيُّ الْاَمِيْنُ۔ (سورة القصص، آية : ٢٦)

"(No doubt) the best of men for you to employ is the strong, the trustworthy". (28:26).

Ahadith - A View

Number of Ahadith are there in which it is made clear that Prophet (peace be upon him) himself in his life time employed persons, and assigned different works to them to be performed. For example, he employed persons as treasurers, and persons to shepherd sheeps. He employed not only Muslims but non-Muslims also and assigned different works to them. He (peace be upon him) employed for short period as well as for long period to work. He engaged servants not only for doing immediate work, but assigned works which were to be performed after passing specific times. For example, employed persons to work after one year. The significance lies on the point that whatever contract entered, it was to be executed honourably.

Prophet (peace be upon him) employed servants or labourers, for services to be rendered during Holy battles. Thee were case where persons were employed to work for specific period, without telling the nature of work to be performed by them. This is also justified by Qur'ãnic injunction '28:28' also.

Prophet (peace be upon him) employed persons for house repair purposes, to work upon midday or up to Asr-prayer or even thereafter. Services of porters and brokers were also utilised by him (peace be upon him).

Justifying the employment of the servants we will study some of the relevant Ahadith[I] as follows:

رعی الغنم علی قراریط

حدثنا احمد بن محمد المکی : حدثنا عمرو بن یحیی، عن جده، عن ابی هریرة رضی الله عنه۔ عن النبی صلی الله علیه وسلم قال : ما بعث الله نبیا الا رعی الغنم، فقال اصحابه : وانت؟ فقال : نعم، کنت ارعاما علی قراریط لا هل مکة۔

Narrated Abu Huraira (R.A.): the Prophet (peace be upon him) said, "Allah did not send any prophet but shepherds sheep." His companions asked him. "Did you do the same?" The Prophet (peace be upon him) replied, "Yes, I used to shephered the sheep of the people of Makkah for some Qirats."

استئجار المشرکین عند الخرورة، او اذا لم یو جد اهل الا سلام

وعامل النبی صلی الله علیه وسلم یهود خیبر۔

The employment of pagans (by Muslims) if necessary, or if no Muslim is available for that purpose. And the Prophet (peace

I. XXXVI - 'The Book of Hiring', The translation of the Mening of Sahih al-Bukhari, Arabic-English, Volume III, by Dr. Muhammad Muhsin Khan, I.U. Al-Madinah - Al-Munawwara.

be upon him) employed the Jews of Khaibar (for the purpose of land irrigation).

اذا استاجر احیرا لیعمل له بعد ثلاثه ایام، او بعد شهر، او بعد سنة جاز، وهما علی شرطهما الذی اشترطاه اذا جاء الا جل۔

It is legal if someone hires someone to work for him after three days or after one month or after a year. When that period elapses they should carry out their contract.

حدثنا یحیی بن بکیر: حدثنا اللیث من مقیل: قال ابن شهاب: فاخبرنی عروة بن الزبیر ان عائشة رضی الله عنها زوج النبی ﷺ قالت: واستاجر رسول الله ﷺ و ابوبکر رجلا من بنی الدیل مادیا خریتا وهو علی دین کفار قریش، فدفعا الیه راحلتیها ووعداه غار ثور بعد ثلاث لیال براحلتیهما صبح ثلاث۔

Narrated 'Aisha (R.A.) the wife of the Prophet (peace be upon him): Allah's Apostle (peace be upon him) and Abu Bakr (R.A.) hired a man from the tribe of Bani Ad-Dil as an expert guide who was a pagan (follower of the religion of pagans of Quraish). The Prophet (peace be upon him) and Abu Bakr (R.A.) gave him their two riding camels and took a promise from him to bring their riding camels in the morning of the third day to the Cave of Thaur.

الا جیر فی الغزو۔

Narrated Abu Hurairah (R.A.): The Prophet (peace be upon him) said, "Allah said, "I will be an opponent to three types of people on the Day of Resurrection:—

1. One who makes a covenent in My Name, but proves treacherous;
2. One who sells a free person and eats his price; and

3. One who employs a labourer and takes full work from him but does not pay him for his labour."

All these Ahadith above quoted make it clear that employment of servants in permissible under Islamic Law. The term used for servants in 'Hireling'. Categories of Hireling are noted below.

Classification of Hirelings

According to Islamic law hirelings (servants) can be classified under two heads:

(1) Common hirelings, and

(2) Particular Hirelings.

Under the first category, are persons who are hired, and are not restricted by condition such as not to work for anyone other than the hirer.

In Hedaya, it has been explained as:

"A common hireling is one with whom a contract of hire is concluded for work of such a nature as may be perceived by examining the subject:— and in this instance there is no occasion for any mention of a term; nor is he entitled to his hire or recompense until the work he has engaged for (such as dying or falling) be executed, because the work is the only thing contracted for, where he engages to perform it in person, or the effect of such work, when he has not particularly engaged no perform it in person - It is therefore lawful him to work for the public at large, since no particular person has any claim to his service; and accordingly, he is termed 'Ajeer Mooshtarik'(اجیر مشترک) that is, a general or common hireling".

Examples may be cited of a 'porter' an 'Auctioneer', a 'tailor', a 'jeweller', a 'port boatman', a lackney carriage driver, and a village shephered who are all common hirelings (servants). They are not confined to, or special to any specific person. Such hirelings servant may work for anyone who engages them for work.

As referred above, the right of the common employee to pay arises on the work being done.

Under the second category are persons specially employed. They are hired to work for the hirer alone and not anyone else. Person getting monthly wages may be included under this class. The person who is specially employed for a specific period for the hirer alone, during that time, he becomes a private hireling.

Similarly, when a porter, a carriage driver, or a boatman are hired to work particularly to the hirer, and not to work for anyone else upto a particular place or destination, are private hirelings until the specific assigned work completed.

In Hedaya, a particular hireling has been explained as:

"A particular hireling signifies one who is entitled to his hire in virtue of a surrender of himself during the term of hire, although he does no work; as for instance, a person who is hired as a servant for a month, or to take care of flock for a month, a certain rate, under a condition that he shall not serve or tend the flocks of any other person during that term - An hireling (servant) of this description is denominated an Ajeer Wahid, or singular hireling, because the advantage of has service belongs exclusively to a single person during the term of his engagement, and the wages he received are opposed to such advantage:- and as the hireling, in this instance, is entitled to his hire in virtue of his surrender of himself, for the term of hire, he is entitled to his wages although he does not work, or although his work be afterwards, undone, as where, for instance, a person is hired to make up a dress, and he sew it accordingly, and the sewing be afterwards ripped out, in which case he is nevertheless entitled to his hire."

Several persons also, being regarded as a single person, can be the hirer of a special employee in the same way as one person can be.

Illustration can be given where the residents of a village have hired a shephered by a single contract to be special to themselves, that sphered becomes a private employee, but in case of their having made it lawful for him to watch the animals of people other than themselves, he becomes a common employee.

The private servant (particular hireling - Ajeer Wahid) is entitled to receipt the payment of his wages only when he is found ready for the work at the time for which he has been hired. He should not refuse to do the assigned work at a proper time and place if so directed. If he does not comply with the direction and fails to perform his job, he is not entitle to receive his wage.

In cases where the wage has not been determined prior to the work done by the servant, then if he is of the kind of a person who works for wages, he takes the equivalent wage. If someone asks another to work for him for some days and says to him that he would buy a pair of particular thing as his wage, giving of that thing is not necessary to pay hire equivalent to the work.

Further when a person has been employed to do a work himself, then he cannot employ another to do the work on his behalf. Personal assignment is performed by the hireling personally.

Where there is no condition binding on the hired person, in the matter of the thing which are consequences of the work, as regards those, the use and custom of the town is made to be observed. There is no necessity to feed the person hired unless there is custom to this effect in the town.

Responsibility of Hireling

According to Islamic law, an article delivered to a common hireling is a deposit (ودیعت, trust) in his hands. Imam Abu Haneefa (Rahmatullah Aleh) said that if there is a damage or loss of property while it is in the possession of the servant, he is responsible for such loss or damage. But, according to him, there will be no liability in case where the article is lost or destroyed or damaged by any irremediable and irresistible accident, such as fire conflagrations burning down his house, or robbers forcibly entered his house, looted the property and he was incapable to repeal them.

Hazrat Ali (R.A.) and Hazrat Umar (R.A.) were also of the opinion that a common hireling was responsible for the loss or destruction of property while it is in his possession because the care of the property is incumbent on him; as without such case he cannot perform his work upon it.

However, if there is no negligence on the part of the servant, if the property or article perishes, he would not be responsible. When the article is lost due to a cause which could be avoided, such as usurpation or theft of the property, this proves his negligence, and in consequence, he is "responsible in the same manner as a trustee who lets to hire the deposit (ودیعت) in his hands, - It is otherwise where the article is lost from some unavoidable cause, such as fire, sudden death, and so forth, since in this case he cannot be accused of negligence - The argument of Imam Abu Haneefa (Rahmatullah Aleh) is that the article is merely a deposit in the workman's hands, the possession of which does not involved responsibility, in as much as he took possession with consent of the proprietor, and, accordingly, if it were lost from any unavoidable cause, he is not responsible, - where as, if his possession of it involved responsibility, he would owe a compensation for it at all events, in the same manner as in a case of usurped (misappropriated) property, - The care: moreover, of the article is incumbent upon the proprietor dependently and not essentially, and accordingly no hire is due for such case. This case is different from that of an hired trustee; for the care of the deposit (ودیعت) is essentially incumbent upon a trustee who acts for hire, because of the wages he receives." (Hedaya).

Destruction of Property in the Course of Employment

Islamic jurists have two views on this point. The first view is: "a common hireling is responsible in case of loss or destruction of any article in the course of his work; as where a dyer or fuller tears the cloth entrusted to him, or a porter stumble, or the tying of his load breaks, or the girth of a camel breaks, and thus the goods with which he is loaded fall to the ground, or a boat sinks from the mismanagement of the boatman".

Those who advocate the second view maintain that the hireling is not responsible in those cases, because the hirer had ordered him to work in an absolute manner, and hence his order extends as well to dangerous as to safe operations, - in other words, to operations which subject his property to damage, and also to operations under which it continues uninjured - The hireling in question, therefore, is the same predicament with a particular hireling, or any assistant of a workman.

This has been criticised by the Islamic jurists as: "that the orders of the hirer do not extend to any operations but what are mentioned in the contract; and those are to be supposed of a safe - nature, since in virtue of them is obtained the thing contracted for, namely, the effect of them, hence it is that if this effect be obtained through the work of any other than the hireling, still the recompense is due. The orders of the hirer, therefore, do not comprehend any operations that may be injurious, since through such the thing contracted for, namely, the effect, cannot be produced. It is also otherwise with respect to a particular hireling, as shall be hereafter - (It is to be observed that the breaking of a camel's girth, or so forth, is supposed to originate with the hireling, in as much as the accident maybe attributed to his want of care) - A common hireling, therefore, is responsible for any thing which may be destroyed in the course of his work, excepting, however, where a man is destroyed, either by the sinking of a boat, or falling from a camel or other animal (although those accidents should have been occasioned by the driving of the camel or the navigating of the boat); for in this instance, the hireling is not responsible as responsibility of a man cannot be incurred in virtue of a contract, or in virtue of anything but a 'janayet', or offence against the person, hence, it would be due, in this instance, not from the hireling, but from his 'Akile' who however, cannot be made responsible by a contract."

In case where a porter has been employed for bringing some glass-jars, and the proper when bringing those jars with him, falls down on the ground, and in consequence breaks all the glass-jar. Under these conditions porter is a trustee. The question is that in such a case, would he be liable for breach of trust. The learned opinion in such a case is that it is a violation and the porter is responsible for breaking the glass-jars. The hirer has two options in such a case: First, to take the value of jar in accordance to the cost which the jars had at the place from where it were taken. In this case the porter is not entitled to any recompense; or Secondly, the hirer has an option to take compensation for the value it bore at the place where it was broken, paying the porter a proportionate hire.

Porter is liable because either due to his stumbling the things were fallen on the ground and damaged or the rope tiding thing proper was broken, in consequence of the property was destroyed. Both the things are attributed to him. It is his failure to take proper caution resulted in harm to the property, hence liable.

In cases when due to servant's wrongful act or default, the property of the master in his possession is destroyed, he is liable. It is a breach of trust.

It is a wrongful act of the servant, if he removes or works contrary to the order of the hirer, clearly given or conveyed to him. If the servant has been assigned for a particular job and direction has been given to him to remain with the property entrusted at a particular place and do not carry the property to any other place, in case he carries to the other place and damage is caused to the property, the servant is liable.

Likewise if someone gives to the tailor a piece of cloth and asks him whether a particular style of coat can be made from the piece of cloth and he replies yes. After cutting the cloth it is not possible to prepare that particular type coat, then whatever loss is caused to the owner, the tailor as trustee liable to compensate him. Here the tailor has both types of liabilities civil as well as penal.

In case, where the servant is negligent in keeping the thing safe, any destruction caused to the property, the servant is liable. When a person has been employed as a shephered to look after the animals, if an animal is strayed from a flock and lost by reason of shephered not going to get it back or make a search of it, in consequence of his negligence and indifferent attitude, loss is caused, the servant is liable, because he has violated the trust reposed in him by his master.

As to the responsibility to a person specially hired or employed known as 'particular hireling' or 'Ajeer Wahid' or 'Singular hireling', he is considered a trustee (custodian امین). If an article which is in his possession lost without his act, he would not be responsible.

Hence for determining the liability we may consider two different situations: First, an article is lost whilst in the hands of a particular hireling, without his act, that is, stolen by thief of taken away by the usurper. Second, an article is lost by his act.

The particular hireling is not responsible in the former case because the article is a deposit (وديعت) in his hands, since he took possession of the article with the owner's consent. This is the learned view of Imam Abu Haneefa (Rahmatullah Aleh). His two disciples also agree with him because they hold that the obligation of responsibility upon a common hireling proceeds upon a favourable construction of the law, in order that men's property may be in security; but as a particular hireling does not engage to work for every person, it is still more likely that the property is safe with such a hireling: and therefore, in this case, the law proceeds upon analogy.

In the second case, the particular hireling (servant) is also not responsible because, as the advantage of this hireling's service is the property of the hirer, it follows that, where he directs him to act with his property, such direction is valid: consequently, the hireling is his deputy; his acts, therefore, are the same as the acts of his principal, the hirer, and of course he is not responsible.'

So much so that when the property is destroyed in his hands without his working on it, there is no liability.

Likewise, when the property is destroyed or damaged or lost by the work done by hyim on it, without any fault or wrongdoing, thee is no liability. Such a case is not treated as breach of trust or violation of rules governing deposits (وديعت).

In cases where the servants have been employed jointly, then a servant is liable only for his own wrongs he has committed or acts negligently done. Whatever destruction, damage, loss or injury caused to the property by his own acts and deeds, he would be liable to that act only and not for the joint injuries or destruction caused.

CHAPTER 4

PART A

"AGENT'S LIABILITY: INDIAN CRIMINAL LAW"

Word agent has not been defined in the Penal Code. For definition we have to see section 182 of Indian Contract Act. Section explains agent as:

> "An agent is a person employed to do any act for another or to represent another in dealings with third persons. The person for whom such act is done, or who is represented, is called the principal."

Emphasis is on the agent's representative character. He is to act on behalf of his principal in bringing about a contract between his principal and a third party. Vivian Bose J.,[1] making observation on the definition said that the 'definition is wide enough to embrace a servant pure and simple, even a casual employee, a man who is engaged by me in the street to black my boots; but it cannot for a moment be contended that they are all to be placed in the same category'. The term 'agent' means a person whose object is to establish contractual relations between his principal and a third party. His representative capacity depends upon his relations with the principal and functions and responsibilities assigned to him as agent.

The relationship between a principal and his agent is normally a consensual one. Such relationship may arise in the following ways:

I. Kalyanji V. Tirkaram, AIR 1988 Nag. AT P. 255.

1. By contract under seal;
2. By contract in writing or verbal;
3. By contract implied from the conduct or situation of the parties;
4. By consent express or implied where there is no contact as the agent is acting gratiously;
5. By ratification - this is where agent has no authority but purports to make a contract with the third party on behalf of the principal and the principal later ratifies expressly or impliedly what agent has done.

Consent plays a vital role. The relationship of principal and agent can be established only by consent. It may be implied even. Although mutual consent of principal and agent in necessary for the creation of agency but thee is no specific requirement that the agreement between the two should be in any particular form. Words and conduct may afford proof as to the creation of agency and relationship between the principal and agent. Agent is not to be appointed in writing. Example may be given where an agent is orally appointed to obtain the lease of a house. Normally the principal will pay the agent for his services. However, agent may agree to act gratuitously, without consideration to effect a contract on principal's behalf.

Agent generally drops out of the picture once the relationship between principal and third party under the contract are established. Agents task completes when he brings the principal and agent close to each other. Thus the rights and obligation contained in the contract are created between the principal and the third party belong to them solely. Agent generally has no rights or liabilities under that contract.

Agent may be of different kinds:

1. Agent may be a servant of his principal;
2. An independent contractor - estate agent;
3. Agent under contract of service with the principal may;
   (a) sales representatives;
   (b) convassers, and
   (c) commercial travellers, if they are under the control of their principals as to how they do their work.
4. Dress agency;
5. Private inquiry agent;
6. Secret agent;
7. Mechanical agent, washing or cleaning agent;
8. Factor, entrusted with possession of goods for purposes of selling them;
9. Broker, a kind of mercantile agent - no possession is given - only negotiates on behalf of principal.
10. Del Credere Agent - another kind of mercantile agent. Function is to effect a contract between principal and third party. Then agent drops out. No liability or obligation on his part under the contract.

Another important point is that it is not an ingredient for someone to have full contractual capacity in order to be agent. A minor can effectively bring about contractual selection between his principal and third party.

However, for a principal it is necessary to be competent to contract and of sound mind. However, a minor principal can also appoint an agent to make a contract on his behalf if the nature of the contract is such which he could validly make himself. Such a contract may be a contract to purchase necessaries.

A wife may also validly act as her husband's agent, provided she has been held out by the husband to others as having his authority to pledge his credit for necessaries or otherwise, by regularly paying his wife's debts to the creditors or traders. Husband will be liable for any contract made by her unless the traders has knowledge that the authority has been withdrawn, or husband has deserted her. In the later situation wife would not be considered as an agent of necessity.

As to obligation of the agent to his principal, agency agreement may contains the terms setting for the express obligations. If governs both the gratuitous as well as the paid agent. Some of the obligations may be summed up as follows:

1. To obey the lawful instructions of his principal;
2. To exercise due care and skill;
3. To act personally;
4. To act in good faith;
    - (a) not to take bribe or have secret profit.
    - (b) not to take bribe or have secret profit.
    - (c) no misuse of confidential information.
5. To account - to keep proper accounts of all transactions he enters into on his principal's behalf, and to keep agency money apart from his own.

With this brief statement about agent, his powers and obligations, let us see his penal responsibilities. In the modern world where countless commercial transactions are being carried out with the help of intermediaries or agents, it's role becomes very significant.

The term agent in this section is not confined to those persons who carry on the profession of agents. What the section 409 requires is that there must be an entrustment of property or dominion over the property in the course of commercial transaction, to a person as agent. Entrustment of property in the course of commercial transaction here means entrustment in the ordinary course of his duty or habitual occupation or profession or trade. Entrustment or dominion over the property must be to him in his capacity as agent. The ingredients of the section would satisfied if the person is an agent of another and that another person entrusts the property or dominion over property for achieving particular purpose for which the person has been appointed as agent. The entrustment of property must be in the course of his duty as agent. If the property has been entrusted or dominion given over, for some other purpose than for which an agent is under a duty to perfore, such entrustment or dominion over would be covered under this section.

The accused must be the complainant's agent. If he is not professionally the complainant's agent, the present section does not apply.[I] A person who is to share profits and losses in the business with another cannot be said as agent.[II] A commission agent who has not been entrusted with property or any dominion over property cannot be held guilty of breach of trust.[III] In order that the section may be applicable accused must be an agent at the time of entrustment of property. The section does not require that he should be still an agent at the

I. 1935 Mad WN 699.

II. ILR (1952) Hyd. 753.

III. 1937 (1) Cr. L.j. L.j. 411 (DB).

time of committing the breach of trust[I] or continue to be an agent at the time of breach of trust.

Director of a company is its agent. The phrase 'in the way of his business as agent' is not limited to persons who carry on profession of agency.[II] IN some respects, the directors are also the trustees.[III]

In Mohanty's case[IV] where an insurance agent, received some money from proper for making payment to L.I.C. and after depositing only a part thereof, kept the balance with himself, if was held that 'the offence was committed unless it was shown, that the balance money was paid back to the prosper.

'The President of co-operative society who was also an ex-office treasurer of the society was held to be an agent of society.[V]

In another case where a bank advanced loans to certain members of a co-operative society to be realised by the society and repaid to the bank, the secretary of the society who collected the amounts from the members for payment to the bank, was held to be the agent of bank.[VI]

Where the government appointed a transport company as carriers for whole year, a breach of trust

---

I. 1937 Cr. L.J. 877.

II. AIR 1962 SC 1821 (R.K. Dalmia).

III. A 1962 SC 1821.

IV. AIR 1967 Ori. 135 (B. Mohanty V. State).

V. 1968 Cr. L.J. (AP).

VI. 1969 Cr. L.J. 780 (DB).

committed by the company, it was held that offence under section 409 committed.[I]

An agent though bond to execute the lawful instruction of the principal but he is not under the direct control or supervision of the principal.[II]

In a case where the 'accused was authorised to lend his master's money and he lent it to himself without his master's permission, it was held that he was guilty of criminal breach of trust.'[III]

In Sultan Mahmud's[IV] case a lambardar collected money from landowners in discharge of their liability to government and lambardar converted that money into his own use, it was held that he was guilty for criminal breach of trust.

'The accused an agent, who was in a fiduciary capacity was bound to account for what he had received. He admitted the receipt of money in the letters he wrote to the petitioner and also agreed to return it. Inspite of a registered notice which was sent to him calling upon him to pay the amount, he did not pay the amount. It was held that a prima facie case in respect of offence under section 409 was made out'.[V]

A debtor who borrowed money from another, returns the money to his creditor by cheque. The debtor hands over the cheque to the creditor's agent to pay the cheque to his principal the creditor. Here the person who receives the cheque

---

I. 1967 Cr. L.J. 124.

II. 1955 (2) SCR 1035 (Chandi Prasad Singh).

III. 1933 MWN 256 (Ramnathan Chattiar V. Duraisamy Ayyanger).

IV. (1939) 20 Lah. 119.

V. 1982 Cr. L.J. 1913 (Deh.), (Jia Lal Sharma).

cannot be consider an agent of the debtor merely because to pass over the cheque to creditor his principal.

A retailer, inspite of an agreement between the government and him for the distribution of food grain through fair price shops, the retailer could not be regarded as agent of government in respect of the good grain received by him from government.[I]

'A person who is the manager of a firm cannot be held criminally liable for breach of trust where there is no personal entrustment of goods to him but to the firm in respect of which the offence was alleged to have been committed'.[II]

'Where a commission agent was employed to sell cotton and he acted according to the custom of the market which made him liable for the price of the cotton on demand being made, it was held he could not be prosecuted under this section for return of the cotton'.[III]

As the difference between agent and servant, supreme court[IV] has clearly laid down that the two are different from each other. A servant acts under the direct control and supervision of the master and is bound to conform to all reasonable orders given to him in the course of his work. But as earlier referred that though an agent is also bound to exercise lawful instruction of the principal but he is not under the direct control and supervision.

As to the distinction between agent and factor, 'a factor is an Agent, but he has got a listen for his commission on the

---

I. 1967 Cr. L.j. 1599 (Ghasi Ram).

II. (1930) 32 Cr. L.j. 149 (Guha SC).

III. (1943) N.L.j. 128 (Gangaram).

IV. AIR 1956 SC 149.

property entrusted to him for sale. The factor does not lose such right by reason of his acting under special instruction from his principal to sell the property at a particular price or to sell in the principal's name.[I]

Different kinds of agents as discussed earlier liable only when they are entrusted with property or any dominion over a property and violated the terms of agreement between them and their principals. Mere retention of money by an agent entrusted to him is not enough to make him liable unless it is proved that he retained the money with a view to misappropriate it. Similarly accounts have been wrongly kept by the agent would not amount to an offence unless misappropriation is proved.

Broker another kind of agent. He is a mere negotiator, and is not, as a general rule, entrusted with the possession of the goods, and therefore, has no such special property or lien. He acts only as a middleman and takes no possession. However, where money has been paid to share broker specially for the purchase of shares, but the broker neither purchases shares nor returns money, would be liable under this section 409 I.P.C.[II]

I. (1883), 25 Ch. D. 31 (38), Stres V. Biller.

II. 1957, Cr. L.j. 265.

PART B

"AGENT'S LIABILITY: ISLAMIC CRIMINAL LAW"

A person may lawfully employ another as his agent (وكيل) to represent him in dealing with third persons under the Islamic law. Prophet (peace be upon him) himself authorized persons to represent him (peace be upon him) in the distribution of things exchanging money and weighing goods, saving thing from spoiling. He also deputed persons to pay Sadaqat-al-Fitr, and to pay debts. He permitted others to give gifts to an agent of some people or to their intercessor. He also deputed to give something on his behalf without restricting the power of the agent how much to pay. Prophet (peace be upon him) also permitted that women may depute the ruler in the matter of marriage. A person authorized to represent another was permitted by him (peace be upon him) to lend something of what is in his custody for specific time. However, he prohibited the sales, if the agent sold something in illegal manner. Prophet (peace be upon him) also authorized person to manage the wakf affairs. He (peace be upon him) deputed someone to sacrifice Budn (camels for sacrifice). He (peace be upon him) also told his deputies to spend wealth or property as Allah directs you. He (peace be upon him) also deputed trustworthy persons as treasurer to the treasury.

Ahadith on Agency

Some of the Ahadith taken from Sahih al-Bukhari[1] may be

---

1. XXXVIII The Book of Representation or Authorization - The Translation of the Meaning of Sahih al-Bukhari, Arabic-English

referred below to show that the agency is permissible and legal under the Islamic Law:

وكـالة الشـريك الشـريك فـى الـقسمة وغيرهاـ وقد اشرك النبى صلى الله عليه وسلم عليا فى هديه، ثم امره بقسمتهاـ

"A partner can deputize for another while distributing things etc. No doubt, the prophet (peace be upon him) shard his Hadis (i.e., sacrificing animal) with Ali and then ordered Ali to distribute them."

حـدثـنـا قبيصة : حدثنا سفيان،عن ابن ابى نجيح، عن مجاهد، عن عبد الرحمن بن ابى ليلى عن على رضى الله عنه قال : امرنى رسول الله صلى الله عليه وسلم ان اتصدق بجلال البدن التى نحرت و بجلودهاـ

Narrated 'Ali (R.A.): Allah's Apostle (peace be upon him) ordered me to distribute the saddles and skins of the Budn which I had slaughtered.

حـدثـنـا عـمرو بن خالد: حدثنا الليث، عن يزيد، عن ابى الخير عن عـقبة بـن عـامـر رضى الله عنه: ان النبى صلى الله عليو وسلم اعطاه غـنـمـا يـقسمها على صحابته فبقى وتود فذكره للنبى صلى الله عليه وسلم فقال: ضح به انتـ

Narrated 'Uqba bin 'Amir (R.A.) that the Prophet (peace be upon him) had given him sheep to distribute among his companions and a male kids was left (after the distribution). When he informed the Prophet (peace be upon him) of it, he said (to him), "Offer it as a sacrifice on your behalf."

الـوكـالة فـى الـصـرف والـميـزان، وقـد وكل عمر وابن عمر فى الصرفـ

To deputize one in exchanging money and weighing goods. 'Umar Ibn 'Umar deputized (a person) in money exchanges.

(   ) Volume III - by Dr. Muhammad Muhsin Khan, Islamic University, Al-Madinah al-Munawwarah.

(وكالة) as legal, we will examine general principles governing it and conduct of the agent when amounts to breach of trust as envisaged by Islamic jurists.

"Vekyalet is for someone to put business of his on another, and to make him stand in his own place in respect of that business.

The person who appoints the other is called "mavekkil" and the person who stands in his place "Vekyl" - Agent, and that business is called "muvekkil beh." Art. (1449).[1]

A person may lawfully appoint another his agent, for the settlement on his behalf of every conduct which he might have lawfully concluded himself, such as a sale, marriage and so forth; because as an individual it is not possible to do or attend each ever matter personally. Sometimes a person is prevented from acting in his own person as result of some accident, sickness or the like. In business to attend every thing in person difficult. Obviously, someone may be employed to look after the business affairs on his behalf. He is therefore admitted of necessity, to appoint another person his agent so that he may expedite the business matters effectively.

"The essence of the appointment of an vekyl - (Agent) is the proposal and acceptance. If the process of proposal and acceptance is complete, the 'vekalat' (Agency) is a concluded contract. The acceptance may be express or may be inferred from the conduct of the Agent. But after the proposal the agent refuses it, the contract is not concluded. If the agent deals with the property after his refusal, the disposition by him of such a property is not valid. However, if a person who has no authority to deal with the property of another person and he sells it without permission and the owner later approves the sale, it would be considered that the person who disposed of property was the agent of the owner of

I. Mejelle page 239.

the property. Ratification by the owner makes the sale as valid and the sellers stands as his agent.

Conferring of the powers by the principal (موکل) upon his agent may be limited or unlimited. If the authority given dependent upon a condition to be fulfilled, powers are limited. For example where the agent is appointed to sell a gold watch and the owner gives a direction that it should be sold for Rs. 1000/-, then the power is limited by a condition. An agent cannot sale it less than Rs. 1000/-.

Sometimes appointment is made dependent on a time. For example, the owner says to his agent that property given possession over it to him is to be sold in the month of April. Then a April he becomes an agent. He can sale it in April and not before April because the power is limited by time.

Competency of Principal and Agent

It is a necessary condition that the person who appoints the agent should be a competent person capable to do the work for which the agent is appointed. If a madman appoints an agent, such appointment is not valid. Similarly, an infant incapable to understand the nature of the transaction appoints an agent, such appointment is not valid.

'An infant who has understanding even if his guardian gives permission, cannot appoint another vekyl for matters which are pure loss as regards himself, like a gift or giving also, but he can appoint another vekyl for matters, which are purely beneficial to him, like the acceptance of a gift or alms, even if he has not the permission of his guardian'.

However, if he is freed from restrain (me'zun) for trading, he can appoint another vekyl in matters which may be beneficial or the cause of loss, like selling and buying.

'If he is not, the appointment of the vekyl is a conclude contract subject to the permission of the guardian of the infant'.

As to the competency of the agent, the requirements are that the agent should be capable to have to reason and understanding (mumeyyiz). Age of puberty is not the requirement.

Therefore, an infect can be an agent if he has understanding capabilities. Further when he is released from restrain (me'zun). But rights under the contract do not affect him. These rights relate to the person who appoints him vekyl.

"Subject Matter in Respect of which Agent Appointed"

An agent may be appointed for doing and discharging of every duty related to the transaction (mu'amlat - معاملات), and for matters which he would be capable to do personally. An agent may be appointed for:

1. Selling or buying;
2. Letting or hiring;
3. Giving or taking a pledge;
4. For depositing or receiving a thing for safe keeping;
5. For making or receiving a gift;
6. For making a compromise;
7. For giving an acquittance;
8. For making an admission;
9. For bringing an action;
10. For claiming a right of pre-emption;
11. For claiming partition;
12. For paying paying and receiving debt; and
13. For the receipt of a thing.

However, appointment of an agent discharge the duties assigned to him in connection with the transaction is subject to the condition that it is necessary, the thing for which he is appointed, should be a certain and known thing.

Contract made by Agent

Contract made by an agent sometimes is incumbent upon the principal, and sometimes not. Under the following condition contract would be incumbent upon the principal otherwise contract would not be good:

a. In gift,

b. In loan,

c. On deposit (ودیعت),

d. On leading money,

e. On entering into a partnership,

f. In mudareba, and

g. In compromising a matter denied by the other side.

Under condition, where there is no provision in the contract that the contract would be incumbent on principal, or the agent contends himself with making it incumbent on himself, contract is good. In the following cases of:

a. Selling and buying,

b. Hiring, and

c. A compromise on the admission of the defendant making a contract made by agent incumbent on the principal does not render the contract invalid. The rights under such contract accrues the contracting party i.e., the vekyl - (agent). However, if it is made incumbent upon the principal, the rights under the contract concerns the principals, and agent (vekyl) in such a case is like a messenger (a person who makes the communication - (Rasul). If a messenger (Rasul) is sent, the rights under the contract affects the person who sends him and and not the messenger.

Trust

Property handed over by the principal to the agent, and when received and taken possession over on behalf of the principal is a deposit (Trust - امانت۔ودیعت). Article 1463 elaborates the law as follows:

> "Proper received, under his appointment as vekyl (agent) by a person, who is vekyl to sell to buy, or to pay or receive a debt, or to receive an existing specific thing is like a thing deposited for safe-keeping."

> Similarly, "property in the hands of a messenger for the performance of his message is also like a thing so deposited (ودیعت)."

Breach of Trust

If the property deposited with the agent either to sell, or buy or to pay or receive a debt on behalf of the principal, is destroyed without any fault, indifference or neglect on the part of the agent, he is not liable.

In case of the agent does not return the assigned property to the principal nor does the discharge his duties concerning it instead misappropriate it, he would be liable for breach of trust.

An agent cannot purchase for himself any specific article which he is directed to purchase for his principal. If a person employees another person as his agent to purchase for him some specific article, in that case agent is not entitled to purchase the article for himself; because this is a breach of trust reposed in him by his principal, and also because it is a dismissal of himself from his appointment which he is not empowered to do, unless in the presence of his principal.

If the agent purchase a thing different in nature from the price specified by his principal, the agent would not be liable. For example, when the principal has specified the price of the article and the agent purchases it for his own use for a price of a different species from that asked by the principal to purchase for him or that the principal not having specified the price, the agent purchases the article not in exchange of money, but for something estimatable by weight or measurement of capacity, the agent such situation would not be liable for breach of trust.

If the agent delegates his power to purchase to another agent, and the second agent purchases, the article in the absence of the primary agent; in all such cases the purchase is held to have been made on behalf of the agent himself, and not of his principal, because of the deviation from his principal's orders - if on the other hand, the secondary agent concludes the bargain in the presence of the primary agent, the purchase the wisdom and judgement of the primary agent is held (in consequence of his presence) to have exerted: and hence there is no deviation from the orders of his principle.

In cases of loss of money by the messenger to pay debt, if the messenger is of the debtor and the money returned to the creditor is lost while still in the hands of the messenger, before it is received by the creditor, in such a case loss would be considered of the debtor. But on the other hand if the money handed over to creditor's messenger and during transit is lost, then it would be considered a loss of the creditor. In both cases if there is no faults or negligent of either of the agents or messenger, they would not be liable.

If someone appoints persons as his agent together, one of them cannot act in the matter for which they are appointed vekyl (agent) i.e., one canot perform the vekyalat.

But if they are appointed agents in cases of:

a. vekyl for itigation, or

b. for returning a thing entrusted (امانت) for safe-keeping, or

c. for paying debts.

One alone cane carry out the vekyalat, there will be no breach of trust. In case if the agent has appointed another person vekyl especially for that either of the above noted work, whoever of them carries out the vekyalat, it is lawful. However, the law is that in matter in which a person has been appointed vekyl, he cannot appoint another person vekyl unless specific permission is obtained for this purpose from the principal. Violation would amount to breach of trust. If permission is given by the principal, then such as agent becomes the agent of the principal.

In cases when the vekyl (agent) buys thing of a different genus, not ordered by the principal, it is considered that the thing is bought by the vekyl (agent), for his own use. It has not been bought for the principal. It is not necessary to enumerate its qualities of that for which the vekyl is appointed to buy. The only requirement is that when the vekyalat is limited by a limitation or specification of an article, the vekyl (agent) must not go contrary to it. If the agent acts contrary, the property bought remains on his account, because of the fact that the act is violative of trust reposed in him.

A vekyl (agent) for sale, without limitations imposed on his powers to sale, can sell the property of his principal for a small or large sum, i.e., for the price which he has seen fit unless the principal has fixed the price. If he sells contrary to the price fixed by the principal, the sale is concluded contract, subject to the approval of his principal.

When the agent sells the property on his own accord for a less sum than that fixed by the principal, he would be liable for breach of trust.

Further the agent authorised by his principal to sell his property and the agent himself buys it, it is not good. Again a vekyl cannot sell the property of principal to persons, who are not allowed by law to give evidence on his behalf. But, it he sells for more than its value, the sale is good. Again if he is made vekyl by a general vekyalat, the principal has authorised to sell to anyone he likes, in that case, a sale by an agent to them for an equivalent price is permitted. In such a case it would not amount to breach of trust.

In case where the person who gives the order has money to receive from the person to whom he gives the order, or when there is money deposited (ودیعت) with him for safe keeping if he makes an order to pay his debt from it, the person ordered is compelled to pay the debt.

But in case the person who gives the order has said, "sell such a property of men and pay my debt," the person who receives the order, if he is a vekyl (agent) without pay, cannot be compelled.

And if he is a paid vekyl (agent), he is compelled to sell that property and pay the debt of the person who gives the order. Non-compliance would be breach of trust.

On the completion of the work for which the vekyl (agent) has been appointed, there is an end of the vekyalat, and the vekyl (agent) is naturally released from his vekyalat.

CHAPTER 5

PART A

"PARTNERSHIP: INDIAN CRIMINAL LAW"

Partnership Defined

Section 4 of the Partnership Act, 1932, defines partnership as:

> "Partnership is the relation between persons who have agreed to share the profits of a business carried on by all or any of them acting for all".

Inference which one draws from the definition is that there must be the following elements which are needed to establish a partnership:

1. A relationship between persons to carry on a business;
2. An agreement to create partnership;
3. Business to be carried on in common;
4. With a view to share the profits of the business; and
5. The business is to be carried on by all or any of them acting for all.

As to the term 'business', it has been explained by section 2 as:

> "business includes every trade, occupation and profession".

If the above definition is taken literally, it would create problem because every occupation cannot be called a 'business'. For example a landowner foes not carry on a business although the management of his estate and the collection of the rents may be his only occupation which keeps him to be extremely busy man.

Thus the term business must be considered in the practical sense which the men of business use it in their day to day business routines. If refers to all such activities which if successful would result in profit. In Coope V. Eyre,[I] it was observed that where certain persons jointly purchased wheat and oil with a view to divide and pay for it equally, they being not interested in profit or loss, were not partners.

If certain persons are co-owners of a land, a mere co-ownership, does not create a partnership although they make all possible efforts to develop the land for their mutual benefit. What is required here is the proof that they go further and carry on business with respect to it.

In Smith's[II] case James Lj, said that 'where members of society formed to purchase investment for their common benefit are not partners because there is nothing to be done by such societies that comes within the ordinary business, any more than what is done by the trustees of a marriage settlement who have large properties vested in them, and who have very extensive powers of disposing of investment, changing the investments, and selling them reinvesting in other investments, according to their discretion and judgement'.

Other illustrative cases of partnership may be:

I. IBI H 37; (1788) 2RR 706.

II. Smith V. Anderson (1880) 15 Ch D. 247 at 276.

Where the owners of a ship use it in the business of carriers of either the goods or the passenger They become the partners in business.

A partnership is constituted where two persons have agreed to produce a film and share the profits of hiring it out.[I]

If a society is constituted 'to speculate in investments with a view to make profit by selling and buying again securities whenever, in the opinion of the management, in turn of the market should make it advisable to do so, then no doubt a partnership would exist because that would be a business, i.e., a buying and selling of property with a view of profit as distinguished from jurist or common ownership.

To be precedise the term business has been used in the partnership Act, in a limited sense as to commercial and professional businesses, calling in which men hold themselves out as willing to sell goods or to provide skilled assistance or other service.

Another important elements is the agreement for creating partnership. Section 5 of the Partnership Act visages that a partnership is created by contract and not as a result of status by operation of law. For example joint family carrying on business, which does not arise as a result of contract rather than by status, operation of law, succession or inheritance.

In Minck's[II] case, it was held that a partnership may exist in a single business deal. Where two persons agreed to produce a film and share the profits of lending it on him, it would be sufficient to constitute a partnership.

I. Monek V. Roslan Lal Shorey, AIR 1931 Lah. 390.

II. Supra N.P.

Apart from business, another element is to carry on business in common. Section 4 of the Partnership Act envisages that the business may be carried on 'by all or any of them acting for all'. It may create the relation like principal and agent, but still they are partners. For example A carries on the business not only for himself but for others also.

Further the business must be carried on with a view of sharing of profits. Merely two or more persons carry on business jointly with a view of sharing of profits is not enough to make them partners, infect, division of profits is essential for the existence of partnership. Partner should have a right to share the profits.

As to rules for determining the existence of a partnership section 6 of the Indian Partnership Act provides two explanations the list of persons who might be interested in the profits of a business, such as, joint-tenants and tenant-in-common, those who share the gross-profit, and the receipt by a person of a sharfe of the profits, but they do not by such relation become partners. They may at best be called as holders of non-partnership interests.

Some of the other cases of receipt of a share of the profits may be, 'a payment of a debt by installments, a contract for the remuneration of a servant or agent, a widow or child of a deceased partner, a loan to a partnership and the sale of the good will of a business'. Such accruing profits do not itself determine the partnership or make them partners in the partnership firm.

To constitute a valid partnership as to maximum number forming the firm, we may have two different categories. In carrying on banking business there cannot be more than ten partners while in all other cases twenty is the maximum limits or partners forming the partnership.

For the formation of partnership it is necessary that a person must have the capacity to enter into a partnership. As to the form of agreement there are no requirement which have to be fulfilled. Minor and unsoundness of mind of a person are exceptions to the general rule for the formation of partnership.

Further the partnership must not be for an illegal purpose. It is also necessary that the number of partners should not exceed the limit laid by law.

Next important issue is the relation of partners to one another. It has been given in section 11 of Indian Partnership Act. According to this section the relations of partners to one another is governed wholly by the terms of the partnership agreement. This gives the partners the liberty to settle their mutual rights and duties by their own voluntary agreement.

The terms of the partnership agreement may be varied with the consent of all partners. Mutual trust and confidence among partners is an assential condition of their relations. Section 9 recognises this principle that the partners are bound to be just and faithful to each others. The statutory obligation thus created cannot be warded off by any agreement to the contrary.

Certain rights are given to every partner of a firm, e.g., as to capital and profits, and as to right to take part in the management of the partnership business though the agreement to these effects is absent between them.

The relation between partners results in certain duties e.g., to render true accounts and full information to each other, account to the firm for any benefit derived by him without the consent of the other partners from any transaction concerning the partnership, or from any use by him of the partnership property, name of business connection, account for profits from competing business, liability of a proper for misappropriation of property entrusted under section 27 of Indian Partnership Act, account for improper imployment of trust property for partnership purposes, etc.

"Breach of Trust"

From such relations and duties of the partners result the criminal liability also. Decision of R.K. Dalmia V. Delhi[I] Administration has now settled that section 405 and 406 are quite wide enough the include within their purview the case of a partner if it is proved that he was in fact entrusted by agreement with the partnership property or with dominion over property, and that he dishonestly misappropriated the property.

'A partner can be held liable for criminal breach of trust if entrustment of partnership property to him is proved or if it is shown that he was given authority to collect monies or property of the firm. Partner is liable only if entrustment in any form is proved'.[II]

Where a sum of money is entrusted to a partner specially for being deposited as a security for tenders, the partner is given exclusive dominion over that money that if he misappropriates the same, the offence under section 406 is prima facie made out against him.'[III]

'In the absence of a specific agreement entrusting a partner with a specific item of property, a partner cannot be

---

I. (1970) 3 SCR 765.

II. 1972 Cr. Lj. 945 (Guj).

III. Ibdi.

held to be guilty of an offence of criminal breach of trust even in respect of a partnership assets."[I]

'Where a person, who was working partner was in charge of the assets of the partnership and he, contrary to the provisions of the partnership agreement prohibiting him from withdrawing the meny for his personal use before the settlement of account at the end of the year, misappropriated certain amount, he was held guilty under section 406 Penal Code.'[II]

A partner in the absence of such a special agreemented cannot be convicted of criminal breach of trust.[III]

For an offence of criminal breach of trust, an entrustment of dominion over property is essential and in partnership there is no entrustment unless there is a special agreement'.[IV]

'Where a partner is given authority by other partners to collect money, he is entrusted with dominion over that property and if he dishonestly misappropriates it, he comes within section 405'.[V]

Where a partner has been authorised to withdraw from only up to Rs. 100/- at a time withdrawing Rs. 3000/- without consulting other partners and misappropriates the same. He will be liable under section 405.[VI]

I. 1968, Cr. Lj. 1074.

II. 1959, CR. L.j. 1302.

III. (1870) 3 SCR 765; 1980 Cr. L.j. 1030 (Cal).

IV. AIR 1965 SC 1433; 1970 SCC (Cri) 221.

V. AIR 1962 SC 1821 (RK Dalmia).

VI. 1954 Cr. Lj. 1202.

In Lok Nath V. Jagri Suri,[I] it was observed that like joint owner who cannot commit misappropriation of property which he holds jointly with other co-owners, the partner also cannot misappropriate partnership's property belonging to him and other co-partners.

In Delhi Prasad Bhagat's[II] case where a partner was asked to give account of the expenditure of money which he received, and had power to spend the money received, failed to make out the accounts satisfactorily, it was held that there was no dishonest conversion making him liable under section 406 Penal Code.

In Koorathalvar Chetty[III] it was observed: 'In the case of a charge of criminal breach of trust against a partner, the criminal court should not entertain the case if the prosecution is unable to prove clearly and beyond reasonable doubt that the accused has acted dishonestly and with a view to enrich himself clandestinely at the expense of those with whom he was working and with whom he was bound by fiduciary relationship.

'A partner cannot be held guilty of criminal breach of trust even in respect of partnership assets.'[IV] 'A partner not rendering account and withholding share of property of other partners is not liable under section 406 I.P.C.[V] In cases of disputes regarding the liabilities of the partners the court will not interfere under this section 406. The court has to be

---

I. 1982 Cr. Lj. 1328 (J&K).

II. Devi Prasad Bhagat V. Nagar Mull. (1901) 35 Cal. 1108.

III. (1920) MWN 346; 1921 Cr. Lj. 309.

IV. ILR (1969) Delhi 178.

V. AIR (1964) Raj. 267.

cautious and careful in proceeding against partners for charges of criminal breach of trust.

In Chiranji Lal V. Raja Ram Singh,[I] it was held that a partner received money on behalf of the partnership did not receive it in a fiduciary capacity. Consequently, where a partner alleged to have had with held the share of the profits of the partnership business said to be due to another partner, could not be prosecuted under this section.

'Where a partner holds property belonging to the partnership he holds it as one of the partners entitled to hold it and until dissolution and accounts it cannot be said that he holds the property in a fiduciary capacity. Unless the relationship of partnership imposes on one partner holding property fiduciary obligations, it cannot be said that the partner, if he holds property of the partnership with the consent of the others, has been entrusted with it, and that he is guilty of a fraud on his trust in not accounting to his co-partners for the property.[II]

In Jai Krishna (1950)[III] it was held that no criminal prosecution is sustainable against a partner for misappropriating partnership money.

Similarly, in State V. Gopal C. Poddar,[IV] 'The money due to the partnership was required to be deposited in bank in the name of the firm. A partner, however, deposited money in the name of a third party. It was held that there was no breach of trust as in the absence of a special agreement a

---

I. (1964) II Cr. L.j. 730.

II. Raghubir Singh (1966) Cr. L.j. 202.

III. 1950, Nag. 379; Shridher.

IV. 1978 Cr. L.j. 425 (Bom).

partner receiving money belonging to the partnership cannot be held to have been entrusted with dominion over partnership properties.'

A partner may be a working partner, not contributed money or capital, even does not share the losses, only shares the profits, his only contribution is his labour. It all depends upon the terms of agreement entered between different partners. In Devkinandan,[1] 'the accused was a working partner and manager of a partnership firm, was in charge of the assets of the partnership agreement he was debarred from making any with-drawals for personal use before the settlement of accounts at the end of the year. The accused misappropriated a certain amount belonging to the partnership and for this purpose he brought about false credit and debit entries in the books of accounts of the partnership showing that he had paid a certain amount to his financing partners. It was held that the accused was guilty of criminal breach of trust.'

To be precise to make a partner liable for breach of trust under section 405 and 406 of Indian Panel Code, following rules must be taken into consideration:

1. Mere dominion over property of a partner is not enough;
2. It must be established that his dominion was the result of entrustment;
3. To prove that dominion over the asserts or a particular asset of the partnership was by a special agreement between the partners, entrusted to the accused partner. In the absence of such a special agreement, no fiduciary relationship can be established and cannot

---

1. (1958) 60 Bom LR 1413; 1959 Cr. Lj. 1302.

be held to have been entrusted with dominion over partnership properties. In order to attract section 405 and 406 the entrustment must be alleged and proved. 'The fact that the partnership property belongs to the firm does not in any way indicate that any partner has entrusted his share to the other partners. Such entrustment cannot be read in the mere relationship of partners.'[1] A special agreement entrusting the dominion over the property and dishonest misappropriation make a partner liable under section 406, I.P.C.

---

1. Raja Kumar G.S.V. Subramaniam Poti 1979 Cr. L.j. 738.

PART B

"PARTNERSHIP: ISLAMIC CRIMINAL LAW"

Islam exhorts man to make efforts, do strive for earning his livelihood, and exert himself in production and exchange of useful goods. He may strive for the welfare in this life but subject to the condition that he should be consistently loyal to the Islamic way of life, individually and socially. The economic activities and the economic ends should all be in the direction to achieve Falah as has been visaged in Qur'ãn and to please the Lord (الله سبحان و تعالى).

Allah says,

قَدْ اَفْلَحَ مَنْ تَزَکّٰی۔
(سورة الا على ،آية: ١٤)

"They are sure to prosper who purify themselves and manage to grow (develop)". (87:14).

Islam is opposed to the materialistic approach but it does not mean that to achieve economic well being or to devote to productive efforts, in any way opposed by Islam. Material well being is an essential constituent of Falah.

Prophet (peace be upon him) once advised:

حدثنی ابو هريرة قال قال رسول الله صلى الله چليو وسلم قعوزوا بالله من الفقر والقلة والزلة وان تظلم او تظلم۔۔۔

(نسائی: كتاب الا ستعاذه۔باب الا ستعاذه من الزلة)

"Seek God's refuge from poverty, scarcity and ignominy."

To earn a livelihood is an obligation. However, when the man indulges in economic activities, he is required to safeguard his religion in belief and practice. Earnings should be rightful, by honest means and inconsonance with the religion. The Prophet (peace be upon him) has emphasized one's obligation to earn a livelihood:

عـن عبـداللـه قـال قـال رسـول الله صلى الله عليه وسلم، طلب كسب الحلال فريضة بعد الفريضة۔

(مشكوة: كتاب البيوع۔ باب الكسب وطلب الحلال مجوالة بيهقى: شعب الايمان)

"To strive to earn a livelihood through right means is an obligation after the main duty (prayer)".

Economic activities pursued in consonance with teaching of Islam, by proper means and for the proper ends are highly venerated and regarded as devout and poetic as devotional prayers. Trustworthiness and honesty should be the basic requirements of business transactions under Islamic concept.

Prophet (peace be upon him) once gave the incentive to the traders:

عـن ابـى سـعيـدن الـخـردى عن النبى صلى الله عليه وسلم قال: التاجر الصدوق الامين المسلم مع الشهداء يوم القيامة۔

(ابن ماجه: ابواب التجارات۔ باب الحث على المكاسب)

"The honest, trustful Muslim trader shall have his rise with Martyrs (on the Day of Judgement).

In the Holy Qur'ãn it has been repeatedly emphasised that all the natural resources have been created by Allah with a view to provide man unlimited possibilities of satisfying his wants and thus maintain his life in reasonable manner. Allah says:

وَلَقَدْ مَكَّنّٰكُمْ فِى الْاَرْضِ وَجَعَلْنَا لَكُمْ فِيْهَا مَعَايِشَ، قَلِيْلًا مَّاتَشْكُرُونَ۔ (سورة الا عراف، آية: ١٠)

"And We have given you (mankind) power in the earth and appointed for you there in a livelihood. Very little do you thank." (7:10).

هُوَالَّذِی جَعَلَ لَكُمُ الْاَرْضَ ذَلُولًا فَامْشُوا فِی مَنَاكِبِهَا وَكُلُوْا مِنْ رِّزْقِهٖ، وَاِلَيْهِ النُّشُورُ۔ (سورۃ الملك، آیة: ١٠)

"He it is Who has made earth subservient unto you, so walk in the paths thereof and eat of His providence". (67:15).

In another ayat Allah says:

وَجَعَلْنَا النَّهَارَ مَعَاشاً۔ (سورۃ النباء، آیة: ١١)

"And We have appointed the day for livelihood." (78:11)

Thus Islam exhorts a man to endeavour for earnings but within Islamic concept. Economic activities beyond and without limits laid sown by the religion would be demand to be contrary to the Islamic Fiqh. Economic activities are not separate from religion. With this brief statement we will examine the concept of partnership agreement are trusts, if so, does violation thereof amount to breach of trust of not?

Definition of Partnership (Shirkat -) شرکت

"Shirkat in its primitive sense, signifies the conjunction of two or more estates, in such a manner, that one of them is not distinguishable from the other. The term Shirkat, however, is extended to contracts, although 'here be no actual conjunction of estates, because a contract is the cause of such conjunction. In the language of the law it signifies the union of two or more persons in one concern." (Hedaya).

Partnership under Islamic law is lawful because in the time of the Prophet (peace be upon him) men were accustomed to have transactions in partnership, and the Prophet confirms their transactions.[1]

Kind of Partnership

In Mejelle, three Chapters, VI, VII and VIII are devoted to this subject. These Chapters are sub-divided into number of sub-sections. These sections defines the different kinds of partnerships and have elaborated the detail rules governing them. Similarly, in Hedaya also Book XIV - has been devoted explaining the Islamic concept of partnership and general principles governing it. According to Mejjelle following is the classification of partnership:

First, partnership by contract (شرکت عقد) shirkat-i-Aqd).

"Shirkat-i-Aqd is further sub-divided between 'Shirkat-i-Mufaveza, that is complete equality in all aspects, and 'Shirkat-i-Inan, without a condition for complete equality.

Again partnership whether Mufaveza or Inan is divided into 'Shirkat-i-Emwal (partnership in property), Shirkat-i-A'mal', (partnership for working together), and Shirkat-i-Vujuh, (partnership for many accounts).

Shirkat-i-A'mal, is sub-dived as: "Shirkqat-i-Ebdan", (partnership of persons - where labour is the capital), Shirkat-i-Sanai" (partnership of Art), and Shirket Taqabbul (partnership for undertaking).

Secondly, Mudarabe, (capital to be found by one, and labour and work by the other); and Thirdly, 'Muzara'a', and 'Mu'saqat.'

---

1. Ibid.

In Hedaya, a different approach has been adopted in explaining the different kinds of partnerships under the Islam. According to it, partnership may be divided between two kinds: First "Shirket-i-Milk', by right of property, and secondly, Shirkat-i-Aqd.

By right of property, Shirket-i-Milk, is divided as: (1) Optional, and (2) Compulsive.

Partnership by contract is classified as:

1. Shirket-i-Mofavizat, partnership by reciprocity, (earlier explained as complete equality in all respects);
2. Shirket-i-Inan, partnership in traffic (same as explained earlier - without a condition for complete equality);
3. Shirket-i-Sinnaie, (partnership in art); and Shirket-i-Woodjooh, partnership upon personal credit; and lastly Mazaribat.

The difference between Mejjelle and Hedaya explaining the classification of partnership is that in Hedaya, under Shirket-i-A'mal, only Shirket-i-Sannai has been discussed. There is no reference to two other kinds of partnership Shirket-i-Ebdan and Shirket-Taqabbul. Further Mudarabe, and Musaqat are not discussed in. We will briefly discuss these partnership and then will examine the concept of breach of trust in relation to partnership under the Shariah or Islamic law.

Partnership by Contract[I]

'Partnership by contract consists of an agreement for association, on the condition that the capital and its benefit be common two or more persons'. (Art. 1329).

I. Shirket-i-Aqd or partnership by contract, is effected by proposal and consent - that is, by one person saying to another, "I have made you my partner in such a property," and the other replying "I

The essence of partnership by contract is an offer and acceptance expressed or implied. For example, if one says to another "I am partner with you to trade with so many piastres". And the other also say "I have accepted". Those is a concluded agreement for partnership by an express offer and acceptance.

And, if one gives the other 1,000 piastres, and says, "you also put, 1000 piastres to this, and buy property" and the other do what he was told; by reason of there having been an implied acceptance, there is a concluded partnership by contract. (Art. 1330).

The gist of the 'partnership by contract' is that there should be a contract between the parties forming the association. Offer and acceptance by the partners are the basic requirements. Offer and acceptance may be either express or implied. Acquisition, arising from such a contract should be participated in by the both parties.

Further every kind of partnership by contract contains a contract of agency and condition for reason and discernment as followed in contract for agency are to be applied in partnerships as well. In other words partners should have reason and being of understanding, that is, Mumeyyiz, capable of knowing that by a sale rights of ownership are lost, and that by purchase they are acquired, and being able to distinguish from a small deceit, a deceit which it is clear has been an excessive deceit, like deceived five in ten. In brief a young person who can make such distinctions. In brief partnership should be competent to contract.

---

consent": and it is a condition of the contract that the concern respecting which it is a condition of the contract that the concern respecting which it is made be of such a nature as to admit of delegation in order that the acquisition arising from it may be participated in established - in order words, the acquisition may become equally the property of both. (HEDAYA, page 217).

It should also be made clear in the contract how the profit is to be divided among the partners. If it is not clear, doubtful or unknown to the partnership than such partnership would be fasid. It is a condition that the shares of the profit, to be divided between the shareholders, be known by division, like a half, or a third or a fourth.

If it is agreed that so many piastres, as a fixed amount, be given from the profit to one of the partners, the partnership is void (batil). (Art. 1337).

As regard the capital of the firm, it is a condition that the capital be some kind of silver or gold money. Brass coins which are currently in use are by custom considered to be silver or gold. It does not mean that the present currency notes cannot be used as a capital investment of the partners in the partnership firm. If there is a use and custom amongst the people to transact their business with gold and silver, which has not been coined, this also is regarded as gold and silver coins. If there is no such use and custom they are regarded as merchandise ('aruz). It is a condition that the capital be a thing, which is known and individually perceptible ('Ayn). A debt which will be received being on accounts of debts due from people, cannot be the capital of a partnership. And if the capital of one is corporeal property ('Ayn) and the capital of the other is a debt, again the partnership is not good.

'A contract of partnership in respect of property which is no considered gold and silver coins, like merchandise, and immovable property, cannot be good, that is to say, these things cannot be the capital of a partnership.

But when two persons wish in this way to make their property, which is not of the nature of gold and silver coin, the capital of partnership, each of them sells to the other the half of his property, and after they have become their common property, they can make a contract of partnership in respect of this property held in common between them.

Likewise, when two persons have mixed together properties, which they have of a kind which is misly,[1] like a quantity of wheat, which each of them have, after it has become 'Shirket-i-Mulk' between they can use as capital that mixed property and make a contract of partnership about it'. (Art. 1342).

If the partners enter into a contract of partnership, with an stipulation in the contract that there is to be a complete equality between the partners, and when they have introduced into the partnership their properties, which are to be the capital in the partnership, if their shares in the capital introduced by them and the profits are equal, there is a Shirket Mufaveza.

Similarly, where someone has died, and his sons use, as principal, the whole of the property left by their father, they can make a contract of 'Shirket-i-Mufaveza', upon the condition to buy and sell every kind of property, and to divide the profits equally between them. But the occurrence of partnership on the terms of complete equality on this way are rare.

And if there is a partnership by contract, without a condition for complete equally being made, it is a Shirket-i-Inan'. A partnership whether it be 'mufazefa' or 'Inan' is either a partnership in property (Shirket-i-Emwel), or a partnership for working together (Shirket A'mal), or it is a partnership for many accounts (Shirket-i-Vujuh).

I. Misly is a thing found in the Bazars and weekly markets, that is to say, a thign to be matched without any difference causing an increase in price. (Art. 145) Mejelle).

Work valued at its worth

'Work is constituted by the way in which it is done. In other words, work is valued by its value which is made known. And the work of one person can be more valuable than the work of another'.

For example - 'When it has been agreed, that the capital of two persons who are partners by a 'Shirket-i-Inan' are to be equal, and that the two of them are to work, if a condition is made to give a larger share of the profit to one, it is lawful. Because the one can be more skilful in business, and more able to work and useful'. (Art. 1345).

In Article 1346, responsibility for work is a kind of work has been elaborated. If someone puts a person who is a skilled artisan in shop, and makes him do work which he has accepted and undertaken; if they make a contract of partnership in skilled labour (shirket sannai), upon the terms, that they are to divide between them, the profit which shall be produced, that is to say, the payment, it is lawful. And the right of the owner of the ship to the half share is by reason of his having become responsible for the work alone, although included in this he takes also for the use of his shop. (Art. 1344-1346).

Further elaborating the point that the right to profit has come sometimes from property or work, so sometimes it arises in consequence of responsibility.

In Mudarebe, the partner who supplies the capital, by the property, and the party who supplies the labour, by the labour, becomes entitled to the profit.

And when one is the apprentice of a skilled workman, if he makes him do the work, which he has undertaken, for half pay, it is lawful.

And as the apprentice is entitled by his work to half the profit, i.e., half the pay taken from the owner of the work, so also by reason of his responsibility and undertaking his master, is entitled to the other half. (Art. 1347).

In cases where property, work and responsibility are absent, there is no right to share the profits. If one says to another, "Trade with you property and let the profits be shared between us," in such a case, no partnership is constituted, and he cannot take a share of the profit.

Division of Profits

Article 1349 deals with the division of profit. The right to profit is determined in accordance to the terms of the contract. The stipulation made part of the contract is alone to determine the shares of the partners. It is not according to the work done. Article further explains that even if the partner, who it was agreed should do that work, does not do the work, he is considered as if he had done the work. Where partners have stipulated that both should work, but only one works and the other, with or without any excuse, does not work, by reason of their being agents for one another, it would be considered as if he has done work. His work is presumed on the basis of performance of the other partner who had done the work and thus the profit in the way stipulated is divided between them.

Partnership by right of Property - optional and compulsive

In Hedaya, partnership by right of property (Shirket-i-Mulk) has been explained under two different heads - optional, or compulsive as - 'where two or more persons are proprietors of one thing; and it is of two different natures, optional and compulsive:- optional, where two persons make a joint purchase of one specific article; or where it is presented to them as a gift, and they accept of it; or where it is left to them, jointly, by bequest, and they accept of it; - or where they both obtain possession, by conquest, of one specific article in an enemy's country; or where they unite their respective properties in such away is that one is not distinguishable from the other (such as the mixture of wheat with wheat) - or where it may be difficult to distinguish them (as in a mixture of wheat with become united without their act, under such circumstances as render it difficult or impossible to distinguish between them; or: where two persons inherit one property. In this species of partnership, therefore, it is not lawful for one partner to perform any act with respect to the other's share, without his permission each being as a stranger with respect to the other's share. It is, however, lawful for either partner to sell his own share to the other partner, in all cases here stated:- and he may sell his share to others without his partner's consent; excepting only in cases of association or a mixture of property, for in both these instances one partner cannot lawfully sell the share of the other to a third person without his partner's permission.'

Liability of Partner for custody of partnership property

Partners are persons entrusted (EMIN - امین) the one by the other. The partnership property in the possession of each of them is like a thing entrusted - (Trust , - Article 762). (Art. 1350).

In Hedaya it has been stated that each partner holds the stock in the manner of a trust. The possession of each of two partners, by reciprocity or in traffic, over the partnership stock, is considered as the possession of a trust - (ودیعت), since each possesses the property with consent of the proprietor, for this reason, that he is to give something in lieu of it, in the same manner as where a person takes possession of a thing with a view to purchase it (not because it is a pledge, as in pawnage). The stock is therefore a deposit (Trust وديعت).

Either of the partners is at liberty to lodge his capital as a deposit (Trust - وديعت) with the other partner, as this is customary, and sometimes necessary, among merchants, or entrust it to the care of a manner, by Mozaribat - each of them is also at liberty to give his capital in the way of Mozaribat, because, as Mozaribat is subordinate to partnership either by reciprocity or in traffic, it follows that a contract of partnership comprehends Mozaribat.

When we consider the consequence of Mudarebe, the 'Mudarib' is a person entrusted (Emin). The capital in his hands is like property deposited for safe keeping (Vedia-Trustوديعت). And as regard his disposing of the capital, he is the agent (vekyl) of the owner of the capital. And if he makes a profit he is a partner in it. Mudarib can deposit the property of the partnership for safe-keeping and make it abide and pledge and take as pledge, and let and hire it.

In case of partnership by contract, if the property in hands of one of the partners is destroyed without fault or neglect, he is not responsible for the shar of his partner. In other words it would not be considered as breach of trust.

All the partners in the partnerships have right to deposit (Trust - وديعت) the partnership property for safe-keeping. Each of the partners may give the property for this purpose to another on the condition that all the profit comes to himself. He can hire a ship and a man to keep the partnership property but except so far as he has the leave of his partner, he cannot mix the partnership property with his own property. Such act of the partner would amount to breach of trust for which he would be accountable to the other partner. Further he cannot make a partnership with another. If he does, and the partnership property is lost, he is responsible for the share of his partner. Again such a case is covered by breach of trust.

Other cases of breach of trust by the partners may be:

In cases of right of partner to borrow and lend, if one of the partners makes loan of partnership property without the leave of partners, he would be liable for. But when he has such a consent of other partners and lends a loan to another from partners property there is no breach of trust.

Further one of the partners may borrow loan for the partnership, for the partnership, and if one has borrowed any amount of money, it becomes also the debt of his partners jointly.

In cases where each of partners leaves the business of the partnership to the discretion of the other, and says, "work according to your discretion" or, "Do what you like," each of them can perform the work which is the subject of their trade, so that each of them can pledge the partnership property, or take a pledge on behalf of the partnership, and can travel with the partnership property, and mix the partnership property with his own property, and can make a contract of partnership with another. However, the above referred conduct of the partner is subject to one condition that the use of partnership property should not be in such a way that the property is destroyed, such a partner would be liable and accountable and may be prosecuted for such damage or destruction caused to the property. Again for lending the partnership property or giving part of the partnership property to another there must be express leave or consent of all the partners. Doing act without such express, any damage caused to the property, makes liable for.

Acts done by one of the partners in violation of express prohibition would also amount to breach of trust. If a partner says to other partner, "Do not go to another country with the partners property," or "Do not sell on credit," and the other, while he is prohibited, does not obey, and goes to another country, or sells the property on credit, he is responsible for his partner's share in any loss which takes place.

The admission of a debt by one of the partners in a Shiket-i-Inan does not affect the other partner. If one of the partner admits that a debt has arisen, out of his own contract and transactions alone, he must bear the burden himself. In other words he must pay the whole of it.

In cases when the debt has arisen from transactions, carried out together with his partner, he must pay his half. If the debt is due in consequence of transactions carried out by his partner alone, nothing is necessary.

'Under Shiket-i-A'mal,' liability is based on the different principles. If the property is delivered to be worked upon is destroyed, or damaged, by the work of one of the partners, he becomes jointly liable with the other partner. The liability is determined among partners according to their respective responsibilities.

If they make a contract of partnership with a condition to accept and undertake on equal terms, the loss also is divided half to one and half to the other. And if they have made a contract of partnership to accept and undertake work by way of two thirds to one, and one third to the other, the liability of the partners is accordingly determined.

In case where partnership is constituted by way of Mudarebe, that is, on condition that the capital is to be found by one, and the labour and work by the other, the liability of Mudarib would be based on the nature of transaction - unlimited mudarebe, and limited mudarebe. For example, where the Mudarebe is not restricted to time, or place, or to one kind of trade, or by fixing the person from whom he is to buy and to whom he is to sell, it is unlimited Mudarebe. But if it is reverse, restrictions have been imposed, then it would be a restricted Mudarebe. Violation of such restrictions would amount to breach of trust, as the Mudarib, according to Article 1413 is person entrusted (Emin). The capital, as said earlier, in the hands is like a property deposited for safe keeping (ودیعت).

In according to the terms of contract of Mudarebe, the Mudarib is authorised to do all necessary things arising out of Mudarebe. He can buy and sell property to make gain. But if he buys property at an excessive loss, he would he liable for. Property at an excessive loss, he would be liable for. Property shall be demand to have bought for himself and not for Mudarebe's account. He can deposit the property of the partnership for safe-keeping but not so as to cause destruction or damage. If his acts result in destruction of Mudarebe, he would be liable. In brief, in a Mudarebe limited by restrictions, whatever may be the restriction and condition made by the owner of the capital, the Mudarib, must respect it. Acts contrary to such restriction's imposed would, as the Mudarib is a person entrusted (Emin) and the property deposited (ودیعت) for safe keeping, create liability for breach of trust.

To precise the discussion, under Islamic law different kinds of partnership are there, and the partners are (Emin), the partnership property a trust - deposit (ودیعت), liability of the partners would be based upon the nature and kind of each partnership and effect of violation of conditions governing such partnerships.

CHAPTER 6

PART A

"PRODECURE: INDIAN CRIMINAL LAW"

"Cognizance"

Section 2 (c) Criminal Procedure Code explains the cognizable offence as offence for which, and a cognizable case means case in which, a police officer may, in accordance with the First Schedule or under any other law for the time being in force, arrest without warrant. As such word cognizance has not been defined in the Criminal Procedure Code, 1973. In fact taking cognizance is a mental act. It is also judicial act.

A magistrate is said to have taken cognizance of an offence when he applied his mind to the contents of the petition with the purpose of proceeding in a particular way. When the magistrate has come to the conclusion that there is a case to be inquired into. (Shivangowda V. Veerappa).[I]

According to First Schedule, Criminal Procedure Code, criminal breach of trust under section 406, 408 and 409, is a cognizable offence triable by the magistrate of the first class.

"Magistrate to take cognizance"

First class magistrate under section 190 may take the cognizance of the offence under the following conditions:

I. AIR 1964, Mys. 129.

(a) upon receiving a complaint of facts which constitute such offence;

(b) upon a police report on such facts;

(c) upon information received from any person than a police officer, or upon his own knowledge, that such offence has been committed.

Thus section 190 Criminal Procedure Code envisages three contingencies upon which magistrate takes cognizance of an[I] offence. In R.R. Chari V. State of U.P. Supreme Court observed that the first contingency apparently is in respect of non-cognizable offences that is, on receiving relates to where the magistrate receives the police report on completion of police investigation, and the third is where the magistrate himself takes notice of an offence and issues the process.

In a case where a complaint is pending before a magistrate, he may either after conducting a judicial enquiry under section 202 Criminal Procedure Code or even without holding such an inquiry, merely by scrutinizing the case diary and other relevant material before him may place the accused on trial. In such a situation he may adopt either of the following two courses:

1. he may call for charge-sheet from the police and take cognizance under section 190 (1) (b); or

2. he may take cognizance on the complaint under section 190 (1) (a).

Where a 'Magistrate takes cognizance on the ground of the charge-sheet, he may say that no further action is necessary on the complaint petition and vice-versa.'[II]

I. AIR 1951 SC. 207: (1951) SCR 612.

II. AIR 1558 Orissa II.

For taking cognizance under clause (a) on a complaint prior investigation is not necessary.

Taking cognizance of an offence does not require any formal action or action of any kind. It may happen as soon as the magistrate applies his mind to the suspected commission of an offence.[I]

Word 'may' in section 190 should not be considered as must because it is discretionary with the magistrate to take cognizance of an offence alleged to have been committed referred in the complaint. He is not bound to take cognizance of an offence merely because there is a complaint petition alleging the commission of an offence. But there may be circumstances when magistrate may exercise his discretion and take cognizance of a cognizable offence. If he uses his discretion he has to proceed in accordance to the provision under Chapter XV, Criminal Procedure Code.

Magistrate may take cognizance of an offence at any stage. However, the examination of the complainant, conducting of enquiry under section 202 and section 156 (3), are all aimed with a view to assist the magistrate to form an opinion whether cognizance should be taken or not. Actually when the cognizance is to be taken or not all depends upon the facts and circumstances of the case.

Magistrate under section 190 (1) has been empowered to take cognizance of an offence upon a police report of facts of the case. A magistrate may also take cognizance of an offence under section 190 (1) (b), even on receiving a negative report from the police. But the magistrate must act in a judicial manner. Conducting of enquiry and trial must be fair to the accused.

I. AIR 1965 Mad. 349.

Once the magistrate takes cognizance of the offence, it is his duty to find out who the offenders are. Summoning of the additional accused is part of the proceedings initiated by his taking cognizance of an offence. In fact the cognizance of an offence is not the cognizance of offenders.[1]

Section 201, Criminal Procedure Code lays down the procedure where the magistrate is not competent to take cognizance of the case. In a case where a complaint has been made to the magistrate who is not competent to take cognizance of the offence, two courses are open to him, that is, he shall -

(a) If the complaint is in writing, return it for prosecution to the proper court with an endorsement to that effect;

(b) If the complaint is not in writing, direct the complainant to the proper court.

"Magistrate to take Cognizance of Offences Committed by Public Servants"

In cases of public servant liable for breach of trust under section 409, a different procedure has been laid in section 197 of the Criminal Procedure Code. When any person who is a public servant not removable from his office save by or with the sanction of the government is accused of any offence alleged to have been committed by him while acting or purporting to act in the discharge of his official duty, no court shall take cognizance of such offence except with the previous sanction.

(a) 'in the case of a person who is employed or, as the case may, was at the time of commission of the alleged

---

1. AIR 1967 SC. 1167.

offence employed, in connection with the affairs of the union, of the central government.'

(b) in the case of a person who is employed or, as the case may be, was at the time of commission of the alleged offence employed, in connection with the affairs of a state, of the state government.

Some exception under clause (2) has been extended to any member of Armed Forces of the Union acting in the discharge of his official duty. No magistrate may take cognificance of an offence unless previous sanction of the central government is obtained.

In Ram Kishan's[I] case it was held that the conviction of a public servant under section 409 without prior obtaining sanction, from proper authority would be illegal. His trial under such conditions would be considered a nullity in law.

Ommission to take sanction necessary for prosecution from a proper authority is not an irregularity but an error fatal to the case and is incurable.

The object of the present section 197 Criminal Procedure Code is to give protection to responsible public servants against possible vexatious criminal proceedings while acting under colour of their office. However, this exception does not apply to all public servants. Its application is restricted to offences committed by public servants of higher ranks. Section 197 provides protection to certain classes of public servants against vexatious and harassing proceedings.[II]

I. 1982 Cr. L.j. (NOC) 21 (P & H).

II. Shilal V. Manmath Kumar Misra, AIR 1960 Raj. 173.

Discussing the significance and efficacy of provision dealing with sanction necessary for prosecution in Indu Bhushan Chatterjee B. State, his Lordship observed:[I]

"The provision of sanction is a most salutary safeguard. The sanctioning authority is placed somewhat in the position of a sential at the door of the criminal courts in order that no irresponsible or malicious prosecution can pass the portals of the court of justice. It is essential that persons charged with the responsible duty of granting sanction which is a duty of deciding whether or not the credit and reputation of another citizen should be put in peril by means of criminal prosecution, should bring to the discharge of their duty a sense of responsibility and the industry required to examine the relevant material".

Sanction authority should consider all circumstances and evidence before it, and to give due thought to them before approving the sanction for prosecution.

Further the act complained should be within the purview of the official duty of the accused. Mere fact that a person is a public servant is not sufficient to avoid the protection given under section 197 Criminal Procedure Code.[II]

'If the acts complained of are so integrally connected with the duties attaching to the office as to be inseparable from them, then sanction under section 197 (1) will be necessary, but if there was no necessary connection between them and the performance of those duties, the official status furnishing only the occasion or opportunity for the acts, then no sanction will be required.[III]

I. AIR 1955, Cal. 430: 1958 Cr. L.j. 1169.

II. Mukand Singh V. Vishnu Prasad, 1956, Alj. 337.

III. AIR 1955 Sc. 309, Vaidya Nath Ayyar V. State of Kerala, AIR 1961, Ker. 175; 1961 Ker. L.j. 52.

Illustrative cases in which to obtain sanction prior to prosecution is necessary may be noted below:

In Amrik Singh V. State of Pepsu,[I] a public servant, whose duty included the disbursement of wages to workmen, drew the amount from the treasury, but falsely entered the name of a fictitious person in the acquittance roll and utilised the amount for himself, their lordship of the supreme court held that sanction for the prosecution against him for an offence under section 409'. Their lordship observed as follows:

"The result of the authorities may thus be summed up: It is not every offence committed by a public servant that requires sanction for prosecution under section 197 91) Criminal Prodecure Code, nor even every act done by him while he is actually engated in the performance of his official duties; but if the act complained off is directly concerned with his official duties so that if questioned, it could be claimed to have been done by virtue of the office, then sanction would be necessary; and that would be so, irrespective of whether it was, in fact, a proper discharge of his duties, because that would really be a matter of defence on the merits which would have to be investigated at the trial, and could not arise at the stage of the grant of sanction, which must precede the institution of the prosecution."

In another case a Famine Relief Supervisors[II] were charged for dishonestly misappropriating government money entrusted to them. It was held that sanction for their prosecution was necessary.

Where the President of a Municipality, a public servant,

I. A 1955 SC 309 (313).

II. 1973 Cr. L.j. 1447 (1450) Raj.

committed criminal breach of trust, sanction for his prosecution under section 409 was held necessary.[I]

if it is established that the offence under section 409 was committed in the discharge of official duty by a public servant, prior sanction for his prosecution becomes necesarry.[II]

Where the breach of trust by a public servant has no connection with the performance of his official duty, no sanction for prosecution under section 409 Criminal Procedure Code is needed.[III]

In the following cases of embezzlement or misappropriation by the public servants, sanction for prosecution was not required:

In Saha SB V. Kochar MS,[IV] a public servant was charged for the offence of conversion of goods and dishonest appropriation sanction of prosecution was not required.

Similarly a Sub-Postmaster[V] was accused of embezzlement of funds entrusted to him by various depositors for credit into their saving bank accounts, prior sanction for prosecution was not held necessary because in the commission of offence he could not be said acting in the performance of his official duty. But in fact performed acts in direct opposition of his duty.

In Gurushidayya Shanti Vivayya,[VI] an officiating village official Kulkarni collected land revenue. He instead of

---

I. A 1961 Gj. 57 (59, 61): 1961 (1) Cr. L.j. 499.

II. A 1950 Raj. 51 (53).

III. A 1967 SC. 1590.

IV. 1979 Cr. L.j. 1367 (SC).

V. Manzur Ali, (1939) 20 Lah. 227 Sannaya (1941) Mad. 258.

VI. (1938) 40 Bom. LR 1286.

depositing the collected money in the government treasury converted that in his own use. He was charged under section 409 without obtaining the sanction for prosecution under section 409 Criminal Procedure Code. It was held 'that the offence was not committed by the accused while acting or purporting to act in the discharge of his official duty and therefore no sanction of the state government under section 197 of Criminal Procedure Code was necessary'.

Contents of section 197 Criminal Procedure Code 1973 and old section of 197, under Criminal Procedure Code 1898 are the same hence all old cases similar in nature applies under the present section also.

In brief the discussion may be summed in the light of supreme court observation as: 'Whether sanction is necessary to prosecute a public servant on a charge of criminal misappropriation, will depend on whether the acts complained of hinge on his duties as a public servant. If they do, then sanction is requisite. But if they are unconnected with such duties then no sanction is necessary'.[I]

"Arrest with Warrant"

Though the offence under section 406, and 408 is cognizable in which case a police officer may arrest a person without warrant, but for breach of trust a warrant of arrest is to be issue by the magistrate. A police officer, like as in non-cognizable offence, has no authority to arrest without warrant.

Under section 41 Criminal Procedure Code any police officer has been authorised, without an order from a magistrate and without a warrant, any arrest any person who has been

I. Supra N.P.

concerned in any cognizable offence or against whom a reasonable complaint has been made.

Whereas in non-cognizable cases under section 155 Criminal Procedure Code when information is given to an officer incharge of a police station of the commission within the limit of such station of a cognizable offence, he shall enter or cause to be entered the substance of the information in a book to be kept by such officer in such form as the state government may prescribe in this behalf, and refer the information to the magistrate. No police officer shall investigate a non-cognizable case without the order of a magistrate having power to try such case or commit the case for trial. On receiving order from the magistrate such police officer would arrest the accused without the warrant for arrest. The magistrate has to apply his judicial mind before issuing the warrant of arrest. Later case is applicable in cases of criminal breach of trust.

A person was arrested at Bangalore by the Police Sub-Inspector of Tiruvattiyar (Madras Province) for an offence under section 406 Indian Penal Code committed within the jurisdiction of the magistrate of Saidapat (Madras Province). He was produced before the sub-magistrate of Saidapat and released on ball. He then went back to Bangalore. On summons being taken for his appearance he appeared on his own accord before the court and pleaded that his arrest at Bangalore was illegal and the court had no jurisdiction to try him for the offence under this section. It was held that the illegality of the original arrest cannot affect the jurisdiction of the court to inquire into the offence committed within its jurisdiction.[1]

I. A 1941 Mad. 181 (181) : 42 Cr. L.j. 320.

Offence under section 409 Criminal Procedure Code are also cognizable but arrest without warrant cannot be made. A magistrate on receiving the complaint against the accused of an offence if after consideration of the facts is of the opinion that there is no ground for proceeding, may dismiss the complaint under section 203 of the Criminal Procedure Code.[1] However, if there are sufficient grounds to proceed with the case, the magistrate may issue the warrant for arresting the accused. It is discretionary with the magistrate not to issue warrant, instead issue summons for the appearance of the accused under section 409 Indian Penal Code. But an accused cannot be arrested for an offence under section 409 Indian Penal Code, by a police officer, without the warrant of arrest.

"Offence non-bailable"

In the first schedule, column five, Criminal Procedure Code, criminal breach of trust has been shown as an offence which is not bailable. Chapter 33 contains the section which provide for bail. These sections contempletes and provides for two kinds of security -

(a) Simple recognizance of the principal; and

(b) Security with sureties. In vernacular the first is known as 'muchalka' while latter is called 'Zmanat'.

Bail is aimed to set the accused at liberty from his arrest and imprisonment on receiving security for his appearance on a day and at a certain place. Such security is known as bail. Under such security a person arrested or imprisoned is delivered into the hands of those who bind themselves for accused appearance on the due date and place as required. The purpose of the bail is to protect the accused from

---

1. (1887) ILR 9 All 666 (671).

imprisonment and also secure from the fear of escape of the accused.

In other words bail means "the setting at liberty of a person arrested upon other becoming sureties by recognizance for his appearance on a day and at a place assigned, he also entering into his own recognizance. The party accused is delivered or bailed by law to be in their custody, they may, if they will surrender him to the court before the date fixed and thus free themselves from further responsibility. The word bail is properly applicable to second kind of security and that is the meaning which has been attached to the word in the practice and procedure of the courts."[I]

The dictionary meaning of the word bail: "to set free or liberate a person arrested or imprisoned on taking security for his appearance." In fact it is a release from restrains with a view to save a man from being in custody during trial, before the conviction, where there is a reasonable doubt as to the allegations made against the accused.

Criminal breach of trust is a non-bailable offence, where the bail cannot be claimed as a matter or right but section 437 lays down certain conditions keeping in view of them the accused may be released on bail. When any person accused of or suspected of the commission of any non-bailable offence is arrested or detained brought before a court, other than the High Court or Court of Session, he may be released on bail. An accused cannot be refused bail mostly on the ground that he may be required during investigation for being identified by witnesses.

If the court at any stage of the investigation, inquiry or trial, as the case may be, that there are not reasonable grounds

---

I. 15 C.W.N. 736: 12 Cr. L.j. 358.

for believing that the accused has committed a non-bailable offence, but there are sufficient grounds for further inquiry into his guilt, the accused shall, pending such inquiry, be released on bail, or, at the discretion of such officer or court, on the execution by him of a bond without sureties for his appearance.

A court releasing any person on bail under sub-section (1), or sub-section (2) of section 437 Criminal Procedure Code shall record in writing his or its reasons for so doing.

It in any case triable by magistrate, the trial of a person accused of any non-bailable offence is not concluded within a period of sixty days from the first date fixed for taking evidence in the case, such person shall, if he is in custody, during the whole of the said period, be released on bail to the satisfaction of the magistrate, unless for reasons to be recorded in writing, the magistrate otherwise directs. (Clause (6), section 437 Criminal Procedure Code).

Further in clause (7) of section 437 Criminal Procedure Code it has been provided that if at any time after the conclusion of the trial of a person accused of a non-bailable offence and before judgement is delivered, the court is of opinion that there are reasonable grounds for believing that the accused is not guilty of any such offence, it shall release the accused, if he is in custody, on the execution, by him of a bond without sureties for his appearance to hear judgement delivered.

The court also takes into consideration the following matters in non-bailable cases in granting the bail:

1. Whether or not there is reasonable ground for believing that the accused has committed the offence,

2. The nature of accusation and the gravity of the charge,

3. The severity of punishment which the conviction will entail,
4. The dangers or like hood of the accused absconding if he is released on bail,
5. The character, means, behaviour and standing of the accused,
6. The danger or likelihood of the alleged offence being continued or repeated.
7. The danger of prosecution witnesses being tempered with or preparation of false defence.
8. The accused has already been in jail for several months.
9. The old age and sex of the accused.
10. The state and health of the accused.
11. The social status or his position which an accused person occupies in relation to other members of his family.
12. The severity of the punishment which the conviction will entail.
13. The nature of evidence in support of the accusation.
14. The opportunity to the applicant for preparation of his defence and access to his counsel.

These are some of the factors which the court takes into consideration for granting the bail in non-bailable cases. But these considerations cannot be claimed as exhaustive. There may be other consideration which may be weighed by the court before granting the bail. All depends upon the facts and circumstances of the case.

The object of bail is to protect the interest of the administration of justice and to prevent its being hampered in any manner. A bail granted may be concealed also and the accused be recommitted to fail if the circumstances in the opinion of the court so demand.

Under section 438, Criminal Procedure Code when a person on reasonable believe that he may be arrested on an accusation of having committed a non-bailable offence, he may apply to the High Court or the court of session for a direction; and that court may, if it thinks fit, direct that in the event of such arrest, he shall be released on bail.

The direction may include such conditions in the light of the facts of the particular case as the court may think fit -

(a) That the person shall make himself available for interrogation by a police officer as and when required;

(b) That the person shall not, directly or indirectly, make any inducement, threat or promise to any person acquainted with the facts of the case so as to dissuade him from disclosing such facts to the court or to any police officer.

(c) That the person shall not leave India without the previous permission of the court.

(d) Such other conditions as may be imposed under sub-section (3) of section 437, as if the bail were granted under that section.

If the magistrate taking cognizance of non-bailable offence decides that a warrant should issue in the first instance against that person, he shall issue a bailable warrant in conformity with the direction of the court under sub-section (1).

Section 439 Criminal Procedure Code gives special powers to the High Court or court of session regarding bail. Under this section any condition imposed by a magistrate when releasing any person on bail may be set aside or modified. A High Court or court of session may direct that any person who has been released on bail under this chapter be arrested and commit him to custody. Section also lays a limitation with a view to make it more difficult for persons arrested of grave offences to get released on bail by an expert order, and be in position to hamper investigation. No court shall grant bail except after giving notice in writing of the application to the public prosecutor. In the absence of such a notice the reasons for not giving such notice are to be recorded in writing.

In brief the grant of bail in non-bailable offences is discretionary, but the discretion is a judicial one and must be exercised in accordance with the well established principles.[I] 'It may be stated that the object of the detention of the accused person during trial is not punitive; it is merely to secure his appearance to abide and serve out the sentence to be imposed by the court and, except where a statutory provision specifically lays down, the principal consideration to weigh with the court in the exercise of its discretion in ganting or refusing bail is the probability of the accused appearing to stand the trial and not his supposed guilt or innocence'.[II]

"Compounding of Offences"

Offences under section 406 and 408 of the Indian Penal Code are compoundable. Section 320, Criminal Procedure

---

I. Emperor V. Abhai R.J. Kumar, 1939 O.W.N. 791: 1939 A.W.R. 144:40 Cr. L.j. 841: AIR 1940, Oudh 8.

II. Krishnan Singh V. Punjab State - AIR 1960 Punj. 307.

Code lays the law relating to offence committed under the above referred section 406 and 408. Clause (2) section 320 Criminal Procedure Code reads as:

The offences punishable under the sections of the Indian Penal Code (45 of 1860), specified in the first two columns of the Table next following may, with the permission of the court before which any prosecution for such offence is pending, be commanded by the persons mentioned in the third column of that Table.' Table is noted below:

I	II	III
Offence	Section of Indian Penal Code	Persons by whom offence maybe compounded
- Criminal breach of trust, where the value of the property does not exceed two hundred and fifty rupees.	406	The owner of the property in respect of which the breach of trust has been committed.
- Criminal breach of trust by a clerk or servant, where the value of the property does not exceed two hundred and fifty rupees.	408	Ditto.

Table above referred shows that the offences under sections 406 and 408 are compoundable subject to three conditions.

Firstly, Prosecution for such offences may be compounded where the value of the property which is the subject matter of breach of trust does not exceed to hundred and fifty rupees;

Secondly, Prosecution for such offences may be compounded with the permission of the court before which the prosecution is pending; and

Thirdly, Prosecution is compoundable by persons referred in the third column of the Table, and by non-else. Here the person referred in the third column is the owner of the property in respect of which the breach of trust has been committed.

Further a case which is legally compoundable can be compromised even where the case has been sent by the police. A compromise petition, after it is filed, cannot be taken back by the parties. A case can be compounded at any stage before the judgement is pronounced. It can even by compromised when revision is pending. The High Court has jurisdiction to allow the parties to compromise the dispute. It is not necessary that proposal for compromise the dispute. It is not necessary that proposal for compromise should be initiated before the lower court. In Kumaraswami V. Kuppuswami,[I] it was held that 'a case cannot be compromised without the permission of the court if the law so requires'. Where the allegations related to matters of serious public interest, require thorough investigation and trial, the order sanctioning compromise can be set aside.[II] Once in a legally compoundable case a compromise has been submitted, the court should order the acquittal of the accused.

I. 1941, Mad. 685.

II. Provincial Govt. V. Bipin Singh, AIR 1945 Nag. 104.

When an offence is compoundable under section 320, Criminal Procedure Code, the abetment of such an offence or an attempt to commit such offence (when such attempt it itself an offence) may be compounded in the like manner. (Clause 3).

In cases when the person who would otherwise be competent to compound an offence under this section is dead, the legal representative, as defined in the Code of Civil Procedure, 1908, of such person may, with the consent of the court, compound such offence. (Clause 4 (b).

Where the accused has been committed for trial or when he has been convicted and an appeal is pending, ho composition for the offence shall be allowed without the leave of the court to which he is committed; or, as the case may be, before which the appeal is to be heard. (Clause 5).

Under Clause 6, section 320 Criminal Procedure Code a High Court or court of session acting in the exercise of its powers of revision under section 401 may allow any person to compound any offence which such person is competent to compound.

Again under this section an accused is not competent to compromise if by reason of a previous conviction, he is liable either to enhanced punishment or to a punishment of a different kind for such offence. (Clause 7).

Lately under Clause 8, of section 320 Criminal Procedure Code, compromise of an offence shall have the effect of an acquittal of the accused with whom the offence has been compounded.

However, offences committed under section 409 of the Indian Penal Code cannot be compounded. Where public servant is an accused for the committing of the criminal breach of trust, there is no law allowing any compromise. Offence in such a case is not compoundable.

"Civil Liability"

It is significant that when dealing with cases of criminal breach of trust the difference between civil and criminal liability must be kept in mind because of the fact that every breach of trust is not criminal. An act done may be intentional without being dishonest or apparently may appear to be dishonest without in fact being so. The general tendency is that the aggrieved party seeks speedy remedies by recourse to criminal proceedings. Results under criminal law is speedier in comparison to civil remedies. In such circumstances it is the responsibility of the courts to move slowly with cautious attitude. It is the mental element of dishonest intention accompanied with the act of misappropriation which constitutes the offence of criminal breach of trust. Whereas the same act done without a dishonest intention would be a civil wrong or tort rendering a person liable under the civil laws.

'Every offence of criminal breach of trust involves a civil wrong in respect of which the complainant may seek redress in a civil court, but every breach of trust in the absence of the requisite means rea is not criminal.'[I]

However, merely on this ground that a civil remedy for breach of trust is available a complaint for criminal breach of trust cannot be refused a fail trial.[II]

'Where there is no dishonet intention but only an illegal demand no criminal breach of trust is committed, and the

---

I. (1951) 52 Cr. L.j. 1178 (1182) Lah.

II. 1980 BLJR 145.

remedy of the aggrieved person is only on the civil side. A case of non-payment of dues demanded at a higher rate is merely a breach of contract.[I] If a banker dishonours depositor's demand, he has got his remedy by way of damages. Where there is no entrustment in a fiduciary capacity the remedy of the aggrieved party is only on the civil side.[II] In another case where a dispute is in the nature of accounting, the proper remedy is a civil suit and not a complaint for breach of trust.[III]

As to pending civil suits between the parties whether criminal proceeding by stayed till the civil court decides the issue? It has been held in different cases that pending civil suits, criminal proceedings cannot be stayed as the dispute in a civil suit would be between the complainant and the accused, while the criminal case would be one between the crown and the accused.[IV] In practice use of criminal courts to litigate civil claims has been condemned and discouraged.

"Investigation"

Chapter XII containing section 154 to 176 Criminal Procedure Code is relevant which deals with the information to the police and their powers to investigation. Section 154 relates to the recording to the 'First Information Report', and

---

I. 1980 BLJR 145.

II. (1926) 27 Cr. L.j. 949 (2) (950) Punj.

III. (1951) ILR 3 Assam. 63 (67) DB.

IV. 1980 All Lj. (NOC) 84; Pannalal (1943) All 27.

(Contract for supply of machines - contract rescinded but case under paid as part - price not refunded - it is not a Prosecution under section 406 queshed). (1978 45 Cut LT 338. (Religious endowment - Accused managing affairs of two them to the uses of the other diety - No Criminal liability (Refusal of the mortagee to return little deeds remediable 405 or section 415) 1972 All Cr. LR 2.

information of the commission of crime given with the object of setting the police in motion. Information indicates that a crime has been committed and thereafter on the basis of receiving such information is bound to start investigation.[I] No enquiry can be contempleted before the information is recorded by the police.

Such an information is usually made by the victim of crime known as complainant or by someone on his behalf. It is essential that the information be given by a person who has personally seen the occurrence of crime or has the personal knowledge of the incident reported.[II]

In Mohanlal V. State,[III] two fold object of the information were observed.

(1) to make a report to the police to set the criminal law into motion,

(2) to obtain early information of an alleged criminal activity to refused the circumstances before there is time for such circumstances to be forgotten or embellished.

Information to police must be clear and definite. Under section 154, it must be an information about the commission of a cognizable offence with an object to set the investigating machinery in motion.

If the information about the commission of crime is oral it must be reduced to wrigng by the officer incharge of the police station or under his direction by a subordinate police

---

I. Bhanuhal Das V. State of Tripura, AIR 1958 Tri. 40.

II. Hallu V. State M.P. AIR 1974 SC. 1936.

III. AIR 1960 Bom. 146.

officer. It must be read over to the informant and signed by the informant. The substance of such an information shall be entered in a book to be kept by such officer in such form as the state government may prescribe in this behalf. A copy of the information as recorded shall be given forthwith, free of cost, to the information.

Any person aggrieved by a refusal on the part of an officer incharge of a police station to record the information may send the substance of such information, in writing and by post, to the superintendent of police concerned who, if satisfied that such information discloses the commission of a cognizable, offence, shall either investigate the case himself or direct an investigation to be made by any police officer subordinate to him, in the manner provided by this code. Such an officer shall have all the powers of an officer-in-charge of the police station in relation to that offence.

In Dwarka V. State,[I] it was held that a confidential information received by a police party that some bad character have assembled at a certain place, is not an information of the commission of an offence and therefore it is not necessary that it should be recorded under section 154 (1), Criminal Procedure Code.

Failure on the part of the police to observe the procedure does not make a statement in admissible, but renders more difficult to prove it.[II]

Essentials are: It must be an information, and must relate to a cognizable offence. If no cognizable offence is disclosed, the police would have no authority to undertake an investigation. If the police without a cognizable offence

I. 1953 ALJ, 580.

II. Mir Rahman V. Emperor AIR 1935 Pesh. 165.

undertakes investigation, High Court may interfere with under section 482 Criminal Procedure Code.

To determine whether an information amounts to be a report or not, all depends upon the facts and circumstances of each case. A telegraphic message cannot amount to first information report. Similarly a telephonic information is not a first information report as envisaged by section 154 (1) of the Criminal Procedure Code. Neither the telegram nor the telephonic message are signed by the informant. It is difficult to place a reliance as to its genuineness. However, in telephonic message received by the police station may be recorded by the station giving the information because a first information report may be merely hearsay. It is not necessary that the person giving the information must have first hand knowledge of the facts.[II] In State V. Rambali,[III] where a person after giving information on phone died after some time, for determining the authenticity, it was held that 'a report was made is relevant, but it cannot be said with confidence that it was made by the person who is said to have made the report or that the contents of the report were correct.'

First information report is, in fact, an important document. It is an information made soon after the occurrence, when the memory is fresh, and when there is no opportunity to fabricate or make consultations to improve upon or add to. The fact that from which source the information came, whether from a stranger, aggrieved person or an eye witness, adds to its significance also. Law attaches great significance to its contents. But it cannot be made a basis either for conviction or acquittal. However, it may be used only for corroboration under section 157 or for contradiction under section 145 Evidence Act.

I. AIR 1941 Rang. 209.

II. AIR 1953 All 163.

First information report is different from complaint. It is given in writing to police officer while the complaint, whether oral or in writing, is made to the magistrate. Information can be given by any person whereas complaint can be made by a person authorised under section 195, 196, 197 and 198, Criminal Procedure Code. First information empowers only the police officer to commence the investigation. On the other hand the report by the police of the same information to the magistrate empowers him to take cognizance of such offence. Thereafter he may direct an investigation or, if he thinks fit, at once proceed, or depute any magistrate subordinate to him to proceed, to hold a preliminary inquiry into, or otherwise to dispose of the case in the manner provided in Criminal Procedure Code.

Police officer's power to investigate also include within it's scope to require attendance of witnesses and examination of witnesses. No statement made by any person to a police officer in the course of investigation under Chapter XII, Criminal Procedure Code shall, if reduced to writing, be signed by the person making it. Statements recorded during police investigation under section 162, Criminal Procedure code are wholly in admissible in evidence except for the limited purpose stated in provision thereto. Under the present amended section 162 both defence as well as prosecution (with the permission of court) may make effective use of such statement to contradict witnesses or to confront hostile witnesses. Such statements are not to be used either by the accused or the prosecution for the purpose of corroboration. Such statements recorded by the police are not to be used as substantive evidence in favour of or against either the accused or the prosecution.[I]

I. Dhaneshawar Thakur V. The State, AIR 1958 Pat. 412.

The object of section 162, Criminal Procedure Code is to protect primarily the interest of the accused against the use of such statements recorded by the police during investigation at the trial on the presumption that such statements were not made under circumstances inspiring confidence.[I]

Section 162, clause (2), Criminal Procedure Code exempts from its operation the dying declarations which are admissible under section 32 (1) Evidence Act. 'A dying declaration made to a police officer during the course of investigation is not subject to the limitation of section 162 Criminal Procedure Code.[II]

'Section 162, Criminal Procedure Code enacts a rule of evidence. This section, is so far as it is material, prohibits, but not so as to affect the admissibility of information to the extent permissible under section 27 of the Evidence Act, use of statements by any person to a police officer in the course of an investigation, in any inquiry or trial in which such person is charged for any offence under investigation at the time when the statement was made.'[III]

Analysing of section 24 to 27, Evidence Act, and section 162, Criminal Procedure Code, together, one may draw the following inferences:

1. A confession made by a person to a police officer either in custody or outside under inducement, threat or promise having reference to the charge against his eminating from a person in authority cannot be proved against the accused in any proceeding;

I. Tahsildar Singh V. State of U.P. 1959, SC. 1012.

II. Rahman V. Emperor, AIR 1932 Lah. 14.

III. State of U.P. V. Deoman Upadhaya, AIR 1960 SC. 1125.

2. A confession made not to a police officer but to some other person while in police custody cannot be proved in any proceeding against him unless made in the presence of the magistrate;

3. An information which distinctly relates to the fact thereby discovered while in police custody whether the information amounts to a confession or not may be proved;

4. A statement which amounts to a confession or not made by a person when he is not in police custody, to another person who is not a police officer may be proved against him if it is otherwise relevant;

5. When a statement is made to a police officer during the investigation of an offence under Chapter XIV of the Code of Criminal Procedure, may not, except to the extent permitted by section 27, Evidence Act, be used for any purpose at any enquiry or trial in respect of any offence under investigation at the time when the statement was made in which he is concerned as a person accused of an offence.

A confession may be admissible in evidence in a criminal proceeding if made by a person not in police custody subject to: that the statement has not been procured in the manner mentioned in section 24, of the Evidence Act, and is not made to a police officer. Section 163 of the Criminal Procedure Code clearly lays down that no police officer or other person in authority shall offer or make, or cause to be offered or made, any inducement, threat or promise as is mentioned in section 24 of the Indian Evidence Act, 1872 (1 of 1872).

Another important procedure laid down in section 165, Criminal Procedure Code relates to the power of search by police officer making the investigation. If the investigating officer has reasons to believe, that anything necessary for the purpose of his investigation may be found in any place within the limits of the police station of which he is in charge, or to which he is attached, and that thing cannot in his opinion be otherwise obtained without undue delay, such officer may, after recording in writing the grounds for his belief and specifying in such writing, so far as possible, the thing for which the search is to be made, search or cause search to be made, for such thing in any place within the limits of such station. The copies of the search list shall be sent to the nearest magistrate empowered to take cognizance. On application a copy of search list shall also be supplied to the owner or occupier of the premises. No cost for such a copy shall be charged from the owner or occupier whose premises has been searched.

The investigating officer may also require an officer-in-charge of another police station to cause a search to be made in any place within the limits of his own station. (Section 166).

A police officer in investigating the officer cannot detain a person in custody for more than twenty four hours in the absence of the special order under section 167, Criminal Procedure Code. When the investigation cannot be completed within the period of twenty four hours and these are grounds that the accusation or information is well-founded, the officer-in-charge of the police-station or the officer making the investigation, if he is not below the rank of sub-inspector, shall forthwith transmit to the nearest judicial magistrate a copy of the entries in the diary and shall at the same time forward the accused to such magistrate. Investigating officer would show the time of arrest of the accused, the grounds for believing that he committed the offence with which he is charged and the reason why the investigation could not be completed within twenty four hours. The magistrate ordering the detention of the accused must record his reasons in writing.[1]

The magistrate to whom an accused person is forwarded under this section may, whether he has or has not jurisdiction to try the case, from time to time, authorise the detention of the accused as such magistrate thinks fit, for a term not exceeding fifteen days on the whole. (Section 167 (1)).

If the magistrate has no jurisdiction to try the case or commit if for trial, and considers further detention unnecessary, he may order the accused to be forwarded to a magistrate having such jurisdiction.

The magistrate may authorise detention of the accused even beyond fifteen days if he is satisfied that adequate grounds exist for doing so. However, no magistrate shall authorise the detention of the accused person in custody for total period exceeding sixty days. (Section 167 (1) (a)).

On exceeding sixty days the accused would be released on bail. A magistrate shall not authorise detention in any custody under section 167 Cr. P.C., unless the accused is produced before him. (Section 167 (1) (b)).

A magistrate of second class, if not specially authorised by the High Court, shall not order detention in the custody of the police. (Section 167 (1) (c)).

Article 22 (2) of the Constitution of India also requires that the accused has to be produced before a magistrate within twenty four hours of his arrest. For further detention in custody the accused should be conveyed the charges for which he is

---

1. 1933 Oudh 315, Dhrew Dev V. Emperor, 32 Cr. L.j. 464.

going to be detained. The magistrate before authorising further custody of the accused person should apply his mind judicially. He should determine after scrutinizing whatever material is in record before him whether the detention of accused person is necessary for the investigation of he case against him.

The object of producing an accused person before a magistrate is to ensure that the arrest and detention of the accused is, at any rate, prima facie justified. Law does not place reliance upon the judgement of police. It is the magistrate who is to decide, though prima facie, on certain material contained in the diary relating to the case, whether or not the detention in prison of an accused is necessary.

In Re Raju Thevan,[1] it was held that at every stage when remand is asked for, the police must satisfy the magistrate that there is sufficient evidence against the accused and that further evidence must be obtained and then, if the magistrate is satisfied, he can direct remand.

Under section 168 Criminal Procedure Code when subordinate officer has made any investigation he shall report the result of such investigation to the officer in charge of the police station.

Section 169 and 170 lay down the procedure of release of accused person when evidence is deficient, and cases to be forwarded to magistrate when evidence is sufficient. Section 171 mentions that the complainant and witnesses are not required to accompany police officer and not to be subjected to restraints.

Section 172 deals with the diary of proceedings in investigation. Significance of the diary lies in that it is a record

---

I. AIR 1966 Mad. 349.

of facts ascertained by a police officer during the investigation of cognizable offence. It is absolutely privileged. But it ceases to be so when the statement by a station house officer under section 162, Criminal Procedure Code is entered in it. It is very effective tool in the hands of the court to check the methods of investigation, the omissions and errors committed by the investigating officer during the investigations. In Local Government V. Mt. Guji,[1] it was observed: 'a delay in making an entry is calculated to throw suspicion on the dairy.'

The accused as of right is not entitle to see any portion of the diary that he may wish to see. However, in two cases the accused may use the diary. Firstly, when diary is used by the court to contradict the police officer who made it, or, secondly, when it is used by the police officer to refresh his memory.

Section 173, Criminal Procedure Code deals with final stage of investigation. It requires that every investigation shall be completed by the police officer, authorised to investigate the offence in cognizable offences, without unnecessary delay. As soon as it is completed, the officer incharge of the police station shall forward to a magistrate empowered to take cognizance of the offence on a police report, a report in the form prescribed by the state government. Report may be of two kinds - in the form of charge-sheet, or a final report. Charge-sheet is submitted when it appears to the said officer that there is sufficient evidence or reasonable ground of suspicion to justify the forwarding of an accused to a magistrate and requesting him to take cognizance of the offence. Such a report is known as 'positive report'. Final report is submitted when it appears to the said officer or to the police officer making the investigation that there is no

---

I. AIR 1935 Nag. 69.

sufficient evidence or reasonable ground of suspicion to justify the forwarding of the accused to the magistrate. Such a report may be called a 'negative report.'

Persons accused of the offences are entitled that the case against them should be investigated as quickly as possible so that they may know what they are being charged with.

To facilitate a fair and speedy trial copies of all material documents and statements in the possession of the prosecution are furnished to the accused under this section so that the accused may prepare himself to meet the evidence to be advanced by the prosecution at the trial. However, if the copies of all relevant documents have been supplied to the accused in advanced, it does not mean that prosecution is barred from relying on any additional evidence that may be subsequently discovered by them.[I]

The investigation is not incomplete merely because that the investigating officer when he submitted his report to the magistrate still awaited the reports of the experts or by some chance, in advertently or by design, he failed to append to the police report such documents or statements recorded under section 161 Criminal Procedure Code, though all such documents were with him when he submitted the police report before the magistrate.[II]

On receipt of the report magistrate is not bound to accept it. He is to scruitinize the material as to whether the facts disclosed will warrant the issue of a process against the accused.[III] If the police submits the final report magistrate may disagree and proceed to take cognizance of the offence

I. AIR 1960 Andh. Pra. 253, Sri Ram Reddi Sinhachalam, in re.

II. State of Haryana V. Mehal Singh, 1978 Cr. L.j. 1810 (F.B.).

III. Abhindandar V. State, 1968 Cr. L.j. 97.

or may direct further investigation. But once the magistrate takes cognizance on police report he cannot direct further investigations.[I]

If cognizance has been taken on police report in breach of mandatory provisions relating to investigation, the result which follows cannot be set aside unless the illegality in investigation can be shown to have caused miscarriage of justice. An illegality committed in the course of investigation dos not affect the competence and jurisdiction of the court of trial.[II]

"Recording of Confessions"

If an accused or a suspected person during investigation volunteers confession, the investigation officer should present him before a magistrate for recording the confession under section 164 of Criminal Procedure Code. It is immaterial that the metropolitan magistrate or judicial magistrate to whom the accused or suspected person has been referred, whether or not he has judisdiction in the case, may record any confession made to him under Chapter XII, Criminal Procedure Code or under any other law for the time being in force. Such a confession should be recorded in the course of investigation at any time afterwards before the commencement of the inquiry or trial. A police officer, although any power of a magistrate has been conferred upon him under any lay for the time being in force, cannot record a confession.

The magistrate before recording the confession must administrator a caution to the accused or suspected person who volunteers to make confession that he is not bound to make a confession and that, if he does so, it may be used as

I. Jitendra Nath V. State, 1976, Cr. L.j. 1296.

II. Manilal V. Delhi Administration, 1971, Cr. L.j. 1153.

evidence against him.

The magistrate shall not record any such confession unless he is satisfied and has reasons to believe that it is being made voluntarily. Any such confession shall be recorded by the magistrate in full himself or where he is unable to do so owing to a physical or other in capacity, under his direction and superintendence. The manner of recording the confession shall be the same as laid down in section 281 of he Criminal Procedure Code. The record shall be, if practicable, be in the language in which the accused is examined or, if that is not practicable, in the language of the court. The record shall be shown or read to the accused. If he does not understand the language in which it is written, shall be interpreted to him in a language which he understands, and he shall be at liberty to explain or add to his answers.

The confession so recorded shall be signed by the person making the confession, and the magistrate shall make a memorandum at the foot of such record to the following effect:

"I have explained to (name) that he is not bound to make a confession and that, if he does so any confession he may make may be used as evidence against him and I believe that this confession was voluntarily made. It was taken in my presence and hearing, and was read over to the person making it and admitted by him to be correct, and it contains a full and true account of the statement made by him." - (Signed) - Magistrate."

In Ram Charan V. State of U.P.,[1] the magistrate recorded the confession under section 164 Criminal Procedure Code and certified at the foot of statement as: "Certified that the statement has been made voluntarily. The deponent was warned that he is making the statement before the first class magistrate and can be used against him.

Recorded in my presence, there is no police here. The witness did not go out until all the witness had given the statement". The supreme court in the case held that endorsement at the foot of statement was not proper.

The language should be simple to explain and not to warn the person volunteering his confession. Here the language and manner adopted by the magistrate is not the same as has been envisaged by Clause (4) of Section 164, Criminal Procedure Code.

"Confession Admissible in Evidence"

The investigating officer in the course of investigation gets valuable information from the confession recorded by the magistrate. But he should not unduly rely on confession. He should try to find out and obtain all circumstantial and oral evidence available in support of the prosecution case. If the investigating officer succeeds in obtaining the all such corroborative evidence it will help him judging the nature and character of the confession.

In Raja Ram V. State,[1] it was held that 'a confession recorded by a magistrate under section 164 after the police completed its investigation and submitted a charge-sheet, but before the magisterial enquiry has commenced, is admissible'.

But it should be proved beyond reasonable doubt that at the time of recording the statement or even before when the accused is in custody of police, no police officer or other person in authority offered or made or caused to be offered or made, any inducement, threat or promise in violation of the provisions of section 163 Criminal Procedure Code and section 24 of the Indian Evidence Act, 1872.

I. AIR 1966 All. 192 (F.B.)

Further that the confession recorded was voluntary, made on his own free will and due caution was administered by the magistrate before confession was recorded. The manner and language used was proper as mentioned in section 164 Criminal Procedure Code. It is also essential that confession was recorded in accordance to the Procedure laid in section 281 Criminal Procedure Code.

Confession made by the accused to police officer while in police custody is irrelevant. When any fact is deposed to as discovered in consequence of information received from a person of any offence in the custody of a police officer, so much of that information, whether the information amounts to confession or not as relates distinctly to that fact thereby may be admissible.

If the above noted conditions are satisfied then confession is admissible in evidence. If the confession is made under threat or promise or inducement, such confession would not be admissible in evidence.

In cases if any court before which confession of an accused person recorded or purporting to be recorded under section 164 or section 281, is tendered, or has been received, in evidence finds that any of the provisions of either of such sections have not been complied with by the magistrate recording the statement, it may not withstanding anything contained in section 91 of the Indian Evidence Act, 1872 (1 of 1872), satisfied that such non-compliance has not injured the accused in his defence on the merits and that he duly made the statement recorded, admit such statement. (Section 463, Criminal Procedure Code).

Non-compliance with the provisions of section 164 or section 281 under this section 463, makes the confession admissible only when it is established that the expediency of justice so requires and the accused in his defence is not prejudiced.

"Charge"

"If there be any principle of criminal law and justice clearer and more obvious than all others, it is that the offence imputed must be positively and precisely stated, so that the accused may certainly know with what he is charged and may be prepared to answer the charge in the best way".[1] It is a first step in the criminal prosecution process of an offence. The charge is aimed at to warn the accused person of the prosecution case against him which he is to answer. The charge is to enable the accused of the allegations which he will have to meet. It is a notice of the matter of which he is accused. It must convey to the accused clearly and accurately the allegations which the prosecution is to prove against him and which he will have to defend himself. Charge is also an information to the trial court of the allegations against the accused person to which evidence is to be directed. In fact it is a basic principle of criminal law to convey to the accused with sufficient clearness and certainly what the precise accusation against him is, before he is asked to defend himself. 'An accused is entitled to know with accuracy and certainty the exact nature of the charge brought against him. Unless he has this knowledge, he will be prejudiced in his defence, specially in cases where it is sought to implicate him for acts not committed by himself but by others with whom he is in company'.

A charge includes facts and law both. Its significance lies in the fact that the charge is a safeguard to the accused against injustice. It consists of the facts or allegations which

---

I. Norris R. J. in Lim Beh V. Opium Farmer, (1842) 3Ky 110, 112.

the prosecution undertakes to prove against the accused and the offence constituted by them in accordance with the law. Chapter XVII of Criminal Procedure Code deals with the charge. According to the requirement of section 211, Crimina Procedure Code, a charge states the offence is to be described in the charge by that name only. If there is no specific definition of the offence in the law with which an accused person is charged then so much of the definition of the offence must be stated as to give the accused notice of the matter with which he is charged. Charge will also include the law and the section of law against which there is a violation.

The charge shall be written in the language of the court. In cases where the accused person has been previously convicted and by reason by previous conviction enhanced punishment or a punishment of a different kind is to be awarded for subsequent offence and it is intended to prove such previous conviction for the purpose of affecting punishment, the fact, date and place of the previous conviction shall be stated in the charge, and if such statement has been omitted, the court may add it any time before sentence is passed. Sufficient particulars of the previous conviction should be mentioned so that the accused may understand why he is liable to enhanced punishment.

The charge shall contain such particulars as to time and place of alleged offence. If will also mention the person, if any, against whom or thing in respect of which, it was committed, as are reasonably sufficient to give the accused notice of the matter with which he is charged.

In cases when the accused is charged with criminal breach of trust or dishonest misappropriation of money or other moveable property, it shall be sufficient to specify the gross sum or, as the case may be, describe the movable property in respect of which the offence is alleged to have been committed, and the dates between which the offence is alleged to have been committed, without specifying particular items or exact dates, and the charge so framed shall be deemed to be a charge of one offence within the meaning of section 219 subject to the requirement that the time include between the first and last of such dates shall not exceed one year.

Provision of section 212 (2) are important and must be strictly observed in framing a charge under section 405 and 406.[I] It must indicate which of the several ingredients of the offence was intended.

1. 'Whether the accused dishonestly misappropriated the property, or
2. Whether he dishonestly converted to his own use, or
3. Whether he dishonestly disposed it of in violation of any direction of law, or
4. Whether he dishonestly disposed it of in violation of any legal contract express or implied, or
5. Whether he wilfully suffered any other person to do any of the acts (1) to (4) referred to above'.

'The charged must state who made the alleged entrustment or who suffered from the alleged breach of trust.'[II]

As we have noted earlier charge must also mention the dates between which the offence is alleged to have been committed."[III]

I. (1913) 14 Cr. *L.j.* 219 (222) (Cal.).

II. (11936) 37 Cr. *L.j.* 439 (440) (DB) (Cal.).

III. A 1957 Madh. Pra 225 (226): 1957 Cr. *L.j.* 1411.

In R.K. Dalmia V. Delhi Administration,[I] it was observed that a charge for criminal breach of trust in different modes is really a charge for a single offence. The charge was:

"That you being entrusted with the funds of B committed breach of trust, by wilfully suffering C to dishonestly misappropriate the said funds and dishonestly use or dispose of the said funds in violation of the direction of the law and the implied contract between you and B prescribing the mode in which such trust was to be discharged."

In this case though the mode of committing was not precisely stated, however, their lordship of the supreme court were of the opinion that the charge was in respect of a single offence and vagueness of charge did not make the trial illegal particularly under the circumstances when no prejudice was caused to the accused.

Where the accused embezzled Rs. 1-11 and Rs. 5/- on 5th August and Rs. 1-3 on 20th May which he had collected from 3 persons but was not charged with three separate offences but with one offence under section 409 Indian Penal Code, the court held that the charge was valid, satisfied the requirement of law.[II]

In another case an accused realised Rs. 103/- by 23 rent receipt and misappropriated Rs. 67/- out of it was tried for it under section 408, Indian Penal Code in one trial for offences falling within the period of one year. It was held that the charge was valid covered by the provisions of section 222 (2) old Criminal Procedure Code (Present equivalent section is 212 (2) of the Criminal Procedure Code 1973).[III]

I. Supra N......... P.

II. (1906) 3 Cr. *L.j.* 138 (DB), Cal., A 1936 Bom. 154.

III. (1905), 1 Cr. *L.j.* 791 (DB) (Cal.).

A charge in respect of an aggregate sum of money alleged to have been misappropriated within one year relating to three items specified as composing the total, was held valid.[I]

A charge under sections 405 and 406 or 408 cannot be joined with a charge for an offence of extortion,[II] or with a charge of falsification of accounts though in respect of the same items.[III]

In criminal breach of trust cases a charge must indicate and specify the gross-sum of money, and dates on which such crime committed.[IV] A charge under section 405 is defective if it does not set out the time and the manner of entrustment alleged with sufficient particularity.[V]

'Where the accused has been charged under section 409, in respect of three separate entrustments of paddy in kind, it would be better if the charge were framed regarding each of the deliveries showing the date and the quality of each entrustment separately. But the failure to do that cannot vitiate the trial unless it is shown that such a defect has occasioned a failure of justice'.[VI]

In Umar Saheb's case[VII] their lordship of supreme court held that 'where the charge under section 406 said to have been committed by the accused persons in pursuance of a criminal conspiracy was with respect to the gross-sum

---

I. (1902) All W.N. 44.

II. A. 1936 Sind 29 (30) : 37 Cr. L.j. 457 (DB).

III. A 1926 Bom 110 (111) : 27 Cr. L.j. 305 (DB).

IV. AIR 1957 MP 225.

V. 1960, Cal. 1316.

VI. AIR 1958 Pat. 27.

VII. AIR 1962, 1 Ker. LR, 544.

embezzled within the period between 6/3/1349 and 30/6/1950, the charge contravenes the prevision to section 222 (2) (S. 212 (2) of the new Code); but the defect does not cause prejudice to the accused and does not vitiate the trial as the charge could have been split up into two charges with respect to periods from 6/3/1949 to 5/3/1950 and from 6/3/1950 to 30/6/1950 and two charges could be tried together at one trial.'

Section 213 Criminal Procedure Code specifically lays down that when the nature of the case is such that the particulars mentioned in sections 211 and 212 do not give the accused sufficient notice of the matter with which he is charged, the charge shall also contain such particulars of the manner in which the alleged offence was committed as will be sufficient for that purpose.

In every charge words used in describing an offence shall be deemed to have been used in the same attached to them respectively by the law under which such offence is punishable. (Section 214).

Under section 215, errors or omissions in the charge cannot be regarded as material unless it is shown by the accused that he had in fact been misled or that there had been a failure of justice as a result of such error or omission.

In Rajindra Singh V.[1] State of U.P. the court convicted the accused for an offence constituted by the facts mentioned in the charge even though not charge with it. It can invoke the aid of section 215 and ignore the error in stating the offence in the charge or in the omission of stating the offence of which he is found guilty.

'A general charge of embezzlement showing the gross sum misappropriated is sufficient under section 212 (2) of

---

I. AIR 1960, All 387.

the Criminal Procedure Code and the conviction would not be bad unless the accused was prejudiced thereby.'[I]

In K. Kunhahammad V. State of Madras,[II] their lordships of the supreme court made observation as follows:

"The failure of the prosecution to split up the first count into sub-counts cannot obviously be regarded as introducing a fatal infirmity in the validity of the trial. It would be noticed that this argument is not one of misjoinder. It is based on the formal requirement prescribed by the provision to section 222 (2) as to how charges of breach of trust should be framed. There is no difficulty in holding that such an irregularity can be cured both under section 225 and section 537 of the code provided of course no prejudice has been thereby caused to the appellants' case".

Section 215 clearly mentions that no error in stating either the offence or the particulates required to be stated in the charge, and no omission to state of the case as material, unless the accused was in fact misled by such error or omission and it has occasioned a failure of justice. However, each case has to be judged on its own specific facts and there cannot be any general presumption that every error or omission in a

---

I. (1907) 6 Cr. L.j. 137 (Lah).

II. A. 1960 SC 661 (663)- : 1960 Cr. L.j. 1013: Charge contravening provison to section 222 (2) old (New - 212 (2) - defect held did not cause prejudice to accused - Trial not is charged under section 408 for misappropriation of the gorss amount during one year and the charge also sets out items with necessary dates and amount it falls within the privisions of section 222 (2) equivalent 212 (2) Criminal Producere Code. If the items are more than 3 in the number, the charge under section 408 I.P.C. and not in respect of charge on several items. (A 1929 Cal. 457 : 31 Cr. L.j. 74 (DB) - Trial involving offences under sectin 406, I.P.C. committed on 5 distinct dates is not bad - (1926) 42 TLR 57.

charge has materially affected a trial or occasioned a failure of justice.

Section 216 of Criminal Procedure Code deals with the alteration of charges. Any court may alter or add to any charge at any time before judgement is pronounced.

Whenever a charge altered or added to the court after the commencement of the trial, the prosecutor and the accused shall be allowed to recall or re-summon, and examine with reference to such alteration or addition, any witness who may have been examined. However, the court if it is of the opinion that either the prosecutor or the accused desires to recall or re-examine such witness for the purpose of vexation or delay or for defeating the end of justice, may refuse such recall of witnesses. The court refusing the recall witnesses is to record its reason for such refusal. Court may also to call any further witness whom the court may think to be material.

As to joined of charges, section 218 to 233 of Criminal Procedure Code provide different conditions under which accused persons may be charged with jointly. In fact these sections are also exception to the general law relating to place of inquiry and trial as given in section 177 of the Criminal Procedure Code. Where in the course of the same transaction, different offences are committed by different accused persons and where they are tried jointly, the court will have jurisdiction to try all the offences together whether they have been within the territorial jurisdiction of that court or not.[I]

For every distinct offence of which any person is charged is accused, there shall be a separate charge and every such charge shall be tried separately. This provision is subjected to that if the accused person by an application in

---

I. AIR 1967 Mys 44 (Venakatesh V. State of Mysore).

writing desires, and the magistrate is of the opinion that such person is not likely to be prejudiced thereby, the magistrate may try together all or any number of the charges framed against such person. Sub section (1) of section 218 shall not effect the operation of the provisions of sections 219, 220, 221 and 223.

Two offences falling under different sections of Indian Penal Code are considered distinct offences. Misappropriation of money on different are distinct offences. For different offences though committed in the same transaction, separate charges should be framed. It may be that those charges will be tried together under sections 218, 219 and 220. Three offences of the same kind within a period of one year may be charged together in one trial (Section 219).

Sections 219, 220 and 221 provide where separate charges are framed for the circumstances in which those charges could be tried together and not separately as required under section 218.

If, in one series of acts so connected together as to form the same transaction, more offences than one are committed by the same person, under section 220 Criminal Procedure Code, he may be charged with, and tried at one trial for, every such offence. When a person is charged with one or more offences of Criminal breach of trust or misappropriation of property as provided in sub-section (2) of section 212 or in sub-section (1) of section 219, is accused of committing, for the purpose of facilitating or concealing the commission of that offence or those offences, one or more offences of falsification of accounts, he may be charged with, and tried at one trial for, every such offence. For certain acts forming one transaction there must be one continued thread of common purpose running through the acts of support a joinder of charge. The question that different offences are committed in the course of same transaction must be determined on the facts of each particular case. There must be sufficient unity of time, place, purpose and action as to so connect the different acts to make them one transaction.

In cases where the charge of criminal conspiracy to commit criminal breach of trust is followed by a substantive charge of criminal breach of trust in pursuance of such conspiracy, there is nothing to prevent the court from convicting an accused under the second charge even if the prosecution fails to establish conspiracy. In such a case no prejudice is caused to the accused as he is aware that thee is a substantive charge against him under section 409 Criminal Procedure Code.[I]

Under section 409, it is essential that a charge for criminal breach of trust must indicate the several ingredients of the offence and also that the accused was entrusted with property in his capacity of a public servant in the course of his employment.

A charge alleging 3 different acts of criminal breach of trust and the different acts of falsification of accounts under section 477 A is an illegelity though all acts committed within 12 months.[II]

Again two charges under section 409 and two alternative charges under section 420 in respect of the same transaction cannot be validly joined together.III

Joint trial of offence under section 5 (1) (c) read with section 5 (2) of Prevention of Corruption Act (which is the

I. 1967 Cr. L.j. 1401: AIR SC 1590.

II. A 1926 Bom. 110.

III. A. 1952 Bom. 177.

same offence as under section 409, I.P.C.) and offence of falsification of accounts under section 477 A both in respect of several items is illegal.[1]

Under section 221 where it is doubtful what offence has been committed an accused may be charged with having committed all of any of such offences, and any number of such charges may be tried at once or he may be charged in the alternative with having committed someone of the said offences. In a case where the accused is charged with one offence and evidence shows a different crime committed, he may be convicted of the offence which he shown to have committed, although he was not charged with it.

For the application of section 222 of the Criminal Procedure Code the following conditions should be proved:

1. When a person is charged with an offence consisting of several particulars, a combination of some only of which constitutes a complete minor offence, and such combination is proved, but the remaining particulars are not proved, he may be convicted of the minor offence, though he was not charged with it.

2. When a person is charged with an offence and facts are proved which reduce it to a minor offence, he may be convicted of the minor offence, although he is not charged with it.

3. When a person is charged with an offence, he may be convicted of an attempt to commit such offence although the attempt is not separately charged.

In cases where the conditions requisite for the initiation of proceedings in respect of that minor offence have not been

---

1. 1970 Raj. LW 529.

satisfied there cannot be any conviction of any minor offence under this section.

Section 223, Criminal Procedure Code, gives a list of persons who may be charged jointly for offences committed, person is accused of abtment or attempt to commit, such offences. Person accused of an offence which includes theft, extortion, cheating, misappropriation, and persons accused of receiving or retaining, or assisting in the disposal of, concealment of, property possession of which is alleged to have been transferred by any such offence committed by the first named person, or of abetment of or attempt to commit any such last named offence may be charge jointly.

Splitting up of the case into several trials should be avoided to where such a course is likely to prejudice the accused in their defence.

The last section 224 of Chapter XVII Criminal Procedure Code relating to charge deals with the withdrawal of remaining charges on conviction on one of framed against the same person, and when a conviction has been had one or more of them, the complainant, or officer conducting the prosecution, may with the consent of the court, withdraw the remaining charge or charges, or the court of its own accord may stay the inquiry into, or trial of such charge or charges, and such withdrawal shall have the effect of an acquittal on such charge or charges, unless the conviction be set aside, in which case the said court (subject to the order of the court setting aside the conviction) may proceed with the inquiry into, or trial of, the charge or charges so withdrawn.

In brief the object of joint trial is to avoid multiplicity of trials. The only limitation which can be placed on joint trials is that justice and fairness should not be prejudiced. Where prosecution desires a joint trial it is for the prosecution to justify. The magistrate has a full discretion to try the accused jointly or separately keeping in view that justice should not be effected and accused's interest is not prejudiced.

PART B

"PROCEDURE: ISLAMIC CRIMINAL LAW"

"Qur'ãnic View"

The Holy Qur'ãn is, no doubt, the fundamental and unchangeable source of Islamic law. Crimes are to be determined in accordance to the commandments and injunctions of Holy Qur'ãn. Next comes the Ahadith. Ahadith as discussed in earlier chapters are the interpretations and elaborations of Holy Qur'ãn. After these two basic sources of Islamic law comes the other sources. In this chapter, a systematic attempt is made to examine the procedure for the administration of justice keeping in view the different sources of Islamic law.

Administration of justice as the basic responsibility of every Islamic state. Justice must be executed in accordance to Qur'ãnic commandments. Allah Ta'ala in surah Sad (ص) says:

يٰدَاوٗدُ اِنَّا جَعَلْنٰكَ خَلِيفَةً فِى الْاَرْضِ فَاحْكُمْ بَيْنَ النَّاسِ بِالْحَقِّ وَلَاتَتَّبِعِ الْهَوٰى فَيُضِلَّكَ عَنْ سَبِيْلِ اللّٰهِ اِنَّ الَّذِيْنَ يَضِلُّوْنَ عَنْ سَبِيْلِ اللّٰهِ لَهُمْ عَذَابٌ شَدِيْدٌ بِمَا نَسُوا يَوْمَ الْحِسَابِ۔ (سورة ص، آية: ٢٦)

"O David (داؤودٌ) ! We did indeed make thee a vicegerent on earth: So judge thou between men in truth (and justice): Nor follow thou the lust (Of thy heart), for it will mislead thee from the path of Allah: for those who wander astray from the path of Allah, is chatisement grievous, for that they forget the Day of Account". (38:26).

This ayat (سورة ص) has laid down the basic concept of administration of justice under Islamic law. God has made us His viceroy on the earth, so follow His commands only, and decide the matters with justice and fair play according to Divine Shariah. It gives direction to those who are responsible for administrating justice that never an infinitesimal part of the wish of the soul should come in the way of judgement of any affair or matter, because this thing leads astray from the way of God. And when a man went astray from the way, then where would be his resort? Reference to David here means a man just and upright, endowed with all the virtues, in whom even the least thought of self-elation has be washed off. Assuredly those who go astrary from the way of God-for them there is a terrible chastisement for that they forget the Day of Reckoning.

Generally the wish is followed because a man forgets the Day of Reckoning. If this thing is present before his soul that one day he will have to go before God and give an account of minutest actions, then he cannot go astray from the path of God. He cannot prefer his wish contrary to the achieving of pleasure of God.

Disputes among believers should be decided in accordance to the commandments of Allah Ta'ala and sayings of Prophet (peace be upon him). There should be no hesitation in accepting the commandments and sayings of Prophet (peace be upon him). Allah Ta'ala in Sura Noor commands:

اِنَّمَا كَانَ قَوْلَ الْمُؤْمِنِيْنَ اِذَا دُعُوا اِلَى اللّٰهِ وَرَسُوْلِهٖ لِيَحْكُمَ بَيْنَهُمْ اَنْ
يَّقُوْلُوا سَمِعْنَا وَ اَطَعْنَا وَاُولٰئِكَ هُمُ الْمُفْلِحُوْنَ۔ (سورة النور، آية:٥١)

"The answer of the believers, when summoned to Allah And His Messenger, in order that he may judge between them, is no other than this: They say, "We hear and we obey. It is such as these that will prosper." (24:51).

The affairs of true Muslims should be subject to the commands of God and His Messenger. In any matter if they are directed to follow they should never hesitate even for a moment whether there is loss or gain to them in it outwardly. At once say: 'We heard and we obeyed'. They should always keep ready to obey the order. In it alone is hidden the secret of their prosperity and abiding welfare. Fraud, hypocracy, and duplicity are of no use. Better way advised to believers by Allah Ta'ala in this Ayat (آيت) is to listen good counsel attentively and carry out in their lives.

This is a general guiding principle commanded by Allah Ta'ala for the administration of justice, that is, hear and obey Allah Ta'ala and His Messenger (peace be upon him) when they may judge their disputed matters between them. The following Ayat (آيت) will make it more clear:

فَلَا وَرَبِّكَ لَا يُؤْمِنُوْنَ حَتّٰى يُحَكِّمُوْكَ فِيْمَا شَجَرَ بَيْنَهُمْ ثُمَّ لَا يَجِدُوْا
فِيْ أَنْفُسِهِمْ حَرَجاً مِّمَّا قَضَيْتَ وَيُسَلِّمُوْا تَسْلِيْماً۔
(سورة النساء، آية: ٦٥)

"But no by thy Lord, they can have no (real) Faith, until they make thee judge in all disputes between them and find in their souls no resistance against thy decisions, but accept them with the fullest conviction". (4:65)

In earlier Ayat (آيت) there was command to obey the directions of Allah Ta'ala and His Messenger both. But in the present Ayat there is specific advice to believers to obey the judgement of Prophet (peace be upon him) in their disputed matters. This is very significant verse which presents the criterion of a full and perfect believer. A perfect believer is that who believes in the authority of the Holy Prophet (peace be upon him) perfectly in all matters of life. The true momins accept the decision of the

Holy Prophet (peace be upon him) from the depth of his heart. They do not find any impediments or narrowness in their souls at the admonitions, instructions, directions and orders of the Holy Prophet (peace be upon him) given in the true traditions. Like hypocrates, they do not claim by tongue and reject by heart. Unless hearts are fully satisfied with the finality of the Holy Prophet (peace be upon him), Eman (ایمان) cannot attain perfection. The principle which can be inferred here that justice in matters of disputes should be administered in accordance to Ahadith. Believers have to obey whatever the decision is whether there is gain or no gain from it.

Allah Ta'ala, again in Sura Maedah, from verse 48 to 50, commands how to decide dispute arising among the believers. He says:

وَاَنْزَلْنَا اِلَيْكَ الْكِتٰبَ بِالْحَقِّ مُصَدِّقاً لِّمَا بَيْنَ يَدَيْهِ مِنَ الْكِتٰبِ
وَمُهَيْمِناً عَلَيْهِ فَاحْكُمْ بَيْنَهُمْ بِمَا اَنْزَلَ اللّٰهُ وَلَا تَتَّبِعْ اَهْوَاءَ هُمْ عَمَّا
جَاءَكَ مِنَ الْحَقِّ لِكُلٍّ جَعَلْنَا مِنْكُمْ شِرْعَةً وَّمِنْهَاجاً وَلَوْشَاءَ اللّٰهُ
لَجَعَلَكُمْ اُمَّةً وَّاحِدَةً وَّلٰكِنْ لِّيَبْلُوَكُمْ فِى مَا اٰتٰكُمْ فَاسْتَبِقُوْا الْخَيْرٰتِ۔

(سورة المائدة، آية:٤٨)

"To thee we sent the scripture in truth, confirming the scripture that came before, it, and guarding it in safety: so judge between them by what Allah hath revealed, and follow not their vain desires, diverging from the truth that hath come to thee, to each among you have we prescribed a law and an open way. If Allah had so willed, He would have made you a single people, but (His plan is) to test you in what He hath given you: so strive as ina race in all virtues."

(5:48)

In verse 49, Allah Ta'ala commands:

وَاَنِ احْكُمْ بَيْنَهُمْ بِمَا اَنْزَلَ اللّٰهُ وَلَا تَتَّبِعْ اَهْوَاءَهُمْ وَاحْذَرْهُمْ اَنْ يَّفْتِنُوكَ عَنْ بَعْضِ مَا اَنْزَلَ اللّٰهُ اِلَيْكَ فَاِنْ تَوَلَّوا فَاعْلَمْ اَنَّمَا يُرِيْدُ اللّٰهُ اَنْ يُصِيْبَهُمْ بِبَعْضِ ذُنُوبِهِمْ وَاِنَّ كَثِيراً مِنَ النَّاسِ لَفٰسِقُوْنَ۔

(سورة المائدة، آية:٤٩)

"And this (He commands): Judge thou between them by what Allah hath revealed, and followed not their vain desires, but beware of them lest they beguile thee from any of that (teaching) which Allah hath sent down to thee. And if they turn away, be assured that for some of their crimes it is Allah's purpose to punish them. And truly most men are revellious".

(5:49)

In verse 50, Allah Ta'ala says:

اَفَحُكْمَ الْجَاهِلِيَّةِ يَبْغُوْنَ وَمَنْ اَحْسَنُ مِنَ اللّٰهِ حُكْماً لِّقَوْمٍ يُّوقِنُوْنَ۔

(سورة المائدة، آية: ٥٠)

"Do they then seek after a judgement of (the Days of) Ignorance? But who, for a people whose faith is assured, can give better judgement than Allah? (5:50)

In these verses Holy Prophet (peace be upon him) is advised to execute and judge according to the Divine Laws revealed to him and pay no heed to the criticism and objection raised by different people of the world. In other words Muslims are advised to follow the constitution of Holy Qur'ãn and execute and judge according to the Qur'ãnic law.

There may be various laws in the world - some secular and some ecclesiastical - but the Muslims should not pay heed to them.

The political leaders and statesmen of the Modern Muslim States should know that the modern laws cannot vie with the Qur'ãnic laws. A momin should please the God and His Messenger, he should not please the rebellious infidels of God and His Messenger.

If they turn away and do not execute and judge according to Qur'ãn and Sunnah and do not promulgate Qur'ãn constitution and laws, it means they are plunged into sins and God wants to punish them for some of their heinous sins in the world and hereafter.

Those who believe in the absolute sovereignty, boundless mercy and unlimited knowledge of God cannot pay heed to order and law of anyone except God. So do they want to go to the darkness of ignorance, whims and caprices, godlessness and infidelity. Obedience to lowly desires and disobedience to Divine commands, always detract the believers from the open way and throw them into dark pits of error and infidelity.

Allah Ta'ala, again commands in verse 44:

وَمَنْ لَّمْ يَحْكُمْ بِمَا اَنْزَلَ اللّٰهُ فَاُولٰٓئِكَ هُمُ الْكٰفِرُوْنَ۔

(سورة المائدة، آية: ٤٤)

"If any do fail to judge by what Allah hath revealed, they are unbelievers". (5:44).

Those who do not adjudicate or execute according o Divine Revelations are unbelievers. In the first case if the executive or judicial authority denies the Revealed Order or Revealed Law and promulgates or judges according to his own wish or other laws, then that authority shall be infidel without doubt. In the second case if the executive or judicial authority has faith in the Divine Order but promulgates or judges according to a law other than Divine Law, then he shall be considered as an infident in action.

Again Allah Ta'ala says:

وَمَنْ لَمْ يَحْكُمْ بِمَا اَنْزَلَ اللّٰهُ فَاُولٰئِكَ هُمُ الظّٰلِمُوْنَ۔

(سورة المائدة، آية: ٤٥)

"And if any fail to judge by what Allah hath revealed, they are wrong-doers". (5:45)

Again in verse 47, Allah commands:

وَمَنْ لَمْ يَحْكُمْ بِمَا اَنْزَلَ اللّٰهُ فَاُولٰئِكَ هُمُ الْفٰسِقُوْنَ۔

(سورة المائدة، آية: ٤٧)

"And if any do fail to judge by what Allah has revealed they are those who rebel". (5:47)

The seeming repetitions at the end of verses 44, 45, 47, 48 and 50 are not real repetitions. The significant words used in these verses are: Unbelievers, wrong-doers, and rebellions. If any one tampers with the revealed law, he is unbeliever. If gives false judgement contrary to the revealed law, he is wrong-doers. And lastly, if he does not follow the commandment of Allah, he is a rebel. The gist is to obey the commands of Allah Ta'ala in all walks of life. Whatever law is revealed judge your disputes accordingly.

The righteous man seeks no other standard or judgement but Allah's will. Allah Ta'ala says in Holy Qur'ãn:

"Say: "Shall I for judge other than Allah? - When He it is who hath sent unto you. The Book, explained in detail". (6:14-15)

It is not possible for believers to listen the talks of others than God, when God has given a perfect and miraculous Book which contains the necessary details and explanation of all fundamental principles. Its tidings are all true, its laws are moderate and just and no one has power to change them. Laws of God possess a universal character and application. In the presence of such Holy laws, perfectly just and truthful, believers need not to listen the conflicting ideas of the modern thinkers.

As to the administration of justice, Islamic concept is what Allah Ta'ala commands. Allah Ta'ala says:

وَاِنْ حَكَمْتَ فَاحْكُمْ بَيْنَهُمْ بِالْقِسْطِ، اِنَّ اللّٰهَ يُحِبُّ الْمُقْسِطِيْنَ۔

(سورۃالمائدۃ، آیۃ: ٤٢)

"If thou judge, judge in equity between them. For Allah loveth those who judge in equity". (5:42)

Command of Allah Ta'ala in this verse is to decide the cases according to the principles of justice whether the contending parties are foes or friends, wicked or virtuous, oppressed or oppressors, relatives of strangers, citizen or aliens, all immaterial. Allah Ta'ala loves those who do justice in their mundance.

In verse 58, noted below, Allah Ta'ala says:

اِنَّ اللّٰهَ يَاْمُرُكُمْ اَنْ تُؤَدُّوا الْاَمٰنٰتِ اِلٰى اَهْلِهَا وَاِذَا حَكَمْتُمْ بَيْنَ النَّاسِ اَنْ تَحْكُمُوا بِالْعَدْلِ اِنَّ اللّٰهَ نِعِمَّا يَعِظُكُمْ بِهٖ اِنَّ اللّٰهَ كَانَ سَمِيْعًا بَصِيْرًا۔

(سورۃ النساء، آیۃ:٥٨)

"Allah doth command you to render back your trust to those to whom they are due; and when ye judge between people that ye judge with justice: verily how excellent is the teaching which giveth you! For Allah is He who heareth and seeth all things". (4:58)

Here in the verse God has again command for administering justice. Justice in fact, is the basis of the Islamic Law.

Allah Ta'ala in Sura-Nahl, verse 90, advises against for doing justice:

إِنَّ اللّٰهَ يَأْمُرُ بِالْعَدْلِ وَالإِحْسَانِ وَإِيْتَائِي ذِى الْقُرْبٰى و يَنْهٰى عَنِ الْفَحْشَاءِ والْمُنْكَرِ وَالبَغْى يَعِظُكُمْ لَعَلَّكُم تَذَكَّرُون۔

(سورة النحل، آية: ٩٠)

"Allah commands justice, the doing of Good, and giving to Kith and Kin, and He forbids all indecent deeds, and evil and rebellion: He instcks you, that ye may receive admonition." (16:90)

Allah again commands:

قُلْ اَمَرَ رَبِّى بِالْقِسْطِ

(سورة الا عراف، آيه: ٢٩)

"Say: My Lord hath commanded justice." (7:29)

Further Qur'ãn has laid down an ideal of justice by referring to Divine Balance - the Balance of Justice. It says:

وَالسَّمَاءَ رَفَعَهَا وَوَدَعَ الْمِيْزَانَ۔ اَلَّا تَطْغَوْا فِى الْمِيزَان۔ وَاَقِيمُوا الْوَزْنَ بِالْقِسْطِ وَلَا تُخْسِرُ والْمِيْزَانَ۔ (سورة الرحمن،آية: ٩۔٧)

"And the Firmament has He raised High and He has set up the Balance (of justice), in order that ye may not transgress (due) balance. So establish weight with justice and fall not short in the balance." (55:7-9)

Again Allah says:

لَقَدْ اَرْسَلْنَا رُسَلَنَا بِالْبَيِّنٰتِ وَاَنْزَلْنَا مَعَهُمُ الْكِتٰبَ وَالْمِيْزَانَ لِيَقُوْمَ النَّاسُ بِالقِسْطِ۔

(سورة الحديد، آية: ٢٥)

> "We sent aforetime our Messengers with clear signs and sent down with them the Book and the balance (of) right and (wrong), that men May stand forth in justice."
>
> (57:25)

Here Divine balance stands for justice. Revelation commands good and forbids evil, justice which gives to each person his due. Men in these verses have been advised to act justly to each other and observe due balance in all their actions. Men should be straight, just and honest. Administer justice even handedly without partiality. Justice is the central virtue, and avoidance of both excess and defect in conduct keeps the human world balanced. The idea presented here is the doing of justice and equity in their dealings with one another. The ideal has not been kept confined within the domain of abstract theory. The Muslim Monarch and rulers tried to imitate it and act upon the Divine plan in practice also. In fact implemented the plan in practice as well.

God does not command unwise things and indecent deed unrecognized by human nature and just wisdom. God commands just path and administration of justice. Where we say justice, it covers all laws of Shariat dealing with human affairs. Thus it is necessary for administration of justice to act upon all laws of Shariat. For not doing justice, those involved would be recreated and accounted for their deeds.

Ahadith

Now we turn to Sunnah to show how much significance attached by Prophet (peace be upon him) to the administration of justice. It is not possible to refer all Sunnah relating to administration of justice in this Chapter. Only few selected are referred below:

عن عائشة رضى الله عنها قالت: سمعت النبى صلى الله عليه
وسلم يقول: ليا تين على القاى العدل يوم القيامة ساعة يتمنى انه
لم يقض بين اثنين فى تمرة و ط۔
(المنتقى من اخيار المطفى: ج۲، ص۳۲ ۹، طرع قاهره ۱۹۳۲ء)

Hazrat Ayesha (R.A.) explaining the accountability of just and honest Qazi for his deeds on the Day of Decision narrated that Prophet (peace be upon him) said:

"That on the Day of Accountability even a just and justice loving Qazi would have to face a moment when he would wish - that it would have been better if he had not decided a dispute even about a date between two persons."

This Hadith shows the significance which Prophet (peace be upon him) attached to the administration of justice. Even an honest Qazi responsible for administration of justice, decides cases justly would be subjected to severe scruitiny by Allah Ta'ala on the Day of Decision. Just imagine what would be the position of a Qazi when Allah Ta'ala subjects him to such an examinations of his deeds. A wish not to had decided a dispute even about a single 'date' shows the severity of the examination. This is in fact a limit of a person's wish.

In another Hadith Hazrat Abu Hurera (R.A.) quoted Prophet (peace be upon him) saying:

عن ابى هريرة رضى الله تعالى عنه: سمعت رسول الله صلى الله
عليه وسلم يقول: ليوشكت الرجل انه يتمنى انه خر من الشريا
ولم يل من امر الناس شيئا۔ (حاكم)

"A time would soon come when a person would wish that it would have been better if he had fallen from a star

(ستارہ) rather than taking upon the responsibility of deciding the disputes among the people."

This Hadith also, reflects on the severe accountability of Qazi on the Day of Decision and the significance of administering of justice. Those who are responsible of administering justice would have no escape unless completely accounted for their deeds before Allah Ta'ala on the Day of Decision.

These two Ahadith - truly represent the spirit, significance, and importance Islamic law attaches to the doing of justice. In fact, justice (انصاف) is the first and the foremost principle. Qur'ãn has ordained us to observe this basic concept of justice throughout our lives. Though justice has its impact upon private and individual lives, however, its main concern is social life in general. Whatever we enter into some relationship with others, the question of justice inevitally comes in.

Under Islamic concept of justice, it visualises equality of all persons before law and refutes birth and descent, wealth and possessions, or colour and creed as claims to social distinction and special consideration. It is in these respects justice appears to be synonymous with equality.

A balanced approach be adopted in determine the rights of the people and every one's due share should be conscientiously rendered to him. This is, in fact, the Islamic concept of justice.

Place of Trial

The ruler of the state will appoint a Qazi's court at a distance which a person may cover in a day on foot. Distance of a day includes going from and coming back to his house. Considerations before the ruler are: complainant and his witnesses should not cover long distances. There should be no inconvenience in approaching the courts. Easy access for seeking redress is the purpose behind.

As to Mufti, the Ruler of State should appoint him at a distance where Salat-i-Qasar (صلاة القصر) becomes due, i.e., which a person may cover the distance going from his house on foot within three days. In other words the distance from the house of the litigants should not be more than 48 miles.[I]

Thus the residence of the litigant (plaintiff) and his witnesses is a factor in determining the jurisdiction of the Shariah court. The suit lies in the court within the jurisdiction of which they reside, even if the defendant resides in, or the subject matter of the suit situated within the jurisdiction of another Qazi. Preference is to be given to the complainant's (plaintiff) residence because the complainant is the aggrieved party.

If the complainant institutes a suit at a different court not satisfying the above requirements, his plaint or complaint may not be heard.

Another factor to determine the jurisdiction is the powers of a Qazi contained in his letter or appointment. Qazi's powers be limited to try only a particular class of cases, or to cover only specific area.

Thus the complainant (plaintiff) should file his suit in a competent court having jurisdiction over the matter and the area.

"Appointment of Qazi"

Appointment of Qazi is a duty incumbent (فرضی) on mankind. It is because that administration of justice is also ferz (فرضی) - a duty incumbent.

I. Adab-ul-Qazi, p. 434.

Allah Ta'ala says:

يَا دَاوُود إِنَّا جَعَلْنٰكَ خَلِيْفَةً فِى الاَرْضِ فاحْكُمْ بَيْنَ النَّاسِ بِالحَقِّ۔

(سورة ص، آية:٢٦)

"O David (داؤد)! We did indeed make thee a vicegerent on earth: so judge thou between men in truth (and justice)". (38:26)

Similarly Allah says to Prophet (peace be upon him):

Thus decide according to law, revealed by God."

Qada (قضاء) means decide cases with justice among mankind and in accordance to God revealed laws.

Institution of Qazi is mot important and significance. Qazi is ornamental in the due discharge of justice to all irrespective of status, dignity, wealth, colour or caste. Administration of justice is the basic need of the society which Qazi honestly executes it. For controlling litigation, giving protection to poor and weak against the cruels and aggressors, to promote good and prevent evils, to control and prevent malpractices, for all this Qazi's services are required.

Qazi is appointment by the King of Khalifa or President of a State. He must be a qualified and honest person, a deserving person who can perform the responsibility with honour and dignity.

"Qualifications"

The authority of a Qazi is not valid, unless he possess the same qualifications as required for a witness. The qualifications are:

1. Free man.
2. Sane person.

3. Adult.
4. A Musalman.
5. Never convicted of Had-e-Qazaf (Not convicted of slander).
6. Capable to speak.
7. Capable to see.
8. Capable to hear, and
9. A Mujtahid (a learned scholar in Qur'ãn and Ahadith).

Whoever possesses competency to be a witness is also competent to be a Qazi, and also, that the qualifications requisite to a witness are in the same manner requisite to a Qazi.

Qazi must be a justman at the time of his appointment. If afterwards, by taking bribes, proves himself an unjust man, he is not discharge by such conduct from his office, but he is, nevertheless, deserves dismission. This is the 'doctrine of Zahir Rawayet.'

However, to Imam Shafi'i, an unjust man is incapable for the office of Qazi, in the same manner as he is incompetent to give evidence.

It is related in the Nawadir, as an opinion of our three doctors, that an unjust man is incapable of discharging the duties of a Qazee.

The appointment of an ignorant man to the office of Qazee is valid. Imam Shafi'e differs with this view. He argues that such appointment supposes a capability of issuing decrees and of deciding between right and wrong. These acts cannot be performed without knowledge.

On the other hand it is argued that the Qazee's business may be to pass decrees merely on the opinion of others. Moreover, he is to render to every subject his just right and this object is accomplished by passing decrees on the opinion of others.

However, it does not mean that an unfit person be appointed. It is the responsibility of the sovereign to appoint a fit person, capable of discharging the duties and passing decrees. He should also in a superlative degree just and virtuous.

Prophet (peace be upon him) has said:

> "Whoever appoints a person to the discharge of any office, whilst there is another amongst his subjects more qualified for the same than the person so appointed, does surely commit an injury with respect to the right of God, the Prophet (peace be upon him), and the Musalmans."[1]

This Hadith makes it clear that the sovereign in appointing a person as Qazi has to take all precautions. He should appoint a qualified, learned person, a Mujtahid, having knowledge of Ahadith, Qur'ãn, and also of social customs and traditions as many laws are founded upon them.

There is no impropriety in selecting for the office of Qazee a person who has a through confidence in his ability to discharge the duties assigned to him because the companions of the Prophet (peace be upon him) accepted this appointment; and also, because the acceptance of it is a duty incumbent on mankind.

Further, selection of an unfit person would be a cause of the propagation of evil.

It is also said that the acceptance of the office of Qazee without compulsion is abominable. As Prophet (peace be upon him) has said:

I. Hedaya, p. 615.

"Whoever is appointed Qazi suffers the same fortune with an "animal, whose throat is mangled, instead of being cut by a sharp knife."

That is the reason that many of Prophet's (peace be upon him) companions used to decline to accept this appointment. In fact, the post of Qazi is full of responsibilities. Any person not fit should not offer himself to accept it. Qazi's accountability in the next world is very great.

Woman Qazi

Can there be a women Qazi?

A woman can be appointed as Qazi. She can hear and decide cases. However, she is not competent to hear cases where the liability is covered either under Ḧud or Qasas. In Qasas and Hudud cases she is not competent and her decision would not be valid. (Adab-e-Qazi, p. 431).

"Investigation"

In Saudi Arbia it is difficult to draw a line between investigation and enquiry. Police makes the investigation. Interrogation or the enquiry is aimed for establishing the suspicion, and preliminary enquiry or investigation for establishing the allegations. The preliminary investigation of crime before the trial is purely administrative in nature and is not subject to any form of judicial restrains.

On a complaint to Qazi, he also makes enquiry into the case with a view to give cognizance to the suit.

Practical difficulties are there. Judges often do not receive the minutes of police investigation. It was suggested in 'Draft Law of the Judicial Authority, that the power of police to investigate crimc should be with drawn and handed over to the prosecution.

Instead of police the prosecution should conduct the investigation. Here we may notice that changing hands does not materially alter the position. Prosecution and police both are responsible for the trial of accused. Transfer of investigating power from one to other makes no change. It should remain vested with police. As to enquiry it should be the part of the court's power. The only thing is that police should forward the minutes expeditiously.

Ahtisab

Ahtisab is connected with Amr-bin-Maroof (امربالمعروف), and Nahe-anil-Munkir (نهی عن المنکر), that is, when people leave doing good deeds (معروف) and indulge in doing evil deeds (نهی عن المنکر). Under such conditions, the Ruler of the State appoints 'MUHTASIB', an officer to check, control, and prevent spreading evils in the society, and promote goods and virtuous things (معروف). It has relations with investigations also.

Although to check, control and prevent spreading evils in the society and promote virtuousness is the responsibility of every Muslim, but in Islamic state a separate officer. Muhtasib is made responsible to take care of all these matters. He is duty bound (فرض) to attend all complaints made to him. He should investigate prevalent evils in the society. He is also authorised, to take such measures necessary to eradicate the evils. He may order the people to do goods deeds and follow the religious and righteous path, and prohibit them doing evil deeds (نهی عن المنکر).

Amar-bil-Maroof (امربالمعروف) are of three kinds:

1. حقوق اللہ - (Haqooq-Allah);
2. حقوق العباد - (Haqooq-ul-Ibad);
3. حقوق عام - (Common-Haqooq).

Again Haqooq-Allah (حقوق الله) are divided into two categories:

1. Applicable to a group of people not less than forty in number, a congration which is sufficient to perform (صلاة جمعه) Sala-te-Juma'a. For example a group of people migrating from a place.
2. Matters connected with individuals, such as individual is indifferent in performing (صلاة) salat intime, delaying it intentionally.

In these matters the Mohtasib may interfere and issue orders as deem necessary.

Haqooq-ul-Ibad (حقوق العباد) may also be classified under two heads:

1. حقوق العباد خاص - (Haqooq-ul-Ibad-Khas), and
2. حقوق العباد عام - (Haqooq-ul-Ibad-Aam).

Haqooq-ul-Ibad-Khas (حقوق العباد خاص) are connected with mutual dealings, rights and duties of individuals to each other in the society. If any person owes any material thing to another and that person has right or claim to take back that thing from him, the person concerned intentionally avoid or delays in the returning of that thing, the Mohtasib may order such person to return the thing so claimed. But this power is subject to one limitation that Mohtasib may order the returning only when the claimant specifically requests him. Without a demand from the claimant, Mohtasib cannot interfere.

Cases relating to 'breach of trust' (الخيانة بالامانه) are also covered under this Head of Haqooq-ul-Ibad-Khas. But Khiyanat-ul-Amanat case relating to Baitul-Mal (بيت المال) and wakf's (اوقاف) may be covered under Haqooq-ul-Ibad-Aam also. On breach of trust, if a demand is made to the Mohtasib for recovery of وديعت (trust), then he would order the violator for return of it. He cannot imprison the violator. That part is covered under the jurisdiction of regular court of Qazi.

Haqooq-ul-Ibad-Aam (حقوق العباد عام) are matters connected with the general welfare of the masses. For example supply of water in any river is effected due to any obstruction, and the masses are adversely effected by the shortage of water, then Mohtasib may take suitable and reasonable steps for removing such obstructions.

As to Mushtrak-Haqooq (مشترك حقوق), such matters as arranging marriages of widow, if they so desire, ordering for the observance of Iddat (عدّة), ordering people not to take more labor from animal beyond their capacity or order to provide feeders to the animals as sufficient for satisfying their hungers are covered under this right.

Nahi-Anil-Munkir (نهى عن المنكر), means evil spreading in the society. It may be divided into three parts:

1. Evils connected with حقوق الله (Haqooq-Allah);
2. Evils connected with حقوق العباد Haqooq-ul-Ibad); and
3. Evils connected with Mushtarik (مشترك).

Again evils connected with Haqooq-Allah are divided into:

1. Evils connected with the method of worship, effecting changes in Sunnah, etc., for example changing (اذان) Azan pattern, or not observing purity of cloths. Coming wearing impure cloths in the Mosque etc., Muhtsib may order them to make corrections.

2. Evils connected with doubts and false allegations about others, for example doubting upon the character of male and female talking in suspicious

circumstances or in privacy. Muhtasib may warn them in such condition because it may give rise to doubts and false allegations about their integrities.

Under حقوق الله و حقوق العباد عام (Haqooq-Allah and Haqooq-ul-Ibad in common) evil includes looking into neighbours house, etc.,

There is one more category, that is, (Mun-ke-rat-Haqooq-ul-Nas, includes when a person constructs something in the neighbours' courtyard or put a slipper over the walls of his neighbour with out his permission. Muhtasib may prevent such construction but only when neighbour makes a complaint to him. He cannot take an initiative in such a matter on his own.

In brief, it may be stated that powers vested in Muhtsib in cases of Ahtisab, that is, امر بالمعروف (Amar-bil-maroof_, and (Nahe-Anil-Munkir) are very wide. Not only investigations of evils, but prevention and control of evils are all included within his power. In Saudi Arabia, where Shariah law is in force, there is no such designation as Muhtasib, but his powers are performed by different committees formed under the Royal Regulations, such as, Forgery Committee, Bribery Committed, Grievance Board, etc., etc.

Under Islamic law Muhtasib in enforcing his orders for preventing the evils may take the assistance of police also. But evil doers cannot be imprisoned by him. Such powers are vested in the courts only.

"Securing the Appearance of Parties in the Court: Islamic Law"

Criminal are divided into two categories with regard to the procedure for bringing action before the Shariah courts. First, those which are tried only on a demand by a private claimant, and are therefore called crimes of private right or Haqq-al-'Abd.

Secondly, those in which action can be brought by anyone, and therefore, are called crimes of the public right, or Haqq-Allah.

The claimant or complainant has to file a (petition) in the Shariah court. Thereafter the court must notifying if the action is of private right, and to inform the prosecution if the action is a public right. The person against whom allegations have been made is to be summoned on a fixed date before the court.

If a person on receiving summons does not appear on the fixed date, it is to be presumed by the court that his case is weak and the opponent's complaint has force in it. But if the summoned person gives reasons for his absence, those reasons must be taken into consideration.

Hazrat Hasan reported that Rasool-Allah (peace be upon him) said:

عن الحسن قال: قال رسول الله صلى الله عليه وسلم، من دعى الى حاكم من حكام المسلمين فلم يجب فهو ظالم لا حق له۔

(سنن الدار قطنی، جلد دوم، ص ۵۱۵، طبع دهلی ۱۳۱۰ھ)

"If a person is called or summoned by any Hakim-e-Adalat, and he does not comply with the order, he is a cruel person and he should not be given any right."

It makes it clear that if a person is summoned by the court which he has received and does not comply with the court's order. He forfeits all his rights. Prophet (peace be upon him) has called such a person cruel. No right be given to him if he makes any claim.

In another hadith, narrated by Hazrat Abu-Musa-Ashari (R.A.) that Hazrat Ma'wia-bin-Abi-Sufian (R.A.) told to him that the procedure which Prophet (peace be upon him) adopted in cases where two persons came to him with a case or dispute, and any date fixed for hearing in consultation with them, and on that fixed date, one of them appeared and the other not, then Prophet (peace be upon him) used to decide the case or dispute in favour of the person appeared and against that person who did not appear."

This also shows the signification of courts' summons. If any one does not appear, knowingly the date fixed for hearing, he loses his right. Prophet (peace be upon him) did decide the case against such an absentee. Islamic law does not favour delaying in delivering the judgement. If must be expedited unless there is a valid ground for delay in delivering the judgement. Thus appearance in the court when summoned is binding.

"Arrest and Bail"

In cases of complaint if the Shariah court is of the view that person be detained or arrested, it may order to this effect. The accused may be taken into custody. But this is required only in cases of serious nature, and where the possibility is that the person may abscond or would avoid attending proceedings in the court against him. If an accused is summoned, does not appear before the court on a fixed date for hearing, the court may compel his appearance. Warrant may be issued against him. Police may arrest and bring him before the court.

Jurists justify the arrest of the accused on the basis of the following hadith:

عن ابی هریرة رضی الله عنه ان النبی صلی الله علیه سلم وسلم
جس رجلا فی تهمة یوما ولیلة استظهارا واحتیاا۔

(حاکم المستدرك علی الصحیحین جلد چهارم، ص ۱۰۲)

"Hazrat Abu Hurera (R.A.) narrated that Prophet (peace be upon him) ordered a person accused of a crime to be detained in custody for one day and night with the purpose to know the reality of the fact and as a pre-cautionary measure."

But detention and arrest should be only on serious charge. In breach of trust cases, arrest and detention of an accused may be ordered only when the nature of the offence is serious.

In another Hadith Hazrat Nehreen-Hakeem narrated that his father quoted his father (grand-father) that:

عن بهز بن حكيم عن ابيه عن جده ان النبى صلى الله عليهوسلم

جس رجلا فى تهة- (ابو داؤد، ابواب القضاء، جلد دوم، ص ١٠٠)

"Prophet (peace be upon him) detained a person, who was charged for an offence, in custody."

Mulla Ali Qari making observations upon the hadith says that the person was detained either because he gave a false evidence or someone complained against him for the commission of crime or made a claim for debt against him. Prophet (peace be upon him) detained that person so that it might be ascertained whether there was any truth in the claim of the complainant. He was released because no proof could be given against him. For detaining a person in custody it is necessary that the court should take into consideration whether there is a possible prima facie case against him or not. In other words Mulla Ali Qair is of the view that an accused person is not to be arrested or detained in every case. It is necessary that there must exist the possibility of a prima facie case against him.

Arrested person may be asked to furnish bail or KAFALIT. 'It literally means junction. In the language of the law it signifies the junction of one person to another in relation to a claim.'

In other words the person who renders obligatory on himself the claim of another, whether it relates to person or property, is termed kafeel, or surety. Thus under Islamic law for release of a person from custody the accused be asked to furnish bail. If the possibility in breach of trust cases is that he would damage the trust property court may ask bail for security the property also.

It makes clear that bail may be two descriptions:

1. Bail for the person, which is known as 'Hazir-Zaminee', and
2. Bail for property, termed as Mal-Zaminee.

It is all discretionary with the court to release a person on bail. If the circumstances warrant that he should not be released even of furnishing the sureties, the bail may be refused. Court may grant the bail or may not grant the bail. But it is not arbitrary with the judge. Decision either to grant bail or not to grant depends upon the seriousness of the allegations and surrounding circumstances. Refusal to grant bail must be based on reasons.

"Trial"

During Caliph Hazrat 'Umar (R.A.), Farmans were issued to the governors for the guidance of Shariah courts. Once such Farman sent to Abu Musa Ashari, the governor of Kofa, reflects the interest the Caliph was taking in procedural matters of court trial. The purpose was that no one should suffer, and justice be done to all. Farman is noted below:

1. The administration of justice is essential: Treay all men justly and on equal footing when they appear before you in your court so that the weak may not be disappointed from justice and the well-to-do may be hope to get any advantage from you;
2. The burden of proof is on the person who puts forward a claim and oath on the person who denies it;

3. Compromise is allowable provided it does not make a lawful thing illegal, and the illegal thing lawful;

4. A decision passed yesterday regarding a dispute may be revised on the next day so that you may arrive at a correct decision;

5. It there be any doubt on a point and no text or tradition is available, then ponder over it and again ponder over it and try to find out precedents, then try to solve it by ratiocination;

6. When a party desires to produce evidence, fix a date of hearing;

7. If he adduces proof, adjudge his rights in his favour, otherwise dismiss his claim;

8. All Muslims are competent witnesses amongst themselves except those who have suffered the punishment of hadd or have been characterized as liers by the court, or whose clientage is doubtful."[I]

These were some of preliminary instructions issued by the Caliph for guidance of the court. The law at the time was on initial stage. Since then Islamic jurisprudence and rules relating to trial procedure have gone tremendous changes. We will examine some of the Rules governing trial procedure in next following paragraphs.

"Institution of Suits in Shariah Court"

Institution of suits in Shariat court depends upon the nature of crime committed and the category under which it falls. Broadly speaking crimes may be covered either under Haqooq-Allah (حقوق الله), or Haqooq-ul-Ibad (حقوق العباد), or Mushtareq-Haqooq (مشترك حقوق). Again Haqooq-ul-

I. Shibli: "A-Faruq", Part II, pp. 49-50.

Ibad (حقوق العباد) are divided into:

1. Haqooq-ul-Ibad Khas (حقوق العباد خاص) and
2. Haqooq-ul-Abad-Aam (حقوق العباد عام).

Cases under Haqooq-ul-Ibad Khas or Jara'im-al-Haqq-al-Khas can be tried by the court of Qazi only on a demand by a private claimant. While in Haqooq-al-Ibad-Aam, action can be brought by anyone. These are crimes of public nature.

Criminal breach of trust as referred earlier comes under private right, i.e., Haqooq-al-Ibad Khas as well as Haqooq-ul-Ibad-Aam. The procedure followed in institution of suit is simple. Plaint (دعوئ) is failed by the complainant in the competent court of jurisdiction. In the cases of Haqooq-ul-Ibad-Aam any person any file a complaint.

Breach of trust, under Islamic concept, is civil in nature. But it depends upon plaintiff, if he is interested to have criminal trial, then he is to move an application to this effect before the Qazi. As such there is no bar of criminal trial in breach of trust cases.

The plaint (دعوئ), to be filed in Shariah court should fulfil the following requirements:

1. (مدعا ليه) (plaintiff), who files the suit, and مدعا عليهم (defendant), against whom suit is filed, both should be major and of sound mind. A minor not having maturity of understanding cannot file a suit. Similarly, if plaintiff and defendant, both are minors with immature understanding capabilities or insane, there can be no suit filed against either of them. Even if under such conditions a suit is instituted against them, they are not bound to file written statements (دعوئ) in their defence. The rule is that the written statements from the defendants is asked only when

the plaint satisfies all procedural and pleading requirements. When plaint is itself, ib-initio defective and illegal, written statement of the defence cannot be asked to be filed.

2. Cause of plaint should be known, definite and ascertained. Without which it is difficult to produce witnesses and also to give the judgement. In cases of debt or financial claims, the gross-sum or value of property, the nature of loss, and manner how loss caused should also be given in the plaint, then only 'Den (دین)' may be determined.

3. If the issue related to an immovable property, it must be mentioned in the plaint that the property in dispute is in the possession of the defendant (مدعا علیهم) so that he may be made party to the suit.

4. The plaint also include cause of action and redress be specifically demanded by the plaintiff, then only the claim can be determined. If he demands penal action, then court will take into consideration accordingly.

5. The plaintiff should demand redress in his own language unless some disability makes it impossible.

6. The plaint should be instituted in the court room itself and be submitted before in the presence of Qazi. Witness in support also be presented before Qazi sitting in the court.

7. Hearing of plaint (دعویٰ), and proof there to can be only in the presence of the defendant. His presence is necessary.

8. Plaint (دعویٰ) relating to any matter previously decided by the Qazi, cannot be entertained again on the same issue. Matter should also not be pending in another court relating to the same subject matter.

9. Plaint relating to the subject matter which is humanly impossible to attain, for example a claim of a father about

a boy as his son, who is older than the father, cannot be heard.

10. Plaint (دعویٰ) should also include names addresses of the plaintiff and defendant, and should be entered in the court register. Register should also have the date and names and addresses of the witnesses.

The plaint (دعویٰ) should fulfil the above requisites. If these requisites are absent then plaint would not be considered legally valid and sound, and would not be heard by the Qazi. Qazi on receiving the plaint orders to call the person against whom plaint is filed to appear before him and answer the allegations. The defendant is given full opportunity to prepare the defence and file the answer. With this simple procedure the trial begins.

The same procedure is followed in Shariah courts of Saudi Arabia. Crimes are divided into two categories, public and private claims. Party effected under private claim is to file the suit while under public claim anyone can take action.

Since the establishment of the Kingdom of Saudi Arabia, most crimes of the public right have been brought to court by the executive authorities. In Makkah, the vice royalty used to refer such crimes to court. In 1927, King Abdul Aziz objected to the way in which the grand Shatiah court of Makkah accepted cases without their first being referred to it by the vice royalty. He explained that the vice royalty could possibly have some information regarding the case in issue which no private person or other authority had. In 1928, the consultative council decided that the magistrate court must not hear criminal cases until they had been referred to it by the vice royalty.

But the vice royalty was not the only authority which used to bring criminal actions of the public right before the courts in Makkah. The police used also to do so in crimes falling within the jurisdiction of a magistrate court, especially if they were related to minor offences.[1]

When a crime is referred to the court by an executive authority, it must be handled by the appropriate public prosecutor, an authority which is competent to prosecute the defendant in a criminal case.

If a private claimant brings an action and the court discovers that he himself has in some way participated in the crime, the court may take the initiative and try him, without asking the public prosecutor to handle the prosecution. But if the case is so complicated that it requires a preliminary investigation the court must refer it to the police, and after the investigation has been completed the public prosecutor may prosecute the accused. However, Shariah Judges decline to look into any case unless they deem that they are able to do so with complete impartiality.

As to cognizance of the charge, the court do not restrict the receivability of an action to any formal measure. However, the acceptance of an action by the court is subject to three conditions:

1. Tahrir i.e., stating the case adequately,
2. The accused must be a till alive,
3. The time prescribed for trying the charge has not lapsed.

When the court gives cognizance to the charge, then it must immediately fix a date for the hearing. However, adequate consideration to the conditions of defendant be given in fixing the date for hearing. The hearing may be postponed if the parties need long time than that already fixed to produce his evidence.

The law of 1952 (A) also lays down provisions relating to the dropping of a case if the claimant fails to appear the first session

---

1. Statute of Directorate of Public Security, Articles - 8. 71.

without a reasonable excuse. Case may be restored if the claimant moves the court for fixing hearing date again. Even if he does not appear, then case would be dismissed, and can be restored only on High order. The dropping of a case does not mean it's dismissal.

"Charge"

When the defendant appears in the court, the plaintiff or his advocate will explain the allegations to the defendant. Qazi also explains the allegations and ask the defendant to reply. If the defendant accept the claim, Qazi will decide the case accordingly. If he denies the allegations, he will be given an opportunity to prepare the defence and reply the allegations.

Burden of Proof

The general rule about the burden of proof is that a person who alleges a fact must proof it. Thus it is the responsibility of a plaintiff or complainant that he should proof his allegations.

(حضرت عمر بن شعیب) Hazrat Umar bin Shoeeb quotes his father, and father quotes his father Hazrat Abdul bin Umar bin Aas (R.A.) (حضرت عبد البن عمر بن عاص) that Prophet (peace be upon him) during his address (خطبه) said:

عن عمرو بن شعیب عن ابیه عن جده ان النبی صلی الله علیه
وسلم قال فی خطبته : البینة علی المدعی والیمین علی المدعی
علیه۔ (جامع ترمزی، مع ماشیة تحفة الا حوذی، جلد دوم، ص ۲۸۰)

"Responsibility of burden of proof is on plaintiff, and Oath is on defendant". (Tirmizi - P. 280, Vol. II).

عن ابن عباس ان رسول الله صلی الله علیه وسلم قطی ان الیمین
علی المدعی علیه هذا حدیث حسن صحیح والعمل علی حذا
عند احل العام والیمین دلی المدعی علیه۔
(جامع الترمذی جلد دوم، ص ۲۸۰ مع تحفة الا حوذی)

Hazrat Abdullah bin Abbas narrated that Prophet (peace be upon him) said:

"Oath taking is on Defendant".

He further says that it is a correct hadith that it has been in practice among the followers of Prophet (peace be upon him) and all other learned scholars that 'burden of proof is on plaintiff' and 'oath is upon defendant.'

These words that 'burden of proof 'is on plaintiff' and 'oath on defendant' have been repeatedly used in Ahadith and have no doubt about it's correctness.

Men is greedy by nature. If the courts start giving whatever is claimed without proof, there would be chaotic conditions. Therefore, allegations and claims are subject to limitations. Complainant must proof beyond reasonable doubt his allegations. If the plaintiff of complainant has no proof than the matter would be decided on the oath of the defendant. Oath taking is only when the complainant has no proof in support of his allegations and demands oath be given to the defendant.

عن علقمة بن وائل بن حجر الحضرخی عن ابیه قال: جاء رجل من حضرموت، ورجل من کندة الی رسول الله صلی الله علیه وسلم فقال الحضرمی: یارسول الله ان هذا غلبنی علی ارض کانت لابی فقال الکندی: هی ارضی فی یدی ازرعها، لیس له فیها حق۔ فقال النبی صلی الله علیه وسلم للحضرمی: الك بینة؟ قال: لا قال:فلك یمینه۔ قال یا رسول الله! انه فاجر، لیس یبالی ما حلف، لیس یتودع من شئی۔ فقال لیس لك منه الا ذلك۔

(ابو داؤد، ابواب القضاء، جلد دوم، ص ۱۵۳، نولکشور ۱۳۹۳ھ)

We may here a hadith, where two person, one belonging to Haz-re-Mot, and another resident of Kunda, approached the Prophet (peace be upon him) and person belong to Haz-re-Mot told to Prophet that: 'the other one along with him has forcibly taken his land from him. Person belonged to Kunda denied the allegation and said to Prophet (peace be upon him) that land belonged to him and he was cultivating. The Hazrani had no right in the land. Then Prophet (peace be upon him) asked Hazrni, "Do you have any proof about the land!"

Hazrani replied "No", Then Prophet (peace be upon him) told him:

"Then you can ask defendant to take oath".

Hazrani replied to Prophet (peace be upon him) that 'Kundi is a bad character person. He has no regard for his statements. Taking oath is immaterial for him. He is not afraid of God also. He never hesitates doing anything". The Prophet (peace be upon him) said:

"Whatever may be, you have the only right to take oath from him".

This Hadith makes it clear that if the complainant has no proof in support of his allegations than on the oath of defendant case will be decided. If is not of significance that the possibility is that defendant may take a false oah. Only the oath of defendant under such circumstances would determine the suit.

A similar Hadith has been narrated by Hazrat Abu Hurera (R.A.). He narrated that Prophet (peace be upon him) said:

عن ابی هریرة: ان رسول الله صلی الله علیه وسلم قال: البینة ولی من ادعی والیمین علی من ابکر الافی القسامة۔
(سنن الداد قطنی، جلد دوم، ص ۵۱۷، طع دهلی ۱۳۱۰ھ)

"Burden of proof is on person who makes the claim, and oath taking is the responsibility of a person who denies such a claim. But قسامت (Qasamat) is free from it".

(Qasamat) is a kind of (forming opinion on alalogy). It is free from this general law. (Qasamat) applies only is situations when other strong proofs are absent. Thus Qasamat is different from the rule of burden of proof.

These Ahadith make it abundantly clear that 'Burden of Proof' is on the complainant. He is to prove it and then court would determine the liability of the accused.

In Pakistan Islamic Law of Evidence has been condified. This general rule relating to burden of proof has been incorporated in section 81. It reads as:

> The burden of proof shall rest with the person who asserts a right and desires a court to give judgement in his favour in respect of that right."

As to oath taking from the defendant or refusal to take oath, and their effect on the proceeding has been elaborated in Chapter 12, of Draft Ordinance Islamic Law of Evidence.

Section 56, explains oath taking or refusal of oath taking by the defendant as follows:

> "If the plaintiff (مدعی) fails to prove his claim the defendant shall, subject to demand by the plaintiff be given oath, and if the defendant denies on oath the claim of the plaintiff shall be dismissed".

When the complainant fails to prove the allegations than he may demand on oath be given to the defendant. Thus oath taking is subject to the demand made by the plaintiff. If the defendant takes the oath on his own, it would not be covered under this section. Once oath taken by the defendant on demand by the complainant and he denies the allegation, complainant's case would be dismissed.

Procedure of oath taking is further elaborated under the explanation attached to the section.

Explanation Elaborates

> "Oath may be demanded in every such case where oath or refusal to take oath can be made basis of decision".

Exception to the explanation when oath cannot be demanded.

Exceptions

1. "Oath cannot be demanded in case liable to Hadd except in the case of Shriqah (سرقه - theft) where it can be demanded to make a decision in respect of property stolen on the basis of refusal to take oath."

Mode of taking oath is given in clause (2). It says:

2. "Oath shall be given in the name of Allah or attributive names of Allah, such as one should say "Wallah, Billah, Tallah or Birrahmanirrahim (برر حمن الرحيم).

In administering oath under clause (2), no discrimination is to be made on the basis of religion. Same method of oath taking is to be applied to Muslim and non-Muslim alike.

Explanation I reads:

> "The method provided in sub-section (2) above shall be adopted in all cases whether the party is a Muslim or non-Muslim".

The court keeping in view the nature of the case and circumstances if considers proper and also in order to put force in oath, may take the oath at a specific time which Muslims consider sacred, and at a sacred place also. Similarly the court may ask the defendant to take oath by putting hand on Qur'ãn-e-Majid

Explanation II elaborates as:

> "The court, if it deems fit and the nature and circumstances of the case demand, may, in order to put force in oath, take oath from Muslim at sacred time like that of 'asr (عصر) or at a sacred place (like a Mosque), and likewise a Muslim may be made to take oath putting his hand on the Qur'ãn-e-Majid and a non-Muslim on his sacred book".

Clause (B), explains persons who are competent to demand oath on behalf of the plaintiff or complainant, and persons who cannot be subjected to oath. It reads:

3. "The demand for oath may be made by a representative of a party but he, in his representation capacity, cannot be subjected to oath (yamin)".

This point has been further clarified under the explanation.

Explanation:

> "The vakeel (وكيل Agent) of a plaintiff may demand oath from the defendant (مدعا عليهم) but in place of defendant his vakeel or representation shall neither take oath nor have authority to refuse it".

The effect of refusal to take oath are given in section 60 as:

> "In cases relating to Mu'amlat (معاملات) dealings if the party, from whom oath has been demanded by the court, clearly refuses to take oath or remains silent without due excuse, the court shall decide the case against him on the basis of his refusal to take oath, and he shall have no option to take oath afterwards".

Silence due to natural disability would not amount to refusal. In such a case court will resort to other means of ascertaining the intention of the defendant. Explanation I below makes it clear.

Explanation I:

> If the defendant remains silent due to his being def dumb, his silence shall not be regarded as refusal to take oath unless the court is satisfied by resorting to other names such as writing etc., that the defendant does not want to take oath.

In oath taking court has to warn the defendant of consequences of his refusal to take oath. This warning is to be given thrice repeatedly. Even after explaining the consequences of his refusal and repeated warnings if he adheres to his refusal to take oath, the court would decide the case against him. Explanation II given below makes the point clear.

Explanation II:

> "The party concerned be warned by the court thrice and each time informed of he consequences which may arise from his refusal to take oath, but if he, inspite of all this, persits in his refusal, the matter shall be decided against him".

Section 63 deals with oath in cases Tazeer: "The accused shall on demand by the complainant, be given oath when no proof is available in a case liable to Tazeer, and if he refuses to take oath shall be liable to Tazeer.

Provided that no oath shall be given in cases where Tazeer is imposed as a 'Haqqul-ul-Allah (حقوق الله the right of Allah).

Criminal breach of trust cases would be covered under section 63, because in such cases the punishment awarded is Tazeer. Further breach of trust is covered under (Haqqul-ul-Ibad Khas).

It has also been made clear under section 58 that oath is to be given by court. 'The oath shall be given by the court. If the defendant (مدعا علیهم) on demand by the plaintiff took oath on his own accord, before it was asked by the court, it shall not be valid, and he shall be given oath again by the court.'

The established rule according to Hedaya is that the right of demanding an oath from the defendant rests upon the lack of evidence on the part of the plaintiff. To a Western trained lawyer, this law may be strange and unique in nature, or unusual or harsh. A law may be unusual or harsh, but the law is law. Further it should be kept in mind that Islamic law is not separate from one's faith or religion. Under Islamic law the presumption is that no Muslim would tell lie upon oath by putting hand on Qur'ãn or swearing in Allah's name. To a Muslim lying under oath is considered to be the most serious sin which a man may commit. If the defendant on demand takes the oath, the complaint's case is dismissed.

Here we may discuss a situation which may arise during litigation that after the complaint made, it is the responsibility of the complainant to prove the allegations. Suppose he produces one witness only where the requirement under Islamic law is that there should be two male witness or one male and two female witnesses be produced in support. Qazi asks the complainant to produce the other witness also. The complainant regrets his inability to produce the second witness. Question is: Can he demand an oath to be taken from the defendant?

Answer is: "According to Shafi-i, Maliki and Hambali schools of law, "If the plaintiff has only one witness, he may complete his evidence by taking on oath."

"According to Hanafi School of law and some Muslim jurists, the court in its discretion, may disregard the testimony of the witness, and instead may require the defendant to take an oath".[1]

It seems that in case where there is only one witness in support of allegation, then the alternative is that the complainant may be given an opportunity to demand the oath to be given the defendant.

Those who are accustomed to the common law system, this simple procedure of proof makes them surprise. Here we may refer a trial in which an American was made accused and the plaintiff presented only one witness before the Qazi.

Qazi says to the plaintiff:

> "To prove your claim under our law (Islamic Law), you are required to produce two witnesses to testify to the truth of your complaint. You have presented only one witness. Do you have the second one too?".

The complainant said he had not. "The you have one right left to you," the Qazi said, "You may demand the oath".

"I demand the oath", said the complainant.

The accused then turned to the ARAMCO lawyers representing him and whispered.

"What is oath".

The lawyer hesitated, wondering if, in just a few seconds, he could adequately explains this ancient, solemn cornerstone of the Shariah law.

I. Fiqh-al-Sunnah by Sayyeed Sadiq: Vide, Article: 'The Shariah Court: Their Relation to the Development of Islamic Law in the Philoppines', - by Judge Corocoy D. Mason', p. 81.

"It is like this". He said finally: "To a Muslim lying under oath is one of the most serious sins that a man can commit. So, he is asking our to swear that you are innocent, if you do not take oath you will be immediately found guilty. But if you do so, it will be the truth".

The defendant quickly decided, "I will take the oath", he said. A moment later, in English, he repeated after the Qazi the oath prescribed for Christians:

> "I............... in the name of God who gave Jesus, son of Merry, the Holy Bible and, with His Will, cured the sick, the leper and the deaf, swear that I did not kick (complainant's name) in the right leg nor did I call him 'son of a bastard".

As soon as he finished the oath the American was adjudged not guilty and released - freed by an unusual aspect of an unusual system of law, the noble Shariah, a Code of Law that has guided Muslim courts for 1300 years".[1]

In Saudi Arabia, Shariay courts are following this rule. It can be said that the burden of proof with regard to a particular fact lies on the party who alleges that fact. The to begin; that is to say makes the opening speech and renders his make out a prima facie case. The plaintiff or the complainant must render the minimum evidence sufficient to prove his allegations.

Burden of proof on defence may be lighter especially in regard to Hudud. The person who alleges has more responsibility. Burden of proof is heavy upon him. He is to proof the allegations beyond reasonable doubts.

The burden of proof can be dispensed with on cases where the respondent or the accused mixed a confession or by a

---

I. Supra N.P.

presumption. In cases where the defendant denies the allegations, then the burden of proof to refute the charges, and establish his innocence, and legal inability to commit crime would be upon him. But this burden, as said earlier, in comparison to the responsibility of the complainant or plaintiff is lighter in the sense that he is suppose to create a doubt about the truthfullness of the allegations. If he succeeds to create doubt in the mind of the judge, benefit will go to him.

Under English law evidence are categorised under two categories:

1. Evidence as means of proof; and
2. Evidence as not means of proof.

This categorisation is not recognized under the Shariah law applied in Saudi Arabia. Law sometimes recognizes the evidence which is a means of proof and evidence which is not so under one category. Example may be given of real evidence which comes under the evidence of presumptions. Further, under Saudi Arabia law relating to formal confession as means of proof and informal confession as not means of concession are treated on equal footing.

"Confession"

The Islamic law method of proof includes three things:

1. قرائنی قطعیه - Qarain-e-Qat'iyyah - Irrebulattable presumptions.
2. Oath or refusal to rake oath; and
3. Iqrar (اقرار) Confession of Admission.

The first, Qara-in-e-Qatiyyah relates to such inferences as are inferred from the circumstances reaching the degree of certainly. Example can be given whcrc a man agitated with fear comes out of a vacant house with a blood stained dagger in his hand. Soon after, the dead body of a man, who is recently killed, is found in that house. Here from the facts and circumstances as above noted a strong presumption to the degree of certainty may be infrared that the person thus came out was the killer of the deceased.

As to the second method of taking oath or refusal to take oath we have already made necessary references in the earlier paragraphs. It means that if the plaintiff (مدعی) fails to prove his claim, the defendant shall, subject to the demand by the plaintiff, be given an oath and if the defendant denies on oath, the claim of the plaintiff, shall be dismissed. Oath can be demanded in every case where oath or refusal to take oath can be made basis of decision.

The third method of proof is (اقرار) iqrar (confession).

Before giving the details about the confession we will refer some Qur'ãnic verses here to show the significance of testimony. If a person is a witness to a fact when invited to narrate the incidence he should tell the truth. It is obligatory on him and should not conceal anything. Allah commands:

ولا یاب الشهداء اذا مادعوا۔

(سورة البقرة، آية: ٢٨٢)

"The witnesses should not refuse - when they are called on (For evidence) (2:282).

Thus Allah makes it obligatory on witness not to refuse to tell whatever they know about any particular fact.

Again Allah says:

ولا تَكْتُموا الشَهَادَةَ ومن يَكْتُمُها فَانَّه اِثْم قَلْبِهِ واللّٰهُ بِمَا تَعْمَلُونَ عَلِيْمٌ۔

(سورة البقرة، آية: ٢٨٣)

> "Conceal not evidence for whoever conceal it, His heart is tainted with sin. And Allah knoweth all that ye do". (2:283).

Thus to Allah Ta'ala whoever conceals the testimony knowingly he is a sinner. Allah makes it obligatory to give the testimony if you know the facts of a case. Confession is one such testimony upon which the decision depends.

In Hedaya it has been explained that it is incumbent upon witnesses to bear the testimony, nor is it lawful for them to conceal it, when the party concerned demands it from them. The requisition of the party, however, is a condition; because the delivery of testimony is the right of the party, and therefore rests upon his requisition of it, as is the case with all other rights.

Confession is most significant because on the basis this testimony the judge is to pronounce the judgement. After confession it is essential on the judge to give decision. It is inferred from Hadith noted below:

Prophet (peace be upon him) says:

> "Anees go to this woman. If she makes confession of her guilt, execute رجم (rajam) on her".

From the hadith it is made clear that confession will be the basis of judgement. Judge is under obligation to give his decision.

Confession is defined as:

> "Giving of information by a person that he is under some obligation to another person in respect of some right."

> "The person making confession (admission) is called Muqirr (مقر) whose right is admitted is called Muqirr lahu (مقر له), and the right which is admitted is called Muqirr-bihi (مقر به)."

"The saying of a Muqirr that Zaid owes nothing to him, or that he has absolved him of his debt, or right, or that he has relinquished his right, or that he has discarded his right, fall under the definition of Iqrar (confession)."[1]

Valid Iqrar

Under the following conditions confession would be vaid -

1. The person who makes the confession should be of sound mind;
2. Person should be adult; and
3. Independent of Free person.

If a confession is made by an infant, not capable to judge things rightly or wrongly, such a confession would be illegal. Similarly confession made by instance is also not valid.

Prophet (peace be upon him) says: Three person are not competent to make confession. They are:

1. An infant till he becomes major or adult;
2. A person sleeping, till he is not awaken; and
3. مجنون (unconscious or instance) till gets into senses or gains consciousness.

This insane person or person who is unconscious or sleeping, when gains consciousness then can be competent to make confession otherwise not.

If an infant reaching near toe adulthood makes a confession and at the time of confession claims to be adult also, then his confession would be admissible. Muqirr-lahu

---

1. Section 64, Draft Ordinance, Islamic Law of Evidence of Pakistan, 1982.

(مقرله), whose right is admitted, would give proof of his adulthood. The person who makes the confession under a situation would not be governed oath because it has already been declared as minor.

Section 65 of Pakistan Islamic Law of Evidence lays down the following condition for a valid confession:

Clause (1) : "Iqrar must be made by a person who is Aqil and Baligh"

Exception : "A minor who has been authorised by his wali (ولی) or guardian to carry on business and deal with people shall be regarded as adult for the purpose of this section and an Iqrar (اقرار) made by him shall be accepted as valid."

Condition validating Iqrar confession have further been elaborated by three explanations attached to the section.

Explanation I says:

> "Iqrar made by such a minor who has been authorised to do business and deal with people shall be treated like that of an adult in respect of matters relating to business and dealing such as Dain (دین debt), Amanat امانت Ariah (عاديه) Muzarabah (مزاربه), and Ghash (غصب) etc."

Explanation II lays down that matters not connected with trade and business such as dower, offences liable to fine and security matters, a minor's confession would not be valid even if the minor has been authorised to make such confession by his guardian.

Explanation II says:

"In matters not relating to trade and dealings, such as Mahr (مهر Dower), Jinayat (جنايات) - offences liable to fine) and Kifalah (كفالہ security) Iqrar made by a minor shall not be accepted even if so authorised by his Wali".

Explanation third declares that an Iqrar by a minor, lunatic or insane, and by a guardian against the interest of his minor ward shall not be valid and cannot be admitted.

Under clauses (2), (3) and (4), it further lays down that for (مقر له) Muqirr-lahu it is not a condition that he should also be adult and sane. Coercion is anther ground which makes confession in admissible. An Iqrar of a person who is under the influence of intoxication would not be valid in cases where liability is under Hudud.

Explanation III -

"Iqrar made by a minor or a lunatic or an insance person shall not be admissible, and if the Wali or guardian of such persons makes an Iqrar which is adverse to the interests of such persons, such an Iqrar also shall not be admissible.

Clause (2)	:	"Being 'Aqil (عاقل sane) and Baligh (بالغ adult) is not a condition for Muqirr Lahu (مقر له).
Clause (2)		Iqrar made under coercion shall not be admissible.
Clause (3)	:	"Iqrar made under the influence of intoxication shall not be admissible in cases liable to hudud."

Thus a person who makes the confession satisfied the above requisites, his confession would be valid and admissible in evidence. Judge is to pronounce judgement on such a confession.

In Saudi Arabia confession (or admission) is divided into two classes:

1. Formal confession, and
2. Informal confession.

Formal confession is one which is made before the trial court. Whereas informal confession is usually made out side the court. The later one must be proved in the same way as a fact is proved in the court. 'It is not considered a hearsay evidence. It is considered a confession, when proved as conclusive as the formal one is.[I]

"Requisites of a Valid Confession"

In Saudi Arabia formal or informal confessions are to be made only by a party, or his representative subject to the condition that law permits such a representation.

Confession made must be by a sane person so that it may have an effect on him.[II]

In cases where a party or his relatives, claim that the person is not mentally sound, court takes necessary steps to enquire about and it claim is found correct, it does not accept as evidence.[III] Court may reject the claim also if it believes that there is reasonable ground not to receive the confession.

I. Al-Mughni, Vol. XII, pp. 87-88.

II. Al-Yamani V. Al-Zahrani, G.S.C. (M), R. of 1381 (1961-62) Vol. II, p. 9.

III. PP V Al-Yami, P.J., D. No. 447 of 1360 (1941).

The confession made about a crime outside the court under a sudden shock is also admissible although he may claim that he was not aware what he said due to sudden shock.[I]

Attainment of age of majority for making confession is another requirement, that is, when a person attains puberty. Under Islamic law fifteen year is supposed to be the age of majority. In proceedings regarding Tazeer, the confession of a mumeyyiz, i.e., minor who knows reasonably the consequence of his action, may be admitted in the Shariah courts of Saudi Arabia.

Ability to speak is another ground to determine the validity of confession. Confession by a dumb person is controversial. In Tazeer and Hudud, jurists differ on the admissibility of such a confession. However, in Saudi Arabia an admission of a dumb person by signs is not valid, except in Tazeer.

In Shariah court confession of an unconscious person has no evidential value at all. Illustrative cases may cover: statements made during sleep or unconsciousness, or under the effect of anaesthetics or drugs, would be not admissible in evidence.

Confession must be made by a party voluntarily. There should not be any inducement, threat of compulsion. It must be made freely. Judges are very cautious about statements made voluntarily. Unless inducement is proved out of question then only they act upon. There should not be any extortion.

Confession must be express. A statement which falls short of a plain acknowledgment of a fact is not to be attached any weightage. Saudi Arabian law also does not recognize implied confessions.[II]

I. Al-Subay 'I V. Al-Subay'!, G S.C. (R), S. No. 169/1 of 1388 (1969).

II. Al-Amudi V. Bakarim, C.C., D. No. 12 of 1325 (1933).

In cases where the confession does not appear to be completely consistent with the fact in issue, the court on grounds of doubts or suspicion will not receive it as valid confession.

If a confession is made to the police, while in police custody, in such a case police will immediately take him to the nearest Shariah Court where his statement of confession will be recorded. If the arrested person makes the confession not during court working hours, he is to be detained in custody alone not with other arrested persons. The next morning he is to be produced before the court for recorded his statement. He is kept alone because if mixed with other persons then possibility is that others may persuade him not to confess his guilt. Generally recording of confession before the Shariah court is in cases of serious crimes covered under Hudud and Qisas.[I]

Statement may be recorded by the court. It is not necessary that it should be recorded in the trial court. If recorded in any court the trial court will receive it during the trial.

As a caution the court is to ascertain whether the statement of confession made outside was voluntary and duly made on his own. Further where there is no way invalidating the confession, the court has to be absolutely sure, and to satisfy its conscience that the confession is an authentic one.

Apart from cases covered under Hudud, the confession in majority of cases even made outside the court are admissible in evidence. In such 'extra-judicial confession' the procedure followed is that such statements are to be collaborated by witnesses. In other words so long as confessions are proved by the witnesses, they would not be admissible. Generally, confessions made to police during its custody are denied in the court. When trial commerce, the police officer before whom the confession

---

I. L. of Saud of Faisal No. 713 of 18/1/1373 (1953).

was made, would appear before the court as witness. He would give his evidence that the accused made confession before him. If the court is satisfied with the truth of the police officer's evidence, it would accept the confession. Likewise confessions made to ordinary persons are to be treated in the same manner.

In Hudud cases the accused may also retract his confession. Even the judge may hint to the confessor to recall his confession. Ahmad b. Hanbal[1] is one the supporter of this view. Other jurists are of the opinion that it is not only unobjectionable for a judge to make a hint recalling the confession, but it is preferable. Jurists give the Hadith in the support that Prophet (peace be upon him), himself warded a man off several times when he was making confession before him that he had committed 'Zina' (زنا); that the Prophet (peace be upon him) hinted for the man to retract his confession as follows:

"Perhaps you just touched";

That Prophet (peace be upon him) said to a thief who had confessed:

"I do not imagine that you have done so".

On the basis these Ahadith, later Caliph Hazrat Umar (R.A.) and Hazrat Ali (R.A.) followed this practice.

Hanbali law does not concretely prefer or reject the allusion, the judge in Saudi Arabia are left to use their own discretion as to this matter. In judicial practice this rule of allusion to retract confusion is limited to Hudud of Zina (زنا) and theft.

Retraction or calling back the confession is not by words but it may be infered from the conduct of the accused also. An accused who intends to fles when he is being prepared for the

---

I. Al-Mughni, Vol. X, p. 294.

execution of his sentence or after he has received part of the sentence, is to be regarded as having retracted his confession.

If the convicted person recalls his confession before the punishment is implemented, the punishment should not be enforced and the person must be committed back to trial court to consider his retraction.

In cases of crime of Hudud where the accused retracts his confession, the crime may be commuted into a crime of Tazeer, and the retracted confession may then be admissible. The reason is that the rule of retraction of confession does not apply to Tazeer. As the breach of trust cases are covered under Tazeer, hence any confession made in such a case would not be retractable.

In Tazeer cases repetition of confession for its admissibility is not required. Confession may be admissible when it is made even once only, except where it is in regard to the hudud of Zina, theft and highway robbery.

Evidence

Abundant literature on Shahadah (شهادة Evidence) is available. Jurists belonging to all prominent schools of Islamic law have made their observations and comments on evidential law. Even to refer summarily is difficult. The purpose referring Islamic law on (Shahadah) evidence here is to acquaint with the preliminary part of it only. A brief statement on significance, quantum of evidence, its basic requirements and order of examination of witness has been referred here.

Shahadah (شهادة) means to give true information for the purpose of proving any right or fact, in or before a court. Such an information should be recorded in the presence of both the litigant parties or their legal representatives. The procedure is that the witness should utter a word "ASHHADU" (اشهدو) or use any synonymous expression.

The significance lies in the fact that it must be a just and honest information. Justice is Allah's attribute, and to stand firm for justice is to be a witness to Allah, even if it is detrimental to our interest (as we conceive them) or the interest of those who are near and dear to us.

Allah Ta'ala says:

يٰاَيُّهَا الَّذِيْنَ اٰمَنُوا كُوْنُوْا قَوَّامِيْنَ بِالْقِسْطِ شُهَدَاءَ لِلّٰهِ وَلَوْ عَلٰى اَنْفُسِكُمْ اَوِ الْوَالِدَيْنَ وَالْاَقْرَبِيْنَ اِنْ يَكُنْ غَنِيًّا اَوْ فَقِيْرًا فَاللّٰهُ اَوْلٰى بِهِمَا فَلَا تَتَّبِعُوْا الْهَوٰى اَنْ تَعْدِلُوا وَاِنْ تَلْوٗا اَوْ تُعْرِضُوْا فَاِنَّ اللّٰهَ كَانَ بِمَا تَعْمَلُوْنَ خَبِيْرًا۔ (سورة النساء، آية: ١٣٥)

"O ye who believe! Stand out firmly for justice, as witnesses to Allah, even as against yourselves, or your parents, or you kin, and whether it be (against) rich or poor. For Allah can best protect both. Follow not the lusts (of your hearts), lest ye swerve, and if ye distort (justice) or decline to do justice, verily, Allah is well aquainted with all that he do".

(4:135)

This verse shows the significance of Shahadah (evidence) in relation to Islamic concept of justice. Justice in Islam is even more penetrative than the subtler justice in the speculations of the other human laws. It searches out the innermost motives, because a witness is to act in the presence of Allah, to whom all things, acts and motives are known. Some people may be inclined to favour the rich, because they except something from them. Some people may be inclined to favour the poor because they are generally helpless. For a witness partiality in either case is wrong. Allah commands: Be just without fear or favour.

In another verse Allah again commands:

يٰاَيُّهَا الَّذِيْنَ اٰمَنُوا كُوْنُوْا قَوّٰمِيْنَ لِلّٰهِ شُهَدَاۤءَ بِالْقِسْطِ وَلَا يَجْرِمَنَّكُمْ
شَنَاٰنُ قَوْمٍ عَلٰٓى اَلَّا تَعْدِلُوْا اِعْدِلُوْا هُوَ اَقْرَبُ لِلتَّقْوٰى وَاتَّقُوا اللّٰهَ اِنَّ اللّٰهَ
خَبِيْرٌ بِمَا تَعْمَلُوْنَ۔ (سورة المائدة، آية: ٨)

"O ye who believe! Stand out firmly for Allah, as witnesses. To fair dealing, and let not the hatred of others to you make you swerve to wrong and depart from justice. Be just: that is next to piety: and fear Allah. For Allah is well-acquainted with all that ye do". (5:8)

For a witness to do justice and act righteously in a favourable or neutral atmosphere is meritorious enough. However, real test comes when he has to do justice to people who hate him or to whom he has an aversion. In all situations the witness must be just, honest and firm.

Allah is another verse again commands:

وَالَّذِيْنَ هُمْ لِاَمٰنٰتِهِمْ وَعَهْدِهِمْ رٰعُوْنَ۔ وَالَّذِيْنَ هُمْ بِشَهٰدٰتِهِمْ
قَاۤئِمُوْنَ۔ وَالَّذِيْنَ هُمْ عَلٰى صَلَاتِهِمْ يُحَافِظُوْنَ۔ اُولٰۤئِكَ فِيْ جَنّٰتٍ
مُّكْرَمُوْنَ۔ (سورة المعارج، آية: ٣٥ـ٣٢)

"And those who respect their trusts and covenants, and those who stand firm in their testimonies, and those who (strictly) guard their worship; such will be the honoured one in the garden (of Bliss)."

(70:32-35)

If a person knows any truth of any kind, to that he must bear witness, as affecting the lives or interests of our fellow-beings; - firmly, not half-heartedly, without fear or favour, even if it causes loss or trouble to him, or if it loses his friends or associates.

These verses show the significance of evidence in social dealings. A witness must adhere to truth. He should be just, honest, firm and impartial in telling the truth. Allah will reward for his just acts.

"Quantum of Evidence" - (نصاب شهادة)

As to quantum of evidence we will refer the codified Islamic law of Evidence of Pakistan. In criminal cases different (نصاب شهادة) quantum of evidence is required.

According to section 4, the offence of Zina where the accused is liable to hadd (حد), four male witnesses are required. If the number is less than four there would be no conviction.

The eye-witnesses may be non-Muslims who are credible according to their own religion or faith.

The offence of Zina liable to hadd may also be proved by the confession of the accused before a court of competent jurisdiction provided that all the requirements of valid confession are satisfied.

According to section 5, in other offences, such as (سرقه) theft, Harabah (حرابه) Qazf (قذف) Shurbe-Khamr (شرب خمر), Qasas (قصاص) evidence of two male witness is required.

Section 6 lays down that except for offences liable to Hudud (حدود) and Qisas (قصاص) and the matters covered by sections 7 and 8, all other matters, including fiscal matters, shall be proved by the evidence of two male witnesses, and in the absence of two male witnesses by the evidence of one male and two female witnesses. Cases relating to breach of trust are covered under this head.

The evidence of one teacher, male or female shall be admissible in respect of assault having taken place amongst the children studying in an institution.

Under section 7, evidence by a single female witness shall be admissible in cases relating to birth, virginity and such other matters concerning women as are not usually seen by men.

If the defendant is a non-Muslim the female witness may be non-Muslim who is credible according to the faith or religion she professes.

The condition of a female witness in this section does not exclude the evidence of male witnesses.

Under section 8, there can be a single male witness, and his evidence shall be admissible in the following cases:

1. to determine the amount of compensation for the damage caused;

2. to translate the statement or the evidence of a party or a witness in a court of law;

3. to decide, when there is a difference of opinion regarding bai-e-salam (بیع سلام) a kind of commercial transaction) whether the article sold is useable or not;

4. to determine, when the period specified for the payment of amount of a decree has expired, whether the debtor under custody has become insolvent;

5. to decide whether an article, which is a subject of dispute between the seller and the buyer, is defective or not; and

6. to determine the amount of compensation for the injuries caused.

Apart from, there may be a situation where evidence of a single witness coupled with oath by the plaintiff may be admissible. Section 9 deals with such a situation. It arises when the defendant fails to appear before the court although summons were served to him. Plaintiff under such condition may be permitted to produce one witness and may take oath in support of his claim.

In a case where the plaintiff fails to produce a witness but produces documentary evidence the court may, if it is of the opinion that the plaintiff's claim appears to be probably true, decide the matter by giving an oath to the plaintiff. But this is subject to one limitation, that is, the defendant must have been served with the summons three times and the defendant inspite of receiving the summons without any Uzr-e-Sharai (عذر شرعی) fails to appear in the court.

Jurists belonging to different schools have difference of approaches as to the quantum of evidence (نصاب شهادة). Refering all the views is not possible. It requires a separate study all together. A brief reference noted from Adab-e-Qazi is given below:

Under Hanafi School the order of quantum is as follows:

1. Four males witness in case of rape (زنا). Evidence of women witnesses not admissible. However, Ata and Hamad , both belongs to Hanbali school are of the view that three males and two females witnesses are admissible in rape cases. It is only a matter of interpretation.

2. The second category under Hanafi School is relating to matters in which liability is Hudd or Qasas, two make

witnesses are needed. Here also woman's evidence is not admissible.

3. Under third category, according to Hanafi School, comes the cases not covered by the earlier to categories. Here there may be two male witness or one male and two female witnesses. Two female witnesses would be considered equal to one male witness. This category covers the financial cases, divorce and bequeath cases, etc. But Imam Shafi'i differs with this view. According to him, women witness may be admissible in financial cases or related thereto. In other matters it would not be admissible.

4. Fourth category includes cases relating to child birth, and to her confidential matters connected with women, of which male witness cannot be aware of, in such cases according to Hanafi School, evidence of single woman would be sufficient. Shafi'i School differs on this point. According to Shafi's jurists four female witnesses are needed in such cases.

It seems that minor procedural differences exist among jurists of different schools as to the quantum of evidence.

Qualifications of Admissible Witness

Characteristic of witness admissible in evidence, according to Adab-e-Qazi (اداب قاضی) are to be determined according to the stages of Shahadah (شهادة). Stages are:

1. تحمل شہادت Tahmammul-e-Shahadah" - means having knowledge of Mashhud Bihi (facts - مشهود به) by the Shahid (witness), and

2. "Ada-e-Shahadah - " ادائے شهادة " - means giving of evidence in the court by a Shahid (شاهد witness) in respect of mashud bihi (مشهود به).

Capability of a witness to give evidence at the time of Tahammul Shahadah includes such conditions as:

1. witness should be (of sound mind),
2. witness should not be blind,
3. witness should be an eye witness.

He should himself inspect the (مشهود به) Mashud bihi. But in specific cases Tahammul-Shahadah can also be by hearsy. In other words a witness be a person who has witnessed the Mashud bihi except such matters as are provable by hearsy evidence.

On a blind witness there is a difference of approach between Hanafi and Shafi'i law. According to Imam Shafi'i, at the time of (تحمل شهادة) Tahammul-Shahadah, it is not necessary that a witness should not be blind. Witness may be even blind. It would not effect the Tahammul-Shahadah. Same is the position at the time of giving evidence (شهادة), Because a witness may have knowledge of Mahshud bihi (مشهود به) even by listening, if his listening capabilities are perfect. Thus a blind man may be a legally sound witness. However, Hanafi point is different. A blind man cannot be a witness. Sounds my resemble with each other. Unless a person has knowledge by seeing a fact by his own eyes, his witness cannot be sound in law.

For the second stage of Ada-e-Shahadah (ادائے شهادة) the conditions requisites are:

1. Baligh (adult بالغ),
2. Sane person,
3. Baseer (بصير) - having eye-sight,
4. Independent - (not slave),
5. Adil - (عادل),

6. Natiq (ناطق) - having the faculty of talking and
7. Muslim.

The above conditions must be fulfilled otherwise an evidence would not be sound in law. The last condition would not apply in cases where non-Muslims are involved. A non-Muslim evidence according to Shariah is admissible.

Similarly if the minor witness is Muslim, sensible and intelligent enough to understand thing and not has a reputation of a liar, his evidence would be admissible in law.

Under Pakistan law - for proof of actuality of trust, lineage, death etc., and such matters as may be proved by Shahadah-e-Samai (شهادة سماعی) the condition for a witness to have eye-sight shall not apply (Section 12, exception (2)).

Samai-Shahadah (سماعی شهادة) - hearsy evidence), means evidence that is given on the basis of tawatur (تواتر) or information of two Aqil, Baligh, Adil, male persons or one male and two female persons being aqil, baligh and adil. (Section 12 Explanation), provided such persons have given this information by using the word 'Shahadah'.

Exception 3 to section 12 of 'Pakistan Islamic Law of Evidence' relates dumb witnesses. Evidence of a dumb person shall be admissible, except in cases relating to Hudud, only when it is written by the witness himself in the presence of the presiding officer of the court.

Two more exceptions are there which relate to cases where evidence by a non-Muslim against a Muslim shall be admissible only when it relates to will (وصیت) made during the course of a journey when no Muslim Shahid is available, and if the Mashhud'alaih (مشهود علیه) is a non-Muslim the witness.

"Tazkiyaz al-Shuhud - (تزكيه الشهود)"

Tazkiyay -al-Shuhud) is a special feature of Islamic law of evidence. This authority is vested in the court. The court proceeds with Tazkiyah al-Shuhud after the statements of the witness are recorded. 'It is a mode of inquiry adopted by a court for the purposes of declaring a witness Adil (عادل) or Ghair-'Adil (غير عادل).

Tazkiyah al-Shuhud shall be obligatory in cases punishable with Hadd or Qisas, even if Mashhud alaih (مشهود عليه) raises no objection as to the witness being an adil or not.[I]

In all cases of Tazirat and monetary and non-monetary matters, Tazkiyah al-Shuhud shall be conducted by the court only when the opposite party so demand for it.

On enquiry by the court, if Mashhud aliah (مشهود عليه) acknowledges the witness being adil (عادل), then it shall not be necessary to conduct Tazkiyah al-Shuhud.

In respect of Tazkiyah al-Shuhud, two persons, reliable, well-informed and belonging to the same walk of life to which the witness belongs, shall be consulted either openly (عـــام) or confidentially (خـفيـه). It is the discretion of the court to adopt and mode of Tazkiyah al-Shuhud. Court while adopting any mode, that is, open or confidential, has to take into consideration the circumstances of the case also.

In open Tazkiyal al-Shuhud the court shall, in its discretion, summon two persons as (muzakkis - referees) and shall, in the

I. عادل (Adil) means a Muslim who is known for performing prescribed religious duties and abstain from major sins; provided that if the witness is a non-Muslim he should be credible according to his own faith or religion. (Section 2 (j), Islamic Law of Evidence of Pakistan.

presence of the parties, inquire from them about the witness being an adil (عادل) or Ghair-Adil (غیر عادل).

In case of inhability of muzakki to appear in court, a suitable person shall be nominated by the court for conducting Tazkiyah al-Shuhud, and the Muzakki, in the presence of such a nominee, the parties and the witness, express his opinion about that witness being an adil or Ghair adil.

The procedure adopted in confidential-Tazkiyah al-Shuhud, the court writes letter to the Muzakki asking his opinion about the witness to be an adil or Ghair-adil. The letter will contain all detailed particulars about the parties, the witnesses and the nature of the case, so that Muzakki may easily identify them.

The confidential letter, duty sealed, shall be delivered to the Muzakki. He will then write down his own opinion about the witness whether adil or Ghair Adil. Then he will seal the letter and without making his opinion known to anybody, would return back to the court. If the integrity of the witness, either in express words or impliedly is effected by the opinion or no-opinion has been given by the Muzakki, creating doubts, the court shall ask the party concern to produce another witness.

The confidential letter shall be sent to two Muzakkis, but may be sent to one Muzakki only. In case the opinions of he Muzakkis differ the letter shall be sent to a third Muzakki (مذکی).

The Muzakki must fulfil the following requirements:

1. Muslim,
2. Aqil,
3. Baligh, and
4. Adil.

Further requirement is that the Muzakki of a non-Muslim witness may be a non-Muslim who is credible according to his own faith or religion and not has open enemity with the witness. This enemity principle applies to all irrespective of the religion of the witness.

In Adab-e-Qazi, observations of Imam Abu Yusuf and Imam Muhammad have been quoted. According to them in all matters Tazkiyyah al-Shuhud must be conducted. It may be either open or confidential. It is necessary because judgement is based on reasons and reasons are infered from the evidence of Adil (عادل) witnesses. Therefore, Qazi must conduct Tazkiyah al-Shuhud to know whether witnesses are adil or not, and thus Qazi's judgement may be saved from being batil (باطل).

It is also that at the present era adil witnesses are rare. Tazkiyyah al-Shuhud become most essential. In the early period of Islam Tazkiyyah al-Shuhud was generally open (عـام) but gradually, it was converted to confidential Tazkiyyah al-Shuhud to avoid any problem which might result from.

"Examination of Witnesses"

In Shariah court procedure for recording the statement of plaintiff, defendant and witnesses is as follows:

Firstly, the statement of the plaintiff or the complainant is recorded in his own words.

Secondly, the statement of the defendant or the accused is recorded in his own words.

Thirdly, on denial of the claim or charge by the defendant or the accused, the court orders the plaintiff or complainant to produce evidence in support of claim or charge.

Thus the witnesses are examined at the third stage. Their statements are recorded in their own words separately one after the other. When statement of a witness is being recorded by the court the other witnesses cannot be present there. However, if the witnesses are two women their statements may be recorded jointly separation is not required.

The court for purpose of knowing the truth, after it has recorded the statements of parties to the litigation and their witness may put questions as the court likes, and after that the defendant will have to cross-examine the parties and witness. Parties here include plaintiff and defendant or complaint and the accused.[I]

The court may,[II] if the deemds necessary, for the purpose of exploring the facts, re-examine a party or witness after cross-examination.

It shows that it is the responsibility of the court to cross-examine and re-examine the parties and witness for knowing the truth. As such there is no examination-in-chief, or cross-examination or re-examination by the parties. But in practice it is not so. Parties may be cross-examined and re-examined. Similarly witness may also be subjected to the examination-in-chief, cross-examination and re-examination. However, among jurists differences of opinion are there. Some are of he view that court only may cross-examine and re-examine. There is nothing like examination-in-chief. Statements are to be recorded in the words of plaintiff or complainant, and defendant or accused person. Statements of the witnesses are also to be in their words. Further the judges should also be reluctant in putting too many questions to the parties so that it may not create doubts of partiality in the minds of any of the parties.

The second view is that for the sake of justice court may allow parties to conduct examination-in-chief, cross-examination and need be to re-examine witnesses of each other. If by cross-examination of witnesses any thing which is false may be proved, the court may allow the party. Generally for impeaching the credibility and integrity of witnesses, the procedure of examination is allowed by the court.

Two words are used for examination-in-chief and cross-examination, they are:

1. Izhar - اظهار (examination-in-chief).
2. Jirah - جرح (cross-examination).

This procedure of examination was first adopted by the fourth Caliph Hazrat Ali (R.A.) in his period of Caliphat.[1] The witnesses were examined and cross-examined separately so that one may not hear the statement of the other. Since then jurists are using this method. Leading questions are not allowed to avoid the implication that the court is trying to help one party to the prejudice of the other. However, Qazi himself may put question as to remove his confusion though the question may be leading, but not in such a manner as partiality may be imputed to him.

In Saudi Arabia Shariah court judges have very wide jurisdiction which cannot be said to be restricted to any particular method of examination. Examination-in-chief is not the feature of Saudi Arabian Law. Judges themselves may assume this responsibility. Due to this it is said that there is no cross-examination of witnesses in Saudi Arabia judicial system except by the judges themselves. But an indept study of the judicial system may bring this inference that the cross-examination, not only by the judges but also by the opposing party of his representative, does exist in practice. However, it is subject to this restriction that the cross-examination is permissible when either a request to the court to this effect is made or the court itself orders for.

I. Al-Faraq-ul-Hukamia, P. 48.

In practice, the judge of a Shariah court does permit a party to cross-examine a witness of the opposite party for testing the integrity. Those who have occasion of observing the Shariah court proceeding say that the flexibility of the judge to permit not only the parties but also their advocates to cross-examine the witnesses for the opposite is quite noticeable.

In actual practice, a party finds more room in a Shariah court to attack the probity of the witnesses. The role of the judge in cross-examination lies mostly in question which may effect the truth of the evidence, and, to a less degree, the probity of the witness. The Shariah court judge may invite a party against whom an evidence has been given by the witness to attack the probity of the witness. The party may prove by such attach on probity that the witness has an interest or motive behind his testimony or he is not a witness of any credibility or integrity. The testimony of any witness is subject to challenge of a personal motive or interest lies behind his evidence. Thus rule of challenging probity of witness (Adil) is common in Shariah court.

As to re-examination of a witness the judge usually asks questions when doubts are created after the cross-examination of the witness or probity of a witness become doubtful. However, re-examination is not a common practice.

In brief, the order of examination-in-chief, cross-examination, and re-examination is not strictly adhere to in the Shariah court. However, use of examination-in-chief, cross-examination, and re-examination do exist in practice.

- "Agents for Litigation"

Under the Islamic law, a person may lawfully appoint another his agent or representative or vakeel to act on his behalf for the settlement of every contract which he might have lawfully, concluded himself.[I]

Authority to appoint agent is derived from Ahadith reported in 'Nakl-Saheeh'.

In Nakl-Saheeh 'it is reported that Prophet (peace be upon him) appointed Hakeem-bin-Khiram his agent for purchase, in order that he might buy for him a camel to sacrifice.

Similarly on another occasion Prophet (peace be upon him) 'appointed Amir-bin-aum his agent for marriage'.

The reason given for appointing vakeel or agent is that an individual is sometimes prevented from acting in his own person, in consequence of accidental circumstances (such as sickness, or the like), he therefore admitted of necessity to appoint another his agent. It is also aimed to expedite his wants by means of the powers which he derives from such appointment.

It is also lawful for a person to appoint another his agent for the management of suits or criminal prosecutions or for the payment or exaction of all rights (even to corporal punishment or retaliation). However, Hadd and Qasas are exception to this general rule.

Justification to this general rule is same as earlier noted. Further it is argued that every person is not himself capable of managing a business of this nature.

In 'Nakl-Saheeh' it has been mentioned that Hazrat Ali (R.A.), fourth Caliph appointed Hazrat Aqeel his agent for the management of his suits, and when Hazrat Aqeel became old he dismissed him, and appointed Hazrat Abdul-bin-Jafar in his place.

It makes it clear that for management of suits civil or criminal an agent or vakeel may be appointed who may represent the

---

I. Supra N.P.

interests of the parties to the litigation or prosecution. But cases covered under Hudud or Qasas are made exceptions thereto. Appointment of vakeel in such cases is invalid. The reason given is that the "punishment or retaliation are remitted in the existence of doubt; and the absence of the principal creates a doubt; may, the forgiveness of the prosecutor is probable in such a circumstance, for this reason, that it is praiseworthy and laudable to pardon; contrary to where the witnesses only are absent (from the execution), as their non-retractation is most probable; and contrary, also to where the prosecutor is present, as in this case there is no apprehension of his having forgiving."[1]

However, differences among the jurists exist on this point.

According to Imam Abu Haneefa, an agent or vakeel cannot be appointed without the permission of the opposite party in cases where the client is not sick or on journey which may not be for three days or more.

But according to Imam Mohammad, and Imam Abu Yusuf, a vakeel or agent may be appointed in such conditions even without the consent and permission of the opposite party. Imam Shafi'i is also of this view.

This disagreement does not relate to the legality of the agency itself, but to the necessity which operates upon the adversary to answer an agent to whose appointment he has not assented. Hazrat Abu Haneefa being of the opinion that he is not under such necessity; and the two disciples think otherwise.

The argument of the two disciples is that the appointment of an agent is the act of an individual in regard to a right purely his own. Therefore, it should not regard to a right purely his own. Therefore, it should not depend on the

---

1. Supra N.P.

consent of another in the present instance, any more than in a case exacting payment of debt.

Hazrat Imam Abu Haneefa on the other hand, argues that the constituent is himself under the necessity of giving an answer, and must attend in case the magistrate should summon him. Individuals differ with respect to their capacities of managing suits. Therefore, if it were admitted that the appointment of an agent is absolute with respect to the adversary, this would be injurious to the adversary. Hence the validty of the appointment must be suspended on his consent. It is otherwise where the person is sick or absent, for in this case his appointment of an agent is valid without the consent of the adversary, since he cannot himself be compelled to appear under such circumstances.

It is to be noted that the same manner as Hazrat Imam Haneefa holds the appointment, in this particular, of an agent by an absent person to be valid, so also does he holds the appointment by one who is immediately about the tavel.[I]

There is a consensus of all modern jurists on the point that a woman may appoint an agent for litigation in all cases. According to Hazrat Abu Baker (R.A.), the first Caliph, a woman who remains in privacy, and is not accustomed to go to the court of the Qazi, can appoint an agent for the management of her suit, and acquiescence is incumbent on her adversary.

A person under accusation may employ an agent to conduct his defence, and agent may make replies and rejoinders, and the doubt with respect to deputations does not prevent this. If an agent confesses anything against the interest of his client or constituent before the court, his confession is valid and enforceable. Hazrat Imam Abu Haneefa and Hazrat Imam Mohammad, both are of the same view on this point. However, such confession

---

I. Supra N.P.

should be in the court and not outside the court. If the acknowledgment has been made outside the court and not before Qazi, immediately after such a confession, the vakeel or agent shall be dismissed.

According to Hazrat Imam Abu Yusuf even if such a confession is not in the court would be valid and legally enforciable.

But Hazrat Imam Zafer and Hazrat Imam Shafi'i have different view. According to them such a confession under both conditions - made in the court or beyond court, is not valid.

Further it is said that an agent without the consent of his client cannot make any settlement with the adverse party nor can discharge the opposite party from his liability.

The appoint of agent is the discretion of the client. He can also remove him at his will. When a person accused of an offence appoints an agent or vakeel to represent him in litigation or defend him against the accusation, it is implied that such an agent is empowered to make concessions on behalf of his client.

"Although in Islam, a suit can be conducted through a vakeel, it is difficult to ascertain from the history of the law court whether there was any practice of appointing vakeels as 'professional lawyers'. In some book it is mentioned that when Isa bin Abban, a contemporary of Imam Shafi'i was appointed the Qazi of Basra, two brothers came to him. They used to appear as vakeels in cases. Apparently it shows that the practice of 'professional lawyers was in vogue from remote time. This practice is not innovation in Islam.[I]

Qazi Tajuddin Abu Nasr Abdul Wahab observes thus:

I. Al-Qazi-fil Islam, p. 19 (Administration of Justice during the Muslim Rule in India, by Wahed Husain).

"The view is this - those vakeel who are lovers of justice, deserve praise, alothough they charge fees for their labour. But those who desire to encourage litigation and defent the rights of others are liable to condemnation. The duty of the vakeel is to grasp the facts from the client (مو کل), to acquaint himself with the circumstance, and to find out on which side is the truth between the parties .... He should present such documents as he deems to be genuine, or those documents which the client places before him and the vakeel places reliance upon them without the knowledge of the real state of affairs. But if the vakeel after discovering them to be false uses them, his place is in the hell."[I]

Under Islamic law, judge of a Shariah court, gives preference to the parties to suit to present their cases on their own. Because parties are the unable to represent their cases properly either due to nervourness or get confused, or any other inability rendering them unable to meet the points of law raised during litigation, they can entrust their cases to their lawyer (vakeels). But Islam does not favour that professional lawyers be engaged with a view to confuse the real issues, to delay the proceedings, and to avail the best talent for defeating the claim of the opposite party.

"Compounding of Litigation and Arbitration"

Islamic law prefere compromises and compounding of disputes rather than parties contesting in the court. Allah also prefers it. The following verses of Holy Qur'ãn will show the significance.

Allah says:

وَجَزٰؤُا سَيِّئَةٍ سَيِّئَةٌ مِّثْلُهَا فَمَنْ عَفَا وَاَصْلَحَ فَاَجْرُهٗ عَلَى اللّٰهِ اِنَّهٗ لَا يُحِبُّ الظّٰلِمِيْنَ۔ (سورة الشورى، آية: ٤٠)

I. Al-Muqarinat-wal-Maqabile, pp. 51, 52.

"The recompense for an injury is an injury equal thereto (in degree): but if a person forgives and makes reconciliation, his reward is due from Allah: For Allah loveth not those who do wrong." (42:40)

This verse relates to criminal cases of Qasas. Whatever injury is caused, that much injury can be caused to the wrong-doer. However, if the victims forgives or compromises with it is far better. His reward is with Allah. Allah does not love the wrong doers.

In another verse Allah says:

اِنَّمَا الْمُؤْمِنُوْنَ اِخْوَةٌ فَاَصْلِحُوْا بَيْنَ اِخْوَيْكُمْ وَاتَّقُوااللّٰهَ لَعَلَّكُمْ تُرْحَمُوْنَ۔ (سورة الحجرات، آية: ١٠)

"The believers are but a single brotherhood: So make peace and reconciliation between your two (contending) brothers; and fear Allah, that ye may receive Mercy." (49:10).

In this verse also Allah commands to be just and try to compromise the quarrel, for peace is better than fighting.

In family disputes whatever may be the nature Allah commands for making amicable settlement of them. In the following verse Allah says:

وَاِنِ امْرَاَةٌ خَافَتْ مِنْ بَعْلِهَا نُشُوزًا اَوْ اِعْرَاضًا فَلَا جُنَاحَ عَلَيْهِمَا اَنْ يُصْلِحَا بَيْنَهُمَا صُلْحاً وَالصُّلْحُ خَيْرٌ وَاُحْضِرَتِ الْاَنْفُسُ الشُّحَّ وَاِنْ تُحْسِنُوْا وَتَتَّقُوْا فَاِنَّ اللّٰهَ كَانَ بِمَا تَعْمَلُوْنَ خَبِيْراً۔ (سورة النساء، آية: ١٢٨)

"If a wife fears cruelty or desertion on her husband's part, there is no blame on them if they arrange an amicable settlement between themselves; and such

> settlement is best; even though men's souls are swayed by greed, but if ye do good and practice self restraint, Allah is well acquainted with all that ye do". (4:128).

In this verse Allah also commands for self-restrained practices, and do what we can to come to an amicable settlement.

Islamic law not only allows compounding of cases, but prefer also to refer the matter to arbitration for settling the disputes even out side the courts. But refering to arbitration (ثالثی) and to compound (کمپاؤنڈ) offences depends upon the nature of offences. Criminal breach of trust is an offence which is both compoundable and may be referred to arbitration of the parties so desire.

About compounding of cases Hazrat Maharib-bin-Disar narrates that Hazrat Umar-bin-Khattab (R.A.) said:

> من محارب بن دثار ان عمر بن الخطاب قال: ردوا النجموم حتى يصطلحوا، فان فصل القضاء يورث الفغائى بين الناس قال سفيان: ولكنا وضعنا هذا اذا كانت شبهة او كانت قرابة، فاما اذا تبين له القضاء فلا ينغى له ان كردهم۔

> "That the parties to litigation at the initial stage be returned back sot that they may mutually compound (کمپاؤنڈ) their cases. Because sometime just decisions of the court give birth to enimities among them."

This shows the significance attached to the compoundability of the cases. Caliph second preferred compounding of cases rather than contending in court and get judgment thereupon.

Hazrat Sufian Sura commenting upon the observation of Hazrat Umar (R.A.) says:

> "That in our opinion Hazrat Umar (R.A.) by this above referred observation means that efforts be made for

compounding the litigation at a time when there is a suspicion or doubt or parties are related to each other. If it is not so and decision seems to be quite clear, it is not proper for Qazi to return the parties."

Hazrat Sufian Suri made this comment on following grounds:

1. That if all the cases referred to the court, irrespective of knowing the nature of dispute, are returned for compounding the cases, it will result in loosening the confidence in efficacy of courts; and

2. It would also lower down the honour and dignity of Shariat (شريعت) and Shariah courts.

In the period of Hazrat Umar (R.A.) there was no such fear that is why he gave such a general direction. But to Sufian Suri, now it should restricted only to cases where there is no legal ambiguity or the matter referred to the court is not too complicated, or court considers that past relations between the parties were such that compounding of the case be preferred. In such cases where is no hitch in refering back for compounding the cases. But if it s otherwise than court should decide itself.

As to Arbitration Allah commands in Sura-al-Nisa:

وَاِنْ خِفْتُمْ شِقَاقَ بَيْنِهِمَا فَابْعَثُوا حَكَماً مِنْ اَهْلِه وَحَكَماً مِنْ اَهْلِهَا
اِنْ يُرِيْدَا اِصْلَاحاً يُّوَفِّقِ اللّٰهُ بَيْنَهُمَا اِنَّ اللّٰهَ كَانَ عَلِيْماً خَبِيْراً۔

(دورة النداء، آية:٣٥)

"If ye fear a breach between twa-in, appoint (two) arbiters, one from his family, and the other from hers; if they seek to set things a right, Allah will cause their reconciliation: For Allah hath full knowledge and is acquainted with all things. (4:35)

Allah commands that if there is a dispute between husband and wife, refer the matter to the arbitration (ثالثی). The law confers the right upon the litigant parties to refer their disputes to an arbitrator of their choice. Each party may also select arbitrators or its own and if they agree, the arbitrators so selected may decide the dispute referred to them. The decision of arbitrators will be the same as of Qazi. The arbitrator has the power to examine witnesses and administer oath like a court, and give awards according to the facts of the case and in accordance with the law to which the parties are subject. However, there is difference between the decision of arbitrators and a Qazi. The difference is as follows:

1. Matters covered under Hudud and Qasas arbitration is not valid (صحیح).

2. Till the arbitrators pronounce their judgement, it is not enforceable. Before the judgement if any party withdraws from arbitration, such withdrawal is allowed. But if the arbitrators have pronounced their judgement, withdrawal is not valid.

3. If the arbitrators give judgement on any Ijtihadi issue and the matter thereafter is referred to the court where the judge differs with the opinions of arbitrators, the judge may reject or set adide the judgement. If no difference of opinion exists between the judge and the arbitrators, then the judge will pass an order confirming the terms of the award.

The Islamic law requires that the arbitrators should possess the qualifications of a Qazi on the ground that the arbitrator virtually performs functions of the Qazi.

Criminal breach of trust is both compoundable and if the parties desire may be referred for arbitration.

"Non-Muslim and Islamic Law"

Islam is often said to be a totalitarian religion. It is an inevitable result of the very faith in God. A believer surrenders to Almighty completely. His prayers, sacrifices, life and death all are surely for God. He has subjected totally to the commandments of Allah. Thus his faith in God and his social life are not separate. They are intervovine. Law is one part of that integrated self. In other words law and religion are not separate. The question is that when law and religion are integrated self, then what is the position and status of those who do not subscribe to Islamic faith? Are the non-Muslims subjects to law to which they have no faith in?

Answer requires an elaborate discussion. Non-Muslims membership of the nation in an Islamic state is based on contracts or compromises reached between them and the Islamic state. That is the reason that non-Muslims are called 'almu'ahidun', means the contractees. Another term used is "ahl-al-dhimmah, or dhimmis," or Arabic word which means "those whose obligations are a trust upon the conscience and pledge of the state of the nation".

It may be said that their rights and obligations are determined according to:

1. basic texts in the Qur'ãn and the Sunnah; and

2. treaties or compromise entered between them or their ancestors and the Islamic state.

"Holy Qur'ãn and non-Muslim"

Let us examine the position of non-Muslims in the light of Qur'ãnic commandment.

Qur'ãn says:

لَا يَنْهٰكُمُ اللّٰهُ عَنِ الَّذِيْنَ لَمْ يُقَاتِلُوْكُمْ فِى الدِّيْنِ وَلَمْ يُخْرِجُوْكُمْ مِنْ دِيَارِكُمْ اَنْ تَبَرُّوْهُمْ وَتُقْسِطُوا اِلَيْهِمْ اِنَّ اللّٰهَ يُحِبُّ الْمُقْسِطِيْنَ۔

(سورة الممتحنة، آية:٨)

"Allah forbids you not, with regards to those who fight you not for (your) faith nor drive you out of your homes, from dealing kindly and justly with them: For Allah loveth those who are just". (60:8)

Allah clearly commands that you should be kind and just while dealing with non-Muslim unless they are rampant and out to destroy you and your faith.

In verse 1, Sura al-Maida Allah commands that the believers should fulfil their covenants and compromises entered with others. Allah says:

يايها الذين امنوا اوفوا بالعقوده

(سورة المائدة، آية:١)

"O ye who believe! Fulfil (all) obligation". (5:1)

Word (عقود)(uqud) has been used in this verse in a very wide sense. Treaties entered by the state with its non-Muslims inhabitants are parts of the wide ranged covered under it. Every individual living in state and the state itself are bound to see that all obligations express or implied resulted from covenant or treaties or compromise entered into are faithfully discharged. Every man of faith must discharge all such obligations conscientiously. This is how Allah in Qur'ãn commands. Non-Muslim are not to be discriminated. Just and honourable treatment and respect to the obligations and discharge thereto is the basis education of Islam. This law must be such which discharge the obligations with honour and respect.

In another verse Allah commands:

وَاِذَا قُلْتُمْ فَاعْدِلُوْا وَلَوْ كَانَ ذَاقُرْبٰى وَ بِعَهْدِ اللّٰهِ اَوْفُوْا ذٰلِكُمْ وَصّٰكُمْ بِهٖ لَعَلَّكُمْ تَذَكَّرُوْنَ۔ (سورة الانعام، آية:١٥٢)

"Whenever ye speak, speak justly, even if a near relative is concerned; and fulfil the covenant of Allah: Thus do the He command you, that ye may remember."(6:152)

In this verse again Allah commands that if you give words, you should honour those words and do justice there unto, even if it is against a kinsman, and fulfil the covenant of Allah. This is what Allah has commanded and we should happily remember that. Again to honour words and doing justice to the compromises are basic to Islamic law. Laws can be framed only keeping in consideration the basic principle of justice commanded by Allah. In other words non-Muslims are all well-protected and have honoured place in the light of above noted command.

In another verse Allah says:

اِلَّا الَّذِيْنَ عٰهَدْتُّمْ مِنَ الْمُشْرِكِيْنَ ثُمَّ لَمْ يَنْقُصُوْكُمْ شَيْأً وَّلَمْ يُظَاهِرُوْا عَلَيْكُمْ اَحَداً فَاَتِمُّوْا اِلَيْهِمْ عَهْدَهُمْ اِلٰى مُدَّتِهِمْ اَنَّ اللّٰهَ يُحِبُّ الْمُتَّقِيْنَ۔ (سورة التوبة، آية:٤)

"(But the treaties are) not dissolved with those Pagans with whom ye have entered into alliance and who have not subsequently failed you in aught, nor aided anyone against you. So fulfil your engagement with them to the end, of their term: For Allah loveth the righteous".(9:4)

The sacred duty of fulfilling all obligations of every kind, to Muslims and non-Muslims, in public as well as in private life, is a cardinal feature of Muslim ethics. The question what is to be done with those who abuse this principle by failing in their duty but expect the Muslims to do their part is not to be solved (in the case of treaties) by a general denunciation of treaties but by a careful consideration of the cases where there has been fidelity and not treachery. There we are enjoined to give the strictest fidelity, as it is a party of righteousness and our duty to Allah.

Allah again commands:

فَمَا اسْتَقَامُوْا لَكُمْ فَاسْتَقِيْمُوْا لَهُمْ اِنَّ اللّٰهَ يُحِبُّ الْمُتَّقِيْنَ۔

(سورة التوبة، آية:٧)

"As long as they stand true to you, stand ye true to them: for Allah doth love the righteous". (9:7)

This ayat (آیت) again relates to covenant with non-Muslims. Muslims should not break the covenant which they have made with non-Muslims. If non-Muslims respect their covenant Muslims should also reciprocate to them. The character of Muslims should be just in all dealings with non-Muslims. No treachery, no fraud, no dishonesty, no infedility is permissible in the observance of their commitments with non-Muslims. God loves those who are very cautious in the discharge of their commitments and obligations. Islamic law is based on such ideal principles.

To do justice and act righteously in a favourable or neutral atmosphere is meritous enough, but the real test comes when you have to do justice to people who are oppose to your faith. In this connection Allah says:

يَـاَيُّهَـا الَّـذِيْنَ اٰمَنُوا كُوْنُوْا قَوّٰمِيْنَ لِلّٰهِ شُهَدَاءَ بِالْقِسْطِ وَلَا يَجْرِ مَنَّكُمْ
شَنَاٰنُ قَوْمٍ عَلٰى اَلَّا تَعْدِلُوْا اَعْدِلُوْا هُوَ اَقْرَبُ لِلتَّقْوٰى وَاتَّقُوا اللّٰهَ اِنَّ اللّٰهَ
خَبِيْرٌم بِمَا تَعْمَلُوْنَ۔ (سورة المائدة، آية:٨)

"O ye who believe! Stand out firmly for Allah, as witness to fair dealing, and let not the hatred of others to you make you swerve to wrong and depart from justice. Be just: that is next to piety: and fear Allah. For Allah is well-acquainted with all that ye do".

(5:8)

Such a justice, which cannot be disturbed by any ill-feeling, if rightly adopted, can be attained to only by the fear of Allah and His retaliation. When this though is strongly deep-rooted in the heart of a believer that nothing of our deeds and actions is hidden to God, and this idea is always present in his heart and mind, his heart will tremble by the fear of God resulting in total justice in all matters of life and in total submission to the orders of God and His Messenger.

These are some of the golden rules upon which the Islamic law is based. Muslims and non-Muslims, under such a law are all safe and well-protected. No injustice can be done to any person irrespective of caste creed or colour. All stands on equal footing. So far administration of justice is concerned no discrimination is to be meted out to any citizen in Islamic state. Islamic law is based on highly moral ideals.

"Prophet (peace be upon him) and Non-Muslims"

Treatment of non-Muslim by the Prophet (peace be upon him) himself is based on such highly moral ideals preached by Holy Qur'ãn.

Prophet (peace be upon him) says:

> "Beware! Whosoever is cruel and hard on a contractees, or curtails his rights, or burdens him with more than he can endure, or takes anything of his prophet against his free will. I shall myself be a plaintiff against him on the Day of Judgement."

Just imagine, the consequences for a believer, there is nothing moire worst than when the Prophet (peace be upon him) would stand as plaintiff against him on the Day of Judgement, if he is cruel and hard on a contractees, that is, non-Muslim, and takes his property without his free consent.

Prophet (peace be upon him) again says:

"And once they (non-Muslims) are willing to conclude the dhimmah contract, then let it be clearly known to them that all rights and duties are equal and reciprocal between you and them."[1]

From the above Sunnah of Prophet (peace be upon him), it is obvious now that once a contract is concluded with non-Muslim living in Islamic state, law would make no discrimination on the basis of religion. All rights and duties of non-Muslims become at par with Muslims. They stand on equal footings. Among Muslims and non-Muslims rights and duties become reciprocal based on principles of equity.

I. Abdullah Mustafa al-Maraghi, Al-Tashri 'al-islamic li-Ghairoi-Muslimin (Islamic Legislation for non-Muslim, Egypt, p. 64.

Prophet (peace be upon him) further says:

"Only faith fullness, no treachery, with every given pledge."[1]

In this Hadith Prophet (peace be upon him) has given a very highly honurable moral sermon advocating that there should be faithfulness with one's promise, covenants, compromises and pledges with others. Treachery in such matters is prohibited. Islamic law dealings with non-Muslims is based on such honourable and dignified principles.

Said Ramadan, in his book Islamic Law, has high lighted some of the Prophet's practices and dealings with non-Muslims after his migration from Makkah and settling in Madinah. He elaborates:

"In Madinah, only a few weeks after his arrival, he established a kind of city state embracing those who believed in him as a Prophet and those who were willing to accept his authority as a political head. The best outlook and objective of that state were to realise a co-existence between those who choose to have it and a collective defence against any sort of aggresion, external or internal. The constitution of that state was in the form of a long written document designing the inter-relations between Muslim tribes and clans among themselves, on the one hand, and between the Muslim and the Jews, on the other. It was a state of a confederal type due to the multiplicity of populations - groups. A recognition was granted to every group within a common bond that applied in two ways; to Muslims upon the authority of their faith in Islam, and the Jew upon whatever provisions a mutual agreement would include."

1. Said Ramadan, Islamic Law - its scope and equity, p. 123, Edition Published by Muslim Youth Movement of Malaysia, Kuala Lumpur, 1987, Malaysia.

Some translated extracts from this constitutional document are noted below:

Said Prophet: "All Jews who choose to join us shall have all the protection that Muslims have. Neither will they be oppressed, nor may there be a Muslim communal agitation against them. To the Jews their religion, and to the Muslims their religion. The Jews of Bani Awf' constitute a community with the believers. Between all there act of oppression or wikedness shall always be personal. Between them there shall always be a mutual council and advice. There shall also be a joint responsibility for defence against every attack on Madinah and against every aggression directed. Jews shall share with Muslims the expenditure of war as long as fighting continues. None shall leave the city except upon an 'exit permit' issued by the Prophet (peace be upon him). Other jewish clans (eight of whom were specifically mentioned) and their associates and defendants shall have, with this document, the same status as Bani Awf. This written document, however, should by no means be a shelter for any transgressor. Those who chose to leave can leave in safety, and those who choose to settle in Madinah can settle in safety, except if held responsible for injustice or transgressions."[1]

The principles we infer from this first important constitutional document are:

1. Equal protection to Muslim and non-Muslims.
2. No communal agitation from Muslims against the convenant.
3. Jews and Muslims were to practice and follow their religions respectively.
4. Personal responsibility for acts of aggressions.

---

1. Ibn Hisham, 2nd edition, Cairo, 1950, 1, pp. 503-504.

5. Joint responsibility for defence.

6. Both communities to share the war expenses jointly.

7. If any non-Muslim to leave, was to take exist permit from the Prophet (peace be upon him).

8. Associates and defendants of non-Muslims were all guaranteed protection.

9. If any non-Muslim wanted to leave Madinah, could leave safely.

10. Any non-Muslim could settle in Madinah. However, if found responsible for injustice or transgression, would not be permitted to settle in Madinah.

These are some of the inferences from the covenant entered between Prophet (peace be upon him) and the non-Muslims. Equal status in all respect was guaranteed by the Prophet (peace be upon him).

In the later part of Prophet's period number of such other covenants were entered into. Full protection and equal status to the non-Muslims was guaranteed.

Another outstanding treaty is which the Prophet (peace be upon him) entered with the 'Christians of Najran'.[1] Main principles of this covenant were as follows:

1. For Najran and its defendants they have God's enjoined protection and the pledge of His Prophet (peace be upon him).

2. Protection to: Property, life, religion, absent and present, kith and kins, churches, all that they have in hands, little or much.

I. Hamidullah, al-Watha'iq al-Siyasiyyah (Political document), 2nd Edition, Cairo, Lajuat al-Taalif wa'l Tarjumah wa'l Nashr, 1956, pp. 111-112.

3. No interference by Muslims in their Church management.
4. No humiliation.
5. Military service not compulsory to them.
6. Justice shall prevail.
7. Usurious dealings declared act of rebellion,
8. Tax upon non-Muslim was introduced in this document.
9. Responsibility for transgression personal. No one else was responsible for the acts of others.

The another important thing is that in later years, after the Prophet (peace be upon him), all Caliphs had honoured this covenant with the Christians of Najran.

Both the above documents are very important. They clearly indicate that in social dealings Muslims and non-Muslims are all equal. In religious matters they are independent and free. Islamic law guarantees full freedom to the non-Muslims. These documents are important guaranteeing equal status to non-Muslim as an authentic text of Islamic law.

During Prophet's (peace be upon him) time, non-Muslim, in practice, were accorded complete judicial autonomy. They were to be judged with equity and in accordance to their religious laws. Religious Muslim law was not to be applied to them.

During the rule of second Caliph, different nations and races came under his reign. Hazrat Umar (R.A.), the second Caliph issued various ordinances (فرمان - farman) determining and guaranteeing the status of non-Muslims which supplied literature to the Fuqahe (jurists) for developing the law and jurisprudence. Many of the Farmans were collected by Hazrat Imam Abu Yusuf (R.A.) in his book entitled Kitab-ul-Khiraj. One such Farman issued by him to Abu Ubaida, the commander of Army, after the conqest of Syria is noted below:

"Forbid the Muslims so that they may not oppress the non-Muslims, nor commit any damage to them, nor seize their property without a valid cause, and fulfil all the terms and conditions which you have convenanted with them."

There were other covenants also entered with the non-Muslims. In all non-Muslims were guaranteed full freedom of religions, customs and other social matters. They were not to be discriminated.

The most recent example is of Malaysia. After independence, constitution was framed. Before that a compromise reached between the state and non-Muslims residents of Malaysia guaranteeing all type of freedoms. Article 3 (1) of the Federal constitution of Malaysia provides that Islam is the religion of the Federation; the other religions may be practised in peace and harmony in any part of the Federation. Malaysian government respects the agreement based on the understanding and friendship between various communities. Non-Muslims are sharing all sorts of facilities. Even they are sharing power as Ministers of Cabinet. They are given civil services also. As to law, they are being governed by secular laws. Their disputes are decided by secular courts.

From the above discussion jurists have developed law as follows:

1. That Muslims and non-Muslims are equal in the eye of Laws. The blood of the Dhimmi is like the blood of the Muslim,

2. Non-Muslims living in an Islamic state are all secured, in matters of right to property, life, freedom of religion, to be governed by their own religious laws or community customs or by secular laws.

3. No molestation or humiliation on the basis of religion.

4. Non-Muslims are not to be governed by Islamic Law which is purely religion in nature. They are to be regulated according to the precepts of their own faith.

5. Secular portion of the Islamic Legal Code is applicable to non-Muslims. Secular law in the sense that the law which is commonly followed by all nations irrespective of their religion, caste, creed or culture. Islamic law does not interfere in non-Muslims, customs and tradition which they follow as a matter of their faith.

In brief, there is nothing to alarm non-Muslims living under an Islamic state. During Mughal period in India, non-Muslims were not only to be governed by their own laws but were having courts where Brahmines and Pandits were sitting as judges and deciding their cases.

However, they are subject to the Islamic criminal law which is secular in nature as explained above. As to criminal breach of trust, non-Muslims' cases under the Islamic state would be governed by Islamic criminal law if the nature of dispute is secular but if it relates to religion, such as religious endowment, would be governed by their religious precepts.

"Ijtihad"

Dr. Muhammad Muslehuddin[1] explains Ijtihad as:

"Ijtihad (interpretation) in its literal sense in making an effort and technically it is an effort to discover law, from its sources. It is just the opposite of 'taqlid or imitation, i.e., following the opinions of others without scrutiny as to their sources."

---

1. Dr. Muhammad Muslehuddin, 'Philosophy of Islamic Law and the Orientalists', p. 125 (Ph.D. London).

Ijtihad is an Arabic word which is delivered from the Arabic verb, Ijtihada, literally means 'to exert oneself.'

Under these two different definitions, one is connected with efforts to discover law from its sources and Interprete it, and other one to exert oneself. We will examine which is more near to Islamic concept.

On view is that law is contained in the text of Holy Qur'ãn and the Sunnah. By Ijtihad means interpretation of the Holy Text and Sunnah, and it's enforcement and to extend it to given social situations. Thus legislation in Islam is not law making in the modern sense. Further such interpretation should not be the result on one's own reasn our personal opinion but by analogical deduction, i.e., reasoning by way of analogy.

Scope of reasoning by analogical deduction is further sub-divided into two parts:

1. Matters relating to religious observance and worship ('Ibadat) and
2. Social affairs (Mu'amalat).

In the first case, according to Ghazali there can be no scope for legislation, no reasoning in such matters. While in the second legislation or law-making is possible, but it cannot take the form of law-making in the modern sense, for laws are already revealed by God.

The second view to exert oneself has been explained by Prof. Asaf Fazee as: "Creative in nature which functions in the absence of Qur'ãnic and Prophetic texts".[1] But this view does not seems to be correct.

I. Asaf A.A. Fazee, Outlines of Muhammedan Law, 2nd edition, London, Oxford University Press, 1955.

Source of Ijtihad is the following Hadith. It is an authentic tradition narrated by Hazrat Mu'adh Ibn Jabal. He was appointed by the Prophet (peace be upon him) as a judge in Yemen. On the eve of his departure to assume his office there, the Prophet (peace be upon him) asked him:

"According to what shalt thou judge?"

He replied:

"According to the Book of God."

"And if thou findest nought therein?"

"According to the Sunnah of the Prophet of God."

"And if thou findest nought therein."

"Then I will exert myself to form my own judgement."

An thereupon the Prophet (peace be upon him) said:

"Praise be to God who has guided the messenger of His Prophet to that which please His Prophet."[I]

Prof. Fyzee, interpretes the last part of the above hadith, that is, "then I will exert myself to form my own judgement," as of a creative nature.

Al-Ijtihad in no way implies, as some modernists would like to believe, freedom of judgement. Its very nature is a mental process which derives its impetus directly from the Shariah and implies no more than individual opinion. It is in no way creative in the sense of legislation or law making. It only opens gate for intelligent and brilliant reasoning.

I. Abn 'Abd al-Barr, Jar-i-Bayan al-Ilm wa-Fadlhi, Arabic, II, p. 56; Khallaf, 'Ilm Usul al-Fiqh, p. 62.

'The concept of "individual opinion" was even recognized and applied by the Prophet (peace be upon him) with reference to himself. Only what he said, did or agreed to in his capacity as a Prophet (peace be upon him) is to be considered a binding Sunnah. The context of a particular tradition usually indicates and in cases of ambiguity, it becomes for the Muslims a matter of consideration, in which spiritual factors as well s individual and collective reasoning should play the decisive role'.[I] It is said that on some occasion Prophet (peace be upon him) consulted Hazrat Abu Bakr (R.A.) and Hazrat Umar (R.A.), and asked: "Advise for in the absence of revelation I am like you."[II] The jurists from this may infer that consultations and reasoning in worldly affairs are part of the Prophet's (peace be upon him) traditions but does not mean to go beyond the limit of Shariah.

Again Ijtihad may be in two ways:

1. The Ijtihad or interpretation of the text way of analogy of qiyas which may be described as strict analogy if the case is apparent; and

2. Sound analogy or 'tawil' if the cause is not apparent. It means to reach a thing or come to the point, that is, to probe into the inner meaning of the text and discover its intents and purposes. In other words tawil as the interpretation where the possibility of doubtful meaning is dispelled by resource to some authority or proof.

To Mr. Muhammad Muslehuddin: 'Tawil has an amazing capacity to cover the growing needs of society, for the text may be interpreted with reference to its words and the meaning implicit therein, its context and the traditions of the Prophet (peace be upon him). In this way the text is open to useful interpretations to

---

I. Said Ramadan, 'Islamic Law, its scope and equity.' pp. 76-77.

II. Kashf al Asrar, Arabi, II, p. 930.

cope with the situation and to accommodate the various needs and transactions of the modern world. And if anything essential is not covered by such interpretation, recourse may be had to the 'Rule of Necessity and Need.'

To him, 'an analogy, to be should must be supported by some proof and for this purpose understanding of not only the word and its meaning but also of the circumstances in which the text came into existences is necessary'. Mujtahid (person qualified to exercise ijtihad) must, therefore, be fully equipped with the proper knowledge of Arabic, its grammar and literature, principles of jurisprudence and of the source of law, of repealing and repealed text, of the circumstances in which the text was revealed, of the methods of ascertaining Sunnah, sufficient acuteness, sound minds, intelligence and legal acumen to be able to grasp the drift of a speech and its purpose.'

'In view of the difficulty in finding a mujahdi of these qualifications, matters may be decided according to the theory enunciated by Ghazzali-consensus of the community on the fundamentals, leaving the matters of detail to the agreement of the scholars.'[1]

Critics point out that this narrow interpretation of ijtihad, later, resulted in different schools and in blind pursuit of imitation what different Imams had interpreted. Further the qualification required for a Mujtahid also closed the doors of Ijtihad suiting to the needs of new arising problems in the progressive and developing society. Critics rely more on one's judgement and in support say that the early jurist (i.e., companions of the Prophet (peace be upon him), in default of relevant text, relied on their own judgement. But, to them, this liberty of judgement later became progressively restricted to a strict process of analogical deduction.

1. Ghazzali, Wajiz, Vol. 2, p. 216.

But this is an erroneous view. It is also baseless. Companions of Prophet (peace be upon him) never relied on their own judgement in disregard to the revealed text. In fact, they were the first and foremost to adopt analogical deduction to preserve the text in its ideal form. Under the rule of 'necessity and need' some departures at times made by the Caliphs, but in reality it is not so. For example, penalty for committing theft was suspended in time of famine by Hazrat Umar (R.A.). It was all because of necessity. Consensus of jurists followed this rule.

This procedure of 'Necessity and Need', is most appropriate and best calculated to accommodate the needs of the society, preserving at the same time the stability and ideal form of Shariah.

In brief Ijtihaed does not mean freedom of judgement. Mujtahahid must be qualified and must have faith in God and His Prophet (peace be upon him). When Qur'ãn and Sunnah on any point are silent, then the Qazi may use his intellectual abilities to come to a just conclusion within the frame work of Qur'ãn and Ahadith. Qazi if makes Ijtihad keeping in view these guiding principles, Allah will reward him. Hazrat Umar bin-Al-Aas (R.A.) narrated that he heard Prophet (peace be upon him) saying:

> "When a Hakin (حاکم) make Ijtihad when pronounces judgement of the court, and attains correct approach, he gets double reward, and if he commits error in making Ijtihad during judgment, he gets a single reward."

Reward to judge only when Ijtihad does not mean creativeness contrary to Shariah.

CHAPTER 7

PART A

"CRIMINAL COURTS: INDIAN CRIMINAL LAW"

In India there are three categories of criminal courts, i.e., courts contituted by the Constitution of India, courts constituted by Criminal Procedure Code, and by other special statutes:

Courts constituted by the Constitution of India are:

i. Supreme Court - it exercises its jurisdiction as provided by the Constitution.

ii. High Courts - their powers have been laid down by the Code of Criminal Procedure.

Courts constituted under criminal procedure are:

Section 6 of Criminal Procedure Code lays down that besides the High Court and the courts constituted under any law, other than this, there shall be, in every state, the following classes of Criminal Courts, namely:

i. Courts of Session.

ii. Judicial Magistrates of the first class and, in any metropolitan area, Metropolitan magistrates,

iii. Judicial Magistrate of the second class, and

iv. Executive Magistrates.

The revised set up of Criminal courts and allocations of magisterial work are intended to bring about separation of the judiciary from the executive. As a consequence of separation there are two categories of Magistrates, namely, the judicial Magistrate and the executive Magistrates. Judicial Magistrates are under the control of High Court and functions assigned to them are essentially judicial in nature.

Offences relating to criminal breach of trust are triable by the court of Magistrate of First Class. Clause III of Section 26, Criminal Procedure Code as shown in the First Schedule of Cr. P.C., empowers the Magistrates for such Trials.

In every district (not being a metropolitan areas), there shall be established as many courts of judicial Magistrates of the First Class and at such places, as the State Government may, after conculation with the High Court, by notification, specify.

The presiding officers of such courts shall be appointed by the High Court. The High Court may, whenever it appears to it to be expedient or necessary, confer. The powers of judicial Magistrate of the First Class on any member of judicial service of the State, functioning as judge in a civil court.

In every district apart from Magistrates of the First Class thee will be chief judicial Magistrate and Additional Chief Judicial Magistrates. The High Court shall appoint a judicial magistrate of the First Class to be the Chief Judicial Magistrate and also may appoint Additional chief judicial Magistrate who will have all or any of the powers of a chief judicial Magistrate under Criminal Procedure Code or under any other law for he time being in force as the High Court may direct.

The High Court may designate any judicial magistrate of the First Class in any sub-division as the Sub-Divisional Judicial Magistrate and relieve him of the responsibilities specified as occasion requires.

Subject to the general control of the chief judicial Magistrate, every sub-divisional judicial Magistrate shall also have and exercise, such powers of supervision and control over the work of the judicial Magistrates (other than Additional Chief Judicial Magistrates) in the sub-division as the High Court may, by general or special order, specify in this behalf.

Territorial division under the Criminal Procedure Code is:

i. Every state shall be a Session Division, shall consist of sessions divisions.

ii. Every sessions division shall be a district or consists of districts.

iii. Metropolitan area shall be a separate sessions division and district.

iv. State Government may, after consultation with the High Court, divide any district into sub-divisions and may alter the limits or the number of such sub-divisions.

v. The State Government may, by notification, declare that, as from such date as may be specified in the notification, any area in the state comprising or town whose population exceeds one million shall be a Metropolitan area.

vi. The State Government may, by notification, extend, reduce or alter the limits of a metropolitan area but the reduction or alteration shall not be so made as to reduce the population of such area to less than one million.

In every metropolitan area, there shall be established as many courts of metropolitan Magistrates, and at such places, as the State Government may, after consultation with the High Court, by notification, specify. The presiding officers of such courts shall be appointed by the High Court. The jurisdiction and powers of every metropolitan Magistrate shall extend through out the metropolitan area.

As to subordination[I] every chief judicial Magistrate shall be subordinate to the sessions judge.

The chief judicial Magistrates may, from time to time, make rules or give special orders, consistent with the Criminal Procedure Code, as to the distribution of business among the judicial Magistrate subordinate to him.

The chief metropolitan Magistrate[II] and every Additional chief metropolitan Magistrate shall be subordinate to the sessions judge.

Every other metropolitan Magistrate, shall, subject to the general control of the sessions judge, be subordinate to the chief metropolitan Magistrate.

The High Court may, for the purposes of Criminal Procedure Code define the extent of the subordination, if any, of the Additional, chief metropolitan Magistrate, to the chief metropolitan Magistrates.

The chief metropolitan Magistrate may, from time to time, make rule or give special order, consistent, with the code, as to the distribution of business among the metropolitan Magistrates and as to the allocation of business to an Additional Chief Metropolitan Magistrate.

I. Section 15, Criminal Procedure Code.

II. Section 19, Criminal Procedure Code.

Jurisdiction

Section 14 of Criminal Procedure Code explains the local jurisdiction of Magistrate of First Class. The chief judicial Magistrates may, subjects to the control of High Court, from time to time define the local limits of the areas within which the Magistrates appointed under Section 11 may exercise all or any of the powers with which they may be invested under this code. Except otherwise provided by such definition, the jurisdiction and powers of every such Magistrate shall extend through out the district.

Jurisdiction - Venue - In Inquiries and Trials

The jurisdiction of Criminal Court to try a particular offence is derived from:[I]

1. The state creating the court, or
2. from the statute defining the offence.

Further the jurisdiction of Magistrate to inquire into and dispose of criminal cases depends also upon:

Magistrate must be competent to entertain and dispose of the cases. Schedule I of the Criminal Procedure Code determines the competency. Under column 6 of the First Schedule the Magistrate of First Class has been shown as competnet to inquire into the dispose of cases of criminal breach of trust falling under section 406, 407, 408 and 409 of the Indian penal Code.

This competency is different from terrirotial jurisdiction. Criminal Procedure Code under Section 177 to 185 contain provisions regarding the place of criminal trial.

I. Jhakar Ahi V. Proo. of Bihar, AIR 1945, Pat. 98.

Where a court is not empowered to try a particular offence does try, the entire trial is void. In cases of territorial jurisdiction same importance is not attached to it.[I] This is clear from the provisions of Section 185, 188, 197 (4) and section 462 Cr. P. Code.

Territorial jurisdiction is provided as a matter of convenience:

1. With administrative point of view. In this connection work load of the court is to be taken into consideration.
2. With a view of convenience of the accused persons and of the witnesses.

Section 177 of the Criminal Procedure Code embodies this principle within it. According to this section every offence shall ordinarily be inquired into and tried by a court within whose local jurisdiction it was committed.

In Narumal V. State of Bombay,[II] it was held: 'The rule laid down by Section 177, is one of general application and governs all criminal trials held under the provisions of this code.'

The competency of the court under section 177 to take cognizance or to try an offence is determined by the place where the offence is committed. Requirement is that the offences in their nature are local and the jurisdiction of the criminal courts is also local.

A Magistrate is competent to try an offence within whose local jurisdiction an offence is committed. If the offence committed wholly outside the limits of his jurisdiction he is

I. Purshotam Das Dalmia V. State of West Bengal, AIR 1961 S.C. 1589. Vp. 1593.

II. AIR 1960, S.C. 1329:1960 Cr. *L.j.* 1674.

not authorised to take cognizance of and to try the accused. Therefore, the offence of criminal breach of trust may be inquired into or tried by a court within the local limits of whose jurisdiction any part of the property which is subject of the offence was received or retained by the accused person, or was required to be returned or accounted for by the accused person or the offence was committed.'[1]

Section 177 makes it clear that ordinarily every offence shall be tried by a court within whose local jurisdiction it was committed. It does not say that it would be tried by such court except in the cases mentioned in Section 178 to 184 and 188 or in cases specially provided by and other provision of law. In other words sections 178 to 184 and 188 cannot be read as exceptions to the general rule laid down by Section 177. They are rather elaborations of that rule telling where exactly an offence must be taken as committed in different situations and circumstances mentioned therein. Thus it leaves the place of trial open. Its provisions are not peremptory. Keeping this view in consideration it may also be said that provisions of Section 218 to 223 are also not exceptions to the general rule laid down by Section 177 Cr. P.C., if they do permit the trial of a particular offence along with others in one court.

Section 178 deals with situations where it is uncertain in which of several local areas an offence was committed, or where an offence is committed partly in one local area and partly in another, or where an offence is a continuing one, and continues to be committed in more local areas than one, or where it consists of several acts done in different local areas, it may be inquired into or tried by a court having jurisdiction over any of such local areas.

I. D'Mello V. Pereira (1937) 39 Bom LR 620 : 1937 Bom 743. Sattenapalli Goparaju V. Meka Ramakrisha 1970 Cr. L.j. 1290 (AP).

This section contemplates four contingencies. The first contingency as to when it is uncertain in which of the local areas an offence is committed, the type of contingency as envisaged by section 178 has been well explained by the Supreme Court in State of M.P. V.K.P. Ghiara.[1] Facts of the case were that 'the accused was employed as an agent in the company whose head office situated at Nagpur where its books were maintained and the staff located. On 12 September, 1950, he was entrusted at Nagpur with a car belonging to the company for sale. The sale took place in Bombay and the proceeds were paid over to him at Bombay between the 13th and 14th January, 1951. It was clear from the evidence that the accused reached Nagpur on 17 January, 1951 but the sale proceeds were not credited in the company's book nor the money paid over to the company then or thereafter. A charge sheet was filed against him under section 408 Indian Penal Code at Nagpur did not, either specifically or by necessary implication, refer to the embezzlement in Bombay nor did it indicate that it took place in Nagpur. There was no evidence to show that prior to his leaving for Nagpur, the accused had entertained or even been animated with an intention to misappropriate the sale deeds and there was nothing to show that he had utilised the funds during the period of his stay at Bombay for 4 days for his own use.'

It was held that:

1. 'The veneu of inquiry or trial of a case like the present must primarily be determined by the averments contained in the complaint or charge sheet and unless the facts thee are positively disproved, ordinarily the court where the charge-sheet or complaint was filed,

I. AIR 1957 S.C. 196.

had to proceed with it, except where action had to be taken under section 202k, Cr. P.C.

2. In the circumstances, it was uncertain whether the offence of embezzlement was committed at Bombay or Nagpur, and, therefore, section 178, Cr. P.C. applied, and the court at Nagpur had jurisdiction to inquire into the offence.'

In order to attract the provisions of section 178, it is necessary for the prosecution to cover that the offence was committed in one or the other local area of which it was uncertain.

The provisions of section 179 and 180 are quite wide to enable cognizance to be taken either by:

(a) a court where anything was done within the local limits of its jurisdiction, or

(b) a court where the consequences ensued.

'When an act is an offence by reason of anything which has been done and of a consequence which has ensued the offence may be inquired into or tried by a court within whose local jurisdiction such thing has been done or such consequence has ensued'. (S. 179).

Where the accused was engaged in Kanpur as an agent of a firm of Kanpur to sell goods in Bengal and either bring or remit the money to Kanpur; and the accused made some sales and realised the prices at some places kin Bengal but failed to bring or to remit the money to Kanpur; and there was no allegation or evidence that the accused had actually misappropriated or converted to his own use the money by any definite act committed at any particular place, it was held that 'the Kanpur Court had jurisdiction to try him for an offence under sections 408/409'.[1]

Section 405 is in two parts. The first part will apply where it is known that the accused has dishonestly misappropriated or converted to his own use the entrusted property at a particular place, and the jurisdiction to try the accused will be at that place. But when be at that place. But when it cannot be alleged that the misappropriation was actually and definitely committed at any particular place, there the case comes under the second part of section 405, namely dishonestly disposing of property in violation of any direction of law or of any legal contract; and if the legal contract required that the accused should remit or deliver or otherwise dispose of the property at a particular place, then his failure to do so constitute the coffence, and the jurisdiction to try the accused exist at such place. Santosh Kumar V. State[II] may be discussed here as an illustration. A seller at place X undertook to deliver refrigerators to purchaser at place Z after making due repairs of them. The seller delivered unrepaired refrigerators at place Z. Not only this but he also removed some material parts from them. It was observed that courts at place Z were competent to inquire into the offence under section 406 as the seller failed in discharging his trust in the manner undertaken by him. If there is evidence apart from the fact of non-delivery or non-accounting to show where the misappropriation was committed, the trial may be held at that place; but if there is no evidence to show where the misappropriation was committed, other than the fact of non-delivery or non-accounting according to the contract, than the trial may be held at the place where the accused failed to deliver or to account, because that is where the offence was committed.

I. Mahrulal (1935) 58 All 644; Kury Beharilal V. Brahama Datta (1942) ALj 559; (1942) 44 Cr. L.j. 102: (1942) (A) AIR, (A) 439. Hiralal (1956) Cr. L.j. (1165).

II. 1975 Cr. L.j. 734 (All).

Under section 180 Criminal Procedure Code place of trial is determined where act is an offence by reason of relation to other offence. It contemplates two offences. Where an act which is an offence by reason of its relation to any other act which is also an offence, is committed, and the other act which is an offence is also committed, a charge of the first mentioned offence may be tried by the court within the local limits of whose jurisdiction either act was done.[I] The jurisdiction as regards the offence of dishonestly receiving stolen property under section 411 Indian Penal Code, would be governed by section 180, Cr. P.C. under which that offence can be enquired into or tried by a Magistrate within the local limits of whose jurisdiction either the offence under section 407 or the offence under section 411 was committed.[II]

Section 181 deals with place of trial in case of certain offences. Clause (4) is relevant here. It reads that any offence of criminal misappropriation or of criminal breach of trust may be inquired into or tried by a court within whose local jurisdiction the offence was committed or any part of the property which is the subject of the offence was received or retained or was required to be returned or accounted for, by the accused person. Where the offence committed at Gauhati which is outside the local limits of the jurisdiction of any Magistrate of Manipur, but, because the property was handed over by the complainant at Imphal within Manipur, the offence under section 407 I.P.C. can be tried at Imphal.[III]

In cases where offence committed by letters or telecommunication messages, could be tried or inquired by

---

I. In re L.N. Mukerjee, AIR 1961 Mad 126 (DB).

II. Rameshwarlal Bhura Mal V. Dwaraka Prasad, AIR 1959 Manipur 14.

III. AIR 1959 Manipur 14

any court within whose local jurisdiction such letters or messages were sent or were received. (Section 182 Cr. P.C.)

Section 183 is aimed to provide provision against difficulties which may arise while an offence is committed in the course of performing a journey or voyage, the offence may be inquired into or tried by a court through or into whose local jurisdiction that person or thing passed in the course of that journey or voyage.

Place of trial for offences triable together under section 184 is determined where the offence committed by several persons are such that they may be charge with and tried together by virtue of the provisions of sections 219, 220 or 221 or, the offence or offences committed by several persons are such that they may be charged with and tried together by virtue of the provisions of section 223, the offences may be inquired into or tried by any court competent to inquire into or try and of the offences.

Relevant remaining section of Chapter XIII contemplate such situation as power to order cases to be tried in different sessions divisions, High Court to decide, in case of doubt, district where inquiry or trial shall take place, power to issue summons or warrant for offences committed beyond local jurisdiction and offences committed outside India.

The offence of criminal breach of trust is complete as soon as the dishonest intention of the accused is formed coupled with an overtact to show that intention to misappropriate or convert to his own use the entrusted property. The consequence loss, to the owner of the property is not a component part of the offence. Consequently, it is the court within whose jurisdiction the property was received or retained or the dishonest intention formed that has jurisdiction to try the offence and not the court of the place where the loss to the owner or other consequence occurs.[I]

Where neither entrustment nor conversion has taken place within the territorial jurisdiction of a court that court has no jurisdiction.[II]

Warrant case Trials

Criminal Procedure Code lays down three types of trials:-

1. Trial of Warrant Case by Magistrate - Chapter XIX.
2. Trial of Summons - Cases by Magistratre - Chapter XX.
3. Summary Trials - Chapter XXI.

Offence of criminal breach of trust is covered under trials of warrant cases by the Magistrate. Thus the present study is confined to trials of warrant cases by the Magistrate.

Section 2 (x) defines warrant case as a case relating to an offence punishable with death, imprisonment for life or imprisonment for a term exceeding two years. While the summon case has been defined as a case relating to an offence, and not being a warrant case. It may be inferred from the definitions that the nature and measure of punishment which the law prescribes for a particular offences determines the character of summons-case or warrant-case. Cases while are punishable with imprisonment for two years or below 2 years are summon cases. On the other hand offences punishable with imprisonment exceeding 2 years are warrant cases. Later

---

I. A 1930 Bom 490.

II. 1970 Cr. L.j. 332.

category of cases covers the offence of criminal breach of trust.

Under warrant cases, a Magistrate is to follow two different procedures:

1. Where in a case instituted on a police report procedure to be followed has been laid down in sections 238 to 243, and

2. Where any warrant case instituted otherwise than on a police report, the procedure has been specified in sections 244 to 247, Criminal Procedure Code.

In respect of trial condicted by a Magistrate on a police report, the accused either appears or is brought before him at the commencement of the trial, the Magistrate shall satisfy himself whether the accused has been furnished with all documents referred in section 207, Criminal Procedure Code or not. The Magistrate on consideration of those documents and after giving the prosecution and the accused an opportunity of being heard if he considers the charge against the accused as groundless he will discharge the accused; on the other hand if the Magistrate is of opinion that there is ground for presuming that the accused has committed an offence triable. Under Chapter XIX of Cr. P. Code and that such Magistrate is competent to try, he will frame a charge against the accused.

In cases instituted otherwise than on the police report, the Magistrate will frame charge after taking evidence for the prosecution, but the Magistrate may not frame charge if on such evidence the Magistrate thinks that no case against the accused has been made out which, if unrebutted, without warrant his conviction and, in such case, will discharge the accused.

In cases instituted otherwise than on the police report, the accused has the right to reserve cross-examination of prosecution witness till at a later state. The Magistrate has to ascertain from the complaint or otherwise the name of any person to be able to give evidence for the prosecution and shall summon them; the Magistrate cannot discharge the accused without examining all witnesses for the prosecution.

'As a general rule the cross-examination of a witness is to be made immediately after examination-in-chief, but exception to this general rule has been made in cases of trial of warrant cases where the accused is entitled to defer the examination until after the framing of the charge. This right to cross-examine a witness after the charge is framed, is an absolute right and the omission to give the accused the benefit of that right would vitiate the whole proceeding, and then fact that the witnesses were once cross-examined by the accused before the charge is of no avail.

In Habeeb Mohammad V. State of Hyderabad,[1] it has been observed that it is the bounden duty of the prosecution to examine a material witness particularly when no allegation has been made that, if produced, he would not speak the truth. For them observed that not only does adverse inference arise against the prosecution case from his non-production as a witness in view of illustration (g) to section 114 of the Indian Evidence Act, but that the circumstances of his being withheld from the court would case a serious reflection on the fairness of the trial.

'If it is shown that persons who had witnessed the incident, have been deliberty kept back, the court may draw an adverse inference and, in a proper case, record such failure

---

I. AIR 1954 S.C. 51: 1954 Cr. L.j. 338.

as constituting a serious infirmity in the proof of the prosecution case'.[I]

When the accused is not discharge then the accused after examining and cross-examining the prosecution witness shall be called upon the enter upon his defence and produce his evidence; and the provisions of section 243 shall apply to the case.

Offence of criminal breach of trust cannot be tried summarily,[II] and no order under section 360, Crimina Procedure Code can be made on conviction under section 408 Cr. P.C. To discharge frivolous complaints, section 250 enables the court to compensation to the accused if there was no reasonable ground for accusation where civil case had been filed and decreed criminal proceeding after a gap of quite long time under section 406 were not proper and maintable.[III] But merely because there is a civil remedy a complaint for criminal breach of trust cannot be thrown out.[IIIa]

A Magistrate cannot refuse to take cognizance of an offence under section 405 and 406, Cr. P.C. on the ground that the amount mis-appropriated is very small.[IV] (Five rupees).

Being a cognizable case no process fee is payable by the complainant for compelling that attendance of the accused. An order discharging the accused for non-payment of such fee is not sustainable.[V]

I. Darya Singh V. State of Punjab, AIR 1965 s.c. 328.

II. Karnesh Kumar Singh V. State of U.P., AIR 1968 s.c. 1402.

III. Kariraj Basudevananda V. State 1970 Cr. L.j. 632.

IIIa. 1978 Cr. L.j. 609 Punj.

IV. 1974 BLJR 49 (50).

V. ILR (1954) Punj. 645.

Where the facts in a complaint case indicate a fair case under sections 405, 406 against the accused, it is not proper to dismiss the complaint under section 203 of the Criminal Procedure Code.[I]

When allegations in the complaint do not at all constitute the ingredients, to make out a prima facie case under section 406, after acquittal of some the accused, it was held remanding the case of other accused would be meaningless.[II]

A second class Magistrate cannot, in a case falling under section 409, try the case and convict the accused under section 406 Cr. P. Code.[III]

Burden of Proof

The term 'burden of proof' in relation to the judicial proceedings has been used in two senses: (1) a burden of establishing the case, and (2) in the sense of introducing the evidence. First is covered under section 101, and later in section 102 Indian Evidence Act, 1872.

When a person desires and court to give judgement as to any legal right or liability dependent on the existence of facts which he asserts, must prove that those facts exist. When a person is bound to prove the existence of any fact, it is said that the burden of proof lies on that person. If he fails in proving those facts, his suit fails. The burden of proof in a suit or proceeding lies on that person who would fail of no evidence at all were given on either side.

I. A 1952 Ajmer 58.

II. 1976 Mad. LW (Cr.) 70.

III. (1899) - Bom. LR 27 (29) (DB).

Section 101 to 103 of the Indian Evidence Act, 1872 simply explain who is to prove a particular fact and not the extent of proof required in any case. The extent of proof required in any case, infect, depends upon the nature of the case., In criminal cases the standard of proof required is proof beyond reasonable doubt.

The burden of proof is on the party who asserts, not on him who denies. Whoever goes to the court and asserts any fact, he has to prove the fact. In a criminal prosecution the accused is not bound to prove the defence story, it is the prosecution's duty to prove the guilt of the accused beyond reasonable doubt. The basic principle of criminal jurisprudence is that an accused person is presumed to be innocent and the burden of proving the existence of all the facts on which the existence of criminal liability depends always lies on the prosecution. If the prosecution case does not reach this standard of proof, thee cannot be conviction of the accused.[I]

However, the burden of proving a fact, initially on one party may he shifted to the other party in the following conditions:

1. by the proving facts giving rise to a presumption in his favour, (section 107, 108 and 112 Indian Evidence Act).
2. by showing that the subject-matter of a party's

I. Mohindra Singh V. State, AIR 1953 S.C. 415.

Other revelant cases on burden proff: Bhagat Ram V. State of Punjab, AIR 1954 S.C. 621; Sarwan Singh Ratan Singh V. State of Punjab, AIR 1957 S.C 637; Haripada Day V. State of West Bengal, AIR S.C. 757; Gurcjharan Singh V. State of Punjab, AIR 1956 S.C. 460; Shambhu Nath Mehra V. State of Ajmer, AIR 1956 S.C. 404.

allegation is paculiarly within the knowledge of his opponents, (section 106).

3. by proving an admission, and

4. by proving that case of accused comes within exception in the Indian Penal Code (Section 105).

In cases covered under the second category when applied to criminal cases great care and caution is to be taken. 'An accused charged with the criminal breach of trust of his master's property left in his custody is the only person who can account for the property if he has not committed the offence and the burden of accounting the property is on him, if he fails, he may be convicted.

Under section 109 of Indian Evidence Act, when the question is whether person are partners, landlords and tenants or principal and agent, and it has been shown that they have been acting as such, the burden of proving that they do not stand, or have ceased to stand, to each other in those relationships respectively, is on the person who affirms it. Once a relation is shown to be in existence, for a longer, or shorter period, there is a presumption of its continuance till contrary is proved.

The court may also presume existence of certain facts which it thinks likely to have happened, regard being had to the common course of natural events, human conduct and public and private business, in their relation to the facts of the particular case. (Section 114, Indian Evidence Act).

The burden of proof of establishing all the ingredients of the offence such as entrustment, misappropriation, dishonest intention, etc., is on the prosecution.[I] When the

---

I. (1979), 81 PUNJ. l.r. 247.

prosecution succeeds in making out a prime facie case against the accused, the on us will shift to the accused to show how he is not guilty.[I] Once the entrustment of amounts in question is proved by the prosecution it is for the accused to explain how he dealt with the amount.

The prosecution is to give evidence to prove:

1. That the accused was entrusted with property or with dominion over it;

2. That the accused misappropriated the property or converted to his own use or either used or disposed of the property;

3. That the accused did so in violation of any law prescribing the manner in which such trust was to be executed, or any legal contract, express or implied, which he made touching the discharge of such trust, or he wilfully suffered some other person to do;

4. That the accused misappropriated the property or converted it to his own use or either used the property or disposed of it dishonestly.

In Mohd. Yasin's[I] case, 'a coal depot was raided in the absence of the owner of the depot and the entire stock of coal was seized from the munim and entrusted to him for safe custody under Zimmanama executed by him and subsequently the entire stock of coal was found missing from the place where it had been kept, the owner of the depot could not be at tributed with criminal breach of trust unless criminal conspiracy was established between the owner and munim'.

I. 1978 Cr. L.j. (NOC) 293 (Goa).

'The prosecution cannot rest content with proving mere false entries to bring home to the accused that money had been misappropriated without further evidence to prove that the accused attempted to suppress all traces of his embezzlement by any circumstances of the accused which would render probable a case of misapprotiation'.[I]

In Jay Krishnadas it was held that 'conviction of a person for the offence of criminal breach of trust may not, in all cases, be founded merely on his failure to account the property entrusted to him or over which he has dominion, even then a duty to account is imposed upon him, but where he is unable to account or renders an explanation for his failure to account which is untrue, an inference of misappropriation with dishonest intention may readily by made.'

Onus lies on the prosecution to prove not only that money was paid to the accused in trust but also that he did not apply it for the purpose for which it was given. On the indictment for embezzlement, it is not enough to prove that a clerk has received a sum of money, and not entered it in his book, unless there be also evidence that he has denied the receipt of it or the like.

Proof of mode of misappropriation is not necessary. Mere failure to make an entry in account books is not sufficient to establish charge of misappropriation.

Gist of the offence is the dishonest intention. To retain property even temporarily with dishonest intention is sufficient. Where there is no dishonest intention an accused person would not be liable for criminal breach of trust though he may be accountable to a civil liability for damages.

The essential thing to be proved in case of criminal breach of trust is whether the accused was actuated by

---

I. Rame Rao V. Sub-Inspector of Police, Kahasti Station (1937), MWN 566.

dishonest intention or not. However, direct proof of intention is different. In a case of a public servant, charged with misappropriation of moneys, the element of offence of criminal breach of trust will be established if the prosecution proved entrustment of money, which he has under a duty to account and had not done so. If the failure to account was due to circumstances as pleaded by the accused in defence, the then those facts being within the accused's knowledge it is for the accused to explain them.

In accordance to section 106, Indian Evidence Act, if the facts and circumstances are within the knowledge of the accused then he has to prove them. This, however, does not mean that the burden is cast upon the accused person of persons that no crime has been committed. The prosecution has to establish a prima facie case in the first instance. Section 106 of the Evidence Act does not effect the prosecution's initial onus of proving the guilt of the accused. The non-payment by the accused of collection for a longtime may raise a presumption that he has misappropriated the amounts and it is for the accused to explain the delay. Where the evidence creates a doubt whether the accused is guilty or not, he is entitled to the benefit of the doubt.[I]

A, clerk in sub-office drawing money from office for payment of rent to H owner of the building in which office was situated, and sending a receipt by the Head clerk of H for, such payment to head office. Receipt missing in the head office and H denying such payment. In the absence of receipt it was doubtful whether A forged the receipt or the head clerk of H did so, held that A could not be convicted under section 409 I.P.C. or under section 477A, I.P.C.[II]

I. A 1972 SC 521.

II. 1976 Chand. LR (Cri) 206 (Punj).

Dishonest misappropriation is essential for the offence under section 409. Where the accused retained money for 15 days and deposited it at once when demanded, it was held that the case was not that of dishonest intention.[I]

'Amount drawn by principal for Chowkidar not borne on the register but Chowkidar not denying the receipt of payment. It was held that breach of rules not sufficient for conviction.'[II]

In re B.V. Padmanabha Rao,[III] where the prosecution proved that one of the thumb impressions on the M.O. from of the accused but did not prove that the other was not of the payee and the payee also did not state that she did not receive the money but only stated that the thumb-impression on the form were not hers, held, charge under section 409 was nor proved.

In Om Prakash's case,[IV] non-production of written complaints by several affected persons who also appeared as witness made the case doubtful.

'Where the Bank Manager made fictitious entries showing repayments, held the conviction was justified.'[V]

'Where the keys of the safe remained with the cashier and there was no evidence that he parted with the keys, he must be held guilty in case of embazzlement.'[VI]

I. Nageshwar Prasad V. State, AIR 1970 Pat. 311.

II. 1980 SCC (Cri.) 116 (B.B. Lal).

III. AIR 1970 Mys. 254.

IV. 1980 SCC (Cri). 125.

V. 1974 SCC (Cri). 168 (Budh Sigh).

VI. 1972 SCC (Cri). 700 (Surendra).

'Where the accused was charged with criminal breach of trust and falsification of accounts but the documents alleged to have been falsified was missing from the office record, held the accused could not be convicted under sections 409 and 477A Indian Penal Code'.[I]

Examination of Witnesses

The order in which witnesses are produced and examined shall be regulated by the law and practice for the time being relating to criminal procedure code, and in the absence of any such law, by the discretion of the court.[II] the prosection or the complainant begins his case and produces prosecution witnesses and then accused is asked to enter his defence.

Examination of witness has three stages;[III] the first is called, the 'examination-in-chief', second 'cross-examination', and third, 're-examination'.

The evidence of the witnesses is taken in open court in the presence of presiding officer of the court. In certain exceptional cases evidence may be taken on commission also. When the witness appears in the court to give evidence he is first administered the oath to speak the truth and the only truth. A child witness below the age of 12 is not required to take the oath.

The examination of witness is oral in the form of question and answers, but recorded in the narrative form. However, where may question asked is objected by the opposite party but allowed by the court, it is proper to record question and answer both.

I. AIR 1972 SC 521.

II. Section 1325, Indian Evidence Act, 1872.

III. Section 137 - Indian Evidence Act.

The examination of a witness by the party who calls him shall be called examination-in-chief. The examination of witness by the adverse party is known as his cross-examination. The party who has called the witness, subsequent to the cross-examination, if examines the witness again such examination is called as 're-examination'. The order of examination shall be first examination-in-chief, then if the opposite party so desires cross-examination, and thirdly of the party calling the witness so desires to re-examine the witness.

The examination and cross-examination must relate to relevant facts but the cross-examination need not be confined to the facts to which the witness testified on his examination-in-chief.

The main characteristic feature of the examination-in-chief is to tell the story of party calling the witness. It is the responsibility of the counsel to bring out clearly and in proper order every relevant fact in support of his client's case to which the witness can depose. The examination-in-chief's case to which the witness can depose. The examination-in-chief is limited to facts-in-issue and facts relevant to the facts-in-issue. The irrelevant question should not be asked in the examination-in-chief. Ordinarily, leading question should not be asked in the examination-in-chief.

As to cross-examination, the object is twofold: (1) to weaken, qualify or destroy the case of opposite party, and (2) to establish the party's own case by means of his opponent's witnesses. Adverse party impeach the accuracy, the credibility and general value of the evidence given in chief. The object is to detect and expose discrepencises, or to elicit suppressed facts which will support the case of the cross-examining party. In fact, cross-examination is a good method, in the hands of intelligent lawyers, to take every thing out of the mouth of the opponent's witness.

From sections 146 to 152 lay down rules relating to questions which may be asked to shake the credit of a witness by damaging his character.

A witness during cross-examination may be asked questions which tend to:

1. test the veracity of a witness,
2. discover who hie is and what is his position in life, or
3. shake his credit, by injuring his character, although the answer to such questions might tend directly or indirectly to incriminate him, or might expose or tend directly or indirectly to expose him to a penalty or forfeiture.[I]

The court may forbid questions which may be seandulous, indecent, intended to insult or annoy. Court is to decide when question shall be asked and when witness compelled to answer. If any question elates to a matter not relevant to the suit or proceeding, except in so far as it effects the credit of the witness by injuring his character, the court shall decide whether or not the witness shall be compelled to answer it, and may, if it thinks fit, warn the witness that he is not obliged to answer it.

In exercising the discretion, the court shall consider the question proper only when the matter conveyed by the question would serious affect the opinion of the court about the credibility of the witness.

I. Section 146, Indian Evidence Act.

Question would be considered improper (1) if the imputation refers to a matter which is so remote in time or of such a nature that it would affect the credibility of the witness in a slight degree or (2) if the matter asked is in disproportion between the importance of the imputation and the importance of witness's evidence.

The court may, if it sees fit, draw from the witness''s refusal to answer, the inference that the answer if given would be infavourable.

Section 149 and 150 protect the witness from a questions being asked without reasonable grounds. If the court is of opinion that any such question was asked without reasonable grounds, it may, if it was asked by any barrister, pleader, vakl or attorney, report the circumstances of the case to the High Court or other authority to which such barrister, pleader, vakil or attorney is subject in the exercise of his profession.

Section 153 Evidence Act is intended to prevent the litigation being extended to uncertain limit. If everything, what the witness has deposed to allow to be contradicted by the adverse party, there will be no end to the litigation. That is the reason when a witness has been asked and has answered any question which is relevant to the inquiry only i so far as it tends to shake his credit by injuring his character, no evidence shall be given to contradict him; but if he answers falsely, he may afterwards be charged with giving false evidence under section 193 Indian Penal Code.

This section has two exceptions:

1. Where the witness denies his previous conviction, evidence may be given to this effect contradicting his statement of denial.

2. Where the witness is asked any question tending to impeach his impartiality, and answers it by denying the facts suggested, he may be contradicted.

In cases of hostile witnesses, unwilling to answer the questions or it appears to the party who calls the witnesses that the witness is not going to give the truth, the court may be asked by the party to permit to put any questions to him which might be put in cross-examination by the adverse party.[I]

Impeaching credit of witness may be either by the adverse party or with the consent of the court, by the party who calls him.

A witness may, while under examination, refresh his memory by referring to any writing made by himself at the time of the transaction concerning which he is questioned. The witness may also refresh his memory by reference to any document with the permission of the court. An expert may refresh his memory by reference to professional treatises.

Another important section relating to examination of witnesses is section 165 Evidence Act, where the judge has been empowered to cross-examine any witness upon answer given in reply to any question subject to certain limitation laid down in the section itself.

Right to be Defended

Under section 303, Criminal Procedure Code an accused can, as a mater of right, claim to be defended by a pleader of his choice. A conviction following a trial cannot stand if there has been refusal to hear the lawyer. So also an appeal cannot be disposed of ex-paste where the appellant is entitled to be heard by a lawyer assigned to him by the government, who

I. Section 154, Evidence Act.

fails to reach the court in time to conduct the appeal. If the defence lawyer is weak in presenting the case of his client, a duty is cast upon a trial judge to protect the interest of the accused and cross-examine the witnesses of the prosecution himself. The main object of this provision is that the interest of the accused should remain supreme and in no way be prejudiced.

Before the enactment of new Criminal Procedure Code an accused person as stated above had a right to be defended by a pleader. But after the recommendation of law commissions section 304, a new provision was added in the Criminal Procedure Code. According to this section, where an accused person is not represented by a pleader during the trial before the court of session and it appears to the court that the accused has not sufficient means to engage a pleader, the court shall assign a pleader for his defence at the expense of the state and also empowers the state government to extend this facility to other cases.

A similar right accrues to the accused under section 56 Criminal Procedure Code where the accused person arrested by police without warrant should be brought before a Magistrate competent to try or commit with as little delay as possible or release him on bail.

In Madhu's Limaye's case it was observed that the makers of the constitution of India were anxious to provide these safeguards, as intergral part of the fundamental rights. Article 22 of the Constitution of India is relevant here.

Clause (1) of Article 22 is meant to afford the earlies opportunity to the arrested person to remove any mistake, misapprehension or misunderstanding in the mind of the arresting authority and also to know exactly what the accusation against him is, so that he can exercise the sccond right, namely, of consulting a legal practitioner of his choice and to be defended by him.

Clause (2) of Article 22 provides the next and most material safeguard that the arrested person must be produced before a Magistrate within 24 hours of such arrest so that an independent authority exercising judicial powers may, without delay, apply its mind to his case.

PART B

"HIERARCHY OF SHARIAH COURTS"

The Shariah is recognized as one of the main sources of law in almost all Muslim countries. This notion is part of and incorporated in the constitutional laws of countries such as Bahrain, Iran, Kuwait, Qatar, Syria, United Arab Emirat, all from Middle East, and, Malaysia, Indonesia and Pakistan from East. Civil codes of Egypt (1948). Iraq (1951), and Libya (1953) recognise Islamic Shariah as a source of their respective national legal system. Saudi Arabia and Oman also consider the Shariah as the basis of the national law. However, the contemporary legal systems in these countries are nation bound.

Courts of a country have a pivotal role in the implementation of its laws. Islamic courts, thus, are of the elements and symbols where Islamic law comes into action. How far Islamic law is applied in Shariah courts and what is their present structure in different countries of the world, is the aim to examine in the following paragraphs. It is not possible to study the courts structure of all countries. Therefore, our study confines only to the few selected countries.

Court Structure in Saudi Arabia

In spite, of the existence of a constitutional instruments, according to the official statements, Saudi Arabia has the Holy Qur'ãn and other classical Islamic law as the main source of law of the country. The Shariah governs all, even the King. Shariah courts in Saudia Arabia have general jurisdiction in all civil, criminal and family cases.

A study in the history of Saudi Arabia may be divided into three distinct periods: (1) The pre-Islamic era, (2) The Islamic era, and, (3) period beginning with the establishment of the Kingdom of Saudi Arabia. To study all the periods is difficult. Though we will make some references but study confines particularly to the present era.

In the Post Islamic period, Makkah period, Madinah period, the Republic period - Khilafat period, the Ummayya period, the formative period when the development of Islamic law started, downfall of the Abbasids in 656 A.H./1258 - the underlying feature of this period is the closing of the doors of ijtihad (reasoning), the Ottoman period, and ultimately the modern Saudi period are all most outstanding.

The Makkah period is marked by considerable opposition to the rise of Islam and little opportunity for Prophet (peace be upon him) to engage himself in the implementation of Islamic Law. During Madinah period Islamic Laws, Qur'ãn and the precepts of Prophet were given the practical shape and implemented in the day to day life affairs. After the death of Prophet (peace be upon him), comes the Khilafat period, during which period the "consensus of the Community" was established as a further source of Islamic Law, that is, where the Holy Qur'ãn and Sunnah did not provide any specific answer to the new questions, resort was had to the unanimous views of the Muslim Community.

Under the modern period, in the mid-eighteenth century, Muhammad Ibn Abd. Al-Wahhab, a Hambali jurist, began a campaign for the purification of the Islamic faith from the innovations (bedah) prevailing in Hejaz (now part of Saudi Arabia). Muhammad Ibn Sa'ud, the father of the King Abdal Aziaz, joined the Wahabi rigid orthodoxy. This fact had impact on institutions later established after the Saudi Dynasty captured the whole of the Saudi Arabia from the Ottam Empire. Thus after the establishment of the Kingdom of Saudi Arabia, the Hambali school was adopted as the official creed of the state.

The Supreme Judicial Council of Saudi Arabia in the year 1926, made it mandatory by official decree for all courts to rely on Hambali Texts. The council laid down the following order of Hambali Texts as approved sources of law:

1. Sharh Mutaha al-Iradat by al-Bahuti (Mansur, b. Yunus, b. Idris al-Hambali (d. 1051 A.H./1651-52).
2. Kashshaf al-Kina an Matu al-Ikna by the same author,
3. Commentaries of Al-Zad,
4. Commentaries of al-Dalil,
5. If no answer is found them reference may be made to secondary sources in Hambali legal manuals, and
6. If there is no Hambali work to answer the question reference may be made to the authorities in other sunni schools.[1]

The bulk of the law in Saudi Arabia still to be found in traditional sources of Islamic Law.

The second source of law in Saudi Arabia is State Regulations. They may be secular in nature, but it is true that the purpose of State Regulations in Saudi Arabia is not to detract from the Islamic law traditions or change and reform. These Regulations are simply aimed to supplement them. It is said that the Saudi Arabian jurists usually invoke a convenient legal fiction to support the statutes with a view to

1. S.H. Amin, 'The Middle-Eastg Legal Suystem', p. 313.

avoid any appearance of encroaching upon the tradition Islamic law principles. This fact has resulted in a duel legal and judicial system:

1. First is the hierarchy of Shariah Courts, and
2. Second, is the specialised judicial organs and quasi-judicial tribunals.

Shariah Courts exercise the general and universal jurisdiction while specialised tribunals have the jurisdiction to decide the specific issues. Here our purpose is to confine to the study of Shariah Courts only.

Shariah Courts

The Shariah Courts are organised by the Ministry of Justice.[1] At present there is a three-tiered judicial system comprising of:

1. Courts of first instance;
2. Courts of appeal;
3. The Supreme Judicial Council.

Courts of First Instance

The courts of first instance are classified under two categories:

1. The Lower Courts, and
2. The General Courts of organized courts.

According to the law of 1927, two Shariah Courts were established, one in Jeddah and other one in Madinah. Subsequently, this kind of courts began to spread in Saudi

---

I. Surpa N. - I, p.

Arabia, so much so that their number is now greater than that of any other kind of courts.

Number of judges of the Shariah Courts were never fixed. They were to be appointed in accordance to the need of the time. The only exception was the law of 1927 which determined that Shariah Courts of Jeddan and Madinah were to consist of two judges, a first chief judge, and the other a deputy judge.

The Lower Courts

The lower court deal with minor offences and claims, as well as crimes of defamation and drinking, but have no power to impose sentences of death or amputation. These courts have been established in towns outside Hijaz, and in villages under all the provinces. These usually consisted of one judge, who heard cases in any convenient place, even in his home or in the market or in the building of the office of the governor, and at any convenient time, whether during the day or night.

However, at present, every court, even if it is in a village, occupies a building called 'the court' (al-Mehkeme), and cases are decided during office hours.

The General Courts or Organised Courts

Organised or general courts occupies a permanent building and works according to fixed official schedules, such as the courts of Jeddah and Madinah. This general courts have universal jurisdiction over civil and criminal cases. Generally the court comprises of on judge only. But in cases where sentence of death, stoning or amputation are to be pronounced, the court should be comprised and be presided over by a penal of three-judges.

Shariah court may have a large criminal jurisdiction if there is no Magistrates' Court situated in its veneu, but if there is a Magistrate's Court established under the regulations, the criminal jurisdiction of the Shariah Court will be limited. Magistrate Court if existing in area was also to decide cases in accordance to the Islamic law. A single judge in a village which dies not have a Magistrate's court, exercises much greater jurisdiction than a Shariah court in a big city, where a Magistrate's court exists.

Thus Magistrates are also working side by side with Shariah Courts.

Courts of Appeal

The words "tamyiz" and "tadqia" mean the same thing. They have been used in the judicial laws and regulations to mean reviewing a judgement of a court of first instance, by an appellant authority, in order to ensure.[1]

1. That the judgement are delivered in conformity with the Islamic Laws.

2. If judgement is not inconformity with Islamic Law, then the lower court or court of first instance was to be informed about the correct view or correct judgement and instructions are sent not to repeat such errors in future.

3. That the sentence awarded should be inconsonance with Islamic Law. In cases where judges may use their discretions, it is to be reviewed whether the discretions used are interferometry with Islamic Law.

There are two appellate shariah courts one sitting in Riyadh and the other in Makkah. The former has jurisdiction to hear appeals from lower courts sitting in central and Eastern

Provinces, and the later from the courts of the Western Province. The Chairman of the Court of Appeal in selected on the basis of absolute seniority.

The penal comprising of three judges hear the appeals. However, sentences of death, stoning or amputation can only be imposed by a penal of five judges.

Decisions of the applellate courts are final, except in cases where sentence is death or stoning or amputation.

The Supreme Judicial Council ("Majlis al-Qada' al-A'la")

This is the higher judicial body in the hierarchy of Shariah Courts in Saudi Arabia. The judicial council comprises of ten members. Its chairman holds the rank of a Minister.

Powers of the supreme judicial council covers within its scope administrative, consultative, and judicial functions. It functions in the form of two committees.

Traditionally, direct appeals to the King in the form of petitions are permissible to seek redress of grievances. This system of appeal to the King is still in practice and considered to be a very useful procedure for obtaining a fair hearing.

This is in brief judicial hierachy of Shariah courts in Saudi Arabia. Few more points about the powers and functions of Shariah courts may also be referred here.

Firstly, source of Shariah courts is traditionally the Islamic law, jury trials are unknown in the Saudi Arabian legal system.

Secondly, cases are heard by a single judge, known as Qazi. He acts impartially in the role of an investigating magistrate who can examine and cross-examine the disputants and their witness.

Thirdly, upon the completion of trial, the judge decides both quilt and innocance.

Fourthly, in certain criminal cases the actual punishment may be determined by a local shaikh with the advice of a local Muslim jurist or an advisory group of them known as ulema (علماء).

Fifthly, the base year of Saudi Arabian legal system is 1926. Thereafter, reforms in the judicial structure were introduced from time to time. Most outstanding official instructions are of 1927, 1936, 1954, 1957, 1962, 1967, 1970, 1971 and 1973. Under these instructions, the constitution, powers and functions, original and appellate jurisdictions of Shariah courts were determined, and Courts of First Instance, Appellate Courts, and High Judicial Council (Majlis al-Qada, al-Ala) were established. Now at present Saudi Arabia has a well-knit Shariah judicial system administering justice to the people.

'Judicial System of Afghanistan'

Article 50 - 57 of the constitution of 1928, and Article 213 - 226 of the Nizam - name of Basic Organizations 1923 set up three - tiered system of shariah courts in Afghanistan, that is:[I]

1. 'Mahkama-e-Ibtida'iya' - Primary court,
2. 'Mahkama-e-Morafia' - court of appeal, and
3. 'Hay'at-e-Ali-e-Tamiz' - cassation board.

I. Mohammad Hashim Kamali, 'Law in Afghanistan', p. 212.

Primary Court

Primary court was to exist in each administrative district (Lokumat-e-Mahali) court consisted of a Qazi, two Muftis and a clerk.

This court had jurisdiction in all ordinary civil and criminal disputes. In criminal cases court was competent to pronounce judgements and were enforceable immediately except in death sentences and sentences which imposed corporal punishment or which effected the reputation of the convict.

Death sentences were referred to all the three courts and subject to the approval of the monarch before it could be executed.

Defendants could appeal against penal sentences involving corporal punishment or sentences affecting reputation of a person. Fifteen days after the pronouncement of judgement and its communication to the convicted person, an appeal could be made to the higher court of appeal.

Ordinarily, as a rule, sentences of the primary court in felonies (jinayat) were regularly referred for a review to the High Courts.

Court of Appeal

Constitution of the court was that it consisted of a Qadi, four Muftis and two clerks. This court existed in all the capitals of the provinces. Provincial administration was organised at three levels.

a. Wilayat, which was a larger administrative unit,

b. Hokumat-e-A'la (High Governorate), and

c. Hokumat-e-Kalan (Major Districk), a court of Appeal

was to exist was to exist in each.

These courts were of general jurisdictions and also competent to decide all matters falling within the jurisdiction of the primary courts.

Proceedings at these courts were generally governed by the Shariah and the Nizam namas. Against the judgement of this court, in criminal cases, a further appeal could be made within prescribed time to the higher court.

These Shariah Primary and Appellate Courts had different chambers for deciding civil, criminal and commercial cases.

In criminal cases shariah courts were to order punishments in accordance with the provisions of the General Penal Code (Nizam nama-e-Omumijaza).

Cassation Board

According to Nizam nama of Basic Organisation 1923, a Cassation Board was to be constituted which was to work in the country's capital as a final court of appeal for the whole of the Afghanistan. The cassation boart used to sit in combined sessions with the Kabul Court of Appeal. If the judge from Kabul court of appeal himself heard the case and awarded punishment, he could not part-take in the final review proceedings.

The Cassation Board consisted of President and four members. The Minister of Justice was to be the president of the Cassion Board. This Board was the reviewing court. Its powers were confined to scruitinize the decisions of the Primary Courts and the Appeal Courts, to ascertain whether the decisions of the lower courts were in conformity with Shariah and Nizamnama. Board was competent either to confirm the decisions of the lower court or to reverse them. However, it is not to act as a Trial Court.

All the decisions of the Cassation Board were final. But the Death penalties were subject to the final approval of the Monarch.

Procedure of Appointment of Judges

All judges whether of Cassation Board, Appeal Court judges of the Qadis of Primary Courts were to be appointed by the Monarch.[1] Muftis of Primary Court and Appeal Courts were appointed by the Minister of justice on the recommendation of the Appointments Committee (Komission-e-Ta'inat). Provincial Governors were also empowered to appoint Muftis for Primary Courts, and clerical staff in both the primary and provincial courts of appeal.

Criminal Law Applied in Shariah Courts

Hanafi School of Islamic Law was recognized as the main source of substantce law. Cases were to be decided in accordance to the Hanafi Texts, unless there were express state laws to resolve the problem.

Two types of punishment were awarded by the Shariah courts. Firstly, Hadd, the fixed penalties such as capital punishment for murder and cutting of hands for theft. These penaltics were given in accordance to the primary source of Islamic Law and no one could dare to challenge their enforceability. Secondly, Ta'zir, the penalties which were left to the discretion of the judges which were to be decided according to the circumstances of each case.

I. After revolution situation has changed. Under the present system instead of Monarch, the President of the Republic appoints the judges.

King Amanallah attempted to codify the later aspect of Islamic Law punishment - i.e. Ta'zir, in the form of Nizamnama. The ulema, however, did not welcome the Nizamnama reforms. Qadis considered themselves all-powerful as the penalties were not specified prior to the commission of crime and were left to the discretion of the Qadi. Under Ta'zir, Qadis had wide-ranging discretion to award any penalty which they considered appropriate and deemed fit to the circumstances of the case. The Nizamnama reforms restricted their powers.

The quide for judges was compiled by a group of leading ulema under the chairmanship of Maulvi Abdul Wasi Qandhari, then president of the State Council. Its preamable, signed by King Amanullah, reads as follows:[I]

> "It is for the ruler to specify the shariah penalties of Ta'zri which are flexible and have remained undefined. The fiqh Manuals are, moreover, mainly available in Arabic which makes ascertaining the authoritive rules applicable to particular cases a difficult task, not only for government officials in general, but also to the Qazis and Muftis. I, therefore, ordered the ulema to collect and compile the authoritative opinions of the Hanafi school in Farsi, which is the spoken language of Afghanistan".

Preamble makes it clear that the primary aim of Nizamnama was to consolidate the substantive Shariah Law in a codified form. But his codification of Ta'zir penalties was not liked by ulema. Even today owning to political conditions, inspite of possible efforts, in most areas the law of Afghanistan still remains uncodified in the form of either traditional Islamic law or of customary or tribed practices.

I. Supra - N.P.

Thus the Afghan legal system has etained its indigenous character, never influenced by European judicial system. The sources of inspiration have remained purely Islamic. A study of indigenous growth of Afghan Islamic judicial system in modern times would be a unique study. Even today shariah judges in Afghanistan are religious leaders. At the same they also exercise judicial powers. They lead prayers in the mosque, address religious congregations, deliver, sermosn and render advises to the citizens on legal and religious problems. In brief the training of Shariah judges is religious.

Judiciary was again organised and strengthened under the Administration of Justice Act, 1957. Main features, were as follows:

1. Shariah courts were regularised and centralised.

2. Courts of First Instance, with jurisdictions both civil and criminal continued to hear all cases in accordance with Islamic law.

3. In criminal cases, in the absence of an appeal by the interested party, the decisions of the court of First Instance were final. Cases involving minors, life imprisonment, retribution under Islamic rule of Qasas and capital punishment were formed exceptions. Decision in such cases could be appealed to the High Courts.

4. Appeal courts were authorised to hear appeals against the devisions of the court of First Instance.

5. Further the Appeal Courts were also to try cases of important nature which were beyond jurisdiction of court of First Instance.

Again reforms were introduced in the judicial system of Afghanistan under the constitution of 1964 which was amended in 1967, according to which the judiciary was made an independent organ of the state. Since then the hierarchy of the courts is as follows:

1. Supreme Court.
2. The Court of Cassation.
3. The High Central Court of Appeal.
4. The Provincial Courts, and
5. The courts of First Instance at sub-provincial and city level.
6. Under state secular statutes, there are: specialised courts such as Industrial Tribunal, Military Courts and Tax-Tribunals.

The above structure of the judiciary was approved by "The Fundamental Principles of Democratic Republic of Afghanistan", passed by the Revolutionary Government in April 1980.

Shariah Judiciary in Pakistan

Pakistan inconsonance with the provision of the constitution of Islamic Republic of Pakistan has taken an initiative in establishing the Shariah Court. Initiative is not for constituting the and establishing the shariah courts from the grass-root. As such there is no hierarchy of shariah court structure. Under Chapter IIIA, Article 203 c of the above referred Constitution a Federal Shairat Court has been established.

The Federal Shariat Court shall consist of not more than eight Muslim judges including the chief justice. They are appointed by the President of Pakistan (Article 203 c (2).

As to the qualification for appointment to the Federation Shariat Court, Article 203 c (3) lays down that the chief justice shall be a person who is, or has been or is qualified to be a judge of the Supreme Court, and, as regard to other judges the requirement is that a judge shall be a person who is, or has been or is qualified to be a judge of a High Court.

Clause 4 of Article 203 c of the Constitution of Islamic Republic of Pakistan further lays down that the chief justice and a judge shall hold office for a period not exceeding three years, but may be appointed for such further term or terms as the President may determine. Provided that a judge of a High Court shall not be appointed to be a judge for a period exceeding one year except with his consent and except where the judge is himself the chief justice after the consultation by the President with the chief justice of the High Court.

The Principal seat of the court shall be at Islamabad, but the court may from time to time sit in such places in Pakistan as the chief justice may, with the approval of the President, appoint.

Article 203 D of the constitution deals with the powers, jurisdiction and functions of the court. The court may, either of its own motion or on the petition of a citizen of Pakistan or the Federal Government, or a Provincial Government, examine and decide the question whether or not any law or provision of law is repugnant to the injunctions of Islam as laid down in the Holy Qur'ãn and the Sunnah of the Holy Prophet (peace be upon him).

If the court decides that any law or provision of law is repugnant to the injunctions of Islam, it shall set out in its decision:

a. The reason for its holding that opinion; and

b. The extent to which such law or provision is so repugnant and specify the day on which the decision shall take effect.

If any law or provision of law is held by the court to be repugnant to the injunctions of Islam:

a. The President in the case of law with respect to a matter in the Federal Legislative list or the concurrent legislative list, or the governor in the case of a law with respect to a matter not enumerated in either of those lists shall take steps to amend the law so as to bring such law or provision into conformity with the injunctions of Islam, and

b. Such law or provision shall, to the extent to which it is held to be so repugnant, cease to have effect on the day on which the decision of the court takes effect.

Under Article 203 D D, Federal Shariat Court may call for the examine the record of any case decided by any criminal court under any law relating to the enforcement of Hudood for the purpose of satisfying itself as to the correctness, legality or propriety of any finding, sentence or order recorded or passe by and as to the regularity of any proceedings of such court and may when calling for such record, direct that the execution of any sentence be suspended and, if the accused is in confinement, that he be released on bail or on his own bond pending the examination of the record.

In any case the record of which has been called for by the court, the court may pass such order as it may deem fit and may enhance the sentence.

Provided that nothing in this Article shall be deemed to authorise the court to convert a finding of acquittal into one of conviction and no order under this Article shall be made to the prejudice of the accused unless he has had an opportunity of being heard in his own defence.

A party to any proceedings before the court under clause (1) of Article 203 D may be represented by a legal practioner who is a Muslim and has been enrolled as an advocate of a High Court for period of not less then five years or as an advocate of the Supreme Court or by a juriscounsult selected by the party from out of a penal of jurisconsults maintained by the court for the purpose.

For being eligible to have his name borne on the penal of juriscounsults, a person shall be an a'alim (عالم) who, in the opinion of the court is well-versed in Shariat.

Under Article 203 E (6) of the Contitution, a legal practioner of jurisconsult representing a party before the court shall not plead for the party but shall state, expound and interpret the injunction of Islam relevant to the proceedings so far as may be known to him and submit to the court a written statement of his interpretation of such injunction of Islam.

Under clause (7) of Article 203 E, the court is empowered to invite any person is Pakistan or abroad whom the court considers to be well-versed in Islamic law to appear before it and render such assistance as may be required of him.

The court shall have power to review any decision given or order made by it (Cluse , Article 203 E).

Article 203 F gives the right of appeal to any party to any proceeding before the court under Article 203 D. Appeal is permitted in case when the party to the proceeding feels aggrieved against the decision of the court. Party may prefer appeal within sixty day of such decision final order, sentence. Appeal lies against the decision, final order, sentence of the court to the Supreme Court of Pakistan.

The grounds for appeal against the judgement, order or sentence of the Federal Shariat Court, are:

1. If the Federal Shariat Court has on appeal

   (a) reversed an order of scquittal of an accused and sentenced him to death or imprisonment for life or imprisonment for a term exceeding fourteen years; or

   (b) on revision, has enhanced a sentence as aforesaid.

(2) If the Federal Shariat Court has imposed any punishment on any person for contempt of court.

(3) An appeal to the Supreme Court from a judgement, decision, order a sentence of the Federal Shariat Court in a case to which the preceding clause does not apply that shall lie only if the Supreme Court grants leave to appeal (Article 203 F).

For exercising the jurisdiction for hearing appeal against the judgement or order or sentence of Federal Shariat Court, there is constituted in the Supreme Court a Bench to be called Shariat Appellate Bench. It consists of -

1. Three Muslim judges of the Supreme Court; and

2. Not more than two ulema to be appointed by the President to attend sittings of the Bench as ad hoc members thereof from amongst the judges of the Federal Shariat Court or form out of a penal of ulema to be drawn up by the President in consultation with the chief justice.

The decision of the Federal Shariat Court are binding, subject to Article 203 D and 203 F, on a High Court and on all courts subordinate to a High Court.

The Federal Shariat Court has also been empowered under Article 203 j to make rules for carrying out its jurisdictions.

The Federal Shariat Court, no doubt, working effectively. In a recent order of the court, number of statute in enforde in Pakistan has been annulled because the statutes were repugnant to Islamic injunctions of Holy Qur'ãn. But the unfortunate fact is that the court has been establised at the top of judicial structure. No importance has been given to courts of First Instance and appellate intermediary courts. Infects the cases in bulk are dealt with at the lower level. At the higher level only few selected go either in revision or appeal. Thus the process adopted in Pakistan is dead slow implementation of Islamic law. Unless laws are framed in accordance to Holy Qur'ãn and Sunnah of Prophet (peace be upon him) and implemented by lower courts, efficacy of laws in relation to modern condition cannot be assessed properly.

However, it does not mean that Pakistan is not Islamising the laws or not reverting from British Colonial system to its indiginous system. Promulgation of ordinance No. VII of 1990 which amended the Pakistan Penal Code and Code of Criminal Procedure 1898, is a mile stone towards adopting the Islamic law. This Ordinance has made substantive changes in the Pakistan Penal Code. Section 53, Act XLV of 1860, dealing with different kinds of punishments have been replaced by the following kinds of punishment in accordance to the Qur'ãnic injunctions and Sunnah:

"The punishments to which offenders are liable under the provisions of this Code are:

1. Firstly, Qisas;
Secondly, Ta'zir;
Thirdly, Diyat;
Fourthly, Arsh;
Fifthly, Daman;
Sixthly, Death;
Sevently, Imprisonment for life;
Eightly, Imprisonment which is of two descriptions, namely -
(i) Rigorous, i.e., with hard labour;
(ii) Simple;
Ninthly, Forfeiture of; and
Tenthly, Fine".

Substitution of these punishment and their implementation is, infect, a remarkable progress. Apart from amendments made in the Penal Code of Pakistan Government has also enacted the following ordinances:

1. The Offence Against Property, 1979 (VI of 1979)
2. The Offence of Zina (Enforcement of Hudood) Ordinance, 1979 (VII of 1979);
3. The Offence of Qazi (Enforcement of Hadd) Ordinance, 1979 (VIII of 1979);
4. The Execution of the Punishment of Whipping Ordinance Ordinance, 1979 (IX of 1979);
5. The Zakat and Ushr Ordinance, 1980 (XVIII of 1979).

President of Pakistan, from time to time, has also passed orders:

1. The Prohibition (Enforcements of Hadd Order 1979 (P.O. No. 4 of 1979).
2. Baluchistan Prohibition (Enforcement of Hadd) Rules, 1979;
3. Punjab Prohibition (Enforcement of Hadd) Rules 1979;
4. North-West Frontier Province Prohibition (Enforcement Hadd) 1980.
5. North-West Frontier Province Appointment and Powers Rules under Prohibition (Enforcement of Hadd) Order, 1979;

(6) Sind Prohibition Rules, 1979.

Although constitution of Pakistan provides that all existing laws shall be brought in conformity with the injunctions of Holy Qur'ãn and Sunnah, and all laws in the country repugnant to Holy Qur'ãn and Sunnah shall be struck down as null and void by the superior courts, so far only progress made is in regard to cases covered by Hadd, Qisas, Arsh, Daman , 'Qatl-i-Amd', Qatl-i-committed under 'Ikrah-i-Tam' or Ikrah-Naquis, but no remarkable or worth name work has been done in regard to cases cover under Tazir, a kind of discretionary punishment left with judges to awards as deem fit to them. Field covering Tazir cases is still open to work upon and needs greater attention as majority of offences committed in day to day life are covered under this kind of punishment.

Federal Shariat courts' judges are taking keen interest in the process of Islamisatin of laws. They have in their decisions not only laid thc laws repugnant but also have explained the methodology to be followed. In declaring certain provisions of the Pakistan Penal Code, such as Section 302, 304, 326 and 32, as repugnant to the injunctions of Islam as they do not provide for Qisas or payment of compensation.

Justice Aftab Hussain laid down the following quide lines:[I]

Firstly, the judge should find out the relevant verse or verses in the Holy Qur'ãn regarding the question in issue;

Secondly, to find out the relevant Hadith of Tradition of the Holy Prophet (peace be upon him).

Thirdly, to ascertain the intent of Holy Qur'ãnic verses from the Sunnah of Prophet (peace be upon him).

Fourthly, to know the opinions and views of learned jurists on the matter concerned and to assess their analogies in order to determine their harmony with the present day requirements or it possible to formulate them suiting to the demand of the modern age.

Fifthly, to discover and apply as last resort any other option which would no doubt be in harmony with the Holy Qur'ãn and Sunnah.

In cases when the Federal Shariat Court failed to give reasons for Islamization of laws, in appeal before the Supreme Court, case would be referred back again for clear cut opinion on the subject. It is the responsibility of the Federal Shariat Court to give reasons and refer in support specific Qur'ãnic injunctions and Ahadith in Support.

Summing up the discussion on judicial structure in Pakistan, it may be said that Islamization of laws, and substitution the present structure with indiginous Islamic

---

I. Muhammad Riaz V. Federal Government, PLD 1980 F.S.C.I.

judicial system is at preliminary stage. It has to take long travels, them would be preliminary stage. It has to take long travels, then would be able to reckon with. At present there is no hierarchy of courts as such enforcing and implementing the Shariat in its true spirit.

Shairah Judiciary in Iran

After the Islamic Revolution headed by Ayatollah Khomeini, in 1978-79, the First Iranian Constitution of 1906-07 was repealed. A new constitution was enforced. According to principles 4 and 170, of the New Constitution 1979, the Shi'a School of Islamic Law was declared as the main source of law in Iran. Principle 4 of the constitution lays down:

> "All civil, penal, financial, economic, administrative, cultural, military, political and other laws and regulations must be based on Islamic criteria. This principle governs absolutely and universally all the principles of the constitution, laws and other regulations, and any determination of this matter is entrusted to the religious jurists of the Council of Guardians".

This principle recognises Islamic law supreme over all other laws whether constitutional or municipal or customing or conventional international law. In fact, the authorities of Islamic Republic of Iran, has made the supremacy of Islamic law clear either by their statements or by their practices. Thus the Islamic law is supreme over everybody and the state cannot change the law to suit the ever-changing socio-economic-criminals. Society is to adapt itself to the requirements of Islamic Law.

The substantive Penal Law of Iran was codified in the year 1912, which was repealed by the 1926 Criminal Code.

However, this Iranian Criminal Code was again repealed in 1979, and replaced by the Islamic Penal System.

At present we have the following penal stature dealing with criminal cases:

1. The Law of Retribution 1982 (Haddud and Qasas).[I]

2. The Law of Punishment 1983 (Ta'zir),[II] both the laws are based on traditional Islamic Law. In cases where Ta'zir[III] is to be awarded, limits for those crimes which Islam leaves to discretion of the Islamic judge, has also been laid down."

The Criminal Procedure Code was first approved and implemented in 1911, and amended in 1932, was repealed in 1979.

Since then procedure based on Islamic Law has been implemented. Procedure relating to investigation, and punishment are enacted in accordance to Islamic Law.

Supreme Judicial Council

According to principle 157 of the consultation Iran's Supreme Judicia Council is the highest rank judicial organisation. This council, understandably perhaps, is dominated by the clergy. Supreme judicial council has been empowered by the constitution to appoint all the judges of the Ministry of Justice. These judge must be learned in Islamic Law to the degree of Ijtihad as a faquith. Although the law

---

I. Official Gazette, No. 44814, dated 22 June 1361 A.H. (Solar) 13 September 1982 A.D.

II. Official Gazette, No. 57112, dated 14 August 1362 A.H. (Solar) 5 November 1983 A.D.

III. S.H. Amin, Punishmjent in Islam, pp. 218-257.

states that a faqih does have to be "clothed" as a clergymen, none of professional lawyers educated in the law faculties will qualify for several years 'fiqh' and 'usul' (Islamic jurisprudence) in traditional theological schools, usually in Qum or Najaf. The qualifications and suitability of the nominees will be examined by the Imam, the official Iranian title for Ayatollah Khomeini who, according to section 3 (4), confirms their Ijtihad and righteousness.'

The judicial council has exercised "legislative declaratory powers. Number of acts, such as extortion in the sale of necessaries, non-adherence to government recommendations, obstructing public roads, spreading rumours, etc., were declared criminal offences punishable by up to 12 months imprisonment.

The Council ordered the Revolutionary Prosecution Departments as well as the Islamic Revolutionary Courts to enforce its "Legislations".

The Supreme Judicial Council also drafted some 199 articles of the law of Retribution. These Articles were later approved by the Parliament.

Court Structure

Courts and tribunals can be divided into two classes: (a) Regular judiciary, and (b) specialised courts.

Since Islamic Revolution, 1979, five regular courts are operative in Iran:

1. Revolutionary Court;
2. Public Courts -
   - (a) Civil Courts,
   - (b) First Class Criminal Courts, and

(c) Second Class Criminal Courts.

3 Courts of Peace:

(a) Ordinary Courts of Peace, and

(b) Independent Court of Peace (The later have wider jurisdiction).

4. Special Civil Courts, and

5. Court of Cassation.

Revolutionary Courts

Revolutionary Courts, after the revolution, were set up to del with persons responsible for opposing the revolution. Later on these courts heard all criminal cases under Islamic Law.

These courts in the beginning functioned without official authority. However, later on by passing the Administration of Justice Act, 1981, authorising to administer criminal justice according to the Shi'ite School of Islamic Law. Only those persons who were learned and qualified in Islamic Law could be appointed as judges in these courts.

Public Courts

These First Instance Courts were divided under the following categories:

1. Dadgha-i-Bakhsh (District Court),

2. Dadgha-i-Shahristan (Court of Township).

The first category has limited jurisdiction while the second court is the proper court of First Instance for all intents and purposes. These courts were to be presided by single judge each.

The Court of Township, if exercising criminal powers were known as: Dadgahe jonhe. In civil cases these court were knowns as Dadgha Sharistan.

All judgements of Court of First Instance were subject to appeal in 'Dadgah-i-Ostan' (The Provincial Court of Appeal), and second in Divan-i-Tameez (The Court of Cassation).

The Court of Appeal heard the proof again could receive fresh evidence as to the merits of the litigations. Whereas the appeal to the court of cassation was simply designed to ensure the propriety of conduct by the trial courts.

After the Revolution, both Dadgha-i-Shahristans (Court of First Instance), and Dadgha-i-Ostans (Court of Appeal) were dissolved and replaced by the newly-formed Dadgha-i-Umumi (Public Court), as opposed to the special civil courts and the Revolutionary Courts.

The Public Courts became the proper courts of First Instance but the system of appeal was abolished. These courts have both the jurisdictions - civil and criminal. All judgements of public courts are final and no appeal is permitted against them except in cases when imprisonment has been awarded by the Public Court. A conviction of more than two months imprisonment can be appealed to the Court of Cassation.

Public Courts are composed three judges and judgements are pronounced by majority opinion.

Courts of Peace

These courts are manned by secular judges and are the lowest judicial courts. As a court of First Instance, it has limited civil and criminal jurisdictions.

Special Civil Courts

These courts are known in Farsi as Dadghahe Madani-e-Khas. Scope of jurisdiction covers cases relating to Trust, succession and family law. All civil matters are vested in these types of courts.

Court of Cassation

These court after the Revolution was re-structured but still it is the most supreme judicial forum within the Iranian jurisdiction. It has a controlling power over the legal value of the proved facts.

Principle 161 of the Constitution 1979 state:

> "The Supreme Court of the country is formed on the basis of laws that are determined by the supreme judicial council. It is responsible for supervising the correct enforcement of laws in the courts of the land, for creating unity in judicial policy, and for carrying gout, according to law, the responsibilities that have been given to it".

Of particular interest is Principle 162 of the Constitution which states:

"The head of the court of Cassation and the Attorney-General must be just, religious jurists (mujtahid) and must have knowledge of judicial matters. The leadership, in consultation with the court of Cassation judges, will appoint them to those offices for a period of five years".

Special Courts

There are number of special courts with specialised jurisdiction, such as:

Military Court, The State Council, Civil Servants' Penal Court, The Judges Disciplinary Tribunal, Family Courts, Children's Hearning, Imam's Committee/ Court, People's Tribunal, Houses of Equity, and Councils of Arbitration.

These courts have their limited spheres within which they deal the cases.

Shariah Courts in Malaysia

Article 3, of the Federal Constitution of Malay declares that Islam is the religius of the Federation.

In every state other than states not having a Ruler the position of the Ruler as the head of the religion of Islam in his state in the manner and to the extent acknowledge and declared by the Constitution of that state, and, subject to that Constitution, all rights, privileges, prerogative and powers enjoyed by him as head of that religion, are uneffected and uimpaired, but in any acts, observances or ceremonies with respect to which the Confession of Rulers has agreed that they should extend to the Federation as a whole each of the other Ruler shall in his capacity of Head of the religion of Islam authorise the Yang DiPertuan Agong to represent him (Art. 3(2)).

The Constitution of the States of Malacca, Penang, Sabah and Sarawak shall each make provision for conferring on the Yang DiPertuan Agong the position of Head of the religion of Islam in that State (Art. (3(4)).

Clause 4 of Article 3 of the Federal Constitution makes it clear that nothing is this Article derogates from any other provision of this constitution.

With this brief introduction, let us examine the Shariah Court Structure in Malaysia. Article 121, recognises the Shariah Courts and lays down that the courts referred to in cluae (1) shall have no jurisdiction and powers in respect of any matter within the jurisdiction of the Shariah Courts. Clause (1A) Art. 121).

Before, the advent of Britishers in Malay, Shariah Court were existed. Against the judgement of Shariah Court, an appeal could also be made to the Sultan. During British rule Shariah Courts were relegated to the subordinate position. Its jurisdictions were also restricted to family matters and minor criminal Islamic offences.

After achieving independence, the constitution, organisation and procedure of Shariah Courts were matters included in the state list. Now states in Federation of Malay have established Shariah Courts with jurisdiction only over person professing the religion of Islam and in respect only matters included in List II - State List, paragraph (1), but shall not have jurisdiction in respect of offences except in so far as conferred by Federal Law.

According to List II, - State List, paragraph (1), Shariah Court jurisdiction extends to such matters as:

> "Islamic Law and personal and family law of persons professing the religion of Islam, including the Islamic Law relating to succession, testate and intestate, bethrohal, guardianship, gifts, partitions and non-charitable trust, wakfs and the definition and regulation of charitable and religious trust, the appointment of trustees and the incorporation of person in respect Islamic religious and charitable endowments, institutions, trusts, charities and charitable institutions

operating wholly within the state; and punishment of offences by persons professing the religion of Islam against precepts of that religion, except in regard to matters included in the Federal List."

As regard to offences, Shariah Court, as referred earlier, has jurisdiction only to the extent as given by the Federal law, that is, 'Muslim Courts (Criminal Jurisdiction) Act, 1965". This Act authorises the Shariah Court to deal with criminal cases where punishment of imprisonment does not exceed six months or with any fine not exceeding $1000/- or both.

The working of Shariah Courts in Malaysia States has been very learnedly analysed[I] by Shaikh Tan Sri Dato' Prof. Ahmad Mohamed Ibrahim, Dean, Kulliyyah of Laws. International Islamic University, Malaysia. Toi him Shariah Courts were kept in a truly subordinate position. He observed that:

"The subordinate position of the Shariah Courts was emphasised by the provision in some of the State Administration of Muslim Law Enactments that "Save as expressly provided in the Enactment nothing contained therein shall derogate from or affect the rights and powers of the Civil Courts".[II] The Enactments emphasise this by providing "nothing in this Enactment contained shall affect the jurisdiction of any Civil Courts and in the event of any difference between the decision of a court of a Kathi and the decision of a Civil Court acting within its jurisdiction, the decision of the Civil Servant shall prevail".[III]

I. Shaikh Tan Sri Dato' Prof. Ahmad Ibrahim, "The Shariah Court and its Place in the Judicial System," 'Shariah Law Journal,' ISSN 0/27-9033 - December 1989 - Vol. 5 - Page 30.

II. Selangor Administration of Muslim Law Enactment, 1952 - S. 4 (1).

III. Ibid. S. 45 (6).

Above referred observation and reference to the relevant statutes makes it clear that the Shariah Court were kept in subordinate position. Farthing the working conditions of Shariah Court the learned Professor remarked:

> "Many of the courts had no proper houses, many did not have adequate staff. The Kathis, some of whom were University graduates were not give any professional judicial officers in Shariah Courts. The rules of procedure and evidence applicable in Shariah Courts wee unclear. The state Enactments provided for the application of the civil laws of criminal and civil procedure and of evidence but these were not familiar to the Kathis and some of their provisions conflicted with those of Shariah. The result was that the laws were often ignored. There was no provision for appeals from the Shariah Courts to the Supreme Court. Appeals were still heard by Appeal Committees. Decisions of the Kathis' court and Appeal Committees were not reported and there were therefore no precedets to guide and instruct the Kathis."

These unsatisfactory working condition were realised by the government as well by people with the result a committee was set up to improve the existing conditions. Late Syed Nasir Ismail was appointed as Chairman of that committee. The Committee was assigned the task to study the working conditions, powers and status of Shariah Court in the judicial structure of the Court. It was also to study the position and status of the judges of the Shariah Courts.

The Committed in its report made the following recommendations for improving the position of Shariah Courts in Malaysian Judicial set up:[1]

1. The organisation of the Shariah Courts should be separated form that of the Majlis Ulama Islam in the States;

2. That the status and jurisdiction of the Shariah Courts should be improved and increased; and

3. The status and position of the judges of the Shariah Courts should also be increased and a judicial and legal service set up for the judges and officials of the Shariah Court and the prosecutors before the court.

Recommendations of the committed have been given practical shape in some sates while some states are under the process of implementing them. Kelantan Administration of Shariah Court Enactment, 1982, amended in 1985, is one such example which has followed the recommendation of the committee and implemented them in Kelantan State. The Enactment empowers the Sultan to constitute:

1. Shariah Appeal Court;

2. Court of Qadhi Besar;

3. Court of Qadhi Khas; and

4. Courts of Qadhi Jajahan.

The court of Qadhi Besar is presided by the Qadhi Besar. Its jurisdiction includes Matrimonial matters and matters effecting the personal status as well as criminal matters. It

---

I. 'Lapuran Menganai Kedudukan Mahkamah - Mahkamah Shariah dan Taraf Kadi Seluruh Malaysia, 1981.' (Translation and English noted from learned Dean's article referred (in earlier pages).

can try any offence committed by a Muslim and nunishable under the Enactment or any other written law relating to Muslim offences. Court of Qadhi Besar normally try cases which cannot be tried in the courts of Qadhi Khas or a Qadhi Jajahan.

Jurisdiction of Court of Qadhi Khas confines only up to imprisonment not exceeding one year or fine not exceeding $200/-, or both.

The court of Qadhi Jajahan can try offences which are punishable with fine not exceeding $1000/- or imprisonment not more than six months or both.

Both the courts of Qadhi Khas and Qadhi Jajahan have civil jurisdiction also. Qadhi Khas many cases up to the value of $50,000/-, while on the other hand Qadhi Jajahan, only up to the value of $20,000/-, not exceeding the limits respectively.

Appeal against the judgement is made to the Shariah Appeal Board which consists of three members, one of them shall be a Mufti and the remaining two persons are to be chosen from a panel persons appointed by the Sultan.

In the State of Terengganu, a comprehensive law dealing with Shariah Courts, its constitution, powers and jurisdiction was enacted in then year 1986, known as 'Administration of Islamic Religious Affairs Enactment of 1986.[1] Shariah Court under section 2 of the said Enactment has been defined as:

> "Shariah Court means the Syariah Appeal Court, the Shaiah High Court, or Shariah subordinate Court, as the case may be."

---

1. State of Terengganu Enactment No. 12 of 1986.

Thus three types Shariah Courts have been established under the Enactment with different defined jurisdictions and spheres of actions.

Constitution of Shariah Courts

Under section 29, of AIR A Enactments, 1986, His Royal Highness the Sultan may, by notification in Gazette, Constitute:

1. A Shariah Appeal Court, and
2. A Shariah High Courts for the State.

These Shariah Courts shall have their sittings and hear cases at Kuala Terengganu, the capital of the State. His Royal Highness the Sultan may also constitute Shariah Subordinate Courts at such places as he thinks fit and may prescribe the local limit of jurisdiction of such court.

The Shariah High Court shall have jurisdiction throughout the state and shall be presided over the Chief Qadhi or the Deputy Chief Qadhi (S. 31 (1)).

His Royal Highness the Sultan of the State may appoint suitable person as Chief Qadhi and Deputy Chief Qadhi as Chairman of the High Court, and Qadhis to preside over subordinate courts for such cases as may be prescribed (S. 28 (b) (c).

Extent of Jurisdiction of Shariah High Court

The Shariah High Court would have both criminal and civil jurisdictions. In criminal case its jurisdiction extends to try any offence committed by a Muslim and punishable under this Enactment and the Administration of Islamic Family Law Enactment 1985, and may impose any punishment provided for the offence (S. 32 (1)).

In its civil jurisdiction, hear and determine all suits and proceedings in which all the parties profess the Religion of Islam (S. 32 (1)).

Appeals against the judgements of Qadhis sitting in subordinate court are made to Shariah High Court. In its appellate jurisdictione, it hears, and determines all appears (S. 32 (c)).

Under section 33, procedure for appeal has been laid down. Accordingly an appeal from any decision of a Shariah subordinate court may be preferred to the Shariah High Court-

(a) in its criminal jurisdiction, by an accused person or prosecutor who is dissatisfied with the decision.

(b) in its civil jurisdiction, by any person dissatisfied with the decision. Monetary limits have been laid down for appealing purposes.

(c) no appeal shall lie of the decision is made with consent.

(d) in all matters, if Shariah Court gives leave to appeal.

Section 36 further laws down the detailed procedure for criminal appeals. Any person who is dissatisfied with any judgement, sentence, or order pronounced by a Shariah Subordinate Court in any criminal proceedings to which he is party may appeal, to the Shariah High Court on the following grounds:

1. In respect of any error in law, or
2. error relating to facts, or
3. on ground of alleged severity, or
4. on ground of alleged inadequacy of any sentence.

The appeal would be made by fitting or loding a notice of appeal with the court appealed from, addressed to this Shariah High Court, and by paying the prescribed 'Appeal Fee.'

The notice of appeal shall be filed or lodged within fourteen days from the date on which the judgement, sentence, or order was passed or made, unless on application to the Shariah High Court the period of fourteen days in extended.

At the hearing of an appeal the Shariah High Court has been empowered, if it considers that there are no sufficient grounds for interfering with the decision, sentence, or order of the court appealed against, dismiss the appeal, reverse or change the decision of the subordinate Shariah Court.

On termination of the hearing of the appeal, the Shariah High Court shall, either at once or on some future date, which shall either be fixed for the purpose or of which notice shall be given to the parties, deliver the judgement in open court.

As to power of revision, section 58 authorises the Shariah High Court to examine the records of any proceedings in a criminal matter before a Shariah subordinate court for the purpose of satisfying itself that the decision in the proceedings is correct and valid, and that the proceedings were carried out in accordance with the rules of the court.

The Enactment further authorises under section 59 the Shariah High Court in examining the records of Shariah subordinance courts to issue directions for making further inquiries into the matter decided by the Shariah subordinate court.

Shariah Appeal Court

Shariah Appeal Court shall be constituted by His Royal Highness the Sultan. Place of sitting of the court would be at Kuala Terengganu.

His Royal Highness the Sultan may, by notification in the Gazette, any suitable person to be the Sultan shall grant a Tauliah to the chairman and may impose in the Tauliah any condition particularly as regards the limits on the exercise of any power to be conferred.

Shariah Appeal Court shall consist of the three members:

1. Chairman;

2. A person selected from Fatwa Committee, and

3. One other person selected from a penal of ten persons who profess the Religion of Islam according to Mazhab Shafi'i and who are appointed every there years.

Appeal to Shariah Appeal Court

Under section 35, an appeal may be preferred to the Shairah Appeal Court from any decision of the Shariah High Court by any person aggrieved. Appeal would be either the decision given by Shariah High Court sitting as an appellate or against the decision made under its original jurisdiction.

An appeal shall be decided in accordance with the majority opinion of the members of Shariah Court.

Procedure as to criminal appeal and extent of jurisdiction of Shariah Appeal Court, powers relating to revision and issuing directions for revision under its Revision Jurisdiction are same as that of Shariah High Court.

Shariah Subordinate Court

Shariah Subordinate Court is lowest in hierarchy of Shariah Courts. Subject to the provisions of the Enactment, it shall have jurisdiction in respect of civil and prescribed under both. Its local limit of jurisdiction are prescribed under section 29 (2), if no local limits are so prescribed, then it can have jurisdiction within the State, and shall be presided over by the Qadhi appointed by His Royal Highness, the Sultan.

In its criminal jurisdiction, the Shariah Subordinate Courts try any offence committed by a Muslim and punishable under this Enactment, except offences under section 194, 197, 205, 211 and 215 of the Penal Code of Malay, and any offence under the Administration of Islamic Family law Enactment 1985, except offences under sections 35, 36, 125 and 127, and may impose any punishment provided for the offence.

An appeal from any decision of a Shariah Subordinate Court may be preferred to the Shariah High Court, in its criminal jurisdiction, by an accuse person or prosecutor who is dissatisfied with the decision.

Shariah Courts in the State of Kedah

Similar steps as noted earlier are being take in other States of Federation of Malaysia. In the State of Kedah under the Mahkamah Shariah Enactment, 1983, Shariah Court have been established. The Enactment provided for the establishment of a court of appeal and courts of Qadhi for the administration of Islamic Law. His Royal Highness the Sultan appoints the Qadhi, who presides over the Court of Qadhi.

Court of Qadhi in its criminal jurisdiction try any offence committed by the Muslim in violation of State enacted Islamic Law. Qadhi may impose any punishment provided by the Enactment.

The court of appeal constituted of a Qadhi Besar, three Deputy Qadhi Besar and three other persons appointed by

His Royal Highness the Sultan who in the opinion of the Sultan are qualified to sit in the Court of Appeal.

Normally, the Court of Appeal consists of three persons Qadhi Besar, a Deputy Qadhi Besar and one other person from those appointed by the Sultan.

An appeal against the decision of the Court of Qadhi is made to the Court of Appeal. The Court of Appeal hears the appeal and also exercises general supervision. It also exercises the revisionary powers vested in it by the Enactment over all courts of Qadhis.

Efforts are being made in the Federal Territory of Malay to establish the following courts also:

1. Shariah Subordinate Courts.
2. Shariah High Court; and
3. Shariah Appeal Court.

All these efforts show that the State Government are improving the Shariah Courts status in Malaysia. Attempt are being made to raise these courts from its relegated position and have recognition to its officers as well. All round efforts are under development to make the Shariah Judicial Institutions effective.

Shariah Courts in India: Brief Historical Perspective

Necessity of Administration of Justice arose since the dawn of civilization when societies were gradually formed, social and personal disputes were required to be settled, and antagonistic claims adjusted. To the Muslim jurists, the protection of the week and punishment of the wrong-doer are fundamental in the administration of justice.

The basic teaching of Holy Qur'ãn is: "When you decide between people, give your decision with justice". Administration of justice according to Qur'ãnic injunctions are not confined to Muslims only. Its purview extend to the whole mankind. With reference to the cases and concern, of the jews, Holy Prophet (peace be upon him), explained the above noted verse as: And when you give your decision, decide between them (i.e., the jews) with justice: surely God loves those who do justice."

In Holy Qur'ãn Allah Ta'ala has laid great stress on justice. "We have not created the heavens and the earth, and whatever is (contained) between them otherwise than in justice" (15:55). Allah Ta'ala further commands: And He appointed the Balance that he should not transgressed in respect to the balance; wherefore observe a just weight and diminish not the balance (i.e., measure of justice) that men may conduct themselves with equity." (57:25).

In the Holy Qur'ãn, one of the Divine attributes of God, called 'asma-i-husna, is "just". Hence, justice is regarded as integral part of Divine nature of God, and the administration of justice as a divine dispensation. Muslim Rulers in India most obediently adhered to this Divine Dispensation. Judicial set up established in India was aimed to fulfil this Divine dispensation of justice to the mankind irrespective of caste, creed, colour or religion.

When Muslim came to India, a galaxy of scholars, polished writers, cautious chroniclers, laborious historians, venerable theologions and casuistic jurists came along with them. Ulema and Fiqh (jurists) well learned with the functionary of courts were appointed to administer justice in accordance to Qur'ãnic injunction and Sunnah of Prophet (peace be upon him). Under their advise Muslim sovereigns of India took for model the judicial machinery of 'Abbasid Caliphs of Iraq, the Umayyad Caliphs of Spain, and the Fatimide Caliphs of Egypt.[I]

This fact has created confusion in the minds of some thinkers. 'It is ordinarily believered by the common run people that the Muslim sovereigns governed Indian with laws of shara (canon laws of Islam). "Imported ready made from outside India."[II] This is not wholly true. This mistaken notion has arisen and got currency from the off-hand remarks and careless writing of a certain class of historians, who with a little knowledge of Persian and less of Arabic, pose themselves as the exponents of the laws of shara. They do not take notice of the fact that Muhammadan law consists of two parts, religious and secular; and that each portion has its special application. This may be due to ignorance or lack of proper appreciation. But a shrewed suspicion lurks in their writings that their apparent object is to hold up the Muslim rule to ridicule and create racial hatred.'[III]

It should be borne in mind that Islamic Law, religious in nature, applies to Muslims only. The complete Code of Islamic Law does not apply to non-Muslims. Muslim jurists classify the Islamic Law under two distinct heads:

1. Tashri'yi, religious; and
2. Ghair - tashri'yi, secular.

The second class is secular in nature in substance common to all nations, applies to Muslim and non-Muslims

---

I. Wahed Husain, 'Administration of Justice During the Muslim Rule in India, page 10.

II. Sạrkar: "Mughal Administration," pp. 2-4.

III. Supra - N.I.P.

equally. Non-Muslims (Dhimni'i) under Islamic State are not subject to the first category of law which is entirely religion in nature. Non-Muslims are to be governed "according to precepts of their own faith."[I] Prophet (peace be upon him) himself enjoined - "leave alone the non-Muslims and whatever they believe in."

Thus the policy of applying Islamic law during the Muslim rule was: that 'The Hindus, The Budhists and other non-Muslim subjects were governed by their own respective religions and personal law. When the tribunal happened to be the court of Qazi, or the Court of the Sovereign the suits involving the points of personal law of the Hindus, were used to be decided with the aid of the learned Pandits and Brahamanas; in the case of other races, with the aid of their learned men'.[II] It shows that non-Muslims were not governed by the Islamic Law which was purely religion in nature. Non-Muslims under Islamic rule were having full liberty to be governed in accordance to their own faith and religious laws.

Islamic criminal law dealing with religious infringements, was applied to the Muslims only, 'such' as drinking, marrying with the prohibited degree, apostasy, etc. Fur such offences non-Muslims were not held liable to punishment under the laws of shara'.[III]

Only that portion of Islamic criminal law which punishes the acts as crimes in the estimation of all nations, was applied to Muslims and non-Muslims alike.

I. Baillie: "Digest of Muhammadan Law," p. 174.

II. Ibid, p. 174.

Fatawa-i-Alamgiri, Vol. II, p. 357.

III. A. Rahim: "Muhammad Jurisprudence." p. 59. "Sharh-i-Vagaya, Vol. II, Chapter on Qada (Judicial Administration).

'The Qanun-i-Shahi or the Edicts and Ordinance, contained in the farmans and Dastur'ul-Amal for guidance of the officers of the state, were the common law of the people of the country as opposed to the canon law. These Qanun, were binding upon the judicial and excecutive officers, and in compliance therewith the courts of common law were established in India.'[I]

The study of Judicial Institutions under Muslim Rule may be divided under four periods:[II]

1. The period of conquest and military occupation (712-991 A.D.);
2. The period of successive invasions without any attempt to establish a government in India, - From the death of Sabuktagin till the invasion by Muhammad Ghori (999-1206 A.D.);
3. The period of settled government with judicial tribunals - From the time of Slave Dynasty till the death of Sher Shah (1206-1555 A.D.) and
4. The period of well-established government with an extensive judicial and administrative machinery - From the Mughal Rule till the grant of the Diwani (15556-1765 A.D.);

Tracing all periods' judicial institutions is not possible. Only we confine here to some abstracts relevant to our study.

The study may be divided into parts:

I. Supra, p.

II. Division of periods, Table next following borrowed from Waheed Husain's book, Administration of Justice during the Muslim Rule in India, p.

1. Pre-Mughal Period (1206-1555 A.D.);

2. From the Mughal Rule till the gant of Diwani (1556-1765 A.D.).

The first period begins where the Slave Dynasty was settled and established an organized government in India and thereafter history passed through where different Dynasties established their governments one after the other, e.g., Khilji Dynasty, Tughlaq Dynasty, the Lodhi Dynasty, and Sur Dynasty. During this period the judicial institutions were set up to the complete satisfaction of the people and on regular basis. Judicial officers of different ranks and grades were appointed. Judicial courts started functioning in built up court-houses (Mahkume-i-Adalat), observe rules of procedure as found in Law of Shariah, regular hearing of cases and passed and enforced the judgement.

In Kutbuddin Aybak's time the Cheif-Judge (Qazi-ul-Quzat) was first time appointed. He was responsible for supervision of Subordinate Courts of Qadis. Court of Rivision were also established. Kutbuddin Aybak, in fact, was famous for his love to justice. Hasan Nizami in Taz-ul-Masri, remarked:[I]

"He distinguished the flame of discord by the splendour of the light of justice".

Muslim sovereigns themselves were holding courts, hearing and deciding cases personally in this period. 'Al-badayuni points out that Sultan Muhammad Tughlaq constituted himself "The Supreme Court of Appeal", and used to revise the decisions of Qazis and to upset their judgement for the ends of justice.'[II]

I. H.M. Elliot: "History of India," Vol. I, p. 208.

II. Muntakhab-i-Tawarikh, p. 311 (Translated by G.S. Ranking).

The Sultan used to keep four Muftis to whom he allotted quarters in the percents of his own palace.........so that when anyone was arrested upon any charge, he might in the first place argue with the Muftis about his due punishment. He used to say, 'be careful that you do not fail in the slightest degree by defect in speaking that which you consider right, because if anyone should be put to death wrongfully the blood of that man will be upon your head.' Then if after long discussion they convicted (the prisoner) even though it were midnight he would pass order for his execution".[I] This show the love for justice. Even the Sultan was taking pain sitting up to midnight, deciding the cases and ordering for execution of the punishment so awarded after long discussions.

Muslim Sultans of India, although they were sovereign, but found themselves, accountable before courts for their misdeed if any. Sovereign were not above judiciary but subject to judiciary. This fact also shows how much regard was paid to the judicial institutions of the country.

Ibn Batuta made his observations about Sultan Muhammad Tughlaq in the following words:

> "Of all men this King is the most humble and of all men he most love justice...... The Sultan submitted to the decrees of the court passed against himself."[II]

Sultan Razia, the queen transacted court proceedings like King in open courts. 'She used to hold court and dispense justice in person with the assistance of Qazi and Muftis in Public audience Hall.

Ghia'suddin Balban, another King was also famous for dispensing justice to his subjects. He was famous as an

I. "Al-Badayni" - p. 37.

II. Supra - N.P.

impartial judge, who decided cases without showing any partiality towards any of his subject eve if they were closely related to him. He also introduced the system of espionage with a view to make the administration of justice effective and efficient. The persons deputed for espionage purpose were to report about the functioning of court directly to the King. This espionage continued even during the Mughal rule.

Sikander Lodhi another Monarch introduction number of reforms in different government institution including the judiciary the designatio of Qazi-ul-Qazat (Chief Judge) was changed to 'Mir-i-Adl,' and the court of chief-judge was replaced by 'Drul-Adl'.

Sher Shah Suri is famous for introducing judicial reforms during his reign. He divided provinces into Sarkars, which were sub-divided into pargannas. He created a new post of Shiqdars, executive officers, responsible for the administration of criminal justice. For administration civil suits, Munsifs were also appointed. The chief Shiqdar (Shqdar-i-Shiq daran) was responsible for the administration foe ach sarkar, and the Chief-Munsif for civil administration in each sarkar. He also acted as a circut judge. He also posted officers in pargannas and took care not to destroy the autonomy of the village community. A marked thing to be noted is that the civil judges of his period were not necessarily ulema or faqih, and thus introduced common law courts also. Thus in his reign, twosets of courts, canon law courts where Qadis and Muftis sitting and deciding the cases, and common law courts, where ordinary persons sitting as judges, not necessary learned in fiqh.

In brief the judicial set up prior to Mughals during Slave, Khilji, Tughlaq and Lodhi Dynasties could be summarised as follows:

Tribunals	Presiding Officers
1. The Royal Courts	The Sultan
2. The Chief Curt of Justice	The Mir-i-Adl.
3. The Court of Chief Qadi	The Chief Qazi-ul-Quzat
4. The Subordinate Court of Canon Law	The Qazi
5. The Subordinal Court of Common Law	The Adl or Qazi

During the reign of Sher Shah Suri

Tribunals	Presiding Officers
1. The Court of Sultan	The Sovereign
2. The Chief Civil Court	The Munsif-i-Munsifan (Chief Munsif)
3. The Chief Criminal Court	The Siqdar-i-Shiqdaran (Chief Shiqdar)
4. The Civil Court of Common Law	The Munsif.
5. The Criminal Court of Common Law	The Shiqdar.
6. The Court of Canon Law	The Qazi.

"Appeal"

Appeals law from the subordinate courts to the Chief Civil and Criminal Courts respectively and there from the Royal Court.[I]

The above Table shows that a regular and systematic judicial hierarchy of courts was established by the Muslim Rulers of above noted period. Sovereigns themselves took

---

I. Supra - N.P.

interest in dispensing justice. The administration of justice was fair and impartial. For non-Muslims, first time, common law courts were established where they were governed according to their religious faiths.

Mughal Period up to Grant of Diwani

The Mughal period is considered to be the golden age of India. It was a period of property, power and glory to India. Government with elaborate administrative machinery became the most powerful. Judicial and administrative institutions were further reformed. In fact, Mughal rulers were famus for love for justice.

Beginning with Emperor Akbar, he retained his pre-decissor's judicial structure, but added to the State-Machinery the officers Wakil, the Wazir, the Diwan-i-Kul, the Mir-i-Saman, the Bayutal, the Sadr-i-Jahan, the Bakshi, the Sadr, the Mustafy, the Amin, the 'Amil, the Tapukchi, the Mushrif, the Mir-i-Mahal, the Mir-i-Bahr, the Mir-i-bar and many other officials. Here we will explain only those offices connected with the judiciary.

Akbar's regard and love for justice has been bet explained by Mr. Vincent Smith, a historian, by referring A'yin-i-Akbari, where Akbar has been noted saying:

> "If I were guilty of an unjust act, I would rise in judgement against myself."

Mr. Vincent Smith, then, observed:

> "The saying was not merely copy-book maxim. He honestly tried to do justice according to his lights in the summary fashion of his age and country".[1]

---

1. Vincent Smith: "Akbar the Great Mughal," p. 34.

Another historian Peruchi following the authority of Monsewate observe:

> "As to the administration of justice, he is most zealous and watchful ....In inflicting punishment he is deliberate and after he has made over the guilty person to the hands of the judge and court of suffer either the extreme penalty or the mutilation of some limb, he requires that he should be three times reminded by messages before the sentence is carried out".[I]

Mr. Waheed Husain, further elaborates that 'the above quotation one need not run away with the idea that the Emperor used to inflict only two kinds of punishments, viz., of death and mutilation of some limbs. For we find in A'yin-i-Akbari the following instructions to the Subahdar (Provincial Governor):

"He should strive to reclaim the disobedience by good advice. If that files, let him punish with reprimands, threats, imprisonment, stripes or even amputation of limbs, but he shall not take away life till after the most mature deliberation .... Those who apply for justice let them not be inflicted with delay and expectation. Let him shut his eyes against offences and accept the excuse of the penitent ..... Let him object to no one on account of his religious or sect."[II]

Emperor Akbar used to send similar letters of advice to different governors of provinces. He frequently instructed that the capital punishment should be sparingly used. Only in cases of dangerous sedition it could be inflicted but, it was subject that the court record be sent to the Emperor directly. Unless

---

I. Supra - N, p.

II. A'yun-i-Akbari, Vol. II, p. 254.

he approved death penalty was not applied. Similarly in Amputation cases, the penalty was sparingly allowed.

During Akbar's period the Mode of Trial of Criminal cases was that the judicial officers such as Chief Qazi, the Qazi, and the Mir-Adl, used to try cases according to Islamic Law if the offence committed by the Muslims. These officers followed the procedure laid down in the book of Fiqhah. As to non-Muslim, they were tried in accordance to the common law.

The Subahdar and Foujdar being lay-judges were assisted by Qazis and Muftis. They were also to follow the guidance laid down in Shahi Farmans.

Akbar himself used to decide cases and also hear appeals at his Chamber of Audience at his palace (Daulat-Khanah). In the Emperor's court, nobles, the law officers of the crown, the Darogha-i-Adalat (superintendent of the court), the clerks and scribes also used to attend. Decisions, after giving due hearing, were pronounced in consultation with law-officers and his wazirs. Once judgement pronounced it was communicated to the proper authority under the seal of the court for its' execution. The scribe used to take down notes, and the Mir-Munshi to draw up proper order under the direction of the Mir-i-Adl. In cases where the judgement was to be despatched to the Subehdar or the Provincial Governor for implementation and enforcement, a fair-copy used to be sent and also was to be properly stampted under imperial seal.[1]

Akbar also adopted another method of trial by ordeals. It is said that this method was prevalent in India during the Hindu Period. Akbar enforced this method especially at the instance of learned Brahmans who assisted the Emperor in

---

1. Supra - N, p.

the trial of cases of the Hindu subjects. Smith says, that "Akbar encouraged the use of trial by ordeals in the Hindu Fashion."

Precisely during Emperor Akbar's period there were regular court of justice, at the centre, in Provinces, and districts. Hierarchy of courts is graded as follows:

In the Capital I

Tribunals	Presiding Officers
1. The Royal Courts	The Emperor
2. Diwan-i-Adalat or Court of Diwan	The High Diwan or The Chancellor
3. The Court of the Chief Judge	The Qazi-ul-Adl.
4. The Chief Court of Justice	The Mir-i-Adl.
5. The Court of Canon	The Qazi
6. The Court of Common	The A'dl

7. The office of the Mohtasib - who held no regular court but exercised the quasi-judicial power of the Police and the Municipal Officers.

In the Provinces

Tribunals	Presiding Officers
1. The Court of the Subahdar (Popularly known as Nizamat Adalat)	The Subahdar or Nazim
2. The Court of Foujdar	The Foujdar
3. The Court of the Chief Qazi (in some provinces only)	The Qazi-ul-Quzat
4. The Court of Diwan	The Provincial Diwan
5. The Court of Canon Law	The Qazi
6. The Court of Common Law	The 'Adl (civil judge)

I. Supra - N, Table II, p. 38.

The office of Muhtasib as stated above)

After Emperor Akbar, during the periods of Shah Jahan and Aurangzeb, certain changes in judiciary were made suiting to the requirements of the society. Both emperors were holding public courts in Diwan-i-Khas. The were taking personal interests in hearing and deciding the cases.

Emperor's court use to be full of law officers of the crown, the judges of the Canon Law (Qazis), Judges of Common Law ('Adils), Muftis, Ulema, jurists learned in precedents (fatwas) the Superintendent of the Law Court (Daroghe-i-Adalat), and the Kotwal or perfect of the city police. None else among the courtiers was admitted unless his presence was specially necessary. The officer of justice presented the plaintiffs one by one and reported the grievances. His Majesty used gently to ascertain the facts by enquiry, was to take the law from the ulema and, then, was to pronounce judgement accordingly. Many persons had come from far-off provinces to get justice from the highest power in the land. Their points could not be investigated locally, and so the Emperor wrote orders to the governors of those places, urgent them to find out the truth, and either to do them justice there or send parties back to the capital with their reports."[1]

During the period of Emperor Jahangir the most significant feature of the Royal Court were the Golden Chain and bells hung up by the Emperor for administering justice to the masses. This device was adopted with a view that the litigants and aggrieved persons could tie their petitions which had direct reach up to the Emperor without the assistance of intermediary officers. It was aimed that people should had easy and direct access up to the Emperor without undergoing

---

I. Prof. Sarkar: "Studies of Mughal India", pp. 14 and 70.

any harassment of the porters and court - under-lings. In fact Jahangir took keen interest in the administration of justice. Undoubtedly, this sense of justice deserve praise.

The rest of the courts and their hierarchy was as follows:

In the Capital

Tribunals	Presiding Officers
1. The Royal Court	The Emperor
2. Diwan-ul-Mazalim	
Adalat-i-Shari'ya - Court of Canon Law	
1. The Chief Court of Qazi	The Qazi-ul-Quzat
2. The Subordinate Court of Qazi	The Qazi
Court of Common Law	
1. The Court of High Diwan	The Diwan-i-Ala
2. The Court of Mir-i-Adl	Mir-i-Adl or The Chief Justice
3. The Court of Sadri-i-Jahan	The Chief Sadr (Judge)
4. The Subordinate Court of the 'Adl	The 'Adl (Civil Judge)
5. The Subordinate Court of the Sadr	The Sadr (Civil Judge)

Comparing the present table with the earlier table of Emperor Akbar's period, one significant modification in the court structure was that in this period Diwan-i-Mazalin, actual name 'Ad-Diwan-un-Nazr fil Mazalim' was estblished at the top of the hierarchy. This was a Board for the investigation of grievances. It was, in fact, established in the period of Aurangzeb and the King himself presided over. Its main functions were to set right cases of miscarriage of justice which might had occurred in the administration and judicial department. It also exercised control over the judiciary.

As to appeal and revision, courts were authorised to hear them in the following order:

In the Capital

1. The King's Court	Appeals from all courts.
2. Diwan-i-Mazalim	
3. The Court of High Diwan	Appeals from Subordinate Civil Courts
4. The Court of Cheif Qazi	Civil Appeal from the Court of the 'Adl
5. The Court of Chief Qazi	Civil and Criminal Appeals from the Court of Qazi
6. The Court of Sadr-i-Jahan	Appeal from the Court of the Sadr.

The Subordinate Court of Qazi could revise the decision of another Qazi if empowered to do so.

The courts having the power of hearing appeal and also revisional jurisdiction. Thus in Mughal period we find a regular and systematic procedure of appeal and revision was established.

In the Province or Subah

1. The Court of the Nazim	Appeals from Criminal Courts.
2. The Court of the Diwan	Appeals from the Subordinate Civil Courts.
3. The Court of the Chief Qazi	Appeal from the Subordinate Court of Qazi.

Death penalty could not be executed unless an approval of the King was obtained.

A second appeal was allowed from the Provincial appellate court to the High Diwan, or the Mir - Adl, or the 'Qazi-ul-Quzat,' in the capital according to the nature of appeal.

If the paties were not satisfied even with the decision in the second appeal, they could go up to the Royal Court which was the highest court of appeal in the land.[I]

Functioning of Court and Mode of Trial

Waheed Husain in his thesis on Administration of Justice during the Muslim Rule in India has described a working scene of Qazi's court and mode of trial therein which gives the correct picture of functioning of courts of the that period. This scene belongs to Aurangzeb's period, borrowed from Fatawa-i-Alamgiri and other contemporary records of history, the details are as follows:

'In a guardrangle stands the imposing building called 'Darul-Qaza', the court of justice. The 'Iwan-i-Adalat' contains a capacious hall where the Qazi holds trial. The side rooms are for the court officials and court records. On one sinde of the big hall is a raised platform (takht) covered with rich carpet (qalin). This is the seat for the Qazi. On his right and left are the seats for the Mufti and Alim. A carved ivory (and sometimes highly polished wooden) ink-stand and a desk of polished wood for writing, are placed before the Qazi. The floor of the hall is covered with carpets. On one side facing the Qazi's seat is the seat of the clerk of the court (katib-scribe). On another side is the seat of the court vakil (the government advocate). In front of the seat of the Qazi is a table covered with coloured cloth. On this table are heaped up records and files (muhazir and sijilat), plaints and petitions. In front of the Qazi and on the floor sit the parties in two distinct rows. The witnesses and partisans of the litigants sit at the end of the hall. The Darogha-i-Adalat (the Superintendent of the Court) who is the charge of the records

I. Supra - N, P.

brings the files required by the Qazi. The court peon, and orderlies control the crowd'.

This court scene shows that Qazis were having dignified and honourable status. The court's perafernelia reflects that Qazi's court was even superior to the present day District Judge's Court.

It is further stated that 'the plaintiff goes straight to the Katib (scribe), and either hands over the plaint, or states orally the facts of his case. The Katib writes out the plaint in the court register and notes down the name of the Qazi in whose court the case is to be tried. The names and addresses of the parties and of their fathers as well as the particulars of then cases are entered in the register. The court sits from the morning till noon.'

'The Imperial Regulation of Aurangzeb urges upon 'the judges to sit in their offices on Saturday, Sunday, Monday, Tuesday, and Thursday, i.e., five days, while on Wednesday they should attend the subahdar, and Friday alone should be a holiday. From two gharis (about an honour) after day break to a little after midday (i.e., when the sun has begun to decline) the judges should sit in the court room and do justice, and go to their homes at the time of the 'Zuhr prayer.'[1]

This fact also reflects the punctuality and regularity with which the judges attending the court work and disposing them off. Further everything was reduced to writing and registered, and kept in official court record.

When Qazi coming to attend the court, due regard was given by those present in the court and thereafter the Qazi was to attend the day's work. Model Trial is noted below:

I. Mirat-i-Ahmadi, p. 291; Vide Sarkar's 'Mughal Administration', p. 117.

'When the Qazi with his attendants enteres the hall, the audience stands up and bows in obsisance. He goes through the record to see if it is in order. If not, it is returned. The plaintiff or his vakil then states his case. If the defendant is present he will be called to state his defence. If the defendant admits the claim, the case is decided in accordance with law, and the decree is to be drawn up in conformity with the 'mahzur' record of proceedings) and 'sijil' (form of decree). If the defendant denies the plaintiff's claim, then two courses are open to the plaintiff, viz., either he may produce evidence to prove his claim, or he may put the defendant on oath. If he refuses to take oath, and if the plaintiff's witnesses are present, they are examined. The defendant then enters his plea by way of avoidance and is required to prove it by evidence. Both parties are entitled to an adjournment of the case for summoning their witnesses'.[I]

Above observation of court trial makes it clear that the decisions were based on Qazi's capabilities to administer justice inconformity with law. The decrees were also passed in accordance to set forms and principles. Further the decrees or order or judgements passed by the judges were also to be incorformity with the record of the case kept property in court registers and records. In brief Qazis were to proceed step by step in a most systematic way and in conformity with law. It is further stated:

'As the trial proceeds the Qazi is to take down the evidence of the party and his witnesses. He may ask the katib to note their names and addresses. If for any reason the Qazi is unable to take down the depositions, he may ask the katib to do so. But the law of procedure requires that the Qazi should himself take down the depositions. The witnesses are to be

I. Hidaya (Grady), P. 451.

II. Al-Qaza fil islam, P. 66.

examined separately so that one may not know the statements of the others.[II] Cross-examination is allowed. The court may also put questions to elicit facts and tests the veracity of the parties and their witnesses. Then after going through the evidence, if the Qazi finds that plaintiff has established his claim, he enters judgement in his favour. A decree follows, and is drawn up in accordance with the prescribed form.'

The whole proceedings form a record called 'mazhur' and the decree which forms the part of the record is called 'sijil'. It is necessary for the validity of the decree that sijil must conform to 'mahzur.'[I]

The above observation about the mode of trial and procedure followed in Shariah Courts, abundantly makes it clear that they were all at par with the modern procedural laws. Examining and cross-examining the witnesses by the parties separately with a view to determine their credibility and also by the judges to test the veracity are all in line with the natural justice principle. It means justice was administered with due care and caution; with an object before the judges that none of the parties should feel aggrieved. Justice should be given to the justman. Mughal Judicial system, no doubt, is compatable with any modern judicial system with its' present day legality. It was simple free from legal wrangles and technicalities.

Some Characteristic Features of Mughal Judicial System

First, the most systematic and scientific judicial set up was in existence during Mughal period. At the centre there were Appellate Courts. Kings themselves were sitting in courts and dispensing justice to the litigants. At the Provincial level

I. Fatawa-i-Alamgiri, Vol. VI, p. 247.

also there were courts having original and Appellate jurisdictions.

Secondly, aggrieved litigants were had rights to go in appeal twice, first to the provincial courts and second to the central appellate court. Above all even if the party field aggrieved, they were given an opportunity to have direct access to the Emperor and seek redress. Emperors were personally attending the petitions in Royal Court and deciding the petition (jurists Faqih). All grievances were reddressed in accordance with Shariah or Islamic Law, i.e., Qur'ãnic injunctions and Sunnah of Prophet. In their absence, Qyas or Ijmas was resorted to. Thus every litigant had right to appeal Courts were competent to hear appeal, Revision or Reference. Qazi could revise his judgement if any error found in the judgement.

Another note wrong feature is that justice was administered, at the beginning of Islam, in the name of God, or of Caliphate representing the entire Muslim community, but not in the name of Caliph, or Sultan, or Emperor. The author of Musihaj-ul-Talibin points out that "the entire Muslim community is responsible for the administration of justice. After the end of Republic form of Islamic Commonwealth of Caliphs, Kings later started administering justice in their names. The Mughal Emperors loved to pose as the fountain of justice followed the tradition to administer justice in their names."

A noticeable feature was that cases were decided in open courts in public place. During Prophet (peace be upon him) time cases were decided in the Mosque because mosque was a public place where public place where public could had easy access. Then Dar-ul-Qaza was established in separate building, Qazis started hearing cases there. This court was established during Hazrat Umar's (Razi-Allah-Anho) time. Darul Qaza was regarded as public place and was open to all. This practice was followed in India. Shariah Courts were all open courts where public had free access.

Another significant feature of the judiciary was that the Hindus, the Budhists and other non-Muslims subjects were governed by their own respective religious and personal laws. Suits involving personal laws of the Hindus, were used to decide with the aid of the learned pandits and Brahmanas. Similarly, in the case of other non-Muslims, their cases were decided with the aid of their learned men. Islamic law was applied to Muslims only. Islamic criminal law was invoked to Muslims and non-Muslims alike only in cases where the acts which constituted crimes were considered crimes in the estimation of all nations.

If there was religious infringment then, then the Islamic criminal law was applied to Muslims only. In such cases non-Muslims were not governed by Islamic criminal law.

In fact, we find that Muslims and non-Muslims were dealt with the in two different sets of courts - Canon Law Courts and Common Law Courts. First were Shariah Courts while the later were secular courts. Muslim sovereigns were had all regards for the customs and usages of the Hindus although many of them were militant against the Muslim Law. Sovereigns never interfered in personal and religious liberty. No law which could be said external was ever applied to them. The institutions which the Caliphs and other Muslim sovereigns adopted were considered the best and worthy of imitation. For this reason, perhaps, some of the Hindu Rajas also adopted the Muslim judicial and administrative system in their Kingdoms in India.

Wide and elaborate judicial machinery at the centre, province and sub-divisional level were established for administering justice to the subject. But there was paucity of cases. There was no passion for litigation. People lived a simple life, a self-contended life under a strong central government. Ordinary disputes and caste matters were decided by village panch (headman). Muslim sovereign never interfered with the village autonomy. Instead the sovereign encouraged it.

Check upon frivolous litigation is another important characteristic. Appellants were severely fined when their appeals against judgements of the lower courts were if found frivolous and ill-founded.

In cases if the judgement were found unjust, judges were removed from their posts. Aurangzeb when took the charge of the Kingdom, he removed such judges whose judgements were unjust.

As to punishment of death and amputation of limbs we find that the first was totally unknown during Aurangzeb time and the later one was moved with a slow speed. First the culprit was awarded Tazir, kept in prison till he repented. First offenders were not awarded Tazir, kept in prison till he repented. First offenders were not awarded with the punishment of amputation. Even on proof lit was postponed and the culprit was given an opportunity to reform himself. But even if this did not reform him then he was given a prolonged imprisonment. Amputation was the last resort.

The most outstanding feature was that all men, irrespective of caste, creed, colour or religion were treated justly and on equal footing. It was kept in mind by the judges that the poor or weak should not had disappointed from justice and well-to-do might not had hope to get any advantage from.

The burden of proof was upon the party who made allegations. The defendant or respondent was not to be compelled to take oath in his proof. He was at liberty and could plead no guilty and could contest the case. Rules of pleadings were also very advance. There was no concept of King can do no wrong. Rule of law was prevalent. Even, Emperors could be cummoned before court like other ordinary litigants. Court's orders, judgements and decree were to be in consonance with the court records. Evidence law was also well defined. Parties could employ vakeels to represent them before the courts.

These were some of he characteristic features of Mughal judicial system, that is, of Shariah Law and Shariah Courts. The impact of Mughal judicial system is even quite noticeable upon the present day judiciary. Even today almost all the terms concerning the court nomenclature are they same as those of Mughal period. In other words the legal vocabulary and the glossary of law terms daily reminds us of the influence of the Muslim system of judicial administration. Very slight changes have been effected so far.

Such was edifice of Shariah Judicial System but after Aurangzeb its decline started. There was a contest for the crown between the brothers. Later emperors were more titular than real but non of them was powerful enough to save the empire from disruption. Within half a century from the death of Aurangzeb in 1707 A.D. to the grant of the Diwani to the East India company in 1765 A.D. the splendid edifice of the empire gradually crumbled down. India became a theatre of warfares. Judicial system of the country suffered it's worst. When the servants of the East India company took the charge of the administration of the country, they found it in a chaotic condition. Islamic ;civil law was easily superseded, but the penal law was continued to be administered in the criminal courts of the time. Gradually even that law was superseded. Sir Ronald Wilson says:

"The system was gradually Anglicised by successive Regulations, the Muhammadan elements did not entirely disappear till 1862 when the 'Penal Code and the First Code of Criminal Procedure came into force, nor as regards the rules of evidence till the passing of the Indian Evidence Act in 1872".[I]

Critics even do not spare the Islamic judicial system existed up to Aurangzeb. No doubt we can discuss merits and demerits of the system then existing, but it should be clear that it is all due to certain misconception of the historians foreign or Indians. The misconceptions has resulted in good deal of misunderstanding and race-prejudice also. In the words of Mr. Waheed Husain, "These misconceptions have arisen from the haphazard writings, off-hand observations, and sarcastic remarks of a certain class of historians who pose themselves as authentic chroniclers of the Mughal Courts. But their accounts, when critically examined, betray their ignorance and prejudices."[II]

"Present Position"

Shariah criminal courts were abolished during British Rule. At present Muslims and non-Muslims are governed by general Penal Code enacted by the Britishers. In evidential and procedural matters, we have separate Evidence Act and Criminal Code. Substantive Criminal Law is secular in nature. In personal matters such as marriage, dower, divorce, maintenance, guardianship, will, gift, wakf and inheritance, Muslims are governed by their personal law known as Muslim Law. Cases relating there to are dealt with the decided by secular courts. In other words at present there are no Shariah Courts in existence.

I. Anglo-Muhammadan Law, p. 30.

II. Supra - N, p.

CHAPTER 8

PART A

I. "JUDGEMENT : INDIAN CRIMINAL LAW"

Judgement as defined in Kuppusami Rao, is the 'final decision of the court intimated to the parties and the world at large by formal pronouncement of delivery in open court by the trial judge and signing and dating it simultaneously and thereby terminating the criminal proceedings finally.'[1]

The judgement in every trial before criminal court of original jurisdiction shall be pronounced in the open court by the presiding officer of the court. It would be pronounced immediately after the termination of the trial or at some subsequent time of which notice shall be given to the parties or their pleaders.

Judgement may be delivered by the court either as a whole or only operative part is read out explaining the substance of the judgement in a language which is understood by the accused or his pleader.

Judgement when completed, every page of it is to be signed by the Magistrate and also to write the date of the delivery of the judgement in open court. The copy of judgement immediately after the pronouncement shall be made available for the perusal of the parties or their pleaders free of cost.

If the accused is in custody, he shall be brought to hear

---

1. Air 1949 F.C.I. Cr. *Lj*. 625, and 1954 SCR 330 : 1954 Cr. Lj. 475.

the judgement pronounced. If the accused is not in custody he shall be required by the court to attend to hear the judgement pronounced. In cases where during the trial accused's personal attendance has been dispensed with and the sentence is one of fine only or he is acquitted, accused's presence at the delivery judgement is not required. (S. 353, Criminal Procedure Code).

When there are more accused than one, and one or more of them do not attend the court on the date on which the judgement is to be pronounced, the presiding officer may, in order to avoid undue delay in the disposal of the case, pronounce the judgement notwithstanding their absence.

Judgement delivered by any criminal court shall not be deemed invalid on ground of:

1. The absence of any party or his pleader on the day or from the place notified for the delivery thereof, of

2. any omission to serve, or defect in serving on the parties or their pleaders, or any of them, the notice of such day and place.

Every judgement referred in section 353 Cr. PC shall be written in the language of the court. It shall contain:

1. point or points for determination, the decision thereon and the reasons for the decisions.

2. the offence (if any) of which, and the section of the Indian Penal Code, or other law under which, the accused is convicted and the punishment to which he is sentenced.

3. the offence of which the accused is acquitted and direct that the accused be set at liberty.

4. indoubtful cases where it is not clear under which of the two sections or two parts of the same sections of the Indian Penal Code an accused can be convicted the court shall distinctly express the same, and pass judgement in the alternative.

5. reasons for passing different sentences in accordance to the requirements of laws. Even where a statute lays down a minimum sentence for an offence but given discretion to the court to impose a lesser sentence for reason to be given, the fact that the accused was on bail for a pretty long time, would be a relevant ground in using the discretion to impose a lesser sentence.

Every case in the final determination has to depend upon its own facts. No court is permitted to alter or review its judgement or final order disposing of a case when it is signed except as otherwise provided by the Criminal Procedure Code or by any other law for the time being in force.

The original judgement shall be filed with the record of the proceedings and where the original is recorded in a language different from that of the court and the accused so requires, a translation thereof into the language of the court shall be added to such record.

In cases tried by the court of session or a chief judicial magistrate, the court or such magistrate, as the case, may be, shall forward a copy of its or his finding and sentence, if any, to the District Magistrate within whose local jurisdiction the trial was held.

II - 'Punishment: Indian Criminal law'

Section 406, Criminal Procedure Code provides punishment for criminal breach of trust which is defined in section 405. Punishment provided in the section is imprisonment of either description for a term which may extend two three years, or with fine with both.

Procedure for sentencing has been laid down in section 248 Criminal Procedure Code. In cases where charge has been framed, the Magistrate finds the accused not guilty, he shall record an order of acquittal.

Where the Magistrate, in any case, finds the accused guilty, but does not proceed in accordance with the provisions of section 325 or section 360 Criminal Procedure Code, he shall, after hearing the accused on the question of sentence, pass sentence upon him according to law.

Clause (3) of section 248 deals with cases of previous conviction where the accused denies, the Magistrate may, after he has convicted the accused, take evidence in respect of the alleged previous conviction, and shall record a finding thereon. Before taking evidence, convictions under clause (2) section 248 is necessary.

The court before passing the sentence is to weigh the merit of each case, the mitigating circumstances, and facts which differ from case to case. In one case where a long time had elapsed since the offence took place it was held that a heavy sentence of fine was sufficient to meet the requirements of justice.[1]

In another case where the secretary of a co-operative society was held guilty under section 406, and the treasurer who appeared to be in collusion with him was not prosecuted and all amounts received were correctly entered in the account book, the court reduced the punishment to a fine.

---

1. 1968 Cr. Lj. (983 Andhra Pradesh)

Under extenuating circumstances some time severe punishment is rendered unnecessary. In a case where the hirer under a hire-purchase agreement disposed of the property, but payment of instalment, the insurance and other expenses were not disrupted. It continuously paid by the hirer. It was observed that a simple imprisonment was sufficient.

Offence of Criminal misappriation and breach of trust by the chairman of cooperative society must be viewed seriously and no sentence should be shown, yet, in the instant case where transfer of amount was merely from one branch of the society to another branch lenient view taken was held correct.[I]

However, where the accused is a man of position and the secretary of a co-operative society, a sentence of fine of Rs. 175/- and imprisonment till the rising of the court was held in adequate and the fine was raised to Rs. 1000/-. But the jail sentence was held unnecessary under the circumstances of the case.[II]

If a man makes a criminal misappropriation of property of another valued for Rs. 2000/-, it is in no way be an extenuating circumstance to plead that the accused and the victim are close relations; the extenuating circumstance would be that there has been no real misapplication.[III]

In a case where amount of criminal breach of trust is large and the offence has been committed by a member of the legal profession in which the litigating public must repose

---

I. 1970, Pat Ljr 600.

II. A 1923 All 598 : 24 Cr. Lj. 620.

III. (1926) Cr. Lj. 331 (Mad).

entire trust and confidence calls for severe sentence. Under the particular circumstances, it was held that the ends of justice will be simply met by a sentence of nine months rigorous imprisonment.

Analysing the above cases it can be observed that there is no fixed criteria to determine the liability of the accused when his guilt is proved by the prosecution. Sentencing is discretionary with the court and differs from case to case. All depends upon the extenuating circumstance in individual cases. Courts sometime take a lenient view while on other occasion a serious view. Punishment thus may be severe or lenient as the ease may be.

Same approach is to be adopted in cases considering under section 408 when offence of criminal breach of trust has been committed either by the clerk or servant. In Kassim Pillai Abdul's[I] case, the accused, a clerk-cum-accountant, file to deposit various sums amounting to Rs. 100/- in the treasury as required by the rules. He during enquiry explained that as there was no safe in the office he had kept money in his drawer from where it was stolen. The accused was allowed to re-imburse the amount. In appeal, on question of sentence the supreme court held that considering the inexperience of the accused court held that considering the inexperience of the accused and the fact that he reimbursed the misappropriated amount the sentence could be reduced to the period already undergone.'

The fact that the servant lost the benefit of his service is no ground for mitigating the sentence for the crime.[II]

I. 1978 Cr. *Lj*. 1994 (SC).

II. (1890) 13 Mys. LR. No. 421 p. 656.

Where the accused was 18 years of age and a person of good character and the offence was due to unpardonable laxity in management and his own miserable pay, a sentence of one year was held sufficient.[I]

Where a clerk of many years standing and in a position of trust misappropriated large sums of money, it was held that a sentence of 5 years rigorous imprisonment was not too severe.[II]

Section 408 Indian Penal Code authorises the court in criminal breach of trust cases involving either the clerk or servant to punish with imprisonment of either description for a term which may extend to seven years, and shall also be liable to fine. A sentence passed by the High Court under section 408 can be reconsidered by the High Court under its powers under section 482 Criminal Procedure Code which is not limited by section 362 of the Criminal Procedure Code.[III]

A young law graduate as an employee committed his first offence of misappropriation. Supreme court held that no serious notice needs to be taken of the lapse. He was sentenced to a nominal sentence of 1 month's Rigorous Imprisonment and fine Rs. 500/-.[IV]

Offence under section 406 Indian Penal Code, involving servant or agent, etc., is considered most serious and an accused person shall be punished with imprisonment for life, or with imprisonment of either description for a term which may extend to ten years, and shall also be liable to fine.

I. A. 1937 Sind 242: 39 Cr. Lj. 6.

II. A. 1934 All. 173: 35 Cr. Lj. 617.

III. A. 1927 Lah. 139: 28 Cr. Lj. 239.

IV. A 1979 Sc. 1195: 1979 Cr. Lj. 912.

'Where separate trials were held in respect of various items misappropriated and sentences passed in each to run consecutively (totalling 11 years) it was held by the Supreme Court that the sentence could not be attacked as too severe having regard to the fact that the accused was holding a responsible post.'[I]

However, it is not desirable as a general rule to proceed with an indefinite number of trials and impose sentences to take effect one after the other.[II]

As the offence under section 409 Indian Penal Code is punishable with imprisonment for life. Hence the benefit of section 4 of the Probation of Offenders Act cannot be available of by an accused under this section.[III] The breach of trust by clerk or public servant is of an aggravated nature calling for substantial punishment.[IV] Misappropriation by public workers, held sentence must be severe.[V] But having regard to the large number of cases against the same person accused with respect to acts committed at different places and at different times, the sentences of 5 years rigorous imprisonment awarded in each case were allowed to run concurrently and not consecutively as the cumulative effect would be too severe.[VI]

'The admission of the accused of his guilt and his paying up the amount misappropriated before the filing of charge-sheet and the lapse of a long period after the date of the offence, are all matters which may be considered in

---

I. A 1965 Sc. 1248: 1965 (2) Cr. Lj. 253.

II. A 1938 Cal. 697: 40 Cr. Lj. 90 (DB).

III. (1970) 76 Punj. Lr. 103.

IV. A 1950 Lah. 1969 (222) (FB).

V. 1959 Cr. *Lj*. 1197.

VI. 1958 Cr. *Lj*. 15 (DB).

awarding the sentence.[I] The fact that the amount misappropriated was deposited during the pendency of the appeal may also be considered by the appellate court.[II] (Sentence reduced to period undergone and fine).

A sentence of imprisonment is obligatory for an offence under this section. While a sentence of fine is not obligatory.

In a case where the accused was acquitted by the trial court but sentenced to 4 months rigorous imprisonment by the High Court. The Supreme court on appeal, reduced it to the period of 19 days already served, in view of the fact that the accused had secured another job after this acquittal and was working at it.[III]

An accused convicted of an offence under section 409 Indian Penal Code. Trial Court only admonished the accused and warned him to be of good conduct in future as: (1) he pleaded guilty of speaking the truth; (2) promptly deposited the entire amount involved; (3)aa he was not a previous convict and was physically invalid. High court in this case refused interfere to revision.[IV]

An accused convicted under this section cannot be released under section 360 of the Criminal Procedure Code.[V]

From the above cases it is clear from sentencing pattern that punishment is awarded keeping in view the mitigating conditions though criminal breach of trust under section 409, Indian Penal Code by public servant is specially of serious

---

I. A 1954 Sc. 715 (719).

II. A 1974 Sc. 2336.

III. A 1972 Sc. 1618.

IV. 1970 All Wr (HC) 11 (DB).

V. A 1946, Mad. 178.

nature and requires severe punishment. Court before awarding the punishment is to take into consideration the gravity of the offence, the impact on the public and particularly the persons who were deprived of their properties.

"Rules Governing Sentences"

Once a sentence is awarded the general law that a sentence commences to run from the time it is imposed, but section 427 (1) engrafts an exception to this general rule in the case of a person who is already undergoing a sentence of imprisonment. A discretion is given to the court to direct that the subsequent sentence shall run concurrently with the previous sentence. However, the court would not be competent to exercise the discretion conferred by section 427 (1) Criminal Procedure Code after the final judgement is passed.

Section 428 of Criminal Procedure Code provides that the period of detention of an accused as an under trial prisoner shall be set off against the term of imprisonment imposed on him on conviction.

When any person has been sentenced to punishment for an offence, the appropriate government may, at any time, without conditions or upon any conditions which the person sentenced accepts, suspend the execution of his sentence or remit the whole or any part of the punishment to which he has been sentenced. This part is to be studied in relation to other remaining clauses of section 432, Criminal Procedure Code.

Section 433, Criminal Procedure Code, authorises the appropriate government to, without the consent of the person sentenced, commute a sentence of imprisonment for life, for imprisonment for a term not exceeding fourteen years or for fine. A sentence of rigorous imprisonment, for a simple imprisonment for any term to which that person might have been sentenced, or for fine.

The powers conferred by sections 432 and 433 upon the state government to remit or commute a sentence, in any case where the sentence is for an offence which involved the misappropriation of any property belonging to the central government, or which was committed by a person in the service of the central government while acting or purporting to act in the discharge of his official duty, shall not be exercised by the stage government except after consultation with the central government.

Where persons prosecuted for offences, under the laws in the state field and some in the union field and sentence to separate terms of imprisonment to run concurrently, the stage government. Sometimes, remitted the whole sentence without a reference to the central government, the person cannot be released unless the central government also remits the parts of the sentence to an offence in the central field.

PART B

"JUDGEMENT: ISLAMIC CRIMINAL LAW"

When a judge adjudges a thing dependant upon the rights of the litigant parties, it is an essential condition that there must be a claim made by one party against the other. Judgement must be given after formal hearning or trial. It must be prepared by Shariah court judge personally in his own hand-writing. The preparation of the judgement should not be handed over to others. It is also a condition that the two parties be present at the time of pronouncing the judgement.

But when one person has claimed something and the defendant has voluntarily admitted the claim, the judgement may be pronounced in the absence of the defendant also.

Similarly, when the defendant denies the claim, the witnesses of the plaintiff have been examined in his presence, and before the credibility of witnesses has been examined, and the judgement to the given, the defendant leaves the court, the judge may pronounce the judgement even in his absence.

The judgements may be classified into:

1. Judgement on the merit;
2. Judgement by default;
3. Judgement on the pleading;
4. Judgement upon compromise;
5. Judgement upon confession; and
6. Judgement upon on oath.

These judgement are based upon certain principles. These principles, which a judge while preparing the judgement is to adhere with, are:

"Judgement based upon Shariat"

The most important rule in that every judgement should be in accordance to Shariah. It means that the disputes be decided in the light of Qur'ãnic injuctions. If there is no injunction on a particular point, the disputes be decided in accordance of Ahadith, that is, the traditions of Prophet (peace be upon him). Even if there is no hadith, then the judge is to determine the issue according to Ijma and Qiyas. Even if the Ijma and Qiyas, are absence, then on the opinions of honest Muslims, and ultimately if nothing is there then the judge Shariah is free to make an Ijtihad. In other words, in the end, ultimately, he may form his own opinion which should just and best suiting to the circumstances.

First prefence is to Qur'ãnic injuctions. Allah Ta'ala says:

وَمَنْ لَّمْ يَحْكُمْ بِمَا اَنْزَلَ اللّٰهُ فَاُولٰئِكَ هُمُ الْكٰفِرُوْنَ۔

(سورة المائدة، آية: ٤٤)

"If any do fall to judge by What Allah Hath revealded, they are unbelievers." (5:44)

At another place in the same sura, Allah has again commanded:

وَاَنْزَلْنَا اِلَيْكَ الْكِتٰبَ بِالْحَقِّ مُصَدِّقًا لِّمَا بَيْنَ يَدَيْهِ مِنَ الْكِتٰبِ
وَمُهَيْمِناً عَلَيْهِ فَاحْكُمْ بَيْنَهُمْ بِمَا اَنْزَلَ اللّٰهُ وَلَا تَتَّبِعْ اَهْوَاءَهُمْ عَمَّا
جَائَكَ مِنَ الْحَقِّ، لِكُلٍّ جَعَلْنَا مِنْكُمْ شِرْعَةً وَّمِنْهَاجاً وَلَوْشَاءَ اللّٰهُ
لَجَعَلَكُمْ اُمَّةً وَّاحِدَةً وَّلٰكِنْ لِّيَبْلُوَكُمْ فِى مَااٰتٰكُمْ فَاسْتَبِقُوْا الْخَيْرٰتِ

(سورة المائدة، آية: ٤٨)

"To Thee We sent the scripture in truth, confirming the scripture that came Before it, and guarding it in safety: So judge Between them by what Allah hath revealed, and follow not their vain Desires, diverging from the truth that hath come to thee. To each among you have We prescribed a law And an Open Way." (5:48)

In another verse Allah commands:

وَلْيَحْكُمْ اَهْلُ الاِ نْجِيْلِ بِمَا اَنْزَلَ اللّٰهُ فِيْهِ وَمَنْ لَّمْ يَحْكُمْ بِمَا اَنْزَلَ اللّٰهُ فَاُوْلٰئِكَ هُمُ الْفٰسِقُوْنَ۔ (سورة المائدة، آية:٤٧)

"Let the people of the gospel judge by what all hath revealed therein. If any do fail, to judge by what Allah hath revealed they are those who rebel."

(5:47)

In sura An'am again Allah says:

اَفَغَيْرَ اللّٰهِ ابْتَغِى حَكَماً وَهُوَ الَّذِى اَنْزَلَ اِلَيْكُمُ الْكِتٰبَ مُفَصَّلاً وَالَّذِيْنَ اٰتَيْنٰهُمُ الْكِتٰبَ يَعْلَمُوْنَ اَنَّهُ مُنَزَّلٌ مِنْ رَّبِّكَ بِالْحَقِّ فَلاَ تَكُوْنَنَّ مِنَ الْمُمْتَرِيْنَ۔ (سورة الانعام ، آية:١١٤)

"So should I make now any other as judge beside God though He sent down to you the Book distinctly clear, and those woom We have given the Book know that it is sent down from the Lord truly, so be not thou of the doubtors." (6:114)

Again Allah says:

وَتَمَّتْ كَلِمَتُ رَبِّكَ صِدْقاً وَّعَدْلاً لَا مُبَدِّلَ لِكَلِمٰتِهٖ وَهُوَ السَّمِيْعُ الْعَلِيْمُ۔ (سورة الأ نعام، آية:١١٠)

> "And the word of thy Lord is perfect in truth and justice. No one is the changer of His word, and He is the Hearer, Knower." (6:115)

It is not possible for the Prophet (peace be upon him) and his followers, who have accepted God as the Supreme Sovreign and the Sole Judge in all their affairs, to listen to the greasy talks of anyone leaving God aside.

It is never possible, because they have received from God a perfect and miraculous Book which contains the necessary details and explanation of all fundamental principles and important souvenirs.

Its tidings are all true. Its laws are moderate and just and no one has the power to change them.

In the presence of such a grand Book and perfect and guarded laws how the Muslims can fall prey to fallacies of mind and reason and the betraying conjectures, particularly when they know that God, whon the Muslims have recognized as the Supreme Sovereign and chose Book has been accepted as the final constitution and authority.

Allah knows the talents of all human beings and hears all their demands made by their internal talents and knows well those conditions and circumstances which will take place in time and space and knows well what laws should be given to mankind best suited to those conditions and circumstances in time and space.

When the laws of God possess a universal character and applications then the Muslims of today also need not listen to the conflicting ideas of modern thinkers in the presence of the perfectly just and truthful teaching of the Holy Qur'ãn.

Thus the judgement of Shariah court should based on Qur'ãnic injunction. If there is no injunction, then resort to sunnah.

Prophet Muhammad (peace be upon him) asks Hazrat Ma'aaz bin Jabal (محاذ بن جبل) when he was appointed Qazi of YAMAN, 'how would you decide the cases'.

ان رسـول الله صلى الله عليه وسلم بعث معاذا الى اليمن، فقال: كيف تقضى؟ فقال: اقضى بـمـا فـى كتاب الله قال: فان لم يكن فى كتاب الله؟ قال: فبسنة رسول الله قال ان لم يكن فـى سنة رسـول الـلـه صـلـى الله عليه وسلم؟ قال: اجتهد رابئى قال: الحمد لله الذى وفق رسول رسول الله۔ (جامع الترمذى، ج۲، ص ۲۷۰-۲۷۶ مع شئ تحفه الا حوزى)

He replied, "I will decide the cases in accordance to wherever is given in the Qur'ãn."

The Prophet (peace be upon him) asked, "If there is no verse is Qur'ãn relating to that matter then."?

He replied, "Then I will decide in accordance to Sunnah of Allah's Prophet."

Prophet (peace be upon him) "Then I will decide in accordance to Sunnah of Allah's Prophet."

Prophet (peace be upon him) again asked, "If there is no sunnah on that point then"? He said, "Then I will decide whatever is just and best in my opinion. I will ijtihad (اجتهاد).

Prophet (peace be upon him) hearing this 'reply thanked God that the Prophet's representative had been bestowed with such an ability."

This Hadith makes it clear that the judgement of the court should be based upon Qur'ãn and Ahadith. In the absence of any specific injunction relating to the matter concern, then Ahadith should be consulted. If no answer found then Ijma, Qiyas, and Ijtihad, of the Qazi. them only judgement would be perfect.

Similar view was expressed by Hazrat Umar (r. a) the second Caliph in his letter addressed to Qazi Shariah. He advised the Qazi:

> "First whatever is there in Holy Qur'ãn. decide the cases accordingly. If Qur'ãn is silent on any particular point, then decide according to Prophet's (peace be upon him) Sunnah. If no answer in Ahadith, then, decide according to such precedents laid down by Honest men of Muslim umma (مسلم امت). It still you do not find any answer either in Qur'ãn, or Sunnah or the opinion of learned and honest persons of Muslim umma (مسلم امت), then decide yourself. Do Ijtihad. It will be better for you."

Now it is clear that Qazi during Caliphat period were following the same principle. The most significant thing is that decision not based on Shariat would not be valid in law. Judges have to adhere to the above procedure laid down by Allah and his Messenger both.

"Judgement based on Justice"

The second most honoured and significant principle is what has been laid down in Surah al-Maida, verse 42, surah al-Araf, verse 29, sura al-Nisan, verse 58, surah al-Nahl, verse 90, that is, whatever, a decision given it must be based on justice. Whims or desires or liking, disliking of a judge should have no place in the judgement. Order of the judge must be impartial and just.

"Judgement based on Qarain (قرائن) - Signs"

Judgement on the basis of Qarain (قرائن), that is, analogical deductions from the facts of the case. Some passages from sura Yusuf are generally cited in support.

It has been revealed in Qur'ãn-e-Pak that the brothers of Hazrat Yusuf (A.S.) prepared a plot against him to kill, and tell their father a false story about his death. Thus plotters carried Joseph (يوسف) and pushed him into a well, and thereafter returned to father a Jacob with a false story. They came after sun set so that they could convince their father that they made all possible efforts to search him but failed. They wanted to make out that they were not negligent of Joseph. The story told was when they were having games, exercise, and racing, Joseph was that left behind. Meanwhile wolf came and devoured him. In fact, they told that they were busy in racing that prevented them from seeing the wolf.

Joseph wore a garment of many colours, which was a special garment peculiar to him. Brothers produced blood-stained cloths before father, with a view that father could be convinced that Joseph had been killed by a wild beast. But the stains on the garment were stains of 'false-blood'.

The above arguments could not convince their father. This story has been narrated in Qur'ãn as follows:

وَجَاءُو اَبَاهُمْ عِشَاءً يَّبْكُوْنَ. قَالُوا يَاَبَانَا اِنَّا ذَهَبْنَا نَسْتَبِقُ وَتَرَكْنَا يُوْسُفَ عِنْدَ
مَتَاعِنَا فَاَكَلَهُ الذِّئْبُ، وَمَا اَنْتَ بِمُؤمِنٍ لَّنَا وَلَوْ كُنَّا صٰدِقِيْنَ۔ وَجَاءُوْ عَلٰي
قَمِيْصِهِ بِدَمٍ كَذِبٍ، قَالَ بَلْ سَوَّلَتْ لَكُمْ اَنْفُسُكُمْ اَمْراً فَصَبْرٌ جَمِيْلٌ وَاللّٰهُ
الْمُسْتَعَانُ عَلٰى مَا تَصِفُوْنَ۔ (سورة يوسف، آية: ١٦، ١٧، ١٨)

"Then they came to their father in the early party of the night, weiping." (12:16)

"They said: "O our father! We went racing with one another, And left Joseph with out things; And the wolf devoured him. But thou wilt never believe us. Even though we tell the truth." (12:17)

"They stained his shirt with false blood. He said: "Nay, but your minds have made up a tale (that may pass) with you, (for me) patience is most fitting: Against that which ye assert, it is Allah (alone) whose help can be sought........" (12:18)

Plotters were surprised that Jacob received the story about the wolf with cold incredulity. So they grew petulen, put on an air of injured innocence. Therefore, they also had shown the blood-stained shirt. Jacob did not believe that also. These are some of the verses from which learned jurists deduct that (قرائن) analogy can be one of the basis of judgement.

Similarly, sura-Yusuf, verses 23 to 29, are referred by jurists, on the basis of which they consider Qarain (قرائن) as basis of judgement. Verse are quoted below in which a false charge was made against Joseph for act of immorality and how Joseph was declared innocent:

وَرَاوَدَتْهُ الَّتِى هُوَ فِى بَيْتِهَا عَنْ نَفْسِه وَغَلَّقَتِ الْاَ بْوَابَ وَقَالَتْ هَيْتَ لَكَ قَالَ
مَعَاذَاللّٰه اِنَّهٗ رَبِّى اَحْسَنَ مَثْوَاىَ اِنَّهٗ لَا يُفْلِحُ الظّٰلِمُوْنَ وَلَقَدْ هَمَّتْ بِه وَهَمَّ بِهَا لَوْلَا اَنْ
رَّاٰبُرْهَانَ رَبِّه كَذٰلِكَ لِنَصْرِفَ عَنْهُ السُّوْءَ وَالْفَحْشَاءَ اِنَّهٗ مِنْ عِبَادِنَا الْمُخْلَصِيْنَ
وَاْسَتَبَقَاالْبَابَ وَقَدَّتْ قَمِيْصَهٗ مِنْ دُبُرٍ وَّاَلْفَيَا سَيِّدَهَا لَدَا الْبَاب قَالَتْ مَا جَزَاءُ مَنْ اَرَادَ
بِاَهْلِكَ سُوْءًا اِلَّآ اَنْ يُّسْجَنَ اَوْ عَذَابٌ اَلِيْمٌ قَالَ هِىَ رَاوَدَتْنِى عَنْ نَّفْسِى وَشَهِدَ
شَاهِدٌ مِنْ اَهْلِهَا اِنْ كَانَ قَمِيْصُهٗ قُدَّ مِنْ قُبُلٍ فَصَدَقَتْ وَهُوَ مِنَ الْكٰذِبِيْنَ وَاِنْ كَانَ
قَمِيْصُهٗ قُدَّ مِنْ دُبُرٍ فَكَذَبَتْ وَهُوَ مِنَ الصّٰدِقِيْنَ۔ فَلَمَّا رَاٰقَمِيْصَهٗ قُدَّ مَنْ دُبُرٍ قَالَ اِنَّهٗ
مِنْ كَيْدِكُنَّ اِنَّ كَيْدَكُنَّ عَظِيْمٌ يُوْسُفُ اَعْرِضْ عَنْ هٰذَا وَاسْتَغْفِرِى لِذَنْبِكِ اِنَّكِ
كُنْتِ مِنَ الْخٰطِئِيْنَ۔ (سورة يوسف،آية:٢٣ ،٢٤،٢٥ ،٢٦،٢٧ ،٢٨،٢٩)

"But she is whose house he was, sought to seduce him and she fastened the doors, and said: "Now come", He said: "Allah forbid! Truly (the husband) is my lord! he made my sojourn agreeable! Truly to no good come those who do wrong." (12:23)

"And (with passion) did she desire him, and he would have desired her, but that He saw the evidence of his Lord: thus (Did We order) that We might turn away from him (all) evil and indecent deeds: For he was one of our servants chosen." (12:24)

"So they both raced each other to the door, and she tore his shirt from the back: They both found her lord near the door. She said "What is the (fitting) punishment for one who formed an evil design against thy wife, but prison or a grievous chastisement?" (12:25)

"He said: "It was she that sough to seduce me from my (true) self." And one of her household saw (this) and bore witness, (thus):- 'If it be that his shirt is torn from the front, then is tale true, And he is a liar". (12:26)

"But if it be that his skirt is torn from the back, then is she the liar, And he is telling the truth!". (12:27)

"So when he saw his shirt,- that it was torn at the back, - (her husband) said :"Behold! It is a snare of You women! Truly, might is Your anare!" (12:28).

"O Joseph, pass this over! (O wife), ask forgiveness - for thy sin, for truly thou hast been at fault!", (12 :29).

This is another example of judgement pronounced on the basis of (قرائن) - analogical deduction from the facts of the case. In this case woman was proved a liar, and Joseph was acquitted of the false charge. Judges of the Shariah Courts follow this as basis of the judgements. In other words, judgers form their opinions on (قرائن) and decide the cases.

On قرائن (Qarain), a hadith has been reported in Sunan Ibn-Maja, in which Hazrat Nimran bin Jaria quoted his father who told that once a group of persons came to Prophet (peace be upon him) with a dispute that related about a hut. Both the parties were making claim to that. Prophet (peace be upon him) after listening the matter referred that to Hazrat Hazefa bin Aleeman and asked him: 'to go, and inspect the site and give the decision'. Hazrat Hazefa bin Aleeman after inspection of the hut decided: 'that the, hut belong to those in whose side its' bamboos were standing and returned back to Prophet (peace be upon him). Then Prophet (peace be upon him) asked about his decision. He narrated in details of his judgement. Prophet (peace be upon him) praised him and said: "You gave a correct decision."

Most probably on this case the parties were not having proof in their support and Hazrat Hazefa bin Aleeman decided the dispute on the basis of Qarain (قرائن).

Thus it is an approved method when the both have no proof in their support, Shariah Court Judge may give his decision on the basis of analogical deduction from the facts of the case.

"Judgement based on Farasat (فراست)"

Judge Shariah Court may also base his judgement on the basis of فراست (understanding) also. It means that if the judge after examining the facts fairly comes to any conclusion which he considers correct, may give his judgement. Hazrat Abu Hurera (R.A.) reported that Prophet (peace be upon him) said to him: That two women while going with their children, all of a sudden came across a wolf which took away one of their children. Both started disputing and claiming the remaining child. One women said to the other: 'Your child had been take away and the remained one was her. The other said: 'No! your child had been taken away! They carried the matter in dispute to Hazrat Daud (A.S.) Hazrat Daud after hearing the case, decided in favour of the elder lady. Then both of them, after feeling unsatisfied with the judgement went to Hazrat Sulaiman bin Daud (A.S.) and narrated the whole story. He asked them to bring a knife and said that he would cut the child into two and would give half to one and half to the other. Upon hearing this, the younger one immediately reacted and said,: "No, No, do not cut. The child belong to the elder woman" Thereupon, Hazrat Sulaiman bin Daud, basing his judgement on his فراست(understanding) gave the child to the younger lady and decided the case accordingly.

This the intelligence and understanding capabilities of the judge also have due place in coming to correct judgement. Under Islamic Law basing judgement on such understanding is an approved practice. From the above quoted Hadith, jurist declare (understanding capability) of a judge a correct approach to decide the case

Judgement based on Qura قرعه

Hazrat Saeed bin Almuseed narrated that Prophet (peace be upon him) said:

If both the parties have produced equal number of witness in the court, then judgement should be given on the basis of Qura قرعه ".

This is one way of deciding the case. Where number of witnesses of both parties are equal in number and weight and credibility than Prophet (peace be upon him) permitted hat judgement can be given on the basis of Qura قرعه ".

Prophet (peace be upon him) also allowed in such cases to declare the property in dispute as joint property of both the parties.

"Judgement based on Possession"

This matter requires a lot of detail discussion which is not possible to summarise it in this thesis. Only it may be said that possession of the party may be considered a ground for declaring the ownership of one of the parties. But it is not always the ground justifying possession as proof of ownership. It may be or may not be depend upon case to case. When the complainant has no proof in support of his allegations, then the defendant if having possession over the disputed thing or dominion over the disputed thing and (takes an oath in support, then matter may be decided in his favour.

Hazrat Adi bin Adi al-Kandi narrated that his father told him that two persons came to Prophet (peace be upon him) with a dispute. One of them said to Prophet (peace be upon him) that land in dispute in his land and he is the owner of it. The second one said, that the land belong to him. He had cultivated it also and the crop standing thereupon belonged to him. Prophet (peace be upon him) administered the oath to the person who had possession over the land and thereafter decided the case infavour of him'.

(سنن الداد قطنی، جلد دوم۔ صفحہ ٥١٤، طبع دھلی، ١٣١ ھ)

Thus when complainant has no proof in his support and the defendant is having possession over the disputed land, his possession can be basis for giving judgement in his favour. But it is always not so. The defendant may also be administered oath. On taking oath, judgement would be given in his favour.

"Judgement based on apparent conditions"

Judgement can be given on apparent conditions and such a decision would be sound under Islamic Law.

Hazrat Um-Salama (R.A.) narrates that Prophet (peace be upon him) said: "See! I am also a human being. You come to me with your disputes. It is possible that some of you may be eloquent, more sharp and intelligent in arguments in comparison to others. I base my judgement whatever I hear. Therefore, if on the basis of arguments of one, I give my judgement on any issue in favour of a person who does not deserve to that right. Then he should not take that because it is a place of fire cut by my hand, fallen and received by that men."

(بخاری: کتاب الاحکام، ص ۱۰۶۲)

(صحیح مسلم، کتاب الا قیضه، ج۲، ص ۷٤)

It is clear that court may base its judgement on apparent force of argument of one party to a dispute and that party may receive the right to which, infect, he is not entitled, in such circumstances he should give thing to the true claimant. But the judgement based on such apparent force of argument would be valid under the Islamic Law.

"General Governing Rules"

A judgement should not be given when the judge is angry. He should pronounce the judgement when he is cool and composed.

Judgement must be given in writing after hearing both the partes. Judge should himself write the judgement. It should not be left to some other person.

Further judgement shall clearly state the facts and the law on which it is based. Judgement based on merits of the case the shall become final.

Judgement upon a compromise is that where the parties have agreed and that agreement has been submitted in the court. The court may give effect to such agreement. However, the compromise should not be opposed to social morals, law, custom, public policy, public order and public interest.

Judgement may be based upon confession made by the accused. Such a confession must be free, voluntary, and not obtained by inducement, fear, fraud, violence or intimidation. On confession of guilt, judgement would be given to the other party.

Judgement on oath is based upon, when the complainant has no witness in support, he may challenge the defendant accused to take an oath, and if the later takes the oath, judgement shall be rendered in his favour. However, if the defendant accused refuses to take the oath and the complainant affairs his claim under oath, judgement will be given in his favour. If the complainant refuses to take oath, the case shall be dismissed.

If a Qazi happens to able inefficient and unable to make analogical deduction, he may take the opinions of learned persons or refer the matter to known Islamic jurist for his opinion. On receiving such an opinion he may give his judgement. Opinions of (experts) can also be taken into consideration.

In fatawa-i-Alamgiri, it has been observed: "If in any case the Qazi be prefixed by opposite proofs, let him consult other able lawyers, and if they differe after weighing the argument let him decide as appears just".

To avoid any miscarriage of justice, we find that with every court a Mufti is also attached who advices the judge with legal opinion.

If a Qazi is learned in Islamic jurisprudence, and efficient in making his own opinion by resorting it Ijtihad (اجتهاد) he may decide the case on his conclusions taking into consideration all the facts and circumstance and rules of equity and justice.

The judges of the Shariah Court should not delay in delivering the judgement. If he intentionally delays, he will be sinner and may be removed from the post also. Thus judgement must be expeditiously delivered. However, if there is any reasonable course, it may also be delayed.

II. "Punishment: Islamic Criminal Law"

Crime under Islamic Law 'consists in legal prohibitions imposed by Allah, whose infringement entails punishment prescribed by Him'.[1]

Legal prohibition entails within in the acts and omissions both. An act and omission would amount to crime only when it is orohibited by Shariah. When a person does an act which is prohibited or omits to do an act, commanded or for doing which he is under a legal obligation, commits crime - 'jannayat'. Shariah imposes punishment for such violations.

Punishment is prescribed for a crime with a view that people may refrain from committing it. Without punishment, prohibition or command is of no use. It is the fear of punishment which contained people within limits. They obstain from committing offences, from acts detrimental to social order, beliefs, individual's life, property and honour. They refrain from causing disturbances, acting harmfully, and doing evil acts. Punishment is recognized in the society only in the public interest.

In brief Islamic Law has declared certain acts as crimes and has prescribed punishments with a view to protect general interest and the system on which the entire social edifice rests and the enable to safeguard moral values, peace, tranguality and harmony. Disobedience to Allah's commands and injunctions does not effect Him. He is always kind and merciful to His servants.

---

1 Mawardi - Al-Ahkam-ul-Sultania, p. 92.

These commands and injunctions, prohibition and restraining human beings from sin and inducing to obey Allah are aimed to guide the mankind and bring them out from darkness to light.

Modern law concept of punishment and of Shariah are inconsonance as far as both aim to safeguard the social system from lawlessness, but Shariah regards moral virtues as the principal base of society, and modern law does not. Modern law ignores moral values unless such values directly prejudice the interest of the community and the society at large. Further Shariah has been revealed by Almighty. Modern law is man made.

Law punishing crime, not only emanate, from Holy Qur'ãn, but from the traditions and acts of Prophet (peace be upon him). Still there are acts not covered under either Qur'ãn or Sunnah, may be declared offences and punishment may be laid down by the body of authority or on the basis of Ijma and Qiyas of ulamah. However, under Islamic law, no authority has been given power to do whatever it chooses. No authority has power to declare any act as offence and prescribe punishment thereto contrary to Qur'ãnic injunction or Sunnah of Prophet (peace be upon him).

The effect is that Islamic law has assumed immutable, everlasting and universal character. Another effect of divine character of Islamic law is that it is highly respected. Ruler and ruled both consider it sacred. They believe that the laws have been revealed by Allah and it is incumbent upon them to respect and regard it.

"Nature of Punishment"

Islamic law classifies the crimes under there heads:

1. Crimes falling under Huddud;
2. Crimes falling under Qisas, and Diyat; and
3. Tazeer.

This classification of punishment is based on the severity and mildness of punishment.

The 'Hud' (حد) is defined as the punishment prescribed as the right of Allah.[1] Under this category both the quantity and nature of punishment are determined and specified. It does not admit and degree of flexibility. Prescribed as right of Allah here means that the punishment as laid down cannot be altered or annulled by any individual or community or authority. Number of offences covered under Huddud are also limited and prescribed; such as, adultery, false allegiance of adultery, drinking wine, theft, bloodshed and plunder, apostasy and, lastly rebellion.

Qisas and Diyat coves such crimes as:

Wilful murder, suspected wilful murder, murder committed by error, intentional wrong other than murder and unintentional wrong other than murder.

"Tazeer"

The third category punishment is known as Tazeer. Islamic law does not lay down any limited for such crimes as we have noted under the above two categories. In fact, these cannot be any limited to this category. Punishment under this category is ranging from light to harsh one. It is a sort of corrective and preventive punishment awarded by the judge keeping in view the circumstances and seriousness of the situation. Further awarding of punishment is left to the discretion of the Shariah court judge.

As breach of trust is covered under the penal punishment known as Tazeer. We will have some details study about it here.

I. Fathul-Qadeer, Part IV, pp. 112-113.

Al-Ahkam-ul-Sultaniyah, pp. 192-195.

Tazeer means prohibition, and also instruction. In Hadayat it has been explained as: "in law it signifies an infliction undetermined in its degree by law, on account of the right either of God or of the individual, and occasion of it is any offence for which Huddud (stated punishment) has not been appointed; whether that offence consist in word or deed.

Tazeer has been defined by the jurists (فقهاء) as:[I]

هو تأديب على دنوب لم تشرع فيها هدوداى هو عقونبة على جرائم لم تضع الشريعة لا تيها عقوبات معينة محدودة۔

Means to punish a person for an offence not covered by Hud and for which Shariah has not prescribed the punishment.

Imam Zalee (امام ذيلعى) in his book explains Tazeer as:[II]

التعزير يكون فى كل معصية الخ، ليس فيه شئى مقدر، وانما هو مفوض الى رأى الا مام على ما تقتض جتايات الناس و اجس الهم..

For every crime (معصيت) there will be Tazeer and for Tazeer no quantum is prescribed. It depends upon the discretion of Hakim (حاكم). He will decide keeping in view the nature of the offence and circumstances in which the crime is committed."

In ' المهذب ', Fiqh Shafi'i,[II] Tazeer has been explained as:

من الى معصية لا حدفيها ولا كفارة، عزر على حسب مايراه السلطان

I. احكام السلطانيه ،مادردى، ص ٣٠٥، طبع اول،

الردالمختار، برحاشيه ردالمختار، ج٣، ص٣٤٥۔محوله بالا

II. الزيلعى، محوله بالا ، ج٣، ص٢٠٨

"A person who commits an offence not covered under Hud, he will be punished with Tazeer, according to the discretion of (حاکم) Hakim whatever he considers, appropriate."

"In مواهب الجليل Fiqh Maliki,[I] Tazeer has been defined as:

"Except offences covered under Hud, in other cases Tazeer is incumbent (تعزیر واجب هے). It depends upon the (اجتهاد) Ijtihad of Hakim (حاکم). Hakim will award Tazeer in offences against right of God or Masiat (معصیت) against God. "خدا کی معصیت یا حق العباد"

Some of the Tazeer offences are mentioned in the divine injunctions, such as:

'Breach of Trust' usury, abuse and bribery. Detailed Qur'ãnic injunctions on breach of trust have already been discussed earlier in Chapter I.

These are the crimes treated always as such. "Decision in respect of the crimes of penal nature have been left to the discretion of people in power. But the Shariah has not conferred on the rulers unqualified power of determining crime and has laid down conditions that an act should be treated as penal crime consistent with the situation obtaining in the community and its existing set up so as to safe-guard its interests and maintain public order. Moreover, the treatment of an act as a penal crime should not be in compatible with the provisions of Shariah and the fundamental principles thereof. Conferring the right of law-making on the rulers by the Shariah within these limits is designed to organise the community, guide it in the right direction, safeguard its interests

---

I. المهزب، ج۲، ص۳۰٦ محوله بالا

and to prepared the people to guard collective interests and deal with changing conditions".[1]

Actually Tazeer (penal punishment) under Islamic law is a corrective measure for which for which no huddud have been laid down in the Shariah.

"Kinds of Tazeer"

There are three types of Tazeer:

Firstly, Tazeer for offences (Sins):

Secondly, Tazeer for offences (misdemeanours).

The first category includes the cases of (معصيت). that is acts prohibited by Shariah or declared by Shariah as (حرام), the commission of which is a crime (SIN).

The following Qur'ãnic verses contains such injunctions:

In Sura-al-Nisa',verse 58 Allah commands:

إِنَّ اللّٰهَ يَأْمُرُكُم أَنْ تُؤَدُّوا الأَمٰنٰتِ إِلٰى أَهْلِهَا وَإِذَا حَكَمْتُم بَيْنَ النَّاسِ
أَنْ تَحْكُمُوا بِالعَدْلِ. (سورة النساء، آية:٥٨)

"Allah doth command you to render back Your trusts to those to whom they are due; and when Ye judge between people that ye judge with justice." (4:58)

In another verse Allah prohibits as:

إِنَّمَا حَرَّمَ عَلَيْكُمُ الْمَيْتَةَ وَالدَّمَ وَلَحْمَ الْخِنْزِيْرِ
(سورة البقرة، آية:١٧٣)

I. Abdul Qadir Oudah Shaheed, 'Criminal Law of Islam, Vol. I, p. 87.

"Forbidden unto You (for food) are carrion and blood and awine flesh". (2:173).

Similarly Allah commands:

وَلَا تَقْرَبُوا الزِّنٰى اِنَّهٗ كَانَ فَاحِشَةً وَّسَاءَ سَبِيْلًا.

(سورة الاسراء، آية: ٣٣)

"An come not near adultry.Lo! It is an abomination and an evil way". (17:32).

In sura-al Maida. verse 90. there is another prohibition:

يٰاَيُّهَا الَّذِيْنَ اٰمَنُوا اِنَّمَا الْخَمْرُ وَالْمَيْسَرُ وَالْاَ نْصَابُ وَالْاَ زْلَامُ رِجْسٌ مِنْ عَمَلِ الشَّيْطٰنِ فَاجْتَنِبُوْهُ لَعَلَّكُمْ تُفْلِحُوْنَ۔

(سورة المائدة، آية: ٩٠)

"O ye who believe! In-toxicants and gambling. an abomination- of satan' s handi work : Eschew such (abomination). that Ye may prosper".

In there above verses we find that Allah has prohibited certain type. of food stuffs, adultry, intoxication, gambling, any idolatrous or superstitious practices, violation of these verses amount to offence. There are similar number of others verses in which Allah has commanded to do, Violation of which would be an offence.

We may also make a distinction here between absolute prohibitions and desirable prohibitions under the first the inhiditory and injunction constitutes an absolute command, the act involved is unlawful. If the injunction for doing an act is imperative, that act is a duty, violation is an offence. Where act is undesirable, one is required to abstain therefrom, but injunction prohibiting is not imperative. The above referred injunctions are all absolute prohibitions. Doing an act contrary is a crime.

The second type of Tazeer has been explained as penal punishment enjoined for deeds which in themselves do not constitute prohibited acts but assume the character of such acts on account of certain qualities. These acts in fact, constitute exception to the general rule.

Penal punishment may be awarded for an act if the public interests so requires although such act may not be crime in itself as defined by the Shariah, with no injunction declaring it unlawful. These crimes are not possible to be listed in advance as they are not intrinsically unlawful but are treated as such because of a certain quality in them. When this quality predominant these acts become unlawful, when absent, they are some their normal legitimate character. Only criteria is that punishment is awarded in the public interest. If the acts detrimental or prejudicial to the public interest, maintenance of public peace, law and order may be termed as crime under this head.

Punishment in such cases is justified on the basis of an hadith. Holy Prophet (peace be upon him) is reported to have once imprisoned a person accused of stealing a camel. But the accused was not found guilty and was released.[1] Holy Prophet has treated such practice as madatory and justification for it is public interest and maintenance of public peace. To keep a person till his guilt is proved.

Practice of Hazrat Umar (R.A.) is also a precedent. He justified penal punishment for protecting the public interest. Once he over heard a woman saying, "I wish I could drink wine or have access to nasr bin Hujjaj. Hazrat Umer (R.A.) sent for Nasr who was very handsome person. He got Nasr's head shaven. By that

---

I. Sharh 'Fathul Zadeer' Vol. IV, p. 117.

he became more charming and handsome. The Caliph then externed him to Basra lest the women of the city, fascinated as they were by his masculiar beauty, should become licentious. It was all done in public interest.

Penal sentence in such cases is not authoritative. The court is empowered in such cases to impose any sentence provided the act is potential danger to the public interest.

Further penal punishment (Tazeer) in the public interest also pure supposes injunctions of the Shariah. This makes it clear that no provision can be more flexible to suit social requirement then the present one. The presence of such "flexible provision, makes it easy to act promptly when public interest so requires".

Under the third head are acts which Shariah prohibits as such but describes their commission as misdemeanour or 'mukhalafat and not as a crime or sin. These acts are known as mukhalafat-e-Shariah, and not called as معصیت (masiat). Jurists favour punishment for misdemeanours only in cases when minor acts are repeated and not generally. Precedent followed again is from Hazrat Umar (R.A.) that once he saw a man who was about to slaughter a goat, he tied goat first and then sharpened his knife. Hazrat Umar (R.A.) scold him and said: "Why did not you sharpen your knife before hand."

However, even if the act is not repeated, a person may be punished if the act is detrimental to the public interest. It should not be harmful to the common good or the social order.

Offence of 'Breach of Trust' is covered under the head absolute prohibitions, violation of which is معصیت (crime).

"Rules governing punishment"

Fundamental rule governing punishment under Islamic Law is:

> "Unless relevant provision exists, no judgement can be passed on the actions of a sensible person".

It means that a sane and responsible person would be liable for acts or omission when a provision exists either prohibiting or commanding the doing of an act. No act can be declared illegitimate unless it is contrary to law in existence.

The other fundamental rule is:

> "Thing and actions are legitimate in themselves."

It means that acts or omission are not illegal unless a provision forbidding such a course of action exists. If no provision exists, a person is not accountable for his acts or omission.

The third governing rule is"

> "A person legally under obligation is one who is able to understand the reason for being so. He is also capable of being under legal obligation in respect of whatever is declared obligatory. Again, according to Shariah a person is deemed to be under obligation and the person in question knows so much about it that he can be prevailed upon to carry out his injunction".

Thus the requirements are that a person should be under legal obligation. He should be capable of understanding the obligation and lastly should be capable of performing his obligation also. Further the obligation should be such which may be capable of carrying out. Impossible things would not create any liability. Again a thing which is beyond his power to perform would also entail no liability. Person should also be sensible, capable of knowing his obligation. He should know that provision exists by which he is made duty bound to do an act. Disobedience will make him liable for punishment.

As to the sources of the above noted rules, jurists infer from Qur'ãnic injunctions. Some of the injunctions are noted below:

In سورة نبی اسرائیل (sura Bani Israil) Allah says:

وَمَا كُنَّا مُعَذِّبِيْنَ حَتّٰى نَبْعَثَ رَسُوْلًا۔

(سورة الا سراء، آیة : ١٠)

"Nor would we punish until. We had sent a messenger (to give warning)". (17:15)

Again is Sura al-Qasas:

سورة القصص Allah says:

وَمَا كَانَ رَبُّكَ مُهْلِكَ الْقُرٰى حَتّٰى يَبْعَثَ فِى اُمِّهَا رَسُولًا يَّتْلُوْا عَلَيْهِمْ ايٰتِنَا (سورة القصص، آیة:٥٩)

"Nor was thy Lord the one of destroy a town until He had sent to its centre A messenger, rehearsing to them our signs". (28:59)

In سورة الانعام (Sura al-Inam) Allah says to his Prophet (peace be upon him):

قُلْ اَىُّ شَىْءٍ اَكْبَرُ شَهَادَةً قُلِ اللّٰهُ شَهِيْدٌ بَيْنِى وَبَيْنَكُمْ وَاُوحِىَ اِلَىَّ هٰذَا الْقُراٰنُ لِاُنْذِرَكُمْ بِهٖ وَمَنْ بَلَغَ۔ (سورة الانعام، آیة:١٩)

"Say: "What thing is most weighty in evidence"? Say: "Allah is witness between me and you; This Qur'ãn hath been revealed to me by inspiration, that I may warn you And all whom it reaches". (6:19)

In Sura al-Baqr سورة البقرة again Allah says:

لَا يُكَلِّفُ اللّٰهُ نَفْساً اِلَّا وُسْعَهَا لَهَا مَا كَسَبَتْ وَعَلَيْهَا مَااكْتَسَبَتْ۔

(سورة البقرة، آية:٢٨٦)

"On no soul Allah place a burden greater that it can bear .... Our Lord! lay not on us a burden greater than we have strength to bear". (2:286)

We have referred only few of the illustrated verses from which the jurists (Faqih) analogically deduce the above noted principles.

It is clear that under Shariah no act can be considered as a crime and no punishment can be awarded for it unless a provision to that effect exists. No doubt Shariah requires that these principles be applied to all crimes but the procedure varies with different crimes.

In Hudud cases there is no crime and can be awarded no punishment without a provision to this effect.

Similarly no crime and no punishment under cases involving Qisas and Diyat unless provision exists.

Under the third category covering cases of penal punishment (Tazeer), same principle is applied - no crime and no punishment without a provision. It is a fundamental principle of Shariah and in cases involving Tazeer, it cannot be overlooked. However, Shariah does not apply in the same manner in Tazeer as it does to cases involving Huddud, Qisas and Diyat. In Tazeer we find the application of the general rules have wider scope keeping in view the demands of public interest and penal character of such crimes. But this wider sphere of operation relates only to punishments to the exclusion of the penal crimes themselves. The wider sphere of operation under Tazeer is due to the fact that Shariah does not lay down such specific punishments as may be binding upon the judge to award as in the case of Hud and Qisas. Judge, in fact, is free to choose any punishment most fefitting and appropriate to the crime committed and the circumstance under which it is committed. He may reduce the punishment or award more severe punishment, all is included within his jurisdiction. This makes the operation sphere of Tazeer much wider in comparison of crimes involving Hud, Qisas and Diyat.

Another important principle governing punishment under Shariah is that if the 'public interest is in jeopardy, there is nothing inhibiting the combination of a penal punishment with a hud. On this there is an agreement among the jurists of all the four schools.

Imam Malik deems it fit to add penal punishment (تعزير) to Qisas for wilfully committing any offence involving qisas except death sentence. Argument in support given is that it is the right of the aggrieved person whereas penal punishment is a corrective measure and it is the right of the community as distinct from the right of an individual.

Imam Malik does deem it proper to combine Qisas and corrective measures in cases of wilful murder, since the latter would serve no purpose along with death sentence. But if the Qisas is annulled for some reason or other penal punishment (Tazeer تعزير) may be awarded. Imam Shai'i also allows the combination of corrective punishment with hud. Tazeer may be awarded in addition to Diyat also.

"How Shariah determines Tazeer (Penal Punishment)"

In Hedaya, explaining larceny and the punishment awarded therefor, 'Breach of Trust' has also been discussed. It has been made clear that breach of trust is not larceny because the requisites of larceny are absent in the former. Hence a person charged for the offence of 'Breach of trust' cannot be subjected so same degree of punishment as for larceny. In breach of trust amputation of limbs con not be awarded. It has been explained as:

'A 'Breach of Trust' (in Arabic language knows as khianit), by a trustee secreting any property committed to his charge, does not induce amputation; as a deposit is not in custody of the proprietor. In the same manner, the hand of a plunderer, or of one who snatches away anything, is not struck off, as the act of such is not theft, since those carry away the property openly, and not in a secret manner; and the Prophet (peace be upon him) has said:

"The hand of a plunderer, or a snatcher taking away property, or a 'Breach of Trust' is not to cut off".[1]

Secretly taking away another's property out of his possession without consent are the requirements for punishing a person for larceny. These elements are absent in breach of trust. Entrustment or deposit or giving dominion over the property voluntarily to another who accepts the thing or property so entrusted are the basic requirements which are not inconsonance with the elements of larceny. Hence Breach of trust is not covered under the same criterial which is applied or taken into consideration when awarding the punishment for larceny.

Turning to general principles governing the award of punishment for Tazeer cases, we can admit in the beginning that Shariah contains provisions by which Tazeer crimes are determined. We have already discussed in earlier paragraphs provisions under which at constituting penal crimes are declared as illegitimate. Similarly, Shariah has also laid down the principles for determining the punishment for offences covered under Tazeer.

I. Supra N.P.

Determination of Tazeer may be studied with reference to injunctions of Shariah.

"Chastisement"

Chastisement is wide in scope. It includes different methods or oral or corporal punishments. Injunctions as to these punishment are found in the Holy Qur'ãn as well as in Sunnah. Allah Ta'ala says:

وَالّٰتِی تَخَافُوْنَ نُشُوزَهُنَّ فَعِظُوْهُنَّ وَاهْجُروهُنَّ فِی الْمَضَاجِعِ وَاضْرِبُوْهُنَّ فَاِنْ اَطَعْنَكُمْ فَلَا تَبْغُوْا عَلَيْهِنَّ سَبِيْلًا اِنَّ اللّٰهَ كَانَ عَلِياً كَبِيْراً۔ (سورة النساء ، آية: ٣٤)

> "As to those women on whose part ye fear disloyalty and ill-conduct, Admonish them (first), (Next), refuse to share their beds, (And last) beat them (lightly); But if they return to obedience, seek not against them means (of annoyance): For Allah is Most High, Great (above you all). (4:34)

From this verse, jurists infer three different kinds of punishments:

1. Admonition or exhortation or warning;
2. Separation to beds; and
3. Corporal punishment or beating lightly.

Disobediene of women is an offence not covered under Qisas or Hud, thus jurists draw an inference that these punishment may be applied to all cases excluding Hud or Qisas.

It is argued that leaving women alone to their beds is a punishment confines to wives only but there are other kinds or separation or boycott too. The Holy Prophet (peace be upon him) ordered boycott of three of his companions who did not join him at the Battle of Batook.

Similarly, cases are available in which Hazrat Umar (R.A.) also followed the procedure of Prophet (peace be upon him) and ordered boycott of a Sahabee (صحابی).

However, boycott comes to an end if the women or man realises her or his mistake and repents thereupon.

Other Ahadith on chastisement may be noted below:

Prophet (peace be upon him) says:

"May Allah have mercy on the man who hangs his filth in a house at a place where it could be seen by the members of his family."

In another tradition, Prophet (peace be upon him) says:

"Do not raise stick against family".

Again Prophet (peace be upon him) says:

"Teach your offspring how to offer prayer till the age of seven and beat them if they give up saying prayer at the age of ten".

Again:

"The man who takes the penalty of a non-hud crime to the degree of hud is a transgressor".

From these Ahadith jurists infer two kinds of punishment:

1. Warning of punishment and intimidation;
2. Beating with a stick and scouraging.

The last of the above injuctions legitimize is couraging for crimes other than entailing huddud. A jurists holds that this injunction prescribes the higher limit of corporal punishment. However, there is difference of opinion on this point. Some jurists say that higher degree of corporal punishment is prescribed by the last injunction quoted above. Others are of the view that higher degree of corporal punishment is left to the discretion of the person in power.

It is, however, clear that Qur'ãn and Ahadith, no doubt, have presented limits in Tazeer also. A judge is to award penal punishment within limits, that is, exhortation, warning, boycotts, intimidation, scourging physical punishments, fine, and imprisonment.

The reason for imposing Tazeer is that men should not become habituated to the commissions of such acts. If permitted to perpetuate such acts may make them habitual and to be more atrocious in the criminal behaviour. Thus the design in the award of Tazeer is correction of the offencer. That is the reason that in Fatawa-e-Tamoor-Tasbee of Iman Sirukhsh, it is written that in Tazeer, or chastisement, nothing is fixed or determined, but the degree of it is left to the discretion of Qazi. However, this discretion for the purpose of correction, is not without limits. Qur'ãnic and Ahadith injuctions are certainly impose limitations on the power of Qazi.

Abdul Qadir Oudah Shaheed is of the view that Qur'ãnic injunctions and Ahadith lays down limits. To him, 'exhortation and warning constitute, by nature, punishments with a single limit and the limit of boycott as has already been indicated, is the repentance of the person boycotted'.[I]

I. Supra N. P.

Rebu-king a person is also a kind of punishment which we infer from sunnah of Prophet (peace be upon him).

Hazrat Abu Zar (R.A.) narrates that he approached Prophet (peace be upon him) and told him:

> "I reproached a man, wounding his pride by speaking ill of his mother's lineage".
>
> "Didst thou speak ill of his mother?" said Prophet (peace be upon him).
>
> "Thou still hast the vestiges of the days of Ignorance".

Thus, from the above Sunnah of Prophet (peace be upon him), jurist infer rebuke also as a penal punishment (Tazeer). About chastisement another governing tule has been laid in Fatawa-e-Shafee. 'It is said that there are four orders or degrees of chastisement; - first, the chastisement proper to the most noble of the noble - (or, in other words, princes, and men of learning), which consists merely in admonition, as if Qazi were to say to one of them, I understand that you have done thus, or thus", so as to make him ashamed'.

'Secondly, the chastisement proper to the noble, (namely commanders of armies, and chiefs of districts), which may be performed in two ways, either by admonition, (as above), or by 'Jirr', that is by dragging the offender to the door and exposing him to scorn.'

Thirdly, the chastisement proper to the middle order, (consisting of merchants and shop-keepers), which may be performed by 'Jirr', as above noted and also by imprisonment; and

Fourthly, the chastisement proper to the lowest order in the community, which may be performed by Jirr, or by, imprisonment, and also by blows.' (Hedaya)

This also shows that the award of Tazeer is discretionary with the judge, but jurisdiction is not without limitations. Classification under four heads makes it that the judge is to use the discretion within certain prescribed limits.

Another rule governing Tazeer is that the Sultan may punish by means of imposing fine upon the offender proportionate to the offence committed. This is the learned view of Imam Abu Yusuf (R.A.) but some jurists differs on this point. Further the amount of fine should be small and proportionate to the crimes. In other words fine should not be excessive not warranted by the crime.

In case where crime relates to the violation of the right of God, chastisement may be imposed by any person. It is with a view to remove evil. Prophet (peace be upon him) has authorised every person to remove evil with the hand. Prophet (peace be upon him).

> "Whoever among ye see the evil, let him remedy it with his own hands; but if he be unable so to do, let him forbid it with his tongue."

This type of chastisement is peculiar in nature. Generally on a complaint it is the responsibility of the magistrate to chastise an offender. But Islamic law permits that chastisement can be by a private individual even, if it relates to an evil effecting the rights of God.

Chastisement (Tazeer), is to be inflicted only when authorised by law or when the Imam consider it advisable to chatise the law breaker.

Chastisement is not inflicted in cases where a person calls the other as dog or ass. But the modern jurists are of the view that in the present day conditions, such words are held to be 'abuse' Circumstances and status of the person to whom addressed arc to be taken into consideration then a decision is to be taken whether chastisement can be inflicted or not.

Imprisonment and execution are other ways where the offencers are punished. The source of these types of punishments is the practice of the Prophet (peace be upon him).

It is reported that Prophet (peace be upon him) imprisoned a man found guilty of slander and hanged another named Abu Nat at the top of a mound.

Execution of offenders is inferred from the saying of Prophet (peace be upon him):

> "If you arrive at consensus on the choice of a man and someone comes to undermine your solidarity and seeks to disintegrate your party, then kill him."

Again,

> "If someone seeks to cause a split in the ranks of the ummah, then slay him with a sword."

It should be kept in mind that death sentence is intended for dangerous crimes.

As to the inflicting of Tazeer chastisement by stripping a person, there is a difference between different jurists as to the minimum or maximum limits. However, blows or stripes may be inflicted from the most lenient to the severiest degree depending upon the nature of crime serious or a misdemeanour.

If a person dies in consequences of inflicting chastisement in according to the order of the Magistrate, the latter is not liable because whatever is done for which the magistrate was authorised and it was all done in the enforcement of law.

Lastly, another principle governing Tazeer is that imprisonment may be added to scouraging or inflicting stripes depended again on the nature of the crime. It is lawful to unite imprisonment with blows.

"Crimes and Punishment in Tazeer Pre-Suppose Provisions in Shariah"

Abdul Qadir Oudah Shaheed makes his observations about crimes and punishment in cases of penal punishment (Tazeer) pre-suppose provisions in Shariah as follows:

> "It is clear that the Islamic law contains provisions pertaining to all the penal crimes and corresponding punishments which have been so subtly and comprehensively determined that the judge cannot award punishment for an act that has not been declared unlawful by the Shariah, nor can he pass such a sentence as has not been provided for; nor can be overstep the limits laid down for him."[1]

Often it is said that in case, of Tazeer, the Shariah judge is having authoritative and unlimited powers. It is wrong. It is only because of lack of understanding and ignorance of the Shariah.

In the earlier above noted discussions, we have seen that there are specific shariah injunction on different crimes and the judge performs his duties accordingly. He pronounces punishment corresponding to the injunctions relating to crime and punishment. If he finds that the injunction is applicable, then he may pass a sentence.

However, Shariah judge has power to choose any of the numerous penalties presented for the crime. For this purpose a judge is to take into consideration, the following:

1. Antecedent of the accused;

---

1. Supra N. P.

2. Extent of the effect of punishment on the offender,

3. Possible impact of the crime on the community.

Shariah also allows a judge to inflict any punishment he likes. He may also unite imprisonment with stripes. He may award lenient punishment as well as serve and harsh or rigorous punishment. He may admonish, threaten, warn to resist from doing criminal acts, fine or impose imprisonment. The judge also has the power to suspend the execution of any sentence passed.

Thus the assumption that the Shariah has no determined penal crimes in baseless. Judge in Tazeer case does not enjoy absolute powers. Shariah does not confer powers on the judge or upon anybody also to declare an act a crime which Shariah does not treat as one. Further the judge is not empowered to award a punishment for any crime which is not prescribed by the Shariah.

Criminal breach of trust is one such crime absolutely prohibited by Qur'ãnic and ahadith for which Tazeer is prescribed. As to quantum and type of penal punishment to be awarded, a judge is allowed to select according to the nature of crime and the gravity of the circumstances, it's effect on the offender from corrective point of view, its impact upon the community, and his Ijtihad that is on the basis of analogical reasoning.

CHAPTER 9

PART A

"APPEALS, REFERENCE AND REVISION : INDIAN CRIMINAL LAW"

Chapter XXIX, Criminal procedure Code guarantees the rights of appeal either against acquittal or conviction of accused persons involved in the commission of crimes. Section 372 laws down that no appeal, shall lie from any judgement or order of a criminal court except as provided for by this code or by any other law for the time being in force.

Section 374, clause (2) incorporates the right to appeal to the High Court by person convicted on a trial held by a sessions judge, or an additional sessions judge or on a trial held by any other court in which a sentence of imprisonment for more than seven years has been passed. Any other court includes the court of magistrate of the first class.

A person convicted on a trial held by a metropolitan magistrate or assistant sessions judge or magistrate of the first class, or of second class, or sentenced under section 325 or section 360 by any magistrate may appeal to the court of session.

Thus against a conviction by a first class magistrate an appeal lies to the sessions judge irrespective of the sentence imposed. Previous to the enforcement of new code, such appeals were made directly in the High Court if the sentence was one of the imprisonment for more than four years.

In cases where the accused person has pleaded guilty and has been convicted on such plea, there shall be no appeal except as to the extent or legality of the sentence.

Notwithstanding anything contained in section 374 there shall to be appeal by a convicted person where a court of session or metropolitan magistrate passes only a sentence of imprisonment for a term not exceeding three months or of fine not exceeding two hundred rupees, or of both such imprisonment and fine or where a magistrate of the first class passes only a sentence of fine not exceeding one hundred rupees.

Section 377 explains rule governing appeals by the state governing against in adequacy of sentences. It is not permissible to alter the conviction to an aggravated category of offence for which the accused was not convicted.

The central government or the state government may direct the public prosecutor file an appeal to the High Court in respect of cases investigated by the Delhi special police establishment against sentence on the basis of its in-adequacy.

State government may in any case of acquittal direct the public prosecutor to appeal to the High Court from an original or appellate order of acquittal passed by any court other than a High Court.

Section 378 provides for appeal by: (a) a state government; or (b) the central government; or (c) the complainant in a case instituted upon a complaint, provided that special leave from High Court under sub-section (4) has been obtained.

Right of appeal against acquittal rests primarily in the government for all cases. The complainant before filling the appeal has to obtain special leave from the High Court. As the leave may be granted or refused, therefore, it cannot be claimed by the complainant as a matter of right. Government's right to appeal is unrestricted against all cases of acquittal.

The responsibilities of a complainant in prosecuting the complaint after conviction ceases and that of the state begins. The corresponding right of this responsibility primarily vests in the state and not in the complainant for being heard in an appeal against conviction though there was no bar to a complainant also being heard if he was present in the court.

In an appeal under section 378, Criminal Procedure Code the High Court has full power to review the evidence upon which the order of acquittal is founded but the findings of the trial court which has the advantage of seeing the witness and hearing their evidence can be reversed only for very substantial and compelling reasons.[I]

Section 379 gives the right of appeal against conviction by High Court in certain cases. Where the acquittal order has been reversed and the accused convicted to imprisonment for life or to imprisonment for a term of ten years or more, he may appeal to the supreme court. Hearing of appeal in the supreme court would be in accordance to the provisions of Article 136 of the Constitution.

Section 380 gives special right of appeal in certain cases when more persons than one are convicted in one trial, and an appealable judgement or order has been passed in respect of any of such persons, all or any of the persons convicted at such trial shall have a right of appeal.

Every appeal shall be made:

1. In the form of a petition.
2. Petition will be in writing.

I. Surajpal Singh V. State, Air 1952 Sc. 52 : Ajmer Singh V. State of Punjab AIR, 1953 SC. 76.

3. Presented by the appellant or his pleader.

4. Every such petition shall (under the court to which it is presented otherwise directs) be accompanied by a copy of judgement or order appealed against. (Section 382 Criminal Procedure Code).

If the appellant is in jail, he may present his petition of appeal and the copies accompanying the same to the officer incharge of jail, who shall there upon forward such petition and copies to the proper appellate court. (Section 383, Criminal Procedure Code).

If, upon examining the petition of appeal and copy of the judgement received under section 382 or section 383, Criminal Procedure Code, Appellate court considers that there is no sufficient ground for interfering, it may dismiss the appeal summarily.

Supreme court in Mustak Hussein V. State of Bombay,[I] held that in case which, prima facie, raises no arguable issue, summary dismissal of the appeal may be justified but, in an arguable case, a summary rejection order must give some indication of the views of the High Court on the points raised.

The question as to whether the appellant has been given opportunity of being heard under section 344, Criminal Procedure Code, is not only an arguable point but also a substantial and important one.[II]

I. AIR, 1963 SC 282: 1953 SCr 809: 1953 Cr. Lj. 1127. Same view was followed in the later noted cases also: Shrekantiah Ramayya Munipalli V. State of Bombay, AIR 1955 Sc 287, 1963 Sc. 1996: (1964) 3 SCR 237; AIR 1968 SCR 88: 1968 SCD 675: 1968 Cr. Lj. 657; AIR 973 Sc 2187.

II. (1968), 2 SCR 88.

A jail appeal shall not be dismissed summarily without recording reasons and before the times for filing a regular appeal has expired.

Section 385,[II] Criminal Procedure Code, lays the rules governing the procedure to be followed by the appellate court for hearing appeals not dismissed summarily.

Section 386 deals with the powers of the appellate court. The court has the power to examine the record and hear both appellant or his pleader, if he appears, and the public prosecutor, if he appears, and if it considers that there is no sufficient ground for interfering in the judgement of the lower court may dismiss the appeal. In cases under section 377 where an appeal has been made by the state government against

---

I. Procedure for hearing appeals not dismissed summarily - (1) if the Appellate Court does not dismiss the appeal summarily, it shall cause notice of the time and place at which such appeal will be heard to be given -

i. to the appellant or his pleader;

ii. to such officer as the state government may appoint in this behalf;

iii. if the appeal is from a judgement of conviction in a case instituted upon complaint, to the complainant;

iv. if the appeal is under section 377, or section 378, complainant and accused, with a copy of grounds of appeal.

(2) The appeal court shall then sent for the record of the case, if such record is not already available in that court, and hear the parties:

Provides that if the appeal is only as to the extent or the legality of the sentence, the court may dispose of the appeal without sending for the record.

(3) Where the only ground for appeal from a conviction is the alleged severity of the sentence, the appellant shall not, except with the leave of the court, urge or be heard in support of any other ground.

sentence passed by the lower court or an appeal under section 378 against acquittal the appellate court has the power after perusal of record and hearing of appellant accused, if he appears, to dismiss the appeal if it considers that there is no sufficient ground for interfering.

The appellate court has also the power in an appeal from an order of acquittal to reverse such order and direct that :

(a) further inquiry be made, or

(b) the accused be re-tried, or

(c) committed for trial, as the case may be, or

(d) find him guilty and pass sentence on him according to law.

In cases of appeal from a conviction the appellate court has the power firstly to reverse the finding and sentence and acquit or discharge the accused, secondly, to order him to be re-tried by a court of competent jurisdiction subordinate to such appellate court, or thirdly committed for trial or fourthly, to alter the finding, maintaining the sentence, or fifthly, with or without altering the finding, alter the nature or the extent, or the nature and extent of the sentence but not so as to enhance the same.

1. reverse the finding and sentence and acquit or discharge the accused, or

2. order him to be re-tried by a court competent to try the offence, or

3. alter the finding maintainining the sentence, or

4. with or without altering the finding, alter the nature or the extent, or the nature and extent, of the sentence, so as to enhance or reduce the sentence.

In cases of an appeal from any other order, alter or reverse such order and make any amendment or any consequential or incidental order that may be just or proper subject to the limitations:

1. that the sentence shall not be enhanced unless the accused has an opportunity of showing cause against such enhancement;

2. that the appeal are court shall not inflict greater punishment for the offence which in its opinion the accused has committed, than might have been inflicted for that offence by the court passing the order or sentence under appeal.

The above discussion shows that the powers of the High Court in an appeal against the acquittal and against conviction are not different. High Court in such appeals may examine all questions of fast and law and reach its own conclusions on evidence provided it pays due regard to the fast that the matter had been before the session court and the sessions judge had the chance and opportunity of seeing the witnesses deposing the facts. High court in reversing the judgement of the sessions judge, must also pay due regard ti all the reasons given by the sessions judge and must dispel these reasons effectively before taking a contrary view of the matter.[1]

The rules contained in Chapter XXVII as to judgement of a criminal court of original jurisdiction shall apply, so far as may be practicable, to the judgement in appeal of court of session or chief judicial magistrate, unless the appellate court

---

I. AIR 1968 SC 1390 (Luxman Kallu Nikalji V. State of Maharashtra).

otherwise directs, the accused shall not be brought up, or required to attend to, to hear judgement delivered.[I]

Whenever a case is decided on appeal by the High Court under Chapter XXVIII, it shall certify its judgement or order to the court by which the finding, sentence or order appealed against was recorded or passed. When the judgement or order is communicated to the lower court having original jurisdiction shall there upon make such orders as are conformable to the judgement or order of the High Court, and if necessary, the record shall be amended in accordance there with.[II]

Section 389, Criminal Procedure Code lays down the procedure for suspension of sentence pending the appeal and release of appellant on bail. Similarly section 390 deals with the arrest of accused in cases of appeal from acquittal.

Under 391, Criminal Procedure Code, appellate court may take further evidence itself or direct to be taken by the magistrate or when the appellate court is a High Court, by a court of session or a magistrate. The court of session or magistrate, as the case may be, who has recorded the additional evidence on such direction shall certify such evidence to the appellate court, and thereupon such court shall proceed to dispose of the appeal. The accused or his pleader shall have the right to be present when the additional evidence is taken. The taking of evidence under this section shall be subject to the provisions of Chapter XXIII, as if it were an inquiry.

Where an appeal is heard by the High Court before a bench of judges and they differ with their opinions, in such a situation in accordance to section 392 Criminal Procedure Code, the appeal shall be laid before another judge of that court, and that judge, after such hearing as he thinks fit, shall

I. Section 387, Cr. P.C.

II. Section 388, Cr. P.C.

deliver his opinion and the judgement or order shall follow that opinion. Provided that if one of the judges constituting the bench, or where the appeal is laid before another under this section, that judge so requires, the appeal shall be re-heard and decided by a large bench of judges.

Judgement and orders passed by an appellate court upon and appeal shall be final. Exceptions are provided in sections 378, 384 (4) of Chapter XXX. Appellate court may hear and dispose of, on the merits:

a. an appeal against acquittal under section 378, arising out of the same case, or

b. an appeal for the enhancement of sentence under section 377, arising out of the same case.[I]

A new provision has been added that an appeal[II] against a conviction and sentence of imprisonment will not abate on death of the appellant if his near relatives, within thirty days of the death of appellant, apply to the appellate court for leave to continue the appeal and obtains it. Phrase near relatives means parents, spouse, lineal descendant, brother or sister.

"REFERENCE AND REVISION"

"Reference"

Power of making a reference in respect of any question of law involving validity of a statutory provision rests in sessions judges and in all metropolitan judges. Under section 395 Criminal Procedure Code, where any court is satisfied that a case pending before it:

I. Section 393 - Criminal Procedure Code.

II. Section 394 - Criminal Procedure Code.

1. Involves a question as to the validity of any Act, ordinance, or Regulation, or

2. of any provision contained in an Act, Ordinance, or Regulation, or the determination of which is necessary for the disposal of the case, and

3 the court is of opinion that such Act, Ordinance, Regulation or provision is invalid or inoperative, but has not been so declared by the High Court to which that court is subordinate or by the supreme court, the court shall state a case setting out its opinion and reasons therefor, and refer the same for the decision of the High Court.

Under clause (2) a court of session or a metropolitan magistrate may, if it or he thinks fit in any case pending before it or him to which the provisions of sub-section (1) do not apply, refer for the decision of High court any question of law arising in the hearing of such case.

When a question has been so referred the High Court shall pass such order thereon as it thinks fit, and shall cause a copy of such order to be sent to the court by which the reference was made, which shall dispose of the case conformably to the said order.[I]

"Revision"

Section 397, Criminal Procedure Code contains the revisional powers. Section is most important hence reproduced below:[II]

I. Section 396, Criminal Procedure Code.

II. Calling for records exercise of powers of revision:

1. The High court or any session Judge may call for and examine the record of any procedding before any inferior criminal court

Powers of revision at the district level have been given only to the court of session and not to the chief judicial magistrate. Where a case proceeds a police report, a private party has no locus standi. However, section 397 Criminal Procedure Code contains very wide provisions and court can take up the matter even suo motu.

As to revisional powers the sessions judge and the High Court have concurrent revisional jurisdictions. Generally the practice of all High Court do not entertain an application for revisions except on some special grounds unless a previous application has been made to the session judge. However, there is no legal bar to a party coming directly to the High Court without first moving the sessions judge. High

---

the record of any proceeding before any inferior criminal court situated within its or his local jurisdiction for purpose of satisfying itself or himself as to correctness, legality or propriety of any finding, sentence or order, recorded or passed, and as to the regularity of any proceedings of such inferior Court, and may, when calling for such record, direct that the execution of any sentence or order be suspended, and if the accused is in confinement, that he be released on bail or on his own bond pending the examination of the record.

Explanation - All magistrates, whether Executive or Judicial, and whether exercising original or appellate jurisdiction, shall be deemed to be inferior to the Sessions Judge for the purposes of this sub-section and of section 398.

2. The power of revision conferred by sub-section (1) shall not be exercised in relation to any interlocutory order passed in any appeal, inquiry, trial or other proceeding.

3. If an application under this section has been made by any person either to the High Court or to the Sessions Judge, no further application by the same person shall be entertained by the other of them.

Court of Kerala has been entertaining such petitions in the High Court directly.[1]

Section 397, Criminal Procedure Code is important as to revisional powers of the session judge and of High Court. Under this session either the sessions judge or the High Court may call for any record from court subordinate, situated within his or its local jurisdiction and examine the same with a view to satisfy himself or itself as to correctness, legality or propriety of the finding, sentence or order, recorded or passed and also as to the regularity of any proceedings of such inferior court. The sessions judge or the High Court may, or calling such record, direct that the execution of any sentence or order be suspended, and if the accused is in confinement, that he be released on bail or on his own bond pending the examination of that record.

Section explains that all magistrates, whether executive or judicial, and whether exercising original or appellate jurisdiction, shall be deemed to be inferior to the sessions judge for the purposes of section 397 and 398.

Clause (2) of section 397 is important. Before the enactment of this new Code, the High Court could interfere in revision in respect of interlocutory order also. But this clause makes it clear that the powers of revision conferred by sub-section (1) shall not be exercised in relation to any interlocutory order passed in any appeal, inquiry, trial or other proceedings. Fact is that the interference in revision against interlocutory orders was extensively abused and because of interference was the major factor in delaying the disposal of pending cases in the inferior courts. Once the sessions court or High Court interfered under its revisionary powers all proceedings in the lower court were to be stayed and caused

I. S. Narayanan V. Kannamma Bhargavi, AIR 1969. Ker. 126 (F.B._; ILR (1968) 2 Ker. 138: 1968 Ker. Lj. 601.

delay and sometime resulted in injustice also. This facility was availed of mostly by the rich men, industrialist, corrupt officials, and the like who were able to delay disposal of cases against them almost indefinitely. During such pendency sometime witnesses died or lost interest in the case and sometimes even the prosecution lost its keeness. Such revision petitions against interlocutory orders, therefore, not only delayed justice but sometimes defeated it. Interlocutory orders have, therefore, been specifically excluded in section 397 of the new Criminal Procedure Code.

Clause (3) of section 397, Criminal Procedure Code is also significant. It bars the same party to file a second revision. If a revision petition under this section has been made by any person either to the High Court or to the sessions judge, no further application by same person shall be entertained by the other of them. Thus where the new code gives the choice of forum for filing a revision petition to a party, at the same time, it bans the same party from filing a second revision petition to the other forum after his application is dismissed by one forum. However, where an application has been withdrawn from the sessions judge court, a fresh application before the high court is maintainable.

The revisional powers of the High Court and the sessions judge have been enumerated in sections 397 to 402 Criminal Procedure Code. These sections are to be read together. Section 398 deals with power to order inquiry after examining any record called for under section 397 Criminal Procedure Code. Sections 399, 400 and 401 authorize the sessions judge, additional sessions judge and the High Court with powers of revision that is to examine the accuracy, correctness and legality of any judgement or order of the inferior court and pass such orders as may deem fit and proper.

In fact, it is a discretionary power which has to be exercised in aid of justice.

In Amar Chand's[I] case High Court observed that the jurisdiction under section 401, Criminal Procedure Code is to be exercised only in exceptional cases where there is a glaring defect in the procedure or there is a manifest error on point of law and there has been flagrant miscarriage of justice. Power of revision conferred either upon the sessions judge or the High Court, indeed, with an object to set right grave injustice. These extra-ordinary discretionary powers vested in the susperior courts is to see that the justice is done in accordance with the recognised rules of criminal jurisprudence, and the subordinate courts have not exceeded their jurisdiction or abused the power conferred on them by law.

In Akalu Akhir,[II] it was held that section 397 to 401 Criminal Procedure Code though confers wide ranging discretionary revision powers in the superior court but these sections do not contemplate any interference, with the conclusions of facts of the inferior courts in the absence of serious legal infirmity and failure of justice.

The court vested with powers of revision is not empowered to pass order which may prejudice the interest of the accused or other person unless he has had an opportunity of being heard either personally or by pleader in his own defence.[III]

Similarly nothing shall be deemed to authorise a High Court to convert finding of acquittal into one of conviction.[IV]

I. Amarchand V. Shanti Bose, AIR 1973 SC. 799 : 1973 Cr. Lj. 577.

II. Akalu Ahir V. Ramdeoram, AIR 1973 Sc. 2145.

III. Clause (2) Section 401, Criminal Procedure Code.

IV. Clause (3) Section 401, Criminal Procedure Code.

Further where an appeal lies under the Criminal Procedure Code and no appeal is brought, no proceeding by way of revision shall be entertained at the instance of the party who could have appealed.[I]

Where under this code an appeal lies thereto but an application for revision has been made to the High Court by any person and the High Court is satisfied that such application was made under the erroneous belief that no appeal lies thereto and that it is necessary in the interest of justice so do to, the High Court may treat the application for revision as a petition of appeal and deal with the same accordingly.[II]

When the revisional powers of the High Court against an order of acquittal has been invoked by a private party under section 401, such powers are not to be lightly exercised. It is no ground to reject it because the state government was having power of appeal but did not prefer it. In K. C. Reddy's[I] Case supreme court made observations that the High Court is certainly entitled in revision to set aside the order of acquittal even at the instance of private parties, though the state may not have thought fit to appeal, but it was emphasised that this jurisdiction should be exercised only in exceptional cases when there is some flaring defect in the procedure or there is a manifest error on a point of law and consequently there has been I a flagrant miscarring of justice. The power being discretionary, it has to be exercised judiciously and not arbitrarily.

Over and above these wide powers of revision vested in the High Court, where no remedy is available under any

---

I. Clause (4) Section 401, Criminal Procedure Code.

II. Clause (5) Section 401, Criminal Procedure Code.

III. K.C. Reddy V. State of Andhra Pradesh, AIR 1962 SC. 1788.

provision of the Code, in order to prevent miscarriage of justice or abuse of process, High Court can invoke inherent jurisdiction under section 482 Criminal Procedure Code.

Further, if a criminal court acts;

a. without jurisdiction or

b. in excess of jurisdiction, or

c. fails to exercise the jurisdiction vested in it, or

d. commits an illegality or irregularity, or

e. acts in breach of rules of natural justice.

High Court can interfere under Article 227 of the Indian Constitution.

PART B

"APPEAL, REVISION, REFERENCE : ISLAMIC CRIMINAL LAW"

In this section we will study the law relating to appeal, revision, and reference.

Appeal and Revision

Concept of appeal is not alien to Islamic law. Sufian Suri says:

عن الثوری قال: اذا قضی القاضی بخلاف کتاب الله او سنة نبی الـلـه ، او شئ مجتمع علیه فان القاضی بعده عرده، فان کان شیًا یرای الناس لم یرده ویحمل ذلك ما تحمل۔
(مصنف عبدالرزاق، جلد ھشتم، ص ۳۰۲)

"That when a Qazi gives a judgement contrary to Qur'ãn or Sunnah of Prophet (peace be upon him), or against any order upon which there is consensus, then the later Qazi may quash such a judgement. But if it relates to public opinion or Ijtihad, then it should not be rejected. Let the person who has made Ijtihad bear the responsibility".

From this observation of Hazrat Sufian Suri (سفیان ثوریؒ) it is clear that the judgement or order of a subordinate or the same court may be quashed if it is inconsistent with:

1. Book of Allah - Holy Qur'ãn; کتاب اللـه.
2. Sunnah - Rasool - Allah; سنت رسول اللـه.
3. Ijma - اجماع.

Any other order upon which community (قوم) has reached to a consensus (اجماع.) by means of assembly decision or a decision by political authority or on any controversial or Ijtilihadi matter decided by an Adil Ruler (عادل حاکم), it becomes enforceable and binding on all. Abut if it is such a controversial and Ijtihadi matter in which Qazi has been left to use his discretion and he decides such an issue, in such a case there will be no appeal or revision.

Hazrat Imam Bukhari (R.A.) says:

اذا قضی الخاکم بجور او خلاف اهل العلیم فهورد.
(امام بخاری صحیح بخاری: کتاب الاحکام، ص ١٠٦٦)

"If any hakim (حاکم) decides a case arbitrarilly or cruelly or against (اجماع.) (consensus) of learned scholars, then such a decision may be reversed."

These above noted observations of Imam Bukhari and Sufian Suri make it clear that against cruel and arbitrary decisions or orders, or orders contrary to Qur'ãn, Ahadith and Ijma, of the judges there can be an appeal and such decision may be reviewed, changed and reversed.

The question is: What is the basic source from which these learned scholars have inferred this principle of appeal and review?

The answer lies in a Hadith. It has been quoted that "in a certain case parties approached Prophet (peace be upon him) and complained against the judgement of Hazrat Ali bin Abi-Talib, who was then judge in Yemen appointed by Prophet himself. Then Prophet (peace be upon him) heard the statements of both the parties and he affirmed the judgement."[1]

I. Makur, M.S., al-Madkhal-l;i-al-Fiqh al-islami, Cairo, 1960, p. 322.

This hadith shows that if appeal had no place in Shariah than Prophet (peace be upon him) should had rejected the complaint out rightly in the very beginning. Instead he heard both the parties and then confirmed the judgement. It means that in Islam appeal is permitted. Any aggrieved person may approach to the higher authority in appeal and that higher authority may review the case.

Hazrat Umar (R.A.), the second Caliph, in his letters to the governors and judges of the provinces, laid down some of the most important basic rules of judicial procedure. In his letter to Hazrat Abu Musa al-Ash'ari, he instructed him in the following words:

"Let not a judgement in a case which you have given, but which you reviewed again in your conscience, and were guided in it to a more sound judgement, be a hinderance to you from returning to the decision which you know is right, for what is right can never be annulled by anything."[II]

However, the answer is not so easy. Two conflicting views of jurists are there. One uphold, the appellate review as valid according to Islamic law, the other denies the right of appeal. In other words the second group of jurists are of the view that there is no provision for appeal or review under the Islamic law.

Professor Dr. Mohammad Hashim Kamali in his article, 'Appellate Review and Judicial Independence in Islamic Law',[III] has pointed that appellate review has two opposing responses, one which denies the validity of such review and other upholds it. He discusses both the points of views in his article in quite a detail. To quote him:

II. Waki, M.B.K.B.H., Akhbar al-Qudar, Cairo, 1947, pp. 283-284.

III. Prof. Kamali, is Professor, at Kulliyyah of Laws, International Islamic

> "Many observers have drawn the conclusion that the Shariah does not vest any superior jurisdiction with the authority to review the decisions of the Qazi (Judge). This view calls in support historical evidence to the effect that no court of appeal came into being during the life time of Prophet Muhammad (peace be upon him), nor during the ensuring period of the pious Caliphs (Khulafa-e-Rashidun c. 621-665 A.D.)."

He further quotes in support of the argument A.A. Fazee, commenting concerning Qazi that "His judgement was decisive, there being ordinarily to appeal from it".[I]

He refers another observer with regard to penal sentences in which "there is no appeal (Murafa'ah) against the sentence of a qazi. The punishment is executed without delay or resistance............"[II]

Prof. Kamali also refers in the article the observations of Al-Nubhani who "is categorical in stating that Islamic law makes no provision either for appellate jurisdictions (mahakim Isti'naf) or cassation court (mahakim tamyiz). For adjudication of disputes before the court is rendered in a single himself no another Qazi has the authority to reverse it. The reason for this is the consensus of companions. The first Caliph Hazrat Abu Bakr, his successor Hazrat 'Umar bin-al Khattab, the fourth Caliph Hazrat Ali, and other companions have all adjudicated cases on the basis of their

---

University, P.J. Selangor, Malaysia (He read this article in Kulliyyah of Law lectures programme, organised by the Kulliyyah of Laws, IIU). Published in Islamic Studies Quarterly Journal, International Islamic University, Islamabad, Pakistan.

I. A.A. Fazee, Outlines of Muhammadan Law, New Delhi: Oxford University Press, 1974, p. 328.

II. Muhammad Iqbal Siddiqni, The Penal Law of Islam, Lahore, p. 183.

personal reasoning (Ijtihad). They have disagreed with each other, but such disagreements have on no occasion affected the validity of their judicial decisions. None of the leading companions has reversed the judgement of a fellow companion on grounds of a mere difference of opinion and personal judgement."

Prof Kamali also refers learned views of jurists in favour, upholding the validity of appellate review under Islamic law. He observes that "The foregoing needs, however, to be qualified in that it is valid in so far as the clear injunctions (nusus- نصوص) of the Qur'ãn and Sunnah are concerned. Foe only in such cases where the Qazi merely declares the existing law and ascertain its application to a particular case."

He refers Fathi 'Uthman who observes that those who maintain Islamic prescribes appellate review have themselves acknowledged the circumstances in which judicial decisions are liable to reversal under Islamic law."[I]

According to another observer the argument that in "Islam there is no provision for appeal is simply fallacious. To remove error that leads to evil and injustice is one of the fundamental teachings of Islam and a foremost function of its administration of justice."[II]

We have noted two different views referred in the article. But views of jurists supporting denial of appellate review do not seem to be accurate. The author has already cited a case which was submitted before Prophet (peace be upon him) for review in the earlier pages which he heard and decided. This is an authentic proof that appeal is permissible under the Islamic law. It is not so

---

I. Fathi 'Uthman, Al-Fikr al-Qanuni al-Islami: Bayn Usul al-Shariah wa Turath al-Fiqh, Cairo: Maktabah Wahbah, n.d., p. 314.

II. Ghulam Murtaza Azad, Judicial System of Islam, Islamabad: Islamic Research Council, 1987, p. 100.

than Prophet (peace be upon him) should had refused the hearing of complaint of Yemeni Parties. Though the judgement of Hazrat Ali bin Abi Talib was confirmed by the Prophet (peace be upon him) but it only when both parties were given proper opportunities to explain their view points. It also makes it clear, that the argument that during Prophet (peace be upon him) time no appellate courts were existing is false. Tradition of the Prophet (peace be upon him) is an ample proof that there could had been appeal also against the judgement of the Qazi.

It is also to be noted that the denial that no appellate court were existing during Khulafa-e-Rashideen (Four Caliphs) is also baseless. Hazrat Umar's (R.A.) instructions to Hazrat Abu Musal al-Ash'ari, quoted earlier, is a proof. During their period also appeals against the decisions were allowed. No doubt, for a sound judicial judgement, it is necessary that if any error left in judgement that must be remedied. This is the principle of natural justice. Islam is the strongest advocate for the administration of justice.

In original books of Muhammadan Law, for appeal word 'Marafi'at' was used. This word not only included appeal but review also. In Sharh-i-Viqaya,[I] discussion on Marafi'at, refers the observation of certain jurists that 'Qazi of a higher court can revise the decision of a lower court in a point of law also'. In the 'Administration of justice on Muslim Law', Dr. Muhammadullah has also made similar observations.[I]

Some jurists claim that the court of Wali al-Mazalim had appellate jurisdiction, and had exactly the same jurisdiction as that of the supreme court in the modern time. However, its power were restricted. It was to execute the judgements expeditiously. It also had original jurisdictions in some matters. However, anyone

---

I. Sharh-i-Viqaya, Chapter III, Discussion on Marafi'at.

well learned in Islamic jurisprudence cannot deny that Muslim jurists have recognised appeal in principle.

Muslim monarchs, especially the Mughal Emperors established regular courts of appeal and revision. The Lubbat-i-Tawarihk-i-Hind gives the following description:

"But if the offenders were discovered, the local authorities used generally to them on the spot where the offences had been committed according to law and in concurrence with the officers; and if any individual dissatisfied with the decision passed on his case, appealed to the governor or the Diwan or to the Qazi of the Subah, the matter was reviewed and the judgement awarded with care........ If the parties were not satisfied even with the these decision they appealed to the Chief Diwan or to the Chief Qazi on matters of law."[II]

The above statement shows the during Muslim Ruler's period there existed courts of different grades for appeal and revision.

In Saudi Arabia a royal writ[II] was issued in 1932 declaring that if either of the two parties to litigation felt aggrieved by a decision below, the party had the right to appeal against this decision. In cases of dismissal by the lower court, an appeal was permitted if the aggrieved party so desired.[I] In 1971, the Ministry of Justice made it known that anyone aggrieved with the decision of the lower court may go in appeal.[II] The right of appeal in criminal case judgement has been recognized by the judges fully.[III]

Review in the Shariah Court, in Saudi Arabia may be classified into:

I. Dr. Muhammadullah : "Administration of Justice in Muslim Law", p. 67.

II. H.M. Elliot: "History of India", Vol. VII, pp. 172-178.

III. Royal WIll - No. 39 of 21/1/1351 (1932).

1. Automatic; and

2. Ordinary review.

The automatic review lies in cases involving death sentence, mutilation, or nay punishment imposed upon a juvenile. It is applied in breach of trust cases committed by trustee of endowment (Waqf), or principal of Bait al-Mal (بيت المال), and in decisions concerning real estate, and decision given by default.

Appeal to grand Shariah court from the decision of a magistrates court comes under this category, since the latter court, used to commit some of its criminal decisions to the former for revision before 1957, even without request from either party.

The original court of jurisdiction must automatically refer any decision which comes under this category to the appropriate appellate court, which must in turn review it.

The ordinary review is that which does not arise without demand from the party who has the right to appeal. Thus when, dealing with this question of how to appeal against a conviction, reference will be made only to ordinary review.

In appeal, generally speaking, judgement of lower court may only be reversed when it contradicts the Qur'ãn, the Sunnah, or consensus (Ijma), or when it is against what the trial judge believes to be a proper judgement, in cases where determination of the sentence is left to the judge himself. The Mufti and the President of the judiciary of Najd, having acted as an appellate authority, maintained that the decision of the trial judge ended the case, that the grounds just mentioned were the only valid grounds for reversal.

I. Maj., P. 29, L., of P.J. to Vic. No. 3185 of 125/11/1357 (1938).

II. D.M.J., C. No. 98/1/T of 1391 (1971).

III. Al-Mansur V. B. Masud, C.C. (R), D. No. 116/2 of 1389 (1969).

Other grounds which may be considered are:

1. Violation of rules regarding evidence,
2. The non-observance of the rules concerning trial.
3. Court reaching on a wrong judgement.
4. Excess of jurisdiction with regard to the type of offence, and
5. Newly discovered evidence, or evidence which is not produced before the trial court.
6. In tazeer, no change to be made by the appellate, court, but if the Tazeer awarded on the basis of a wrong presumption, can be changed.

These are some of the grounds which the appellate court may take into consideration and may reverse the order or judgement of the lower courts in Saudi Arabia.

In Pakistan also appeal against the judgement of lower court is recognized as a matter of right of the aggrieved party.

In Malaysia criminal appeal is permitted against the judgment of the lower courts.

Section 36, lays down detailed procedure for appeal against the judgement of the lower courts. Clause (1) of section 36 says:

> "Any person who is dissatisfied with any judgement, sentence, or order pronounced by a Shairah subordinate court in any criminal proceedings under this Enactment[1] to which he is a party may prefer an appeal to Shariah High Court against the judgement, sentence, or order in respect of any error in law or in fact or on the ground of alleged severity or alleged inadequacy of any sentence, by filling or lodging a notice of appeal with the court

appealed from, addressed to the Shariah High Court, and paying the prescribed fee."

The notice of appeal shall be filed or lodged within fourteen days from the date on which the judgement, sentence or order was passed or made, unless on application to the Shariah High Court the period of fourteen days is extended.

Thus the grounds, envisaged for appeal in the section may be divided:

1. Error in law or fact, and

2. Alleged severity or alleged leniency or inadequacy of any sentence.

On these grounds appeal from lower court the High may be made. Then time limitation within which the appeal is to be filed and the detail procedure to be followed in that connection has been laid down in the section 36.

At the hearing of an appeal the Shariah High Court may, if it considers that there are no sufficient grounds from interfering with the decision, sentence, or order of the court appealed against, dismiss the appeal.

Appellate Shariah High Court is also empowered that it may in an appeal against an order of acquittal, reverse the order and direct that further inquiry be made or that the accused be retried, or find him guilty and pass sentence on him according to law.

In an appeal against conviction or in an appeal against sentence the court may reverse the judgement and acquit or discharge the accused, or order him to be retried, or alter the

---

I. Administration of Islamic Religious Affairs Enactments 1986, Malaysia.

decision, confirm the sentence or, with or without altering the decision, reduce or enhance the sentence or alter the nature of the sentence.

In an appeal against any other order, the court may alter or reverse the order (Section 44).

Shariah High Court is also empowered that in dealing with any appeal, the Shariah High Court, if it thinks that further evidence is necessary, may either take such evidence itself or direct it to be taken by the court appealed from.

Where further evidence is taken by the court appealed from, it shall certify such evidence to the Shariah High Court which, as soon as possible thereafter, shall proceed to dispose of the appeal.

Unless the Shariah High Court otherwise directs, the accused or his counsel shall be present when the further evidence is taken (Section 45).

On the termination of the hearing of the appeal, the Shariah High Court shall, either at once or on some future date, which shall either be fixed for the purpose or of which notice shall be given to the parties deliver judgement in open court (Section 46).

Section 48 further gives a chance to the aggrieved to go in appeal second time against the judgement of Shariah High Court. Appeal. Maylie in two ways:

1. Against the judgement of Shariah High Court under its' original jurisdiction, and

2. Against judgement after hearing an appeal against the judgement, sentence or order passed or made by the subordinate Shariah Court.

An appeal can be made by the accused or by the public prosecutor, as the case may bc, to the Shariah High Court. It means both the parties are allowed to go in appeal if either of them feel aggrieved. The decision of the appellate court will be inconformity with Shariah or Islamic law.

Now after examining the provisions relating to appeal in Saudi Arabia and Malaysia, it is clear that not only in theory the law for appeal exists but in practice it is being implemented. In fact, Islamic concept of justice is realised only when confidence among the masses about the performance of judiciary is created and that is possible when for all errors, there are remedies available.

Reference

The constitution of Shariah Courts as we can study from the record of History, is that it has always been composed of at least two judicial officers, that is, Qazi and Mufti. Sometime we find more than two, that is, ulema are also included in. Thus the Qazi is assisted by Mufti, learned in Islamic law, and by a Alim (عالم) also. Islamic law also permits to appoint two Qazi to sit together in the court. In such circumstance one of them cannot decide the case. Both conjointly are to take a decision.

The procedure is that Qazi is to consult Mufti on the point of law. But if he disagrees with the opinion of the Mufti, he must refer the matter either to the higher court for decision, or to a full court consisting of the Qazi, Mufti, the Muhtasib and a scholar learned in law. After discussion their opinion is binding in law. This shows that under Islamic law provision for reference exists.

Similarly when two Qazis are sitting together in the court and there is a difference of opinion among them, the matter may be referred to another learned scholar or jurists or may be referred to the higher authority and thus judgement on receiving the opinion may be given.

Mr. Waheed Hussain,[I] in his book quoted a letter of the committed of circuit to the council at Fort William dated 15th August, 1972, which clearly explain how the Shariah court were applying the law relating to reference. The letter reads as:

"The Cazee is assisted by the Mufti and Muhtassib in this court. After hearing the Parties and evidence, the Mufti writes the Fatwa, or the law applicable to the case in question, and the Cazee pronounces judgement accordingly. If either the Cazee or Muhtasib disapproves the Fatwa, the case is referred to the Nazim who summons the Ijlas or general assembly, consisting of the Cazee, Mufti, Mubtasib, the Darogha of the Adawlat, the Moulvis and all learned in the law, to meet and decide upon it. Their decision is final."

It is commented upon this letter that it throws a flood light on the mode of reference and holding a full court.

In Sharh-i-Viqaya[II] it has been reported that when a complicated point of law arises the Qazi can refer it to another Qazi for his opinion. But if the Qazi differs from the opinion of the second Qazi, or if the opinion of the latter conflicts with a well-known juristic principle, the matter may be referred to a third Qazi for his opinion.

In a case where Qazi feels difficulty in forming an opinion because of complications involved in the issues, two ways are open for him. First he should take decision on his own. But it will be better that he refers the matter to the jurists (فهقاء) and consult them. Secondly, if there is a difference of opinion among jurists (فهقاء) of that time, then he should form his own opinion which may be more nearer to the truth and justice. Even his opinion is in conflict with the jurists (فهقاء) of that time, he may do so,

---

I. Administration of Justice during the Muslim Rule in India, p. 76.

II. Vol. III, Section on Marafi'at

and may give judgement accordingly. But he should not do it hurriedly. If he gives the judgement without due consideration, it would not be valid and Allah would not be pleased with it. (ادب قاضی).

To conclude, the above discussion makes it clear that in Islam, law exists relating to appeal, revision and reference. Those who deny, their approach is not correct.

CHAPTER 10

PART A

"RECAPITULATION"

The present study if analysed with little sense of justice bring one to the conclusion that the general impression of the legal experts educated in western environment about the criminal law of Islam that it is not in tune with the modern conditions and does not come up to the standard of modern laws is based on sheer ignorance. In fact, this notion of western educated people is far from being true. Criminal law of Islam has been abandoned and thrown into oblivion without any reason. The modern curriculum of academic institutions include 'Personal Law' of Islam only and criminal law of Islam has been made totally obsolescent. This is the reason why the modern scholars of law are absolutely ignorant of the provisions relating to the criminal law of Islam. This study, though confined to a minor part of criminal law has shown the fallacy of the notion. Each and every principle and doctrine of the Islamic law referred in the study gives the lie to it. The view declaring the Islamic criminal law as incompatible with the demands of the Islamic law referred in the study gives the lie to it. The view declaring the Islamic criminal law as incompatible with the demands of modern age is unwarranted and untenable, as it is not the result of academic research or logical reasoning.

Criminal breach of trust in Islamic criminal law is different from human laws or man made laws. The provisions and rules contained therein are universal and flexible which could be applicable to all the problems arising in every age, in every phase of social development and in ever changing conditions of the society and could fulfil the multifavious social needs at all time to come. It is immutable, everlasting and perfect, characterized by permanence.

Comparing the Islamic Criminal Law with Indian Criminal law in relation to breach of trust, the fundamental difference between the two is that the former is Divine Revealed Law and the later in man-made law. In fact, there is no comparison between the two. Islamic law has been made by the Creator of Universe Himself and reflects the Maker's perfection, glory and the light of omniscience which covers the past and the future. It is based on perfection, sublimity and permanence. However, in the light of the present study, the researcher has inferred some resemblances and differences between the two which are analysed below.

The basic principle which is common between two laws is that 'no commission or omission of an act would be grant amount to crime unless a provision exists either prohibiting or commanding it and also prescribing punishment for it'. Under Indian Penal Code Criminal breach of trust has been defined and explained in section 405. Section 406 prescribes the punishment for breach of trust cases. The remaining section 407 to 409 deal with other aspects related to the breach of trust.

Similarly under Shariah Qur'ãnic Injuctions and Sunnah of Prophet (peace be upon him) explain the nature of trust and breach thereof. In the light of Qur'ãnic injuctions and sunnah, later Islamic law scholars (Faqih) developed and propounded definitions of breach of trust and also rules governing thereto. Explanation of breach of trust by the jurists is based on very sound principles and rules prepared relating thereto are quite exhaustive.

As to punishment, the Qur'ãnic injunctions and sunnah have restricted the powers conferred upon Qazi (Judge). His jurisdictions are ineffective beyond the limits laid therein.

However, the difference lies between the two that the provisions of Shariah or Islamic law have assumed immutable and everlasting character, not withstanding their diversity, it has emanated from one source that is divine revelation. No change of ruler or government makes any difference in them. These provisions are rather linked with religion and faith which do not admit of any change. Believers must exploit every method and system to enforce it. On the other hand Indian Law can be subjected to successive modifications. The change of government may be an adequate justification for the amendment of laws.

Under Indian Law a trust is a relationship of a fiduciary character. Such relationship is with respect to property, not one involving merely personal obligations. It involves the existence of equitable obligations imposed upon the holder of the title to the property to deal with it for the benefit of another and such obligations arise out of confidence reposed in and accepted by the owner, or declared and accepted by him, as a result of a manifestation of an intention to create the relationship.

Any act or neglect on the part of a trustee which is not authorised or excused by the terms of the trust instrument or by law is treated as breach of trust.

It requires entrustment of property or dominion over property to any person, and such entrustment must be in trust. Such person should misappropriate or convert to his own use such a property or using or disposing of that property, or wilfully offering any other person so to do in violation of any direction of law prescribing the mode in which such trust is to be discharged or of any legal contract, express or implied, which he has made touching the discharge of such trust. The important element is that such misappropriation or user or disposal must be dishonest. There is no criminal breach of trust if dishonest intention to misappropriate or converts is not proved. It is in fact this element of mental condition of fraudulent misappropriation or conversion that distinguishes an act of embezzlement which is a civil wrong or tort, from the offence of criminal breach of trust. Every breach of trust in the absence of menswear, that is, dishonest intention cannot legally justify a criminal prosecution.

As to scope the term of the section explaining breach of trust are very wide. Section 405, Indian Penal Code applies in cases where a person is in any manner entrusted with property or dominion over property. Except in cases where the trust is the result of a contract, it is not required that it should be in furtherance of any lawful object. However, where a trust is created by a contract, all the valid requisites be satisfied. Proposal and acceptance, age of majority, sound mind, and no compulsion or fraud in creating trust should be fulfilled.

Further the entrustment may be in any manner, not necessarily what implies a trust to be in the sense of a law relating to trust. The accused may get dominion over the property in any manner. What is contemplated by the section is that the person charged for criminal breach of trust should receive the property.

Criminal breach of trust involves a civil wrong, the relief available to the complainant is that he may seek his redress for damages in the civil court, but criminal prosecution is not barred even if the amount involved in the breach of trust is very small. However, if a civil case is pending on the same issue in a civil court, thee cannot be a criminal prosecution.

Under Islamic law the concept of trust and conditions violations trust are very wide. It's nature is spiritual, civil as well as penal. The redness available may be divine chastisement, civil compensation or a criminal liability. Qur'ãnic injunctions and Ahadith do not make any distinction between civil and criminal breach of trust. Unlike Indian law, Islamic law defining breach of trust, do not demarcate a line between civil and criminal aspect.

The same definition and governing rules thereto may cover both aspects. The whole edifice of the nature of trust and breach of trust may be summed up as:

Trust results from Divine and spiritual covenant between God and human beings. It may result from treaties and covenants entered into either during peace or war with enemies or enemy countries. Further trust may be created by the conduct of human beings either by covenant or without covenants. The last part is being compared with Indian Law.

As to the requisites of a trust there is no much difference between the two laws. A person empowers another to keep his property, the proprietor of thing is termed as Modee (مودع) the depositor, the person so empowered, the Mode (مستودع) or trustee, the property so left with another for the purpose of keeping it, is named widdeeyat (ودیعت). Literally, the thing in question is left with the trustee.

Reposing confidence, fiduciary relationship, entrustment, giving dominion over the property, proposal, and acceptance, express or implied (by implication - بدلالت), creating equitable obligations are essential ingredients of Islamic law as well as Indian Law.

Like Indian Law, under Islamic Law also, for breach of trust, there must be mensrea, a dishonest intention with which a person misappropriates or converts the property. The trustee (مستودع) should use or dispose of entrusted property or allows any person so to do involution of any Qur'ãnic commandment or Ahadith directing the manner in which such trust is to be executed or discharged. Violation may also be in regard to any lawfully entered contract which may be express or implied laying down conditions of discharge of such a trust. But such misappriation, user or disposal either by himself or allowing some other person so to do must be with criminal design. Islamic law does not determine any liability for any act or omission unless done or omitted with criminal intention. So far there is no difference between the two systems.

However, difference lies between the manner entrusted the property to the trustee. Indian law envisages any manner of entrustment whether moral of immoral. A person would be liable for breach of trust even in conditions where he obtained the possession illegally. But under the Islamic law, the manner of entrustment must be moral. Immorality has no place under the Islamic law. Manner of entrustment must be inconsonance with Shariah. Morality, religion and law are not separate under Islamic law.

As to trust created by contract both the laws have the same resembling governing rules except a difference as to the age of majority. Under the Islamic law, it is a condition that the person, who deliveres the thing to be kept, and the person, who accepts it, be of sound mind and capable of contracting (mummeyyiz). Unlike Indian law it is not a condition that they should be of full age. Under Islamic law an infant who is not capable of contracting to deliver a thing for safe keeping, or to accept a thing delivered for safe-keeping is not competent to contract. But a delivery for safe keeping, and the acceptance of a thing delivered for safe-keeping by an infant, who is capable of contracting and freed from control (me'zun) is good. A person is competent to contract, though young if capable to understand selling and buying, that is, by sale rights of ownership are lost and that by purchase they are acquired and able to distinguish between small deceit and excessive deceit, like being deceived five in ten.

Under Indian law the combination of proposal and acceptance characteries the notion of the trust. But under Islamic law sometime trust is inferred by implication (غاصب) only and more proposal is enough to create the trust.

For example where the owner of the property says to the usurper example where the owner of the property says to the usurper (بدلالت), 'I entrust thing usurped as trust.' Usurper is immuned from the liability as Usurper of the thing though he may not have accepted the proposal. Another example may be where a person sitting in a gathering leaves behind his property at the place of sitting, all those present become trustees though there is neither proposal nor an acceptance. Such a trust is created by implication under the Islamic law. Whereas under Indian law trust is an obligation annexed to the ownership of property, and arising out of a confidence reposed in and accepted by the owner, or declared and accepted by him, for the benefit of another or of another and the owner. Proposal and acceptance are basic requirement. However, proposal and acceptance may be express or implied.

Law relating to breach of trust is contained in sections 405 to 409 Indian Penal Code which is precise and brief. But it has been elaborated by the decided cases. In Indian the principle of precedent is followed. Governing rules relating to precedent rest on the doctrine of stare decisis et non quieta movers ('Let it stand as decided and what is fixed should not be moved'). Some jurists interpreate it as stare rationibus decidendis ("keep to the rationes decidendi of past cases"). Stare decisis results from decisions of the superior courts only. Decisions of the higher courts are cited as authority for deciding similar facts on that principle, or by an analogy in lower courts. It includes ratio decidendi, the ground of a decision, and obiter dictum, an opinion not necessary to the courts' judgement.

Contrary to it, Islamic law relating to breach of trust has been laid down by Qur'ãnic injunctions and Ahadith. One feature is common among both the laws that they are precise and brief. But unlike Indian law, under Islamic law, it has been elaborated by citing decided cases as authority. Precedent has no placc in

Shariah. However, precise and brief Qur'ãnic injunctions and Ahadith have been elaborated by Faqih (Muslim jurists). They have laid down elaborate governing rules relating to breach of trust cases. These elaborated and detailed rules are all inconsonance with the spirit of Qur'ãnic injuctions and Ahadith. Nothing contrary can be added by the jurists. Every case is to be decided in the light of Qur'ãn and Ahadith afresh. Past decided cases have no relevance.

Another basic feature of the two laws is entrustment of a thing but under Islamic law it has some wider horizon, such as, that emanate is a thing found with someone, who is considered to be in charge of it. Further it may be an emanate in a contract requiring compensation for loss, like a thing taken on hire, or a thing received as a loan for use, and whether it passes as an emanat into the hands of someone without contract existing or a design formed. It the property of a neighbour falls into the house of someone on account of the wind, by reason there being no contract, that property is not property entrusted with another for safe-keeping, but it is an emanat. This distinguishes the Islamic law relating to breach of trust from Indian law where in entrustment and dominion over the property are the basic requirements. Comparatively the scope of trust under Shariah is wider.

Finder's Liability

Comparing some specific situations, we may begin with the Finder's Liability relating to the lost goods. Under Indian Law if a person finds a thing on the high road, not knowing to whom it belongs; he picks up and appropriates it, he is neither liable for breach of trust nor for misappropriation. It is not breach of trust because in such a case there is no entrustment.

In a case where a person finds a letter on the road, containing a bank note. From the direction and contents of the latter he learns to whom the note belongs. He appropriates the note. He is liable for misappropriation but not for breach of trust. In this case also there is no breach of trust.

But under Islamic law, under both the situations above referred, finder is liable for breach of trust if he appropriates the picked up good. The law is that if someone finds a thing on the road, or in any other place and takes it for the purpose of giving it to its owner, if its owner is known, in his hand it is pure emanat. It is necessary that he should deliver it to its owner. If he appropriates it in his own use, he is liable for committing breach of trust. Similarly, if its owner is not known, it is a thing picked up by a chance, still it is an emanat (trust) in the hands of the person who picks it up and takes it. He should make efforts to know the owner of the lost good. Until the owner appears, he keeps it with himself as an emant - (trust).

Loan

As to loan whether it amounts to trust, and non-repayment a breach of trust, depend upon the facts of each case. According to Indian Law, the relationship between debtor and creditor is not a fiduciary on and the advance of a loan is not an entrustment of money. Once the money advanced after the grant of loan, it becomes the property of the debtor. A failure to repay the loan is not a breach of trust. However, there may be transactions between debtors and creditor where there may be entrustment also. It may be in cases where the money is to be disposed in a particular manner.

On the other hand Islamic law recognizes Arriyyat (عاريت), the thing let for use is emanat in the hands of the borrower. It signifies an investiture with the use of a thing without a return. The borrower is made entitle to use and utilise the usufructs arising from the property borrowed without return. There is no consideration. A loan is gratitiously given for use. If the borrower violates the conditions agreed, he would be liable for breach of trust.

Pledge

Comparing the law relating to pledge in connection with breach of trust, according to Indian law, it may be explained as that pledge or pawn is a bailment of goods by a debtor with his creditor to be kept as security till the payment of the debt, and the relationship thus resulted are fuduciary in character between the pledge and the pledgee, a dishonest conversion or misappropriation of the property pledged, thus would amount to a criminal breach of trust.

A sub-pledge by the pledge to the extend of his interest (in the absence of any condition to the contrary in the contract of pledge) would be fully within the rights of the pledgee and would not constitute a breach of trust. It may be otherwise if it is made in violation of a condition in the contract of pledge.

Under Islamic law, pledge, like deposits or loans cannot be taken as trust. However, it is lawful, that both pledger and the pledgee may agree to deposit the pledge with an honest, upright person. Such a person known as 'adil' (عادل) would act as trustee for both. But Imam Malik (R.A.) is of the opinion that it is not lawful.

Hire Purchase Agreement

As regard to 'Hire-purchase Agreement' cases there is no different between Islamic and Indian Laws. Under this agreement a person agrees to bind himself with the terms of agreement, that is, to pay the instalment for the article purchased under the agreement, till the payment is made for the instalments agreed, not to assign, underlet, or part-with the property during the period of hire, if he violates the terms he would be guilty under both the laws for breach of trust because simply he is entrusted with the property, ownership still remains with whom he has entered the agreement for hire-purchase. In case if the hirer pledges, or disposes off the hired-property in violation of hire-purchase agreement, he is responsible to criminal breach of trust.

Both the laws agree that a mere transaction of sale is not an entrustment. The fact that the purchaser subsequently denies receipt of the goods does not make him guilty of the offence of criminal breach of trust.

Liability of Joint-Owners

Indian Law as to the liability of joint-owners of the property for breach of trust is different from Islamic Law. According to Indian Law a co-owner of property cannot be considered to be entrusted with the joint-property in the absence of an agreement of entrustment, hence no liability for breach of trust. But on the other hand Muslim co-owners are not joint-owners and the principle above noted is not applicable in their cases. They own separate shares, any misappropriation by either one may amount to criminal breach of trust.

Husband and Wife

Indian Law for determining the liability of husband and wife for criminal breach of trust has two conflicting views. Firstly, that the wife is in joint possession with her husband and cannot therefore be convicted or say that a woman's stridhan property becomes a joint property with her husband on entering into the matrimonial relations. Stridhan property of a woman may be pledge in the custody of either of her husband or in-laws, but they are treated as trustees and are bound to return the same when demanded by her. If the stridhan is mis-appropriated or conversed by the in-laws or husband, they would be considered guilty for breach of trust.

Under Islamic law for making the spouses liable for breach of trust there are two governing rules. The first is that the things which are in the house by custom in the hands of either the wife or husband and the nature of the things is perishible, if either one disposes off without the consent of other one, there would in liability for breach of trust. Secondly, if the thing is exclusively in the use of either husband or wife, and anyone disposes or parts with would be liable for breach of trust. For example if a thing is not found is the hands of the wife, like a horse, and some one borrows it from the wife without the persmission of her husband, in case of loss or destruction, husband can make both of them liable for breach of trust. Things received by the wife as gifts from in-laws, at the time of marriage, exclusively is the property of the wife, if the husband is in possession misappropriates or convers it to his own use without her consent, he would be guilty for breach of trust. On this later principle both the laws are the same.

Liability of Auctioneer and Superdar

The law relating to the liability of Auctioneer and superdar appointed by the court for a particular purpose is the same under both the laws.

Servant's Liability

There are two categories of servants under the Indian Law, that is, ordinary servant, and public servant. Consequently the liability is to be determined according to two different sections 408 and 409 of the Indian Penal Code respectively.

Who is servant, a definite precise answer is not possible. It is said that a person is a servant who by implied or express contract of service executes the orders and submits to the control of his master in the course of business. It is his responsibility and a duty to transact the business as directed. The generally accepted test of the relationship of master and servant is that of a contract, and contract of service is thought to be one by virtue of which the employer cannot only order or require what is to be done, but how it shall be done. But this test is criticised on the ground that control trust seems to be more of a fiction than of fact. There are other tests also discussed earlier under relevant chapter, but no single test can be claimed as appropriate to cover all cases. Question is ultimately one of fact differing from case to case.

The requisites to make a servant liable are: Firstly, being servant or employed as servant; secondly, entrusted with property in any manner in the capacity of a servant; or any dominion over the property; and thirdly, servant commits criminal breach of trust in respect of that property.

The basic requirement is that the person must be a servant. Offence is committed when the act of the servant is to cause wrongful loss to his master for a temporary period even.

Word whosoever used in section 408 includes a minor above the age of 12 years, so long his case is not covered under section 82 and 83 Indian Penal Code.

A servant is bound to carry out all the orders of his master, but orders must be reasonable and in the course of business for which he is employed.

Where a person serves as servant, though there is no contract binding him to work, so long as he performs the duties his acts would be covered by section 408.

Where a servant deputed to receive money for a particular objcct and spent on did not utilize it for that object inspite of the fact that he was called to account for, but gave a falsc statement that he used the received money for that particular object is liable for the commission of criminal breach of trust.

What is important to make servant liable is that there should be dishonest intention, entrustment or dominion over property and conversion to his own use. These elements make the servant liable for criminal breach of trust. If these elements are absent, he would not be liable under section 408 Indian Penal Code.

As to the liability of public servant under section 409, sone requirements are to be satisfied. Further it must be proved that he has authority to receive the property in his capacity as a public servant.

Separate section is devoted because the responsibilities of public servant are of highly significant character. It involves greater control and care because of secrecy and confidentiality. If there is a breach of trust, it may lead to serious public and private loss. It is necessary that criminal liability make be strictly proved.

There is a controversy about the application of section 409, I.P.C., after enforcement of a new provision under the Prevention of Corruption Act, 1947. It is said that section 5 of the said Act, after its enforcement, concerning offences by the said Act, after its enforcement, concerning offences by public servants has pro-tanto repealed section 409, I.P.C. However, the controversy has rested with the decision of supreme court in Veereshwar Rao., 1957, that the offence of criminal misconduct punishment under section 5 (2) of the Prevention of Corruption Act, is not identifal in essence, import and content with an offence under section 409 of Indian Penal Code.

Another important feature for the prosecution of a public servant for criminal breach of trust is that for prosecution either under section 409 I.P.C. or section 5 (2) P.C. Act, Prior sanction for prosecution must be obtained from the appropriate authority.

Without prior sanction, trial of a public servant would be illegal. Section 197 Criminal Procedure Code has laid down the procedure to be followed in such cases.

Under Islamic law, there is no distinction between an ordinary servant and a public servant. No separate privileged class for public servants exists. No discrimination between servants is to be made.

According to Qur'ãnic injuctions and Ahadith, it is justified to employ servant for work in according to the directions of the masters.

There term used for servants under Islamic law is hireling. According to the nature of work for which they are employed, they may be called common hirelings and particular hirelings. This classification is not the same as exists in Indian Law. Prior sanction for prosecution for any class of hireling is not required.

An article delivered to a common hireling is a deposit (ودیعت - trust) in his hands. Such a hireling is responsible for any loss or destruction of the entrusted property, if the loss has been caused due to his fault. He is liable for breach of trust. However, if no negligence, no fault of his own; he is not liable. Further loss must be caused to the entrusted property of his master in the course of his work.

Contract for service, employment for work, payment of wages, control over the servants' conduct of the master, work done in the course of business or for which employed, entrustment of property or giving dominion over the property to the servant by the master, and dishonest misappropriation or conversion by the servant to his own use, and causing loss to the master, all these elements are common among both Indian and Islamic Law. There is no difference on these ingredients.

Agent's Liability

Agent, according to Indian Law, has a representative character. He is to act on behalf of his principal in bringing about a contract between his principal and a third party. In other words agent means a person whose object is to establish contractual relations between his principal and a third party. His representative capacity depends upon his relations with the principal and functions and responsibilities assigned to him as agent.

Agent, generally, drops out of the picture once the relationship between principal and third party under the contract are established. Agent generally has no right or liabilities under the contract.

A minor agent can effectively bring about contractual relations between his principal and a third party. Age of majority or full contractual capacity is not the requirement for an agent.

To make an agent liable under section 409, the requirement is that there must be an entrustment of property or dominion over the property in the course of commercial transactions to a person as agent.

If the property has been entrusted or dominion given over, for some other purpose than for which an agent is under a duty to perform, such entrustment or dominion over would not be covered under this section. The accused must be the complainant's agent, if not, then the case would not be covered under section 409 I.P.C. A commission agent who has not been entrusted with property or any dominion over property cannot be held guilty of breach of trust. He should be an agent at the time of entrustment of property. The section does not require that he should be an agent at the time of committing the criminal breach of trust.

In a case where the accused was authorised to lend his master's money and he lent it to himself without his master's permission, it was held that he was guilty of criminal breach of trust.

Agent is bound to exercise lawful instructions of the Principal but he is not under the direct control and supervision as in the casc of a servant. If entrusted property is dishonestly misappropriated, he is liable for criminal breach of trust.

Under Islamic law a person may lawfully employ another his agent to represent him in dealing with third persons. Prophet (peace be upon him) himself authorised persons to represent him in the distribution of things, exchanging money, weighing goods and saving thing from spoiling. Thus agency under Islamic law is legal and permissible.

As to competency of the agent, the requirements are that the agent should be capable to have reasons and understanding (mumeyyiz). Age of puberty is not the requirement. Here on this point Indian Law and Islamic Law differs. Under Indian Law even a minor can be an agent. Maturity of understanding is not the requirement. The only consideration is that he must be above twelve years of age. Under Islamic law to be of mature understanding is the basic requirement.

Principal should be competent. If he is not, the appointment of the agent is a concluded contract subject to the permission of the guardian of the infant.

The rights and liabilities accruing under the contract do not effect the agent. These rights relates to the person who appoints him as agent.

The property, handed over by the principal to the agent, when received and taken possession over on behalf of the principal is a deposit. Here on this point there is a similarity with the Indian Law.

Again there is no difference between the two laws where in a case if the agent does not return the entrusted property to the principal nor does he discharge his duties concerning it, instead misappropriates it, he would be liable for breach of trust.

An agent cannot purchase for himself any specific article which he is directed to purchase for him principal. If he does so, he commits the breach of trust, for which he is liable under the Islamic law. Hence also there is no difference between the two laws.

Under Islamic law when the agent sells the property on his own accord for a less sum than that fixed by the principal he would be liable for breach of trust. On completion of entrusted work, the agent is released from the agency.

In brief it may be said that on basic principles governing agency and breach of trust, both laws mostly are similar with slight difference on some points as discussed above.

Liability of Partners

Another area compared is partnership under Indian and Islamic laws. Indian concept of partnership has been explained as relation between persons who have agreed to share the profits of a business carried on by all or any of them acting for all. Word business includes every trade, occupation and profession. However, literal meaning of word business creates problems. Therefore, this word is to be construed in the practical sense which the businessmen use in their day to day transactions and dealings. The term business includes all such activities which if successful would result in profit. The second important element is the agreement for creating partnership. Partnership is created by contract and not by status. The third element is to carry on business-in-common. It may be carried on by all or any of them acting for all. Last comes the sharing of profits. Merely, two or more persons carry on business jointly with a view of sharing of profits is not enough to make them partners. Division of profits is essential for the existence of partnership. Partners should have a right to share the profits. As to number forming the firm, it has two different categories: Banking business where number cannot be more than ten partners, while in all other cases twenty is the maximum limit of partners. For formation of partnership, partners must be competent to enter into partnership contract. Further partnership must not be for an illegal purpose. Limit of number of partners as laid down by law should not exceed. Another significant point is the relationship of partners to one another. Such relationship is wholly governed by the terms of partnership agreement. Partners are bound to be just and faithful to each other. The statutory obligation thus created cannot be warded off by any agreement to the contrary. The agreement made between partners results in giving them certain rights, and inconsequent imposing certain duties upon them, violation of them make then liable.

Islamic law signifies the conjunction of two or more estates, in such a way that one of them is not distinguishable from the other. Further, the term Shirkat (partnership) extends to contracts, although there may be no actual conjunction of estates but the contract is the cause of such conjunction. It signifies the union of two or more persons in one concern. Thus according to Islamic law to form partnership two different methods are adopted, one by conjunction of estates, and another by contract. The last element is common between both the systems of laws.

Partnership by contract under Islamic law consists of agreement for association, on the condition that the capital and its benefit be common between two or more persons. The essence of partnership by contract under Islamic law is an offer and acceptance expressed or implied. Further the partners should be competent to contract the formation of association. Participation-in-common and sharing of profits are other significant elements of

Islamic law of partnership (Shirkat). Further every kind of shirkat by contract contains a contract of agency and condition for reason and discernment as followed in contract for agency are to be applied in partnership as well. Division of profits should be made clear. If it is doubtful or unknown to the partnership than such partnership would be fasid. All these requisites for forming a Shirkat (partnership) are identical between both the laws under consideration.

Under Islamic law it is a condition that the capital be a thing, which is known and individually perceptible (Ayn). A debt which will be received being on accounts of debts due from people, cannot be the capital of a partnership. If the capital of one is corporeal property (Ayn) and the capital of the other is a debt, again the partnership is not good.

The right to profit may come from property or work of sometimes in consequence of responsibility. When one is the apprentice of a skilled workman, if he makes him do the work, which he has undertaken, for half pay, it is lawful. So also by reason of his responsibility and undertaking his master shares to the other half is also legally justified. In Mudarebe, the partner who supplies the capital, by the property, and the party who supplies the labour, by the labour, becomes entitled to the profit. In cases where property, work and responsibility are absent, there is no share the profits, no partnership is continuted, and he cannot take a share of the profit.

As to number of partners forming partnership, unlike India Law, Islamic law does not lay down any categorisation or any minimum or maximum limit. Partnership may comprise of any number of partners, whether it is partnership by contract (شركة عقد), or Shirket-i-Vujuh (partnership for many accounts) or Shirket-i-'Amal, etc.

As to liability the general law in India relating to partnership is that like a joint owner who cannot commit misappropriation of property which he holds jointly with other co-owners, the partner also cannot misappropriate partnership's property belonging to him and other co-partners. A partner cannot be held guilty of criminal breach of trust even in respect of partnership assets. A partner not rending account and withholding share of property of other partners is not liable under section 406 Indian Penal Code. In cases of disputes regarding the liabilities of the partners the court will not interfere under this section 406 I.P.C. The court has to be caution and careful in proceeding against partners for charges of criminal breach of trust. If a partner receives money on behalf of the partnership, he does not receive it in a fiduciary capacity. Consequently, where a partner alleged to have had with held the share of the profits of the partnership business said to be due to another partner, could not be prosecuted for criminal breach of trust.

However, in R.K. Dalmia V. Delhi Administration, discussed in earlier chapters in detail, it has now been settled that section 405 and 406, Indian Penal Code, are quite wide enough to include within their purview the case of a partner if it is proved that he was in fact entrusted by agreement with the partnership property or with dominion over property, and that he dishonestly misappropriated the property.

Thus for making a partner liable the prosecution must prove clearly and beyond reasonable doubt that a special agreement entrusting or giving dominion over property does exist and the accused has acted dishonestly in misappropriating the partnership property at the expense of those with whom he was working in partnership.

The mere fact that the partnership property belongs to the firm does not in any way indicate that any partner has entrusted his share to the other partners. Such entrustment cannot read in the mere relationship of partners. A special agreement entrusting the dominion over the property and dishonest misappropriation make a partner liable for criminal breach of trust.

Islamic law on partner's liability is totally oppose to India Law. According to this the partners are persons entrusted the one by the other. The partnership assets or property in the possession of each of them is like a thing entrusted - (Trust - ودیعت).

Each partner holds the stock in the manner of a trust. The possession of each of the two partners, by reciprocity or in traffic, over the partnership stock, is considered as the possession of a trust - . Since each possesses the property with consent of the proprietor, for this reason, that he is to give something in lieu of it, in the same manner as where a person takes possession of a thing with a view to purchase it (not because it is a pledge, as in pawnage); The stock is therefore a deposit (Trust - ودیعت).

Each of the partners is at liberty to lodge his capital as a deposit (trust - ودیعت) with the other partner. In Mudarebe, the Mudarib is a person entrusted (Emin - trustee). The capital in his hands is like property deposited for safe-keeping (vedia - ودیعت trust).

All the partners in the partnership have right to deposit (ودیعت - trust) the partnership property for safe-keeping. One partner cannot mix the partnership property with his own property. He cannot make a partnership with another. If he does, and the partnership property is lost, he is responsible for the share of his partner. Such acts of a partner would amount to breach of trust.

Acts done by one of the partners in violation of express prohibition would also amount to breach of trust. Any partner makes loan of the partnership property without the leave of other partners, he would commit breach of trust. Consent of other partners for lending a loan is the essential requirement.

Partnership by way of Mudarebe may be limited or unlimited based on the nature of transaction. If it is a restricted Mudarebe, violation of such restrictions would amount to breach of trust as the Mudarib is a person entrusted (Emin - trustee).

Precisely it may be said that the liability of the partners would be based upon the nature and kind of each partnership and effect of violation of conditions governing such partnerships.

Procedure

Analysing the procedure aspects both the laws have some resemblances and differences. Under both the laws administration of justice, maintenance of law and order, protecting the week from the aggressors and providing redress to the aggrieved persons are the basic responsibilities of every state.

Under Indian law in criminal cases justice is administered according to the penal law of the land while under Islamic law it is executed in accordance to the commandment of Holy Qur'ãn and Ahadith, in the absence, Ijma and Qiyas is followed.

Cognizance

The first important step according to Indian law in the prosecution of the offenders is cognizance of the offence. Although word cognizance has not been defined in the criminal procedure code, infact, it means a mental act and also a judicial act. A magistrate is said to have taken cognizance of an offence when he applies his mind to the contents of the petition with the purpose of proceeding in a particular way. When the Magistrate comes to the conclusion that there is a case to be inquired into, he proceeds with the prosecution.

Magistrate take cognizance of the offence upon receiving a complaint about the commission of crime, or upon a police report, upon information received from any person than a police officer, or upon his own knowledge, that such offence has been committed.

Upon receiving such information the magistrate before whom a complaint is pending may adopt either of the two courses. Firstly, he may conduct a preliminary inquiry under section 202 Criminal Procedure Code or secondly, may scrutinize the case diary and other relevant material before him. Then if he is of the opinion that the offender be prosecuted, he may place the accused on trial. Further he may call for charge-sheet from the police and take cognizance under section 190 (1) (b), or he may take cognizance on the complaint under section 190 (1) (a) Criminal Procedure Code.

Taking cognizance of an offence does not require any formal action or action of any kind. It may happen as soon as the magistrate applies his mind to the suspected commission of an offence.

It is with the magistrate's discretionary power either to take cognizance of a case or not to take cognizance of a case. But the magistrate must act in a judicial manner. It should be clear that the cognizance of an offence is not the cognicance of offenders. Once the magistrate takes cognizance of the offence, it is his duty to find out who the offenders are.

Another important point relating to cognizance of offence is that the magistrate must be competent to take cognizance. If he is not competent, then, he should either if the complaint is in writing, return it for prosecution to the proper court with an endorsement to that effect, or if the complaint is not in writing, direct the complainant to the proper court.

The law relating to take congnizance for the offence of breach of trust committed by public servants under section 409

Indian Penal Code is different. Section 197 of the Criminal Procedure Code has laid down the procedure to be followed in such cases. When any person who is a public servant not removable from his offence save by or with the sanction of the government is accused of any offence alleged to have been committed by him while acting or purporting to act in the in the discharge of his official duty, no court shall take cognizance of such offence except with the previous sanction of either the central government or the state government as the case may be. The object of the prior sanction is to give protection to responsible public servants against possible vexatious criminal proceedings while acting under colour of their offices.

Under Islamic law the crimes are divided under three categories: Haqooq - Allah (حقوق الله), Haqooqul-Ibad (حقوق العباد), and common Haqooq (مشترك حقوق). These are further sub-divided. However, for procedural convenience crimes related to these Haqooq may be classified under two heeds: Private right or Haqooqul-Ibad (حقوق العباد), those which are tried only on a demand by a private claimant, and public rights or Haqooq Allah (حقوق الله), those in which action can be brought by any one.

The claimant or complainant has to file a دعوىٰ (petition) in the Shariah court. Then the court is to take cognizance of the offence and is to notify if the action is of private right, and to inform the prosecution if the action is of a public right. The person against whom allegations have been made is to be summoned on a fixed date before the court.

The inference from the above discussion is that cognizance of offence is common in both the systems with minor procedural differences. Under Islamic law preliminary inquiry or scruiting of diary by the court are not required. Merely on private or public complaint or complaint made by the police the court takes the cognizance of the offence and summons the offender.

Further for taking cognizance under Islamic law no distinction between servant and public servant in made. Both are treated equal before the law. For the prosecution of public servants no special sanction either of the central government or the state government is needed. Simple complaint petition is required to prosecute the public servants also. There is no distinct class or category privileged because of the nature of service.

Warrant of Arrest

The procedure for the appearance of the parties under the two systems is different.

Under Indian law, though the offence under sections 406, and 408 is cognizable in which case a police officer may arrest a person without warrant, but for breach of trust a warrant of arrest is to be issued by the magistrate. A police officer, has no authority to arrest without warrant. Magistrate before issuing the warrant of arrest has to apply his judicial mind.

Offence committed under 409 I.P.C. by a public servant, then, under such a situation it is discretionary with the magistrate not to issue warrant, instead issue summons for the appearance of the accused. But arrest without warrant cannot be made. Police has no authority to arrest the offender without obtaining warrant of arrest from the magistrate.

Islamic law follow a different procedure which is more simple and less humiliating. When the complainant files the petition, the court on receiving it will not issue a warrant of arrest for committed breach of trust. Instead it would issue summons to the offender for his appearance in the court on a fixed date.

If a person on receiving summons does not appear on the fixed date, court presumes his case weak and the opponent's claim has force in it. However, if on receiving summons the offender abstained and gives reason for such absence, then court must take such reasons into consideration.

There is another situation where in cases of complaint, if the Shariah court is of the view that person he detained or arrested, it may order to this effect. But this is required only in case of serious nature, and when the possibility is that the person may abscond or would avoid attending proceeding in the court against him.

If an accused is summoned, does not appear before the court on the fixed date for hearing, the court may compel his appearance. Warrant of arrest may be issued against him. Then police may arrest and bring him before the court. Thus the procedure of arrest is totally different from the Indian procedure of arrest. Under Islamic law emphasis is on summoning the accused rather than issuing the warrant of arrest against the accused.

Bail

The next thing requires comparison is the release of the accused on bail. Bail is aimed at to set the accused at liberty from his arrest and imprisonment on receiving security for his appearance on a day and at a certain place.

Under Indian Law Criminal Breach of Trust has been shown in the first schedule, column five, Criminal Procedure Code, as an offence which is not - bailable. In such a case bail cannot be claimed as a matter of right but section 437 criminal procedure lays down certain conditions keeping in view of them the accused may be released on bail. The court releasing any person under sub-section (1), or sub-section (2) of section 437

Criminal Procedure Code shall record in writing his or its reasons for so doint.

Non-bailable cases not concluded within a period of sixty days from the first date fixed for taking evidence in the case, such person shall, if he is custody during the whole of the said period, be released on bail to the satisfaction of the magistrate, unless for reasons to be recorded in writing, the magistrate otherwise directs.

Again after conclusion of trial of a person accused of a non-bailable offence and before judgement is delivered, the court is of the opinion that there are reasonable grounds for believing that the accused is not guilty of any such offence it shall release the accused, if he is in custody, on the execution by him of a bond without sureties for his appearance to hear judgement delivered.

In cases where a person on reasonable believe that he may be arrested on an accusation of having committed a non-bailable offence, he may apply to the High Court or the court of session for a direction; and that court may, if it thinks fit, direct that in the event of such arrest, he shall be released on bail. Such direction may be conditional which the accused released on bail is to abide with.

It is also be noted that the object of the detention of the accused person during trial is not punitive, it is merely to secure the accused appearance. The court, no doubt, has discretion in refusing or granting bail in non-bailable offences but it is to take into consideration the probability of the accused appearing to stand the trial and not his supposed guilt or innocence.

Under Islamic law bail may be of two descriptions. Firstly, bail for person, and secondly, bail for property. It is all discretionary with the court to release a person on bail. If the possibility in breach of trust cases is that the released person would damage the trust property the court may also ask bail for securing the property as well.

If the circumstances warrant that he should not be released even on furnishing the sureties, the bail may be refused. Court may grant the bail or may not grant the bail. However, it is not arbitrary with the judge. Decision to grant bail depends upon the seriousness of the allegations and surrounding circumstances. Refusal to grant bail must be based on reasons.

Under Islamic law there is no such division as bailable offence or non-bailable offence as existed under the Indian system. Simply the judge, without involving in the techmicalities of law, take into consideration certain relevant factors effecting the release and the proceedings of the case and form his decision either to release or not to release a person on bail.

Jurisdiction - Venue

The magistrate taking cognizance of the offence must be competent to entertain and dispose of the cases. In India Schedule I of the Criminal Procedure Code determines the competency. Under Column 6 of the First Schedule the magistrate of first class has been shown as competent to inquire into and dispose of cases of criminal breach of trust falling under section 406, 407 and 409 of the Indian Penal Code.

As to place of trial, Criminal Procedure Code under section 177 to 185 contain provisions regarding the place of trial. Every offence shall ordinarilly by inquired into and tried by a court within whose local jurisdiction it was committed.

Competency of the court to try an offence depends upon its local jurisdiction within which an offence is committed. If the offence committed wholly outside the limits of its jurisdiction court is not authorised to take cognizance of and to try the accused. Where a court is not empowerd to try a particular offence, does try, the entire trial is void.

The offence if criminal breach of trust may be inquired into or tried by a court within the local limits of whose jurisdiction any part of the property which is subject of the offence was received or retained by the accused person, or was required to be returned or accounted for by the accused person or the offence was committed.

Section 177 of the Criminal Procedure Code has incorporated a general rule. Section 178 to 184 and 188 are elaborations of this general rule. These sections are not exceptions. Similarly section 218 to 223 are also not exceptions to the general rule laid down by section 177, Cr. P.C.

Where an act is an offence by reason of anything which has been done and of a consequence which has ensued the offence may be inquired into or tried by a court within whose local jurisdiction such thing has been done or such consequence has ensued. Detailed study has already been made of all the provisions under the head jurisdiction and venue in inquiries and trials.

Briefly it may be summed up that the offence of criminal breach of trust may be inquired into or tried by a court within whose local jurisdiction the offence was committed or any part of the property which is the subject of the offence was received or retained or was required to be returned or accounted for, by the accused person. Where neither entrustment nor conversion has taken place within the territorial jurisdiction of a court that court has no jurisdiction.

Shariah courts are appointed by the ruler of the state at a distance which a person may cover in a day on foot. Distance of a day includes goint from and coming back of complainant to his house.

Considerations for determining the venue and jurisdiction of Shariah courts are:

1. Complainant and his witnesses should not cover long distances.

2. There should be no inconvenience in approaching the courts, and

3. Easy access for seeking redress is the purpose behind.

The suit lies in the court within the jurisdiction of which they - complainant and his witnesses reside.

Defendant's residence or the subject-manner of dispute situated within the jurisdiction of another court is not the consideration for determining the jurisdiction and place of trial by the court. Because complainant is the aggrieved party.

Another factor which determines the jurisdiction of Shariah court is the powers of Qazi contained in his letter of appointment. Such letter may limit the jurisdiction of the court to try specific class of class, or to cover specific area.

It is a basic requirement under Shariah requirement under Shariah also that the complainant must file his petition in a competent court in whose jurisdiction the matter in dispute and the are is covered in.

Thus on competency of court in relation to jurisdiction and the place of trial there is a similarity. In India statutes determines the jurisdiction and the limits. Under Islamic law the ruler determines them. But both based on the same principle of convenience of the litigants.

Investigation

In India Chapter XII from sections 154 to 176 Criminal Procedure Code deals with the information to the police and their powers to investigate. This information is known as 'First Information Report' about the commission of crime with the object of setting the police in motion. Such information is usually made by the victim of crime known as complainant or by someone on his behalf. The information be given by a person who has personally seen the occurrence of crime or has the personal knowledge of the incident reported.

It must be an information, and must relate to a cognizable offence. If no cognizable offence is disclosed, the police would have no authority to undertake an investigation. If police without a cognizable offence undertakes investigation, High Court may interfere with under section 482 Criminal Procedure Code. Criminal breach of trust is a cognizable offence, hence covered under this provision.

First information report is different from complaint. If is given in writing to police officer while the complaint, whether oral or in writing, is made to the magistrate. The report by the police of the same information to magistrate empowers him to take cognizance of such offence. Thereafter he may direct an investigation or, if he thinks fit, at once proceed, or depute any magistrate subordinate to him to proceed, to hold a preliminary inquiry into, or otherwise to dispose of the case in the manner provided in the Criminal Procedure Code.

Police officer's power to investigate also include within its scope to require attendance of witnesses and examination of witnesses.

No statement made by any person to a police officer in the course of investigation under Chapter XII, Criminal Procedure Code shall, if reduce to writing, be signed by the person making it.

Statement recorded during police investigation under section 162, Cr. P.C. are wholly inadmissible in evidence except for the limited purpose stated in proviso thereto. However, recorded statement under section 162, Cr. P.C. may be used both by the defence as well as by the prosecution to contradict witnesses or to confront hostile witnesses. Such statements are not used for corroboration purposes. The object of section 162. Cr. P.C. is to protect primarily the interest of the accuse against the use of such statements. Section 162 clause (2), Cr. P.C. example from its operation the dying declarations which are admissible under section 32 (1) Evidence Act.

Section 162, Cr. P.C. enacts a rule of evidence. The relevant sections of Evidence Law are 24 to 27, dealing with the recording of confession and its evidential value while the accused is being investigated during police custody.

Another important rule laid down in section 165 Cr. P.C. relates to the power of search by police officer making the investigation. Further a police officer investigating the offence cannot detain a person in custody for more than twenty four hours in the absence of special order under section 167, Criminal Procedure Code. When investigation cannot be completed within the stipulated time of 24 hours and the keeping the accused in police custody if further required than the matter is to be referred to the nearest magistrate. The magistrate may order the detention of the accused beyond 24 hours, but he must record his reasons in writing. No magistrate shall authorise the detention of the accused person in custody for total period exceeding sixty-days.

Further details related to investigation covered under section 168, 169, 170, 171, 172 have already been discussed. Any refines would be a repetition of the same. Lastly, section 173, Cr. P.C. lays down the final stage of investigation. It should be completed without unnecessary delay. As soon as the investigation is completed, the officer-incharge of the police station shall forward to a magistrate empowered to take cognizance of the offence on a police report, a report in the form prescribed by the state government. Such a report may be in the form of charge-sheet, or a final report.

On receipt of the report magistrate is not bound to accept it. He is to scrutinise the material whether the facts disclosed will warrant the issue of a process against the accused. An illegality in the course of investigation does not affect the competence and jurisdiction of the court of trial.

In Saudi Arabia where Islamic law is inforce, it is difficult to draw a line between investigation and enquiry. Police makes the investigation. Interrogating is aimed for establishing the suspicion. This preliminary investigation of crime before the trial is purely administrative in nature. It is not subject to any form of judicial restrains. Police makes the investigation only on receiving the complaint of commission of crime. Procedural technicalities as to first information report as we noticed in Indian system is not found in Saudi System.

Qazi, judge of Shariah Court, on receiving complaint also conduct an investigation into the case with a view to give cognizance to the suit. Here also no distinction, like India, is drawn between inquiry and investigation. Qazi simply enquires to know whether any prima facie case exists against the accused or not.

Under Islamic law another peculiar feature related to investigation is that there is an institution of Ahtisab (احتساب) headed by Muhtasib, who is also responsible to make investigation. It is connected with 'Amar-bil-Maroof (امر بالمعروف), and Nahe-Anil-Munkir (نہی عن المنکر), that is, when people leave doing good deeds (معروف) and indulge in doing evil deeds (نہی عن المنکر). Under such conditions the ruler of the state appoints Mohtasib (محتسب), an officer to check, control, and prevent spreading evils in the society, and promote good and virtuous things. It is imperative (فرض عين) upon him to attend all complaints made to him and investigate them. However, Mohtasib in Haqooq-ul-Ibad-Khas (حقوق العباد خاص), moves and investigates only when a complaint is made to him. Without receiving such information, he is not to move or take any action. No doubt, it may be stated that powers vested in Mohtasib, in cases of Ahtisab (امربالمعروف) and (نهی عن المنكر) are very wide. Not only investigation of evils, but prevention and control of evils are also included within his power. In Saudi Arabia, there is no such designation as Mohtasib, but his powers are performed by different committees formed under the Royal Regulations, such as, Fogery Committee, Bribery Committee, Grievance Board, etc. etc.

Referring again to police powers to investigate in Saudi Arabia, we find that there are some practical difficulties. Although police is authorised to investigate the crimes committed, but judges often do not receive the minutes of police investigation. Keeping in view the difficulties. The Draft Law of the Judicial Authority, suggested that the power of police to investigate crime should be withdrawn handed over to the prosecution. It should be conducted by the prosection instead of the police.

Investigation system under Islam is there but not on lines with the Indian law. In fact, Qazi is responsible under Islamic law to investigation also.

Trial

In India three types of trials are there, such as, 'Trial of Warrant Cases', Trial of Summon Cases', and lastly 'Summary Trials'. Breach of trust is covered under the first one. Under the trial of warrant cases offences punishable with death, imprisonment for life or imprisonment for a term exceeding two years are covered.

It may be inferred from the definitions that the nature and measure of punishment which the law prescribes for a particular offence determines the character of the trial.

In the trials of warrant cases, the magistrate is to follow either of the two procedures:

1. Where in a case instituted on a police report procedure to be followed has been laid down in section 238 to 243, and

2. Where any warrant case instituted otherwise than on a police report, the procedure has been specified in sections 244 to 247, Criminal Procedure Code.

In report of trial conducted by a magistrate on a police report, the accuse either appears or is brought before him at the commencement of the trial, the agistrate sal satisfy himself whether the accused has been furnished with al documents referred in section 207, Criminal Procedure Code or not. The magistrate on consideration of those documents and after giving the prosecution and the accused on opportunity of being heard if he considers the charge against the accused as groundless he will discharge the accused; on the other hand if the magistrate is of opinion that there is ground for presuming that the accused has committed an offence triable under Chapter XIX Criminal Procedure Code and that such magistrate is competent to try, he will frame a charge against the accused.

In cases instituted otherwise than on the police report, the accused has the right to reserve cross-examination of prosecution witnesses till at a late stage. The magistrate cannot discharge the accused without examining all the witnesses for the prosecution.

The right to cross-examine the witnesses after the charge is framed, is an absolute right and the omission to give the accused the benefit of that right would vitiate the whole proceeding, and the fact that the witnesses were once cross-examined by the accused before the charge is of no avail.

When the accused is not discharged then the accused after examining and cross-examining the prosecution witnesses shall be called to enter upon his defence and produce his evidence; and the provisions of section 243 Criminal Procedure shall apply to the case.

To discharge frivolous complaints, section 250, Criminal Procedure Code enables the court to award compensation to the accused if there was no reasonable ground for accusation.

A second class magistrate cannot, in a case falling under section 409, try the case and convict the accused under section 406 Criminal Procedure Code.

Under Islamic law the procedure in relation to trials is simple. There is no such division as trial of warrant cases, or trial of summon cases, or summary trials. There is uniform procedure of trial for all cases. Institution of suits in Shariah courts depends upon the nature of crime committed and the category under which it falls. Broadly speaking crimes may be covered under Haqooq-Allah (حقوق الله) or Haqooq-ul-Ibad (حقوق العباد) Mushtriq-Haqooq. Again Haqooq-ul-Ibad (حقوق العباد) are divided into:

1. Haqooq-ul-Ibad Khas (حقوق العباد خاص), and
2. Haqooq-ul-Ibad-Aam (حقوق العباد عام).

Cases under Haqooq-ul-Ibad-Khas or Jara'im al-Haqq-al-Khas can be tried by the court of Qazi only on a demand by a private claimant or aggrieved party. While in Haqooq-ul-Ibad-Aam, action can be brought by anyone. These are the crimes of public nature.

Criminal breach of trust as discussed earlier comes under private right, that is, Haqooq-ul-Ibad Khas as well as Haqooq-ul-Ibad Aam if the crime is of a public nature connected with (بیت المال) Bait-ul-Mal or public wakfs (پبلك اوقاف).

The procedure followed in the institution of suit is simple. Plaint (دعوی) is filed by the complaint in the competent court of jurisdiction. In cases of Haqooq-ul-Ibad Aam any person including government or police may file a complaint.

Breach of trust in Islamic law is civil nature wrong. It depends upon the plaintiff, if he is interested to have criminal trial, then he is to move an application to this effect before the Qazi. Qazi on receiving such petition will conduct the trial for breach of trust. For a valid petition certain formalities have been laid down by the Islamic law. If those formalities, discussed earlier under the relevant chapter, are not fulfilled the petition or plaint would not be considered by Qazi. It would not be considered legally valid.

Qazi on giving cognizance to the offence on receiving the plaint petition orders to call the person against whom the plaint is filed to appear before him and answer the allegations. The defendant is given the full opportunity to prepare the defence and reply it.

Same procedure is followed in Saudi Arabia in Shariah courts. Since the establishment of the Kingdom of Saudi Arabia, most crimes related to public rights are brought to the court by the executive authorities. But there is no bar if any public man files a suit relating thereto. If a private claimant brings an action and the court discovers that he himself has in some way participated in the crime, the court may take the initiative and try him without asking the public prosecutor to handle the prosecution. But if the case is so complicated that it requires a preliminary investigation, the court may refer it to the police and after the investigation by the police has been completed the public prosecutor may prosecute the accused. Thereafter, giving cognizance to the charge, the date for hearing is fixed. The law of 1952 (A) also lays down provisions relating to the dropping of a case if the claimants fails to appear in the first session without a reasonable excuse. Case can also be restored if the claimant or complainant moves the court for fixing hearing date again. The dropping of a case does not mean its dismissal. The whole procedure of trial is simple. It is not divided into different types of trials as we have in India.

Charge

Charge is a notice of the matter of which a person is accused. It is the first step in the Criminal Prosecution Case against him which he is to answer. The charge is to enable the accused of the allegations which he will have to meet. It must convey to the accused clearly and accurately the allegations which the prosecution is to prove against him and which he will have to defend himself. The offence imputed must be positively and precisely stated, so that the accused may certainly know with what he is charged and may be prepared to answer the charge in the best possible way. Charge is also an information to the trial court of the allegations against the accused person to which evidence is to be directed. In fact it is a basic principle of criminal law to convey to the accused with sufficient clearness and certainly what the precise accusation against him is, before he is asked to defend himself. It includes facts and law both. Significance of charged lies in the fact that the charge is a safeguard to the accused against injustice.

In criminal breach of trust cases a charge must indicate and specify the gross-sum of money, and dates on which such crime committed. A charge under section 405 is defective if it does not set out the time and the manner of entrustment alleged with sufficient particularity.

Errors or omissions in the charge cannot be regarded as material unless it is shown by the accused that he had in fact been misled or that there had been a failure of justice as a result of such error or omission.

As to modification, amendment and joinder of charges if we discuss here it would a repetition. The detailed discussions about them may be read under the head charge.

Under Islamic law where the defendant or accused appears in the court, the plaintiff or is his advocate will explain the allegations to the defendant. Qazi also explains the allegations and ask the defendant or the accused to reply. If the defendant accepts the claim, the Qazi will decide the case according. If he denies the allegations, he will be given an opportunity to prepare the defence and reply the allegations.

Under both the laws the charge is first step in the trial of the offender. It is an information to the accused precisely and accurately about the allegations with which he is to meet.

Burder of Proof

The author has already discussed in details that in India under the Evidence Law, burden of proof in relation to the judicial proceedings has been used in two senses, that is, a burden of establishing the case, and in the sense of introducing the evidence.

When a person desires any court to give judgement as to any legal right or liability dependant on the existence of facts which he asserts, must prove that those fact exist. When a person is bound to prove the existence of any facts, it is said that the burden of proof lies on that person.

In fact, the burden of proof is on the party who asserts, not on him who denies. Whoever goes to the court and asserts any fact, he has to prove the fact. The basic principle of criminal jurisprudence is that an accused person is presumed to be innocent and the burden of proving the existence of all the facts on which the existence of criminal liability depends always lies on the prosecution. However, the burden of proving a fact, initially on one party may be shifted to the obey party in certain exceptional cases.

In criminal breach of trust cases the burden of proof of establishing all the ingredients of the offence such as entrustment, mis-appropriation, dishonest intention, etc., is on prosecution.

When the prosecution succeeds in making out a prima facie case against the accused, the ones will shift to the accused to show how he is not guilty.

Islamic law is also based on the same general principle as Indian law is, that is, the burden of proof is on a person who alleges a fact. He must proof it. It is the responsibility of the plaintiff or complainant that he should prove his allegations.

Prophet (peace be upon him) in his address clearly emphasised the significance of this general rule when he said that the responsibility of burder of proof is on plaintiff, and oath is on defendant. This has been followed by Prophet's followers (صحا بۂ کرام), and all other learned scholars in practice also. These words that 'burden is on plaintiff and oath on defendant have been repeatedly used in Ahadith.

Islamic law makes it abundantly clear hath the burden of proof shall rest with the person who asserts a right and desires a court to give judgement in his favour in respect of that right. So far there is no difference between Indian and Islamic law. But the later part relating to oath taking is totally different from the Indian law.

If the complainant has no proof in support of his allegation than he may ask that the oath be taken from the defendant. Then on the oath of defendant case will be decided. It is not of significance that the possibility is that defendant may take false oath. Only the oath of defendant under such circumstances would determine the suit.

Oath taking is subject to the demand made by the plaintiff or complainant. If the defendant takes the oath on his own, it would not be covered under this section. Once oath taken by the defendant on the demand by the complainant and he denies the allegation, complainant's case would be dismissed.

Oath can be demanded in criminal breach of trust cases and oath or refusal to take oath can be made the basis of decision.

The demand for oath may be made by a representative of a party but he, in his representation capacity, cannot be subjected to oath.

The Vakeel (وکیل - agent) of a plaintiff or complainant may demand oath from the defendant but in place of defendant his vakeel or representative shall neither take oath not have the authority to refuse it.

If the party from whom oath has been demanded by the court, clearly refuses to take oath or remains silent without due excuse, the court shall decide the case against him on the basis of his refusal to take oath, and he shall have no option to take oath afterwards.

In oath taking court has to warn three times the defendant of consequences of his refusal to take oath. Even after warning refuses to take oath, the court would decide the case against him.

This law, though sounds strange, but law is law. Further Islamic law is not separate from one's faith or religion. In case where there is only one witness in support of allegation, then the alternative is that the complainant maybe given an opportunity to demand the oath to be given to the defendant. In Saudi Arabia, Shariah courts are following this law which is totally alien to its Indian counterpart.

Examination of Witnesses

Thee are three stage of examination of witnesses, that is, examination-in-chief, cross-examination, and re-examination. The evidence of the witnesses is taken in open court in the presence of presiding officer of the court. In certain exceptional cases evidence may be taken on commission also. When the witness appears in the court to give evidence he is first administered the oath to speak the truth and the only truth. A child witness below the age of 12 is not required to take the oath. The examination of witnesses is oral in the form of question and answers but recorded in the narrative form. On objection, it is proper to record question and answer both.

The examination of a witness by the party who calls him shall be called examination-in-chief. The examination of witness by the adverse party is known as his cross-examination. The party who has called the witness, subsequent to the cross-examination, if examines the witness again such examination is called as re-examination.

The irrelevant questions should not be asked in the examination-in-chief. Ordinarily, leading questions should not be asked in the examination-in-chief also.

Cross-examination is aimed to weaken, qualify or destroy the case of opposite party, and to establish the party's own case by means of his opponents' witnesses. It is said that cross-examination is a method, in the hands of intelligent lawyers, to take everything out of the mouth of the opponent's witnesses.

From sections 146 to 152, Evidence Act, lay down rules relating to questions which may be asked to shake the credit of a witness by damaging his character.

The court may forbid questions which may be scandalous, indecent, intended to insult or annoy. A witness may be protected from questions being asked without reasonable grounds.

In cases of hostile witnesses, unwilling to answer the question and tell the truth, the court may allow a party, if so demand, to put any questions to him which might be put in cross-examination by the evidence party.

Impeaching credit of witness may be either by the adverse party, or with the consent of the court, by the party who calls him.

A judge has also been empowerd to cross-examine any witness upon any answer given in reply to any question subject to certain limitations laid down in section 165 Evidence Act.

Under Islamic law witnesses are examined at the third stage. First and second stage are meant for recording the statement of complainant and the accused in their own words. On denial of the claim or charge by the defendant or the accused, the court orders the plaintiff or complainant to produce evidence in support of claim or charge.

In Shariah courts, like Indian, the order of examination-in-chief, cross-examination, and re-examination is not strictly adhered to.

Two conflicting views are there. One view advocates the order of examination-in-chief, cross-examination, and re-examination. The other view is that under Islamic Law there is no procedure for examination-in-chief. But in practice use of all the three methods are very common. Izhar (اظهار) - examination-in-chief, and Jirah (جرح) (cross-examination) were first adopted by the fourth Caliph Hazrat Ali (R.A.) in his period of Caliphat.

In Saudi Arabia Shariah court judge, have very wide jurisdiction which cannot be said to be restricted to any particular method of examination. Examination-in-chief is not the feature of Saudi Arabian Law. Judges themselves assume this responsibility. Duty to this it is said that there is no cross-examination of witnesses in Saudi Arabian judicial system except by the judges themselves. But an in-depth study of system may tell that the cross-examination not only by the judges but also by the opposing party or his representative does exist in practice. However, re-examination is not a common-practice. But the rule of challenging probity of witnesses is common in Shariah courts.

In brief it may be said that examination of witnesses is similar to Indian law but not to that extent inpractice which is recognised by Indian Evidence Law.

Confession

If an accused or a suspected person during investigation volunteers confession, the investigating officer should present him before a magistrate for recording the confession under section 164 of Criminal Procedure Code.

Any magistrate whether has jurisdiction or no jurisdiction in the case may record the confession under Chapter XII Criminal Procedure code; or under any other law for the time being in force.

A police officer cannot record a confession.

The magistrate before recording the confession must administer a caution to the accused or suspect who volunteers to make confession and explain to him that, if he does so, it may be used as evidence against him.

The magistrate shall not record any such confession unless he is satisfied and has reasons to believe that it is being made voluntarily.

Recording of confession shall be in the manner laid down in section 281 Criminal Procedure Code. Recording should be in the same language as of the accused, if not then it should be explained and interpreted to him. He shall be at liberty to explain or add to his answers and shall be signed by him. The magistrate shall make a memorandum at the foot of such record and at the end he is to sign the statement.

The investigating officer may get valuable information from the confession recorded by the magistrate, but he is not to rely upon. He should try to obtain corroborative evidences. It will help him in judging the nature and character of the confession.

For making confession admissible it should be proved beyond reasonable doubt that at the time of recording the statement or even before when the accused is in custody of police, no police officer or other person in authority should offer or make or caused to be offered or made, any inducement, threat or promise in violation of the provisions of section 163 Criminal Procedure Code and section 24 of Indian Evidence Act, 1872.

If above noted conditions are satisfied then confession is admissible in evidence. Section 463 Criminal Procedure Code makes the confession admissible only when it is established that the expediency of justice so requires and the accused in his defence is not prejudiced.

Under Islamic law the significance of (Iqrar) confession is proved by Qur'ãnic injunctions and Ahadith. Allah Ta'ala makes it obligatory to give the testimony if a person knows the facts of a case. Confession is one such testimony upon which the decision depends. When the party concerned demands it is not lawful to conceal it.

After a confession is made by the accused the judge is to pronounce the judgement. In other words it is the basis for a judgement.

For a valid confession Islamic law requires that there should be a person who makes the confession. He should be of a sound mind, adult, and independent or free person. If a confession is made by an infant, not capable to judge thing rightly or wrongly, such a confession would be illegal. According to Prophet (peace be upon him), three person are not competent to make confession:

1. An infant till he because major or adult;

2. A person - sleeping, till he is not awaken; and

3. مجنون (unconscious or insane) till gets into senses or gains consciousness.

This principle has been incorporated in section 65 of Pakistan Islamic Law of Evidence. Aqil and Baligh are the conditions for a valid confession.

A confession by a guardian against the interest of his minor ward shall not be valid and cannot be admitted.

Coercion is another ground which makes concession in admissible. An Iqrar of a person who is under the influence of intoxication would not be vaid in cases where liability is under Hudud.

If these conditions are satisfied a confession made voluntarily would be valid and admissible in evidence. Judge is to pronounce judgement on such a confession.

In Saudi-Arabia confession is divided in two parts: formal confession, and informal confession. Formal is one which is made before the trial court. Whereas informal confession is usually made outside the court. The later one must be proved in the same way as fact is proved in the court. It is not considered a hearsy evidence. It is considered a confession, when proved, as conclusive as formal one is.

The confession made about a crime outside the court under a sudden shock is also admissible although he may claim that he was not aware what he said due to sudden shock.

Ability to speak is another ground to determine the validity of confession. Confession by a dumb person is controversial. However, in Saudi Arabia an admission of a dumb person by signs is not valid, except in Tazeer.

Inducement, threat or compulsion should be absent when a confession is made. It must be made voluntarilly and freely.

Confession must be express. Saudi Arabian Law does not recognize implied confession.

If the confession is not consistent with the fact in issue, the court on grounds of doubts or suspicion will not receive it as valid confession.

If a confession, in Saudi Arabia, is made to the police, while in police custody, in such a case police will immediately take him to the nearest Shariah Court where his statement would be recorded. If the confession is made to the police at a time when he cannot be produced before the court, then the person will be detained alone in custody till the next-morning. He would not be allowed to mix with other detainess till he is produced before the court and his statement is recorded. He is kept alone because is mixed with other persons then possibility is that others may persuade him not to confess his guilt.

Generally, recording of confession before the Shariah court is in cases of serious crimes.

Statement may be recorded in any court. It is not necessary that it should be recorded in the trial court.

As a caution the court must ascertain whether the statement made by the accused is voluntary or not. It must be an authentic one.

The extra-judicial confession must be corroborated by independent witnesses, then only would be admissible.

Accused may also retract his confession. Even the judge may hint to the confession to recall his confession.

The retraction or calling back the confession is not by words but it may be inferred from the conduct of the accused also. An accused who intends to flee when he is being prepared for the execution of his sentence or after he has received part of the sentence, is to be regarded as having restracted his confession. If a convicted person recalls his confession before the punishment is implemented, the punishment should not be enforced and the person must be committed back to the trial court to consider his retraction.

In Tazeer cases confession retracted is admissible but not in Hudud cases. In such a situation Hudud cases are converted into the Tazeer. As breach of trust is covered under Tazeer, hence any confession made in such a case would not be retractable.

The above discussion makes it clear that the confession under Indian Law and Islamic Law stands almost on the same basis except in retraction of confession cases. In Indian under the evidence law the mere fact that a confession is retracted may not be a ground for its rejection and to draw inference that it was obtained by improper inducement. A mere subsequence retration of a confession, when the confession as duly recorded and certified by a competent magistrate is not enough to make it inadmissible in all cases. But a retraction may raise a doubt in the mind of court about it's voluntary character and trustworthiness. It is now a settled rule of prudence that before convicting an accused on the basis of confession, which has been retracted afterwards, the court must see that it has been corroborated by some other independent evidence, though, no doubt, that a conviction without corroboration is not strictly illegal.

However, under Islamic law, retracted confession in serious offences cannot be made the basis of conviction. Further, the judge of a Shariah court may give an hint recalling the confession. It is not so in India. Only caution is administered. Hint is not preferred. However, in Tazeer cases even a retracted confession is made voluntarilly can be the basis of conviction. On this later rule no difference lies between Indian and Islamic law except that Indian law requires corroboration of retracted confession by independent witnesses.

In India critics on law of confession in the Evidence Act requires some changes. Where the confessions are generally obtained, not in all cases, by inducement, threat or promise ad even in cases where it is made voluntarily, after getting the advice of the legal profession, it is retracted at the time of trial, they make on observation that in such a situation, 'there is only one remedy, no confession made before the trial begins, should be admitted in evidence. If the person is really penitent, let him confess and plead guilty at the trial.

Evidence

Under Indian Law evidence means and includes - all statements which the court permits or requires to be made before it by witnesses, in relation to matters of fact under inquiry; such statement are called oral evidence; and all documents produced for the inspection of the court; such documents are called documentary evidence.

Generally evidence has been classified under three heads:

1. Direct or indirect which is known as circumstantial evidence;
2. Real or personal; and lastly,
3. Original or unoriginal.

Direct evidence are those which are evidence of the precise point-in-issue. Eye-witnesses are covered under it. On the other hand circumstantial evidences are the evidence of collateral facts and circumstances for which a reasonable conclusion about the question in issue may be drawn which is always based on experience and thereby a relation is established between known and proved facts and the facts sought to be proved. Circumstancial evidence should be such which will reasonably lead to the conclusion that it was the accused who did the act.

The criminal breach of trust case may be proved either by direct or circumstancial evidence alone or with the help of both. So far as admissibility is concerned direct and circumstancial both stand on the same footing.

A real evidence is that which is addressed to the senses of the court. The thing which is an evidence of a fact may be brought before the court or, the judge, in some cases, may go to the spot for the inspection of the thing. Personal evidence is that which is afforded by a human agent, either in the way of discourse or by voluntary signs.

Original Evidence is one which a witness states to have heard or seen through his own senses.

Unoriginal evidence is the second-hand evidence, which has been derived from some other source. It is also known as hearsay evidence. The witness has no first-hand knowledge of the fact.

Hearsay evidence with certain exception is not admissible (see section 60).

Now-a-days tape-recorded statements and dog tracking evidence are produced before the court, the first one has been declared by the supreme court as admissible evidence (R.M. Malkani V. State of Maharashtre, AIR 1973, SC. 157), the later one, in the present state of scientific knowledge, even if admissible, is not ordinarily, of much weight.

Under Islamic law Shahadah (شهادة) means to give true information for the purpose of proving any right or fact, in or before a court. Such statement or information be recorded in the presence of both the litigant parties or their legal representatives. The procedure is that the witness should utter a word 'Ashhadu' (اشهد) or use any synonymous expression.

The significance lies in the fact that it must be a just and honest information. Justice is Allah's attribute, and to stand firm for justice is to be a witness to Allah, even if it is detrimental to one's interest.

So far we do not find any marked difference between Indian and Islamic laws. Under Islamic law it is connected must with the faith, that is, God, rewards or punishes for just or honest and false witness as the case may be.

But as to quantum of evidence (نصاب شهادة) to be produced before the court, Indian and Islamic law differs. Islamic law prescribes different quantum of evidence in different cases based on the nature of offence committed. Indian law does not specify any such quantum for different kinds of offences.

For criminal breach of trust, the fact may be proved by two male witnesses, and in the absence of two male witnesses by the evidence of one male and two female witnesses. Two female witness are considered equal to one male witness. India law does not lay such limits.

There may be a situation where evidence of a single witness coupled with oath by the plaintiff may be admissible. Such a situation may arises when the defendant fails to appear before the court although summons were duly served to him.

Further under Islamic law where the plaintiff fails to produce a witness but produce documentary evidence the court may, if it is of the opinion that the plaintiff's claim appears to be probably true, decide the matter by giving an oath to the plaintiff. But this is subject to one limitation, that is, the defendant must have been served with the summons three times and the defendant inspect or receiving the summons without any uzre-sharai (عذر شرعی) fails to appear in the court. This is another distinguishing feature of Islamic law comparing with Indian Law.

Islamic Law again differs from Islamic law in relation to qualification of admissible witnesses. According to Islamic law, characteristic of witness admissible in evidence are to be determined according to the stages of Shahadah (شهادة). Stages are: تحمل شهادة - Tahammal-e-Shadah, and Ada-e-Shahadah (ادائے شهادة).

Capability of a witness to give evidence at the time of (تحمل شهادة) - Tahammaul Shahadah includes such conditions as: witness should be of sound mind, witness should not be blind, witness should been eye-witness. He should himself inspect the (مشهود به Mashud Bihi). But in specific cases Tahammul-Shadah can also be by hearsay. As to blind witness there are differences between the Imams of different schools as regard to it's admissibility.

For Ada-e-Shahadah (ادائے شہادة) the conditions requisite are: Baligh (adult), sane person, Baseer (بصیر) - having-eye-sight, independent, Adil, Natiq-having the faculty of talking and Muslim. These conditions must be fulfilled otherwise an evidence would not be sound in law.

The last condition would not apply in cases where non-Muslim are involved. A non-Muslim's evidence according to Shariah is admissible.

If the minor witness is Muslim, sensible and intelligent enough to understand thing and not has a reputation of a liar, his evidence would be admissible in law.

Evidence of a dumb person shall be admissible, except in cases relating to Hudud, only when it is written by the witness himself in the presence of the presiding officer of the court.

Tazkiyah-al-Shuhud (تزکیہ الشہود) is an special feature of Islamic law of evidence which is not found under the Indian law. This authority is vested in the court. It is a mode of inquiry adopted by a court for the purpose of declaring a witness Adil (عادل) or Ghair-Adil (غیرعادل). The court proceeds with the Tazkiyal-al-Shuhud after the statements of the witness are recorded. In this connection two persons reliable, well-inform and belonging to the same walk of life to which the witness belongs, shall be consulted either openly (علانیہ) or confidentially (خفیہ). It is the discretion of the court to adopt any mode of Tazkiyah-al-Shuhud.

Compounding of Offences

Offences under section 406 and 408 of the Indian Penal Code are compoundable. But offences covered section 409, Indian Penal Code are not compundable. Section 320, Criminal Procedure Code is a relevant section which permits such compromises. But the offences covered under section 406 and 408 Indian Penal Code are compoundable subject to three conditions.

1. Prosecution for such offences may be compounded where the value of the property which is the subject matter of breach of trust does not exceed two hundred and fifty rupees. It exceeds the limits, no compromise is allowed;

2. Prosecution for such offences can be compounded with the permission of the court before which the prosecution is pending; and

3. Prosecution is compoundable by persons referred in the third column of the table referred in earlier chapter under compounding of offences head, and by non-else. Here the person referred in the third column is the owner of the property in respect of which the breach of trust has been committed.

On the other hand Islamic law prefers compromise and compounding of dispute rather than parties contesting in the court. Allah Ta'ala also prefers it. There is no monetary limitation as to the compoundability of criminal cases as exists under the Indian Law. If the victims forgive or compromise with, it is far better. His reward is with Allah. Allah does not love the wrong-doers. Allah Ta'ala commands for self-restrained practices, and do what we can to come to an amicable settlement.

Islamic law not only allows compunding of cases of breach of trust but also permits to the parties to refer the matters in dispute for arbitration to settle the dispute even outside the courts.

Breach of trust is an offence which is both compoundable and may be referred to artitration if the parties so desire.

However, some Muslim jurists are of the view that if all the cases referred to the court, irrespective of knowing the nature of dispute, are returned for compounding the cases, it will result in loosening the confidence in the efficacy of courts, and, it would also lower down the honour and dignity of Shariat (شریعت) and Shariah court. They suggest that compoundability of cases by restricted only where there is no legal ambiguity or the matter referred to the court is not too complicated, or court considers that past relations between the parties were such that compounding of the case be preferred. In such case there should not be any ethic in referring back for compounding the cases. But if it is otherwise than court should decide itself.

For artitration Islamic law requires that they should possess the qualifications of a Qazi on the ground that the arbitrator virtually performs functions of the Qazi.

This preferential attitude of Islamic law for returning back cases for compounding and permitting arbitration of disputes outside the court distinguishes the Islamic law and Indian Law. In India compoundability of offence is restricted on the basis of value of property involved. Under Islamic law there is no such restriction.

Vakalat - وکالت

Under section 303, Criminal Procedure Code an accused can, as a matter of right, claim to be defended by a pleader of his choice.

A conviction following a trial cannot stand if there has been refusal to hear the lawyer. So also an appeal cannot be disposed of ex-parte where the appellant is entitled to be heard by a lawyer assigned to him by the government, who fails to reach the court in time to conduct the appeal.

If the defence lawyer is weak in presenting the case of his client, a duty is cast upon a trial judge to protect the interest of the accused and cross-examine the witnesses of the prosecution himself. The main object of this provision is that the interest of the accused should remain supreme and in no way be prejudiced.

Section 304, Criminal Procedure Code authorises the court that where an accused is not represented by a pleader during the trial before the court of session and it appears to the court that the accused has not sufficient means to engage a pleader, the court shall assigns a pleader for his defence at the expense of the state and also empowers the state government to extend this facility to other cases.

Islamic law is different from Indian law on this point. No doubt under Islamic law, it is lawful for an accused to appoint another his agent for the management of suits or criminal prosecutions or for the payment or exaction of all rights. However, Hadd and Qasas are exceptions to this general rule. Even on this point there is a differences of opinion among Muslim jurists.

Imam Abu Haneefa (R.A.) is of the opinion that an agent or vakeel cannot be appointed without the permission of the opposite party in cases where the client is not sick or on journey which may not be for three days or more.

But according to Imam Mohammad and Imam Abu Yusuf, a vakeel or agent may be appointed in such conditions even without to consent and permissible of the opposite party. Imam Shafi'i (R.A.) is also of this view.

Argument of the two disciples is that the appointment of an agent or vakeel is the act of an individual in regard to a right purely his own. Therefore, it should not depend on the consent of another in the present instance.

Hazrat Imam Abu Haneefa on the other hand, argues that the constituent is himself under the necessity of giving an answer, and must attend in case the magistrate should summon him.

Individuals differ with respect to their capacious of managing suits. Therefore, if it were admitted that the appointment of an agent is absolute, this would be injurious to the adversary. Thus the validity of the appointment must be suspended on his consent. It is otherwise where the person is sick or absent.

There is a consensus of all the modern Muslim jurists on the point that a woman may appoint an agent for litigation in all cases.

In practice we find that in Islamic countries persons under accusation may employ agent to conduct their defences, and agents may make replies and submit rejoinders, and the doubt with respect to deputation does not prevent this.

It is clear that Islamic law and Indian law on the point of deputing someone as agent or vakeel to defend in prosecution based on different principles. Accused as a matter of right cannot claim to be defended by the lawyer under Islamic law. But on the other hand in India, he may claim to be defended by a lawyer of his choice. Not only this courts have also been authorised to appoint lawyers to defend accused if they are not in the position of engaging a lawyer to defend.

Hierarchy of Courts

In India, at present, there are three types of criminal courts, that is, courts constituted by the constitution of India, courts constituted by criminal procedure code, and courts constituted by other special statutes.

Hierarchy is in the following order:

1. Supreme Court;
2. High Court;
3. Court so Session;

4. Judicial Magistrates of First Class,

   In any metropolitan area, metropolitan magistrate;

5. Judicial magistrates of the second class; and

6. Executive magistrates.

This hierarchy of criminal courts is based on the principle of separation of the judiciary from the executive. As a consequence of separation there are two categories of magistrates, namely, the judicial magistrates, and the executive magistrate.

Offences relating to criminal breach of trust are triable by the court of magistrate of first class.

Considering governing rules relating to jurisdiction, territorial division, etc., would be a repetition of what the author has discussed under Chapter VII Part A of this thesis. Therefore, let us distinguish the hierarchy of courts in India with Islamic courts.

For the purposes of studying hierarchy under Islamic law the author has devoid Part B of the said Chapter in detail. Structure of Shariah courts in different countries have also been discussed. To make a comparision with all is very difficult. In India we are not having Shariah courts. But in the past, during Mughal period Shariah courts were existing. Out study, thus confines to the comparision of Shariah courts existing during Mughal period with that of the present day seculars courts of India.

I. The Royal Court (Diwan-i-Shahi) under Islamic law was the highest court. At that time it was resembling with the British Privy Council. At present it resembles with the Supreme Court of India. It was presided over by the Emperor or Sultan. He used to hear and decide cases personally. Muslim Emperors' decisions were the real decision of the sovereign, not like that or Privy Council's decisions which fictitiously regarded as the king decision. There was no appeal against the decision of the royal court. Same is the position of Supreme Court of India. It is the highest court of appeal. Only Mercy petition may be filed to the President of India against the decision of supreme court. King or Emperor was having original and appellate jurisdictions both.

The Royal court was presided over by the sovereign and decision was given in consultation with the law officers of the crown, the highest state officials and the persons learned in law.

II. The Mir-i-Adl, the High Diwan, The provincial Diwan, these judicial officers resemble the judges of the High Court and of the District courts of today.

They had the original jurisdiction, like the High Court (original side), and as well as the District judges of the present day.

Under Islamic judicial structure judges of the High Court and of Districts had the power of superintendence over the lower courts under their respective jurisdictions. These administrative and supervisory power just resembles with the present High Court powers in their respective Provinces. At the District level resembles with the powers of the District judge.

III. The Qazi-ul-Quzat resembles with the chief metropolitan magistrates or magistrates of the first class.

The chief Qazi also resembles the session judge to some extent, i.e., in his power of hearing criminal appeal and holding session trial exercising original criminal jurisdiction.

IV. The subehdar occupied the position of the governor of a province. The subehdar used to preside over the chief criminal court of province.

V. The Foujdar of the District town or the Parganah resembles the sub-divisional magistrate and had jurisdiction over criminal matters.

VI. The Muhtasib or the public officer used to perform the function of police, and excise officers, as well as municipal supervisors of our time. He was empowered to control and prevent the spreading of evil and vices in the society.

In brief it may be said that Mughal Shariah structure completely resembles with the present day judicial hierarchy. In other Islamic countries also a well-set Islamic judicial structure from bottom to top exists. All these judicial structures resemble with the present modern system.

Punishment

In India punishment for breach of trust has been provided for different situations under different sections. Section 405, Indian Penal Code defines the offence and for violation of conditions enumerated in the said section, punishment has been referred in section 406. Section 408, 409, deals with the offence committed by servants, agents, partners, and public servants and punishments have also been prescribed there in respectively. For every breach of trust, maximum, punishment has been given in the relevant sections up to which punishment may extent.

The court before passing the sentence is to weigh the merit of each case, the mitigating circumstances, and facts which differ from case to case.

Procedure for sentencing has been laid down in section 248 Criminal Procedure Code.

Where the magistrate after framing the charge, finds the accused not guilty, he shall record an order of acquittal.

However, where the magistrate, in any case, finds the accused guilty but does not proceed in accordance with the provisions of section 235 or section 360 Criminal Procedure Code, he shall, after hearing the accused on the question of sentence, pass sentence upon him according to law.

Clause (3) of section 248 deals with cases of previous conviction where the accused denies, the magistrate may, after he has convicted the accused, take evidence in respect of the alleged previous conviction, and shall record a finding thereon. Before taking evidence, conviction under clause (2) section 248 Criminal Procedure Code is necessary.

As to quantum of punishment to be awarded, it differs from case to case. In one case it may be lenient, and in another severe. Sometime in view of extenuating circumstances severe punishment is rendered unnecessary. But for every offence of breach of trust there is a before hand prescribed punishment which the court, after hearing both the parties is to award to the accused.

The breach of trust by a clerk or public servant is of an aggravated nature calling for substantial punishment.

Under section 409, Indian Penal Code, offence committed by the public servant is specially of a serious nature and requires severe punishment.

The court before awarding the sentence is to take into consideration the gravity of the offence, the impact on the public and particularly the person who were deprived of their properties.

Once a sentence is awarded the general law is that a sentence commences to run from the time it is imposed, but section 427 (1) engrafts an exception to this general rule. Exception relates to the case of a person who is already undergoing a sentence of imprisonment. A discretion is given to the court to direct that the subsequent sentence shall run concurrently with the previous sentence. After the pronouncement of final judgement the court is not authorised to exercise this discretion.

Section 428, Criminal Procedure Code provides that the period of detention of an accused as an under trial prisoner shall be off against the term of imprisonment imposed on him on conviction.

The powers conferred by section 432 and 433 Criminal Procedure Code upon the state government to remit or commute a sentence in which public servants of central government are involved cannot be exercised by the state government without consultation with the central government. Where persons prosecuted for offences under the laws in the state field and some in the union field and sentenced to separate terms of imprisonment to run concurrently, both state as well as centre have the power either to remit or commute the sentences.

Under Islamic law crimes are acts or omissions contrary to legal prohibitions imposed by Allah Ta'ala, the infringement of which entails punishment prescribed by Him.

Law punishing crimes not only emanates from Holy Qur'ãn, but from the traditions and acts of Prophet (peace be upon him) also.

Still there may be acts not covered under either Qur'ãn and Sunnah, are declared offences and punishment may be laid down by the body of authority on the basis of Ijma and qiyas of Ulemah.

However, under Islamic law, no authority has been given power to do whatever it chases. No authority has any power to declare any act as offence and prescribe punishment thereto contrary to Qur'ãnic injunctions or Sunnah of Holy Prophet (peace be upon him).

The basic rule governing Shariah punishment is - 'unless relevant provisions exist, no judgement can be passed on the actions of a sensible person.' An Act cannot be declared illegitimate unless it is contrary to law in existence.

The other fundamental rule is - 'things and actions are legitimate in themselves'. In means acts and omission are not illegal unless a provision forbidding such a course of action exists. If no provision exists, a person is not accountable for his acts or omission.

The third governing rule in Islam is - 'a person under legal obligations is one who is able to understand the reason for being so'. It is inferred from this that a person should be under legal obligation, capable of understanding the obligation, and lastly should be capable of performing his obligation, and lastly should be capable of performing his obligations. Impossible things would not create any liability. Further a thing which is beyond his power to perform would also not make him liable. Knowingly disobedient under such conditions will make him liable for punishment.

For all these fundamental rules Holy Qur'ãn is the fountain.

However, as to the application of these principles, the procedure varies with different crimes. No crimes and no punishment in cases involving Hudud, Qisas and Diyat, unless provision exists. Same principle applies to cases covering penal punishment (Tazeer). However, Shariah does not apply in the same manner in Tazeer as it does in case involving Huddud, Qisas and Diyat. In Tazeer cases the application of the general rules have wider scope keeping in view the demands of public interest and penal character of such crimes. The wider sphere of operation under Tazeer is due to the fact that Shariah does not lay down such specific punishment as may be binding upon the judge to award as in the case of Hud and Qisas. The judge, infact, is to choose any punishment most be fitting and appropriate to the crime committed and the circumstances under which it is committed. He may be lenient in awarding the punishment or may award severe punishment as circumstances and facts of a case demands.

If public interest is in jeopardy, there is nothing inhibiting the combination of a penal punishment (Tazeer) with a hud. Further penal punishment may be added to Qisas for wilfully committing an offence involving qisas except death sentence.

Penal punishment, as such under Islamic law, is a corrective measure and it is the right of the community as distinct from the right of an individual.

Tazeer may be awarded in addition to Diyat also.

As to determine the punishment for breach of trust, Prophet (peace be upon him) has said:

> "The hand of a plunderer, or a snatcher taking away the property, or a breaker of trust, is not to cut off".

It means that breach of trust is different from larceny. Breach of trust is covered under Tazeer, which is a reformative and corrective measure. Punishment for breach of trust cases are determined in accordance to the injunctions of Qur'ãn and Ahadith.

Holy Qur'ãn and Ahadith have prescribed limits in Tazeer also. A judge is to award penal punishment within limits, that is, exhortation, warning, boycotts, intimidation, scouraging, physical punishment, fine, and imprisonment. The purpose for imposing Tazeer is that the man should not become habitual to the commissions of such acts. It is discretionary with the judge but jurisdiction is not without limitations. The charge against Shariah that it has no determined penal punishment is baseless. Judge in Tazeer cases does not enjoy absolute powers.

Comparing these general principles with Indian law, it may be inferred that these principles are common under both the laws. There is no difference between the two except that one is a revealed law, and another a man made law. Both intend to protect the society from the wrong-doers.

In breach of trust cases where Tazeer is awarded, in fact, there is no difference. No doubt, under the Indian Law maximum punishment is provided in the relevant sections, but when the judge awards the sentence, he takes into consideration the mitigating circumstances, and it is discretionary to award any sentence befitting the facts of the cases. Same is the position under Shariah. The judge is to take into consideration all extenuating and mitigating conditions and facts of the case, and it is his discretion to award any sentence most appropriate and most suiting to the conditions of the case. This discretion of the judge is not absolute and limitless. He is to act, as in Indian Law, within bounds.

Judgement

Judgement is the final order or decision of the court intimated to the parties and the world at large by the formal pronouncement of delivery in open court by the trial judge and signing and dating it simultaneously and thereby terminating the criminal proceedings finally.

Every case in the final determination has to depend upon its own facts. No court is permitted to alter or review its judgement or final order disposing of a case when it is signed except otherwise provided by the Criminal Procedure Code or by any other law for the time being in force.

As to the general principles governing the judgement there is no difference between the two laws except on issues relating judgement based upon compromise, confession, oath and possession the details of which the author has already given in earlier Chapter on judgement.

Unlike India, under Islamic law judgement may be also based on Qura (قرعه). It must be based upon Shariah, that is, on Qur'ãnic commandments and traditions of Prophet Mohammad (peace be upon him).

The common principle governing judgement under both the laws:

That it must be based upon justice (قرائن) Qarain, (فراست) Farasat, apparent conditions relating to the facts of a case, should be pronounced in the open court, in the presence of both the parties except otherwise where both the laws provides to be so.

The differences between the two are:

When judgement is pronounced in the open court under Indian law, it cannot be changed, altered, modified, etc. Decision pronounced is final even if there is an apparent error in the judgement. Such an error can be corrected only on appeal against such a judgement. But under Sḥariah, for the sake of justice, it may be amended, modified or altered by the judge even after the judgement has been pronounced. Main purpose behind is that no injustice be done to the litigant parties.

Another differentiating point is that the judge in India in lower courts sits all alone and hearts the case. On the other hand judge in Shariah court is assisted by Mufti and Muhtasib. In cases where the judge of a Shariah court is not in a position to form his opinion about any legal issue, he may consult other Islamic known jurists and thus form his opinion. This reference system is not permitted under the Indian Law.

As to judicial activism of the judges, In India, judgements are based on creativeness, giving liberal interpretations and trying to make law cooping with the prevalent conditions of the society. On this point also there is almost little different between the two laws. Under Islamic law if a Qazi learned in Islamic law or jurisprudence, and efficient in making his opinion by resorting to 'Ijtihad' (اجتهاد) he may decide the case on his conclusions taking into considerations all the facts and circumstances and rules of equity and justice, and thus applying the law best suiting to the existing requirements of the society.

Both the laws require that the judges should not delay in delivering the judgement. If, under Shariah, a judge intentionally delays, he will be sinner and may be removed from the post also. Thus judgement must be expeditiously delivered. However, if there is any reasonable cause, it may also be delayed. But in India delay in delivering judgements are often complained of. There is no such provision in Indian Law that if a judge delays in delivering the judgement he may be removed from his office.

Appeal, Revision and Reference

Chapter XXIX, Criminal Procedure Code guarantees the rights of appeal either against acquittal or conviction of the accused person involved in the commission of crimes.

An appeal shall lie from any judgement or order of a criminal court except as provided for by Criminal Procedure Code or by any other law for the time being in force.

An appeal to High Court lies from a judgement or order of a session court or additional session court or any other court which include the court of magistrate of the first class subject to the limitations and restrictions laid down in the chapter above referred which the author has already elaborated under appeal chapter earlier.

In fact, Chapter XXIX comprises section beginning with 372 to 405 which have laid down exhaustive rules governing not only appeal, but revision and reference also. All these rules governing earlier. A reference of those rules would be an irrelevant repetition of the same.

In cases where the accused person has pleaded guilty and has been convicted on such plea, there shall be no appeal except to the extent or legality of the sentence.

Again no appeal in cases where sentence of imprisonment does not exceed three months, or of fine not exceeding two hundred rupees or of both such imprisonment and fine or where a magistrate of first class passes only a sentence of fine not exceeding one hundred rupees.

Government may also go in appeal against the inadequacy of sentences, or against an order of acquittal. It is not permissible to alter the conviction to an aggravated category of offence for which the accused was not convicted.

Section 378 provides for an appeal by - state government, or central government or the complainant provided in the later case special leave obtained from the High Court.

In an appeal High Court has full power to review the evidence upon which the order of acquittal is based. Findings of the trial court can be reversed only for very substantial and compelling reasons.

The appellate court has the power to examine the record and hear both appellant or his pleader and also the public prosecutor. If the court considers that there is no sufficient grounds for interfering in the judgement of the lower court may dismiss the appeal. It may reverse the order and may direct further inquiry be made, or the accused be re-tried, or committed for trial, as the case may be, or find him guilty and pass-sentence on him according to law.

In cases of appeal for enhancement of sentence the appellate court may reverse the finding and sentence, and acquit or discharge the accused or order retrial.

When an appeal is decided by the High Court, it shall certify its judgement or order to the court by which the finding, sentence or order appealed against was recorded or passed and such court shall make orders conformable to the judgement or order of the High Court and record is amended accordingly.

In a case where an appeal is heard by the High Court before a bench of judges and they differ in their opinions, in such a situation the appeal shall be laid before another judge, and that judge after hearing, shall deliver his opinion, and the judgement or order shall follow that opinion provided that if one of the judges constituting the bench, or where the appeal is laid before another judge under this section, that judge so requires, the appeal shall be re-heard and decided by a larger bench of judges.

The judgements or orders passed by the appellate court upon an appeal shall be final.

Power of making reference in respect of any question of law involving validity of a statutory provision rests in sessions judges and in all metropolitan judges. Section 395, Criminal Procedure code gives detailed rules governing reference to the High Court. When the question has been so referred the High Court shall pass such order thereon as it thinks fit and shall cause a copy of such order to be sent to the court by which the reference was made, which shall dispose of the case conformably to the said order.

As to power of revision at the district level, it has been given only to the court of session and not to the chief judicial magistrate. Section 397 of Criminal Procedure Code is the relevant section which gives very wide powers and court can take up the matter even suo motu.

Power of revisions are conferred upon High Court also. Session judge as well as High Court judge have concurrent revisional jurisdictions.

General practice of all High Court have been that the High Court do not entertain an application for revisions except on some special grounds unless a previous application has been made to the session judge. However, there is no bar to a party coming directly to the High Court without first moving the session judge.

Under revisional powers of the session judge and High Court, they may call for any record from any subordinate courts situated within their respective local jurisdictions and examine the same with a view to satisfy themselves as to correctness, legality or propriety of the findings, sentence or order, recorded or passed and also as to regularity of any proceedings of such subordinate courts.

High Court may also interfere in revision in respect of interlocutory order also, but not the orders passed at the stage of appeal.

The court under revisionary powers cannot pass order which may prejudice the interest of the accused or other person unless he has an opportunity of being heard.

Further nothing shall be deemed to authorises a High Court to convert a finding of acquittal into one of conviction.

No proceeding by way of revision shall be entertained at the instance of the party who could have appealed.

If a person files a revision under an erroneous belief that no appeal lies against the order, then court may treat it as appeal and deal with the same accordingly.

Over and above if the powers of revision vested in the High Court, in order to prevent miscarriage of justice or abuse of process, High Court can invoke inherent jurisdiction under section 482 to remedy the errors.

Under Islamic law the concept of appeal, revision and reference is not alien. The judgement or order of a subordinate court or the same court may be quashed if it is in inconsistent with Holy Qur'ãn, Sunnah and Ijma. If any judge decides a case arbitratilly or cruelly or against (اجماع) consensus of learned scholars, then such a decision may be reversed, reviewed or changed.

Thus, the basis of appeal or revision is different from Indian Law. If a decision is contrary to Qur'ãn, Ahadith and Ijma, there lies an appeal against such a decision. Whereas under India conditions of appeal has been enumerated in Criminal Procedure Code. It is generally said that in Islam there is no provision for appeal. This notion is simply fallacious. To remove error that leads to evil and injustice is one of the fundamental teachings of Islam and a foremost function of its administration of justice. Muslim jurists have recognized appeal in principle.

History in India is a witness that Mughal Emperors in the past established regular courts of appeal and revision. If the parties were not satisfied with the decision of Qazi at the district level, the aggrieved party could go in appeal before the chief Diwan or the chief Qazi on matters of law. At present in all Muslim countries, appeal and revision have been recognized as fundamental principles governing the administration of justice. In every Muslim country there exist courts of different grades for appeal and revision.

The rule which are being followed as to appeal and revision in Shariah courts of the present day are almost the same as that of Indian Law.

Both the parties are allowed to go in appeal if either of them feel aggrieved. The decision of the appellate court will be in conformity with Shariah or Islamic law. Detailed governing rules are discussed under the chapter dealing with appeal and revision.

In revision, the Higher Shariah courts have the corrective powers of errors of the lower courts. The procedure adopted in Shariah courts is almost the same as under Indian law.

As to reference, there is a provision under the Islamic law, that in cases where two Qazis are appointed as judges to Shariah court to sit together, hear and decide the cases, if there is difference of opinion between the two judges or Qazi and Mufti, the matter may be referred either tot he High Court for decision, or to a full court consisting of the Qazi, Mufti, the Muhtasib and a scholar learned in law.

In cases of complications on point of law, the Qazi may refer the matter to another Qazi for his opinion or the jurists, learned in Islamic law.

If there is a difference of opinion among jurists (فقهاء) of that time, there he should form his own opinion which may be more nearer to truth and justice. Even his opinion is in conflict with the jurists of that time, he may give the judgement contrary to their opinions.

Islamic concept of justice is realised only when confidence among the masses about the performance of the judiciary is created. It is possible when for all errors, there are remedies available in the form of appeal, revision and reference.

Position of Non-Muslim

Islam is said to be a totalitarian religion. It is an inevitable result of the very faith in God. A believer surrenders to Almighty completely. His prayers, sacrifices, life and death all surely for God. Under such a situation, the question arises whether non-Muslims be also subjected to such a law to which they have no faith in.

The answer to the above question has been elaborated in detail earlier under the head 'non-Muslims and Islamic Law.' Precisely it may be said that non-Muslims membership of the nation in an Islamic state is based on contracts and compromises reached between them and the Islamic state. Once such a contract is entered into and obligations resulted there form, such obligations become trust upon the conscience and pledge of the state or the nation to take care of them.

Thus their rights are determined not only according to the basis text in the Qur'ãn and the Sunnah, but also according to the terms of their contracts entered into. Qur'ãn clearly commands that Muslims should be kind and just while dealing with non-Muslims unless they are rampant and out to destroy them and their faith.

Holy Qur'ãn further commands that the Islamic state is bound to see that all obligations express or implied resulted from covenant must be faithfully discharged. Non-Muslims are not to be discriminated.

Just and honourable treatment and respect to the obligations and discharge thereto is the basic education of Islam. Allah commands that if you give words, you should honour those words and do justice thereunto, even if it is against a Kinsman, and fulfil the covenant of Allah.

Prophet (peace be upon him) also warns that whosoever is cruel and hard on a contractee or curtails his rights, or burdens him with more than he can endure or takes anything out of his property against his free-will, Prophet (peace be upon him) himself would be a plaintiff against such a person on the day of judgement. This Sunnah of Prophet (peace be upon him) enhances the significance of dealings with non-Muslims living in an Islamic state. Prophet's (peace be upon him) practices and dealings with non-Muslims in his life time further adds significance and importance to the dealing with non-Muslims in an Islamic state.

Some of the treaties which Prophet (peace be upon him) entered with non-Muslims are the constitutional landmarks guaranteeing all types of freedoms to non-Muslims in an Islamic state.

According to Islamic law, Muslims and non-Muslims, all are equal and to be equally treated. All non-Muslims living in an Islamic state are well secured and protected in matters of right to property, life and freedom of religion. They are to be governed by their own religious laws or community customs or by secular laws. There can be no molestation or humiliation on the basis of religion. Further non-Muslims are not to be governed by Islamic law which is purely in religion. They are to be regulated according to the precepts of their own faith. Only the secular portion of Islamic Law Code is applicable to non-Muslims. Secular law in the sense, that is, the law which is commonly followed by all nations irrespective of their religion, caste, creed, colour or culture, is to be applied to them.

Islamic law does not interfere in non-Muslims customs and traditions which they follow as a matter of their faith. In brief, there is nothing to alarm non-Muslims living under an Islamic state. They are well-protected and privileged in all respects. During Mughal period in India, non-Muslims were not only to be governed by their own laws but were having courts where Brahmins and Pandits were sitting as judges and deciding their cases in according to their faith and law. This is a significant feature of Islamic law which has no parallel even today in existing penal law of India in hearted from British Colonial Law.

PART B

"PROJECTION"

The comparative study has made it abundantly clear that Islamic criminal law relating to criminal breach of trust is quite comprehensive and exhaustive. There exists a wide scope for legal speculation within the frame work of Islamic law for meeting the challenges arising from the fast changing conditions in the modern era. Execellence of Islamic law has no comparison with any system of law even in the so-called age of contemporary enlightenment.

Islamic law regards the moral virtues as the fundamental base of the society. Religion, morality and law are not separable. But the modern law on the other hand ignores morality and religion. It does not concern itself with them so long as acts repugnant to them do not directly prejudice and adversely effect the individuals, public order, peace and tranquillity. In fact, moral deterioration is the main cause which leads to corruption, malpractices, vices, decay and disintegration of the community. Islamic law provides the solution by integrating religion, morality and law all together.

This study has shown the fallacy of the view declaring Islamic law as incompatible with the requirements of the modern age.

It is an erroneous assumption rather than the result of academic reasoning and research. In fact, such loud thinkings are based on sheer ignorance of law. However, for further familiarising and getting the Islamic law more acquainted with the masses in general, the author makes the following suggestions and recommendation.

Islamic states should solemnly declare as a general principle of state policy that no law shall be repugnant to the teachings of Islam as set out in the Holy Qur'ãn and Sunnah and that all existing laws shall be brought into conformity with these fundamental sources of law.

Researches be conducted by the scholars learned in Islamic law to explore the vast area of the development of Islamic law, through the centuries after the Hejra, in order to bring out the richness of law and essential principles on which the edifice of Islamic law rests.

A community will never gain vigour and vitality until it recognizes the catastrophic consequences of imitating of foreign law, a foreign culture and do everything possible to put an end to this. If the community takes pride in its faith and its heritage is genuine, it must be expressed by adopting its own judicial system. When men recognize the sovereignty of God and the Supremacy of His Law, all false values will be automatically swept away.

Another significant point worth consideration is that Islamic law, no doubt, is very rich. Learned scholars have compiled by treatises. But these treaties are decorative pieces of libraries. Masses in general are un aware of. To make it easily approachable it is necessary that the law should be subject wise codified so that it may increase its accessibility, intelligibility and simplicity, as well as general convenience.

Further the subject wise codified law should be translated in all important languages of the world. It should be the responsibility of all Islamic states to get the codified law translated in languages which are prominently prevalent in respective states.

In all Islamic states, Ministry for Religion, Law and Justice be established and under its auspicious patronage research sections be established where in eminent faqih (learned scholars) and jurists be appointed. They should be assigned the task of conducting researches in different fields and (injunctions) Qur'ãnic or Ahadith be separated, systematised and uniformly consolidated. Such a codified law will be more easily approachable by jurists as well as by the public. Emphasis should be consolidated, uniformed and a logically articulated skeleton for the law.

Deeni Makatib (دینی مکاتیب) should also have separate and independent research wings where researches on different aspects of law concerning the changing environment of the modern society be conducted. However, such researches must be conducted within the permissible limits of Shariah. All suggestions and recommendations must be inconsonance with Qur'ãnic injunctions and Ahadith. No innovation be taken into consideration.

National Universities in Islamic countries, like international Islamic University, Malaysia, should include in its curriculum, and syllabi Shariah Degree and Diploma courses. Study of such courses will improve the competence, efficiency and the professional status of Qazis. It will also make them more confident and not suffer from any inferiority complex.

Learned Prof. Tan Sri Datuk Ahmad Ibrahim, the Dean, Kulliyyah of Laws, International Islamic University, Malaysia, has rightly observed that in order to ensure that the judges in Shariah courts are able to deal with the cases that come before them justly and competently it is necessary to ensure that they are qualified and trained. This is possible only when they learn Shariah and obtain the degrees thereof.

At present Kulliyyah of laws, International Islamic University is imparting education in Islamic law. It attempts to integrate both the Shariah and common law at the L.L.B. degree level and it is hoped that its graduates will be accepted as qualified persons under the Legal profession Act. They may thus be eligible to join the judicial and legal service or to be called to the Bar; and also that some of its graduates, who are competent in Arabic, will be accepted to join the Shariah judicial and legal service and to become judges or Qazis or Pegum Sharie in the Shariah courts also. For Shariah courses study of Arabic language is compulsory. International Islamic University also has provision for Diploma for Qazis where Qazi are trained in procedural laws of Islam.

Thus on similar pattern universities on other countries may also adopt such L.L.B. Degree and Diploma courses which will enhance the significance of studying Islamic Law. In due course of time it would have its own recognition in the society.

With the introduction of such courses expectations for future become very bright. Qualified and trained staff of Shariah courts would again attain dignified status, position, and its lost glory of which Shariah courts and judges were deprived of during colonalism. Honourable Tan Sri Datuk Prof. Ahmad Ibrahim rightly says that "We look forward to a time when judges who are appointed in the Shariah courts will be fully competent in the Islamic law and be able to refer to the original sources of the law in Arabic.' He makes a suggestion that "We need also to have more exchange of decision between the various Islamic countries so that we can learn from each other and work together for re-establishment of the supramacy of the Shariah and the Islamic Law." His emphasis on learning Arabic language, exchange of decisions of Shariah courts and liaison between Islamic countries in this connection are very significant points for promoting and re-establishing the supremacy of Islamic Law.

Efforts be made to raise the status and position of judge or Qazis of Shariah courts through proper selection and recruitment. Recruitment to the post should be through the lawfully appointed commission. It may be given the name of Shariah judicial and legal service commission. Learned scholars in Islamic law should be appointed on competitive merit basis. Appointed persons should also have incentives for future promotions. They should also be well-learned in Arabic language.

Only qualified lawyers in Shariah be permitted to appear before the Shariah courts. Courts may permit legal officers, advocates and solicitors having degree in Islamic law to represent the parties if their presence as lawyer is not contrary to the Islamic law. These measures would improve the status and position of Shariah courts, judges and lawyers. It will also create confidence among the masses about courts, judges and the lawyers.

In connection with Indian Law relating to prior sanction for prosecution of public servant, some modification is needed. It seems as if public servant is a privileged class and if any wrong is committed he is not to be treated alike as layman. Ruler and the rules should be equal before the law. Under Islam law there is no such distinction. Ruler and ruled both are treated alike before the law.

No doubt, principle of prior sanction for prosecution is to avoid any harassment to be caused to the public servant in the discharge of official duty. It is true. When apparently crime has been committed, there should not be any protection extended to the public servants. This breeds corruption and indirectly encourages and perpetuates malpractices.

If there is a fear of harassment and false implication of public servants affecting discharge of official duties, at the most there may be imposed a restriction. Before prosecution departmental preliminary inquiry be made about the conduct and then if irregularity or illegality is found, simple report to the police should be enough authorising police to investigate the complaint. Prior sanction for prosecution should not be the requirement. Therefore, this principle, in cases of breach of trust committed by public should be suitably amended. In fact, section 197 Criminal Procedure Code needs modification.

Another area under Indian Law need consideration is partner's agent's liabilities for breach of trust during the discharge of their respective business transactions. For breach of trust, under both business transaction, specific entrustment is required. If not, there is no liability. Neither agent nor partner is liable under such circumstances. In not, there is no liabilities. Neither agent nor partner is liable under such circumstances. In fact, it is merely a technical requirement, otherwise in both cases there is an implied entrustment. Dishonest misappropriation either by the agent or partner should make them liable for breach of trust. Merely on legal technical grounds, they should not be exempted or exonerated from criminal prosecution. Law needs appropriate amendment. Islamic law does not need any modification in this respect.

Further phrase 'entrustment in any manner' whether moral or immoral under Indian Law needs modification. Law is to protect moral values of the society and not to give incentive and encouragement for promoting immorality. Any entrustment for immoral purpose should have no legal force behind it. Islamic law is not separable from morality. Hence requires no change. Indian law in this regard needs modification.

In breach of trust cases another area under Indian Law needs modification is compoundability of cases. Right is available to the parties but in a very restricted and limited way. It is not enough. Exigency and relations between the parties should be the consideration, because litigation leads to perpetual enemity. There should not be any monetary limit for permitting the parties to have their cases mutually compromised. However, if pubic interest demands that there should be a trial for the committed, then, under such conditions court should not permit the parties to compromise the case outside the court. Law, therefore, needs suitable modification. Under Islamic law compromise in cases of breach of trust is preferred and court itself gives the hint for such compromises, need no modification.

Criminal breach of trust is more in the nature of civil wrong. Therefore, while awarding punishment preference should be given to indemnification and awarding compensation to the victim rather than sending the convict behind the bars. Indian law in this regard needs rethinking. As Islamic law emphasises awarding compensation to the victims rather than punishing with imprisonment needs no change.

In India Lakhs of cases are pending trials in the court. Delay defeats justice. It creates disappointment and no-confidence in the litigantes against the judicial system of the country. The remedy lies that indiginous judicial system should be developed suiting to Indian conditions. Our heritage is rich. Gupta Period and Mughal Periods are known to be the golden periods of the Indian History. They give the best judicial systems to the country. The government should establish a research centre where investigations may be conducted to find out the indigenous laws best suiting our environments and conditions.

Special courts, like family courts or economic courts be established deciding cases in accordance to such indiginous laws.

In fact, legal fictions and technicalities of English doctrines relating to crimes are hurdles in expeditious decisions. When these technicalities are substituted by simplicity, obviously decisions would not be delayed and no disappoint would result.

All communities in Indian have their rich heritage. If they are prosecuted in accordance to their respective simple laws connected with their faiths, it will encourage morality which at present becoming absolute and also will increase the efficiency and expediency in criminal trials.

Though the suggestion may sound strange in an environment where like 'Common Code' is being advocated. Fact is that solution of current problems lies in laws connected with one's faith. In cases where person of two distinct communities are involved in litigation, then only, the secular law should be applied. Indian government is required to consider the matter seriously.

As to Islamic law relating to breach of trust, we have seen that rules governing thereto are quite exhaustive but the illustrations and examples elaborating these governing rules are too old and primitive. These rules should remain as it is but old and primitive illustrations and examples be replaced by illustrations most suiting to the modern conditions. In other words, without effecting the spirit of law, these illustrations and examples be made up to date.

Doors of Ijtihad under Islamic law should remain open. Judges and Qazis of Shariah courts should strive to discover the true application of the teachings of Qur'ãn and Sunnah to particular situations arising in the modern age. However, such interpretations should not go against the plain sense of these teachings. Free thinking should not mean to contravene the commandments of Holy Qur'ãn and Sunnah. These two sources as we discussed earlier, are basically concerned with the general rules that only outline legal speculation. In cases where Qur'ãn and Sunnah are silent, judges have to exert with a view to form an independent judgement on a legal question. But Ijtihad should be subjected to the following considerations:

1. That the judges and Qazis should be learned in Islamic law. They should be Mujtahid;

2. That it may be resorted to only in absence of an applicable (نصوص) injunctions of Qur'ãn and Sunnah;

3. That Ijtihad does not mean to contravene the teachings of Qur'ãn and Sunnah;

4. That Ijtihad should not effect and complicate the simple and plain meaning of Qur'ãn and Sunnah;

5. That the Mujtahid judge or Qazi should be learned in Arabic language. Unless he knows Arabic, he should not resort to Ijtihad.

Unless these basic qualifications are fulfilled, Islam does not give authority either to the judge, Qazi or Mufti in the matters of doctrines and rules to formulate or enact and resort to Ijtihad.

Law relating to court procedure in Islam is very rich. However, it needs streamlining and conditions. Evidence law has been codified in Pakistan. On same like all matters relating to procedure followed in criminal court should also be given statutory shape.

Not only the provisions exist relating to appeal, revision and reference under Islamic law but the courts are following them in practice as well. However, it needs precise consolidation. This measure would further strengthen the confidence of the masses in the Islamic judicial structure.

In Islamic countries where shariah courts exist, case reporting on regular basis should also be introduced. It will help to make law commonly known. It should not remain the domain of only few. Case reporting will popularise the law in masses.

It is also said that in Tazeer (penal punishment) maxim punishment for different offences be prescribed. There should be statutory enactment to this effect. But I do not consider that there is any need for. The determination of Tazeer should be on the merits of case. The judge should take into consideration the extinuating and mitigating circumstances, and facts of the case, and then should determine the sentence most appropriate and befitting to the requirements of each case. It should remain with the judge to decide whatever is needed for the administration of justice in the given conditions.

In an Islamic state if non-Muslims are living, they are to be assured that religious law of Islam is not to apply them and the law with which they are to be governed is secular in nature which applies by all other nations. Further to be assured that Under Islamic law they are to be treated on equal basis with Muslims. No discrimination on the basis of religion is to be made. Their rights, life, liberty and property are all safe. Nothing is to worry about.

As to the accused's right to be defended by a lawyer of his choice, Islamic law does not encourage. Although there is no prohibition. But some jurists do not favour employing lawyers to defend. This discouragement needs to modification but it should not be generalised. In cases where an accused due to some disability is unable to defend himself, he should be permitted to be defended by a lawyer of his choice.

To popularise the Islamic law, the learned scholars should write more and more article and commentaries on different aspects of law and get them published in reputed journals and Magzines. Text books on law should also be written. More comparative research studies be conducted covering different fields of law.

Treatises and classics in Arabic on Islamic law be translated into different languages of the world, particularly in English, so that the critics of Islamic law and may know the worth of it.

Relevant research dates covering the vast and varied field of law from Qur'ãn and Ahadith, and Ijma and Qiyas be classified scientifically and feeded in the computers so that research scholars may have easy excess to the relevant literature suiting to their studies.

In the administration of justice more emphasis be given to Tazkirah-al-Shahud (تزکیه الشهود) to know the credibility of witness.

Institution Ahtisab for controlling and preventing the spread and rise of vices and evils in the society be strengthened and powers of Muhtasib be given statutory recognition.

To summarise if the modifications are made in the light of these suggestions Indian law as well as Islamic law would be far better suiting to the modern requirements. Particularly Islamic law would be far better in excellence to other laws.

This comparative study has proved the fallacy of the notion that the assertion of secularists and western educated scholars that law must be man made if it is to fulfill the changing needs of the changing society has no basis.

The introduction of the traditions, values and laws of the west has corrupted society, bread immorality, destroyed the inherited and traditional values. It has resulted in giving rise to a feeling of inferiority and frustration which is often expressed itself in nihilism and despair.

A law which is not separate from morality and religion can only provide remedy to modern problems.

BOOKS AND REFERENCES

The Holy Qur'ãn (English Translation of the meanings and commentary), Printed at King Fahd Holy Qur'ãn Printing Complex, Al-Madinah al-Munawwarah under the auscies of the Ministry of Hajj and Endowments, the Kingdom of Saudi Arabia. (Yusuf Ali's Translation).

Holy Qur'ãn (Commentaries) تفسير عثمانى

Maulana Shabbir Ahmad Usmani

Ratanlal and Dhirajlal, 'Law of Crimes', 23rd Edition, Vol. II.

V.R. Mohar and W.W. Chitaley, 'Indian Penal Code', Vol. III.

B. Raju, 'Commentaries on Indian Penal Code', Vol. II.

Sir Golden Borrie, 'Commercial Law', Sixth Edition.

S.N. Misra, 'The Indian Penal Code', 2nd Edition.

KL Koh, CMV Clarkson, NA MORGAN, 'Criminal Law in Singapore and Malaysia'.

Paul E. Dow, 'Criminal Law'.

Manohar Chitaley, 'Supreme Court Digest 1950 to 1986', Vol. VII.

Winfield and Jolowicz on Tort.

KWM DIAS, 'Jurisprudence' Fifth Edition.

Avtar Singh, 'Elements of Commercial Law'.

RD Agarwala, 'The Code of Criminal Procedure 1973', 4th Edition.

M.R. Mallick, 'Ganguly's Criminal Court Practice and Procedure;, Seventh Edition.

Mimi Kamariah Majid, 'Criminal Procedure in Malaysia'.

K.K. Singh, 'The Indian Evidence Act, 1872'.

R.H. Maudsley, and E.H. Burn, 'Trusts and Trustees: Cases and Materials'.

Under Hill's, 'Law of Trust and Trustees', 12th Edition.

Maitland, 'Lectures on Equity', 2nd Edition.

Abdul Qadir Oudah Shaheed, 'Criminal Law of Islam', Vol. I - II.

Charles Hamilton's Translation, 'The Hedaya' Commentary on the Islamic Law', Volumes I - IV.

Dr. Tanzelur-Rehman, (Chief Justice, Shariah F. Court, Pakistan), 'Islamic Qanoon' Hudud, Qasas, Diyat and Tazeerat', Vol. II. Said Ramadan, 'Islamic Law - Its Scope and Equity'.

Nisar Ahmad, 'The Fundamental Teachings of Qur'ãn and Hadith'.

C.R. Tyser's, 'The Mejelle'.

Dr. Muhammad Muslehuddin, 'Philosophy of Islamic Law and the Orientalists'.

Shamin, 'Islamic Law and Its Implications of Modern World'.

Maryam Jameelah, 'Islamic Culture in Theory and Practice'.

Dr. M.N. Siddiqui, 'The Economic Enterprise in Islam'.

Edwin B. Firmage, Bernard G. Weiss, John W. Welchi, 'Religion and Law' Biblical - Judaic and Islamic Perspective'.

Waheed Husain, 'Administration of Justice During the Muslim Rule in India'. S.H. Amin, 'Middle East Legal System'.

Alfred Guillaume, 'Islam'.

Victor Danner, 'The Islamic Tradition' and Introduction'.

Dr. Abdul Hamid Ahmad Abu Sulayman, (Hon. Rector, IIU, Malaysia), 'Islam and International Relations'.

السلام اور بین الاقوامی تعلقات
منظر اور لیس منظر
غصب وضمان قبری دکتور سید حسین امین

Longman and New York, 'Islam and Contemporary Society' (Published by Longman, in Association with Islamic Council of Europe).

M.B. Hooker, 'Islamic Law in South-East Asia'.

Mohammad Hashim Kamali, 'Law in Afghanistan'.

Mahmod Ahmad Ghazi, Abdul Raheem Ashraf, Billoch : Tradition, 'Adab-ul-Qazi' - أدب القاضی

Maulana Ashraf Ali Thanwi, 'Bahishti Zewar' (Heavenly Ornaments), (Translated by M. Masroor Saroha).

منهاج الصالحین غرالدین بالیق
(ومن احادیث وسنة خاتم الانبیاء والمرسلین)

Amir Ahsan Islahi, 'Islamic Law Concept and Codification'.

Bayyumi, Muhammad Ahmad Muhammad, 'Islamic Ethic of Social Justice and the Spirit of Modernisation'.

قانون الحقوبات
"تطوراته التشريحية و مذاكراته (الايضاحية)
والدحكام فى مائة عام فتاوىٰ هندىی
ترجمة
فتاوى عالمگيريه
القواعد، الجرائم
تفهيم القران

حسن مادق المرصغاوى
جامعة الاسكندرية مصر
ومن النا السيد امير علك سعمو
داكتر محمد شكرى الى جس الدقق
مولونا مودودى

Dr. Muhammad Muslehuddin, 'Economic and Islam'.

M.P. Jain, 'Outlines of Indian Legal History'.

Terry Calvain and John Seigfraid-Borton, 'Economic Analysis and Anti Trust Law'.

Niyazi-Kausar, 'Economic Concepts in Islam'.

Afzalur-Rehman, 'Economic Doctrines of Islam'.

Joseph Schachi, 'An Introduction to Islamic Law (1964).

S.H. Amin, 'Punishment in Islam'.

Imam Bukhari, 'Saheeh Bukhari, Kitab-ul-Ahkam'.

A.A. Fazee, Outlines of Muhammadan Law.

Fathi Uthman, Al-Fikr-al-Qanuni-al-Islami; Bayn Usul-al-Shariah-wa-Turath-al-Fiqh, Cairo : Maktabah Wahbab.

Ghulam Murtaza Azad, 'Judicial System of Islam: Islam Research Council, 1987'.

Sharh-i-Viqaya.

Dr. Muhammadullah, 'Administration of Justice in Muslim Law'.

H.M. Elliot, 'History of India', Vol. VII, No. 39.

Baillie. 'Digest of Muhammadan Law'.

A. Rahim, 'Muhammadan Jurisprudence'.

Vincent Smith, 'Akbar and Great Mughal'.

Ayin-i-Akbari, Vol. II.

Nisae : Kitab-ul-Istaaza - نسائی: کتاب الاستحاضة

Mushkiwat - مشکوة: کتاب البیوع

Ibn-e-Maja - ابن ماجه: ابواب التجارات

Behaqi - بیهقی: شعب الایمان

Tan Sri Dato' Prof. Ahmad Ibrahim, 'The Shariah Courts and Its Place in the Judicial System', (Shariah Law Journal ISSN - 0127 - 9033, Dec. 1989, Vol. V, IIU, Malaysia).

Dr. H. Maufiq, 'The Role of Judiciary in the Development of Islamic Law: The Indonesian Experience', (ISSN-0122-9033, De. 1989, Vol. V, IIU, Malasia).

C.K.G. Pillay, 'The Role of Islamic Law in Our System', Straits Settlement Times Column - 'You and the Law', Malaysia.

Dr. Ausaf Ali, 'We Fumble and Stumble in the Modern World', ('Forum' - Vol. 6, No. 67, March 1987/Rajab/Shaban 1407, Arabia, Islamic World Review).

Dr. M. Shukri Abdal Jawwad al-Dakkar, Chief Judge, Alexandria, Egypt, 'Issue of Application of Islamic Law in Egypt by Legislator, and Jurisdiction'.

Prof. Dr. Mohammad Hashim Kamali, 'Appellate Review and Judicial Independence', (Public Lecture, IIU, Malaysia).

Dr. Rashid al-Mubarak, 'The Muslim World : An Illness to Cure', (22 Arabia October 1986/Safar 1407).

Tar Sri Jafer Hussein, (Bank Negara Governor, Malaysia), 'Vision for a Full Fledge Islamic System' ('Focus', The Star, Monday, Nov. 4, 1991).

Sarkar, 'Mughal Administration'.

A. Rahim 'Muhammadan Jurisprudence'.

H.M. Elliot, 'History of India', Vol. I.

G.S. Ranking's Translation, 'Muntakhab-i-Tawarikh.'

Al-Badayuni.

Sayeed Sadiq, 'Fiqh-al-Sunnah'. ابوداؤد۔ابواب القضاء جلد دوئم۔

Abu Daud, Abwabul-Qada, Vol. II - سنن الدارقطنی جلد دوم

Sunnah-al-Dar-e-Watni -

Al-Mughni, Vol. X & XII.

Law of Saud to Faisal No. 713 of 1953.

Al-Faraqul-Hukamia.

Nakl-Saheeh.

Al-Qaze-fil Islam.

Saudi Arabia, Royal Will, 1932.

Zaheeria -	ظهيريه
Fatawa-e-Ahle-Sumerqand	فتاویٰ اهل سمرقندی
Muheet-Sarkhasi	محیطؕ سرخسی
Multaqit	ملتقط
Badai	بدائع
Sharah - Tahawi	شرح طحاوی
Tamer - Tashi	تمرتاشی
Fasul Amadia	فصول عمادیه
Behrul-Raiq	بحرالرائق
Muheet	محیط
Tatatar-Khania	تاتارخانیه

ACTS AND STATUTES

The Indian Penal Code - Act No. XLV of 1860.

The Code of Criminal Procedure, 1973, - Act. No. 2 of 1974.

The Gazette of Pakistan, Islamabad, Wed. Sept. 5, 1990. (Amended Pakistan Penal Code and the Code of Cr. P. 1898).

Pakistan Shariat Criminal Laws - (Gazette of Pakistan, Part I, 9th Feb. 1979).

Constitution of India.

Administration of Islamic Religious Affairs Enactments, 1986, (Government of Terengganu Gazette, 26th March, 1987).

Shariah Criminal Procedure Enactment, 1989 (Government of Kedah Darul Aman Gazette, 1989, Malaysia).

Federal Constitution of Malaysia, 15th, September 1989.

Indian Contract Act.

Official Gazette, No. 44814, dated 22 June, 1361, A.H. (Solar) 13 Sep., 1982 A.D.

Official Gazette, No. 57112, dated 14 August, 1362, A.H. (Solar) 5 November, 1983 A.D.

Selangor Administration of Muslim Law Enactment, 1952.

Indian Trust Act

Indian Partnership Act.

Saudi Arabia Stature of Directorate of Public Security.

The Law of 1952 (A), Saudi Arabia.

Jame-Tirmizi, Vol. II - جامع ترمزی۔ جلد دوم

Pakistan Islamic Law of Evidence 1982

(Judge Corocoy D. Mason, The Shariah Court : Their Relation to the Development of Islamic Law in Philippines).

Laws of Saudi Arabia, Official Instructions, 1927, 1936, 1954, 1957, 1962, 1967, 1970 and 1973.